W9-ADD-875

Hannah More

Studies in Nineteenth-Century British Literature

Regina Hewitt
General Editor

Vol. 4

PETER LANG
New York • Washington, D.C./Baltimore
Bern • Frankfurt am Main • Berlin • Vienna • Paris

Charles Howard Ford

Hannah More

A Critical Biography

PETER LANG
New York • Washington, D.C./Baltimore
Bern • Frankfurt am Main • Berlin • Vienna • Paris

Library of Congress Cataloging-in-Publication Data

Ford, Charles Howard.
Hannah More: a critical biography/ Charles Howard Ford.
p. cm. — (Studies in nineteenth-century British literature; vol. 4)
Includes bibliographical references and index.
1. More, Hannah, 1745-1833—Biography. 2. Women and literature—
England—History—18th century. 3. Women and literature—England—
History—19th century. 4. Women authors, English—18th century—
Biography. 5. Women authors, English—19th century—Biography.
6. Women educators—Great Britain—Biography. I. Title. II. Series.
PR3605.M6F67   828'.609—dc20   [B]   95-6770
ISBN 0-8204-2798-5
ISSN 1071-0124

Die Deutsche Bibliothek-CIP-Einheitsaufnahme

Ford, Charles Howard:
Hannah More: a critical biography/ Charles Howard Ford.
– New York; Washington, D.C./Baltimore; Bern; Frankfurt am Main;
Berlin; Vienna; Paris: Lang.
(Studies in nineteenth-century British literature; Vol. 4)
ISBN 0-8204-2798-5
NE: GT

Cover design by James F. Brisson.

The paper in this book meets the guidelines for permanence and durability
of the Committee on Production Guidelines for Book Longevity
of the Council of Library Resources.

Printed in the United States of America.

Acknowledgments

Praising one's own relatives and mentors may be a perfunctory afterthought to most books, but such acknowledgments would be extremely fitting for a critical study of Hannah More, who as a young writer had a knack for cultivating and praising her mature benefactors. Accordingly, I would like to thank my grandmother, Mrs. Doris I. Rapp, for her unconditional emotional and financial support, my parents, Charles J. and Doris I. Ford, for their faith in me, my principal advisor, Dr. James Epstein, for his limitless patience and tolerance, and Drs. Margo Todd and Elisabeth Perry for their invaluable comments and insights. Drs. Matthew Ramsey, Alison Hirsch, Laurence Lerner, Paul Conkin, and Regina Hewitt also kindly read drafts of this biography, and their criticism has appreciably improved the final version. I would also like to thank Professor Barbara Brandon Schnorrenberg for her invaluable comments on my fifth chapter. For useful tips and leads early in the process I am particularly grateful to Drs. Epstein, Todd, Perry, and Conkin, and conversations with fellow graduate students Carol Woodfin, Rhonda Williams, and Ted McAllister proved more stimulating than they may have known. Finally, I would like to thank Kevin Girard for proofreading my final draft and for prodding me to finish this project.

Research for this reassessment of Hannah More was made possible by grants from the Graduate School and Department of History at Vanderbilt University, and by grants especially from my grandmother, Mrs. Doris I. Rapp, and my parents, Charles J. and Doris I. Ford. A year's unemployment provided ample opportunity to read, write and revise, and then a part-time job at J.C. Penney made it possible for me to afford the trip to Nashville to defend my dissertation in March, 1992. Further revision and consequent publication were funded largely by my current position as assistant professor of history at Norfolk State University in Norfolk, Virginia.

I am particularly grateful to the Viscountess Eccles for permission to reproduce extracts from unpublished letters in her Hyde Collection at Firestone Library, Princeton Library. I am also indebted to the staffs of the James Marshall and Marie-Louise Osborn Collection of the Beinecke Rare Book and Manuscript Library at Yale University, the Henry W. and Albert A. Berg Collection of the New York Public Library of the Astor, Lenox and Tilden Foundations, the Historical Society of Pennsylvania, the Special Collections Department of the William R. Perkins Library at Duke University, the Pierpont Morgan Library in New York, the Houghton Library at Harvard University, the Historical Society of Massachusetts, the Folger Shakespeare Library in Washington, D.C., the John Rylands University of Manchester, the East Sussex County Record Office, the Bodleian Library at Oxford University, and the Department of Rare Books and Special Collections of the Rush Rhees Library at the University of Rochester for permission to cite and quote from manuscripts in their possession.

I would also like to thank the following for granting me permission to quote from certain published texts: *Journal of Social History*, University of Wisconsin Press, University of Delaware Press, University of North Carolina Press, Alfred A. Knopf Incorporated, Harvard University Press, University of Toronto Press, Yale University Press, Princeton University Press, Cambridge University Press, The University of Chicago Press, Oxford University Press, and Rutgers University Press. The credit line acknowledging the granting of permission appears in each footnote referring to the relevant quotation.

As for the work that follows, it is perhaps unnecessary to note that although members of my examination committee (and others) shaped quite a few of the most elegant sentences in this study, I take full responsibility for any lingering errors of interpretation, judgment, and style.

Table of Contents

Introduction

This book offers reassessment of the life and works of Hannah More (1745-1833), one of the most prolific and influential authors of her day in England. It is true that More was certainly not neglected by scholars during the nineteenth and early twentieth centuries. Between her death in 1833 and 1952, over a dozen biographies and at least five articles treated More's life and accomplishments. Gifted female amateurs wrote most of these pieces,[1] defending More from prominent male critics such as George Saintsbury who, in 1896, dismissed her and her works as dull and second-rate.[2] Indeed, with the passing of Victorian morality, Hannah More acquired a misleading reputation as an intolerant and minor reactionary whose didactic works had become hopelessly out of phase. On the other hand, apologies for More were generally uncritical and superficial,[3] but the last two to appear—*Hannah More and Her Circle* (1947) by Mary Alden Hopkins and *Hannah More* (1952) by Mary Gladys Jones—were both comprehensive and sympathetic. Hopkins and Jones sensed the complex tensions within More. Jones described Hannah More as "a Tory who championed the radical causes of anti-slavery and the education of the poor, a Churchwoman who attended a Dissenting Meeting House [only

---

[1]Of the nineteenth-century biographies, still worth reading is Charlotte M. Yonge's *Hannah More* (Boston: Roberts Brothers, 1888).

[2]For Saintsbury, see his *A History of Nineteenth-Century Literature: 1780-1895* (New York: Macmillan, 1896), p.45. For the most scathing dismissal of More, see Augustine Birrell, "Hannah More Once More," *In the Name of the Bodleian and Other Essays* (London: E. Stock, 1906). Here Birrell says how he buried an expensive nineteen volume edition of Hannah More's works in his garden. To Birrell, the edition was not worthy of the shelf space and served much better as mulch.

[3]Typically uncritical and superficial is Annette M. B. Meakins's *Hannah More: A Biographical Study* (London: Murray, 1919).

once] and employed Methodist teachers."[4] Both Hopkins and Jones portrayed "a woman of far richer personality and of greater significance" than the one-dimensional conservative depicted by previous scholars.[5]

The rehabilitation of More and her works has stalled in recent years, however. It is true that literary critics have finally recognized More's important contributions to the development of the short story and of the social novel.[6] Historians now regularly note her role in the making of Victorian England[7] and belatedly acknowledge similarities between the "conservative" More and "radical" icons, most notably, Mary Wollstonecraft.[8]

Yet, long caricatured as the lady-like handmaiden of incumbent male elites, More has not fared well in the recent debut of "her-story." More's image as the ultimate traitor to her sex has ensured that no full-length study of More has been published during the rise of women's studies. Feminists have been particularly unwilling to give her life and works the serious examination accorded Georgian authors (both male and female) more in tune with what those scholars consider the advanced ideas of our own day.

This reluctance is extremely ironic as the insights of feminist social historians and literary critics have proved most useful in unlocking the secrets of Hannah More.[9] The desire to see where gender matters in More's life and writings informs this study. For instance, I examine how More overcame the hazards

---

[4]Mary G. Jones, *Hannah More* (Cambridge: Cambridge University Press, 1952), p.183. Excerpt reprinted by permission of Cambridge University Press. All rights reserved.

[5]Ibid., p.ix.

[6]In particular, see Samuel Pickering, "Hannah More's *Coelebs in Search of A Wife* and the Respectability of the Novel in the Nineteenth Century," *Neuphilologische Mitteilugen* 78(1977), pp.78-85.

[7]For example, see Ford K. Brown, *Fathers of the Victorians: The Age of Wilberforce* (Cambridge: Cambridge University Press, 1961), pp.1-11. More is one of Brown's "Fathers."

[8]For instance, see Mitzi Myers, "Reform or Ruin: A Revolution in Female Manners," in Henry Payne, ed., *Studies in Eighteenth-Century Culture.* vol.11., 1982, pp.199-216

[9]Extremely helpful was Margaret Doody's *Frances Burney: The Life in the Works* (New Brunswick, N.J.: Rutgers University Press, 1988), even though Doody (like Frances Burney) dislikes Hannah More.

of being a woman in a man's world. Many of these strategies periodically surface in her works which pulsate with both accommodation and resistance to masculine supremacy. Most revealing is the frequent masking of resistance by apparent accommodation in More's poems, plays, and essays. More's cloaking devices were not unique; ambitious women of every time and place have practiced a similar political artistry.[10] Her success at deftly pushing the envelope, however, was stunning. Although her deepening faith in God made the mature More less hesitant in openly attacking the ungodly gentlemen who ran Georgian Britain, even then she usually sensed just how far and how explicit she could go without drawing a devastating response.[11]

Unfortunately, More's very success has attracted contempt from twentieth-century scholars who tend to appreciate only those women writers of the past whose ideas and tactics resemble current preferences. That success still blinds some scholars to the fact that More was a reformer, not a reactionary.[12] This study unlocks the secrets of her success, deciphering her often coded and ambiguous passages (particularly those passages about feminine place and education). It thus provides glimpses of the sometimes angry woman behind the always proper lady in her life and works.

---

[10]For examples of this kind of political artistry, see Elisabeth Israels Perry, *Belle Moskowitz: Feminine Politics and the Exercise of Power in the Age of Alfred E. Smith* (New York: Oxford University Press, 1987), pp.xi-xiii, 152-60, 217-8. See also Rebecca E. Klatch, *Women of the New Right* (Philadelphia: Temple University Press, 1987), pp.205-8; Arlene Elowe McLeod, *Accommodating Protest: Working Women, the New Veiling, and Change in Cairo* (New York: Columbia University Press, 1991), pp.142-63.

[11]This study in part answers Mitzi Myers' call for a study of Hannah More's "complex rhetorical counterpoint." ("Reform or Ruin: A Revolution in Female Manners," in Henry Paine, ed., *Studies in Eighteenth Century Culture*, vol.11, 1982, p.209.)

[12]For feminist scorn for More and her writings, see in particular Lynne Agress, *The Feminine Irony: Women on Women in Early-Nineteenth-Century English Literature* (Cranbury, N.J.: Associated University Presses, 1978), pp.48-52, 58-74; Beth Kowaleski-Wallace, "Milton's Daughters: The Education of Eighteenth-Century Women Writers," *Feminist Studies* 12(1986), pp.271-93; Doody, *Frances Burney*, pp.96-7; Sylvia Harcstark Myers, *The Bluestocking Circle: Women, Friendship, and the Life of the Mind in Eighteenth-Century England* (Oxford: Clarendon Press, 1990), p.260.

More's career defied not only obstacles of sex, but also of class, religion, and age largely through her political skill of introducing unconventional actions and ideas in conventional packages. Hannah More was obviously a woman, but she was also an ardent protestant drawn from provincial Bristol's middle ranks who chose to remain celibate. All of these qualities made her a cultural outsider to elite Georgian London. Accordingly, the first chapter examines the young More's marginality and her uneasy accommodation to the demands of the fashionable world. A commercially successful beginner writing for elite patrons in the 1770s, More inserted ascetic and woman-centered tropes in seemingly stock tragedies and poems. The need to use subtle codes and to tolerate ridiculous protocols, however, disturbed More. Her gradual conversion to Evangelical Anglicanism eased, but did not immediately eliminate the tensions between practicality and principle within her psyche and writings. Increasingly confident and less self-conscious, the Evangelical More brought Scripture to the stage and a social conscience to society verse. The second chapter discusses her rebirth as a leading critic of the self-indulgence of aristocratic society during the 1780s.

The French Revolution and its threat to the English social order loomed large in the writings of the middle-aged More, testing her skill at introducing reform through familiar values and vehicles. More's linkage of moral renewal amongst the rich and powerful with political and social stability forms the topic of the third chapter. Her appeals to the piety and patriotism of aristocrats were not opportunistic theatrics designed to capitalize on the spectre of revolutionary France, but rather sprang from her long-held belief that aristocratic virtue, whether civic or personal, dictated general morality which, in turn, ensured the soundness of the commonwealth.

In the wake of the crescendo of violence across the Channel, however, More did not remain content to wait for the trickle-down of probity. Between 1795 and 1798 she spoke directly to the lower and middling classes through her *Cheap Repository* tracts, the focus of Chapter 4. More hoped to change the morals and manners of artisans and laborers through lively stories patterned after the usually bawdy chapbook. To promote godly behavior amongst a mass audience she made the self-discipline of activist and ascetic Christianity the salient precondition for charity and patronage in her tracts. Unlike the easygoing, histrionic, and carousing paternalism of the typical Georgian squire, More's paternalism was earnest, corrective, and meddlesome.

Her philanthropy proved more controversial in practice than in literary form. During the 1790s, Hannah More and her sisters set up a number of Sunday schools to teach the poor of Somerset Christian discipline. Local authorities felt threatened by the sisters' assumption of power and were assuaged only by the Mores' manipulation of traditional feminine roles. The Reverend Thomas Bere of Blagdon, nonetheless, saw through Hannah More's facade and aimed to expose the clever, well-connected, and ambitious woman that she was. More answered the Reverend Bere by publically crafting a feminine victim image and by privately playing tough politics. The fifth chapter sympathetically appraises More's feminine exercise of power, first in the establishment of her Sunday schools, and then in detail during the Blagdon Controversy.

Attacked by Bere and others between 1798 and 1802 largely because of her sex, Hannah More focused her writing on feminine education and place in the first decade of the new century. In two popular treatises and a widely read novel, More aimed to enrich the syllabi at ladies' boarding schools without toppling the gender hierarchy of man over woman and without blurring sexual differences. She blamed the typically light curriculum for girls for fashionable androgyny, in other words, for "effeminate" men overly concerned with dress and appearance and for "masculine" women pressing for legal equality. The sixth chapter deals with More's Sisyphean efforts to maintain sexual difference and inequality while upgrading or "masculinizing" the education of women.

Hannah More kept on writing well into extreme old age. In doing so, she spurned the traditional passivity, inactivity and resignation expected of an elderly woman. She reconciled propriety and actuality by projecting these expectations upon her poor and female readers. The final chapter looks at the impact of advancing age on the quality and content of More's last works.

My literary biography does not tell Hannah More's entire story. I do not stray much beyond More's career as a writer. I indulge in pure biography only when More's mastery of resistance masked by accommodation was in danger of being discovered by contemporaries during the bitter Blagdon Controversy. I present her life largely as revealed by her publications and place the patterns and themes of her *oeuvres* in their appropriate historical and biographical context. Thus I have added a strong dose of social/cultural history to this biography in the attempt to delineate the hopes and fears of the complex dynamo that was Hannah More. Yet despite the periodic and necessary detours into historical background and synthesis, the focus is clearly on Miss More. This spotlight is not intended to present her as the definitive female writer or politician, but rather is intended to help historians and critics appreciate the life in the works of Hannah More.

Chapter I

The Ambivalent Moralist

Literary critics and historians usually dismiss the early works of Hannah More as conventional or as derivative. It is true that the early plays and poems of More reflect the general concern for moral regeneration and national identity in Georgian Britain. Hannah More, like most writers, celebrated the godly, self-disciplined layperson who looked out for the common good rather than private gain. She, like most writers, criticized the excesses of decadent court culture and expressed "the passionate feelings of frustrated men and women in an age of torn attachments and uncertain identity."[1] The reputations and incomes of literati such as More primarily depended upon the fickle opinions of Francophile aristocrats and their middling-sort imitators. The ensuing resentment of the quality by "restive and socially sensitive" intellectuals such as More blossomed into a "nationalist Kulturkampf" against their patrons. The prints of William Hogarth, the productions of David Garrick, the essays of Samuel Johnson, and the works of Hannah More juxtaposed their English simplicity, sincerity, piety, and morality with the French extravagance, duplicity, blasphemy, and promiscuity followed by the fashionable.[2] Reverse snobbery appealed to many frustrated imitators of aristocratic vogue such as More whom the great had rebuffed with even more exclusive ways of dress and behavior.

---

[1] Gerald Newman, *The Rise of English Nationalism: A Cultural History 1740-1830* (New York: St. Martin's Press, 1987), p.120.

[2] Ibid., pp 56, 58-60, 63-6, 87-120; Lawrence Lipking, *The Ordering of the Arts in Eighteenth-Century England* (Princeton: Princeton University Press, 1970), pp.328-9; Raphael Samuel, "Introduction: The figures of national myth," in idem., ed., *Patriotism: The Making and Unmaking of British National Identity*, vol.3—National Fictions (London: Routledge, 1989), pp.xxv-xxvi.

Yet scholars overlook the fact that identifying, clarifying, and reforming female roles were central to the young More. In her pronouncements on female education and place, More expressed the ambivalence of a provincial female writer toward the cosmopolitan and androcentric circles which dictated literary success. Released from teaching by a fortuitous annuity in 1772, More became an eminent woman of letters with her second and well-received tragedy *Percy* in 1778. Yet she was torn between the maintenance of aristocratic and patriarchal values for acceptability and the advocacy of moral reforms that rewarded the godly, regardless of sex. Accordingly, she mixed her unconventional views about female education and place with conventional didactic tropes and familiar paternalist attitudes. Her female protagonists are all proper ladies, but they do not emerge victorious as a result of strictly adhering to propriety. More used this type of code to articulate her ambivalence toward aristocratic and masculine supremacy, avoiding crippling controversy.

Translating More's code provides new insights on this literary woman caught between various worlds. Hannah More was marginal in relation to the cultural and social arbiters of the day. She was partly in and partly out. As a marginal individual, More combined inside knowledge with outside perspective, producing perceptive criticisms of prevailing norms.[3]

---

[3]For a perceptive survey of sociological literature on marginality, see Lesley D. Harmon, *The Modern Stranger: On Language and Membership* (Berlin: Mouton de Gruyter, 1988), pp.19-49. For the combination of inside knowledge and outside perspective in marginality, see Everitt Stonequist, *The Marginal Man: A Study in Personality and Culture Conflict* (New York: Russell & Russell, 1937), p.145-8. For women as marginal individuals, see Everett C. Hughes, "Social Change and Status Protest: An Essay on the Marginal Man," *Phylon*, 10(1949), pp.58-65; bell hooks, *Feminist Theory: From Margin to Center* (Boston: South End Press, 1984); Ruth L. Smith and Deborah M. Valenze, "Mutuality and Marginality: Liberal Moral Theory and Working-Class Women in Nineteenth-Century England," *Signs: Journal of Women in Culture and Society*, vol.13, 2 (Winter, 1988), pp.275-98. For the relationships between assimilation and marginality, see Leo Spitzer, *Lives in Between: Assimilation and Marginality in Austria, Brazil, and West Africa, 1780-1945* (Cambridge: Cambridge University Press, 1989), pp.28-37, 129-37.

More subtly exposed the shortcomings of self-appointed male guardians. She furtively scoffed at the absurdities of the great. Yet simultaneously, she eagerly imitated and pleased the powerful whom she wanted to join. She played the roles of dutiful daughter and, later, society fixture, very well. Evenings of elderly sages and Italian operas, however, failed to satisfy her completely. Consideration of her plays and poems of the 1760s and 1770s demands a documentation and assessment of More's uneasy accommodation to the demands of decadent courtiers and literary lions. But first, it is necessary to understand whence she came in order to appreciate what she accomplished.

The religiosity of More's family shaped her identity as an ascetic and activist Christian. Her paternal grandmother was a staunch presbyterian whose brothers were in Cromwell's army. Her paternal grandfather hid dissenting conventicles in his house in Norfolk in the late 1600s. Her mother's family were ordinary rank-and-file members of the languid Church of England, but it was her father Jacob's synthesis of church and chapel that exerted the most influence on the development of her spirituality. In contrast to his parents, Jacob More was a High Churchman. He firmly believed in the authority of the episcopal hierarchy, but he impressed upon Hannah More and her four sisters that the heartfelt religion of their paternal ancestors was possible within the polity of the established church. Jacob More insisted on the importance of family prayers and catechized his children at home. Perhaps in deference to his dissenting parents, he encouraged his daughters to cultivate godliness both inside and outside the Anglican Church.[4] Hannah More and her sisters followed their father's kind of methodism[5] for the rest of their lives.

---

[4]The biographical information of this paragraph rests largely on a letter from one of Hannah More's relatives to her literary executrix after her death in 1833. (Elizabeth Newson to Margaret Roberts, 14 October 1833, William Roberts, ed., *Memoirs of the Life and Correspondence of Mrs. Hannah More vol. 1* (London: R. B. Selley and W. Burnside, 1835), pp.8-10) In addition, see Mary Alden Hopkins, *Hannah More and Her Circle* (New York: Longman, Green & Co., 1947), pp.3-9; Mary G. Jones, *Hannah More* (Cambridge: Cambridge University Press, 1952), p.10.

[5]The word "methodism" in the eighteenth century included zealous High Anglicans who were not necessarily followers of John Wesley. Elie Halevy

Jacob More set an example of moral discipline and integrity for his family. He attributed his virtues to practical and comprehensive instruction in childhood. Like his presbyterian parents, he firmly believed in the power of education to counteract vice and sin; therefore, there was no question in his mind about the advisability of educating his daughters. In contrast to most fathers of his day, Jacob More agreed with the Augustan feminist Mary Wortley Montagu on the feminine aptitude for serious learning. He taught his daughters a wide variety of subjects, ranging from the basics of spelling and grammar through the traditionally masculine pursuits of Latin and mathematics.[6] He wanted to produce literate and cultured laywomen able to contribute to the common good through schoolteaching. He did not want to create female savants and coquettes who used their knowledge for purely private gain.[7] As a schoolmaster, he was well-qualified to realize these goals for his children.

Jacob More's benevolent patriarchy had its limits. The success of precocious Hannah More at the traditionally masculine endeavor of mathematics alarmed her father, who promptly stopped her arithmetic lessons in early adolescence. Although sensitive to the gifts of individual females, Jacob More clung to

---

suggests that in the 1730s and 1740s the most godly Anglicans, such as the Wesleys, strongly believed in the authority of the bishops (Elie Halevy, *The Birth of Methodism in England*, Bernard Simmel, trans. and ed., (Chicago: Chicago University Press, 1971), pp.43-4).

[6]For Hannah More's atypical education, see Roberts, *Memoirs* vol. 1, pp.11-5; Hopkins, Hannah More, pp.12-5. For a psychohistorical and speculative comparison of her education with other female writers, see Beth Kowaleski-Wallace, "Milton's Daughters: The Education of the Eighteenth-Century Women Writers," *Feminist Studies* 12(1986), pp.271-93. For the views of Mary Wortley Montagu on female education, see her *Letters from the Levant, during the Embassy to Constantinople 1716-18, with a Preliminary Discourse and Notes Containing a Sketch of her Ladyship's Character, Moral and Literary* (New York: Arno Press, 1971) as well as Montagu to Lady Mary Bute, 10 October 1752, *The Works of the Right Honorable Lady Mary Wortley Montagu, including her Correspondence, Poems, and Essays* vol.4 (London: Longman, Hurst, & Rees, 1817), p.168.

[7]This steering paralleled the godly education of boys in Bristol. Here the concern was to produce boys "fit for the public life of the city," and to avoid creating both self-absorbed connoisseurs and pedantic men of letters. (Jonathan Barry, *The Cultural Life of Bristol 1640-1775*, University of Oxford D.Phil. thesis, 1985, p.57.)

what contemporaries saw as a divinely ordered hierarchy of man over woman. Everyone had her proper place; Hannah More's unexpected aptitude for mathematics was out of place.[8]

Nevertheless, Jacob More trained his daughters to take care of themselves. He knew firsthand the earthly importance of self-discipline and hard work to those who began a few paces behind in the competitive economy of Georgian Britain. A second son of Norfolk gentry, Jacob More had intended to enter the ministry, and he expected to inherit farmland near the coast of Suffolk. Yet after long and costly litigation with a cousin, Jacob More lost his claim to this estate and could not afford the university education of a clergyman. He then migrated to the western county of Gloucestershire in the early 1730s for reasons that are not clear. Fortunately, his practical industriousness at teaching pleased Norbonne Berkeley of Stoke Park, Stapleton, a prominent landowner and future governor of Virginia in the 1760s. Berkeley arranged for More to become a supervisor of the excise in Bristol, and later the headmaster of a foundation school in a village near Bristol. Jacob More thus overcame his hard luck through the appeal of his self-discipline to an influential patron. His daughters, particularly Hannah, followed Jacob More's way to moderate material comfort even more successfully than he did and later would recommend his brand of virtuous prosperity to a mass audience.[9]

On Easter Monday, 1758, Jacob More's five daughters—Mary, Elizabeth, Sarah, Hannah, and Martha—established a boarding school.[10] The sisters embarked on a typical career path for young bookish women of the middling sort, but tried to transmit their father's atypical religious and moral ideals to the daughters of the slavetraders and merchants of bustling Bristol. Jacob and Grace More followed their daughters' example, setting up a nearby academy for boys. The More sisters excelled largely on their own, however. They offered a welcome alterna-

---

[8]Jones, *Hannah More*, pp.12-3.
[9]For Jacob's struggle, see Hopkins, *Hannah More*, pp.4-6.
[10]The girls were quite young. Mary was nineteen; Elizabeth was seventeen; Sarah was fourteen; Hannah was twelve; Martha was eleven. Sarah's nickname was Sally; Martha's nickname was Patty.

tive to the fashionable froth of conventional education for well-to-do girls.[11]

While the number of governesses and female scholars increased dramatically in the mid-eighteenth century, the quality of female education declined. Girls at English boarding schools learned trivial skills such as dancing, deportment, flower arranging, and a smattering of French. These superficial accomplishments acclimated young ladies to the fashionable world. In the 1750s and 1760s the great imported an exclusionary and, at times, ridiculous social civility from Louis XV's France. Preparing middling-sort girls for this pretentious etiquette was designed to enhance the status of their families, however lowly. Eager parents felt that exposure to at least parts of aristocratic culture helped their daughters on the marriage market. And even if it did not, confirmed spinsters could land good manufacturing and domestic jobs which demanded up-to-date information about the nuances of style.

A growing number of artists and intellectuals criticized the fashionable education of girls for corrupting young minds with artificial French manners. For example, in his periodical *The Mirror* (1779-80), the novelist Henry Mackenzie reported the frequent transformation of industrious daughters of farmers and merchants into useless ornaments who rejected their hard-working parents. He blamed boarding schools for these unfortunate transmutations. Graduates of these institutions, according to Mackenzie, were shallow, lazy, and promiscuous, lacking any preparation for marriage and motherhood. In order to foster feminine morality, Mackenzie and like-minded commentators recommended that mothers should teach their daughters at home.[12] But, as the radical Mary Wollstonecraft noted in

---

[11]c.f. Jones, *Hannah More*, p.7. Jones argues incorrectly that the Mores ran a typical boarding school for girls. For the opening of the Mores' school, see Hopkins, Hannah More, pp.16-7. For an excellent survey of the ideas on female education in the eighteenth century, see Veena P. Kasbekar, *Power over Themselves: The Controversy about Female Education in England 1660-1820*, University of Cincinnati Ph.D. dissertation in English, 1980.

[12]Henry Mackenzie, *The Mirror* vol.2, 1779-80, (London: Parsons reprint, 1794), p.47; Thomas Day, *The History of Sandford and Merton: a Work intended for the Use of Children*, 1785, (New York: Evert Duyckinck, 1818), p.126-7, 202-30; Kasbekar, *Power Over Themselves*, pp.31,70,100,103.

1792, most mothers were unable or unwilling to provide such instruction because they had had no moral or ethical training in their own youth. Many mothers, moreover, could not read. If they knew how to read, they perused descriptions of fashionable life.[13] On the other hand, most fathers were not Jacob More.

The More sisters combined what some writers viewed as uniquely English morals with French manners at their school. They addressed the concerns of the boarding school critics in a marketable way. In particular, Jacob More invited genteel French prisoners-of-war to entertain his daughters, who, in turn, imparted to their charges the elegant politeness of these officers. In the 1760s, the More sisters hired visiting masters to teach the obligatory social graces of dance, music, and French. Yet unlike the curriculum at most boarding schools, this training in etiquette was secondary. The primary focus was on practical moral and ethical instruction which the sisters taught personally. Their curriculum centered on reading the Bible and devotional works as well as drilling students in writing and arithmetic. This unusual alloy of academics, morality, and social polish pleased subscribers and parents. The ducal family of Beaufort (relatives of Jacob's patron, Norbonne Berkeley) underwrote most of the school's expenses. In addition, the Mores drew their clientele from the rich and powerful of Bristol and, later, from the Midlands and Home counties. When Hannah's eldest sisters retired in 1790, the Park Street establishment was one of the most prestigious boarding schools for girls in Britain.[14]

In her first play, *The Search After Happiness*, Hannah More similarly balanced conventional snobbery and moral reform. More had always thought of herself as a writer as well as a teacher and had scribbled epigrams and couplets from the age of three. At the Mores' school, she wrote edifying tales for her pupils. *The Search After Happiness* was one of these. Written in 1762 and published in 1773, this pastoral drama was "a

---

[13]Mary Wollstonecraft, *Vindication of the Rights of Woman*, 1792, Miriam Brody, ed., (London: Penguin Press, 1988), pp.161-3.
[14]For a list of patrons of the Mores' school, see Hopkins, *Hannah More*, pp.17-19.

substitute for the improper custom . . . of allowing plays, and those not always of the purest kind, to be acted by young ladies in boarding schools."[15] More anticipated Jane Austen's concerns in *Mansfield Park* that acting in fickle and fashionable roles might undermine personal integrity.[16] She feared that pupils might assume the morally flexible characters that they played. Such acting complemented the artifice of elaborate court etiquette. More hoped to enlist the potential mimetic effects of role-playing on the side of virtue. If young ladies acted in salutary roles, then they would learn lasting moral sense from their characters. More struck a chord with teachers and parents sick of enervating frivolity from their girls. Priced at a relatively high 1s. 6d., this drama sold nearly ten thousand copies in nine editions by 1787. Performances became common at boarding schools for girls throughout Britain.[17]

The reasons for the contemporary appeal of *The Search After Happiness* are not immediately apparent. While nearly all female authors in the eighteenth century depreciated their own work in the prologue, More's assessment of her piece as "void of wit and free of love" was appropriate.[18] She meant it to be grave and unembellished. She deliberately designed a play with "no comic ridicule, no tragic swagger, not one elopement, not one bowl or dagger, no husband wrong'd, who trusted and believed, no father cheated, and no friend deceiv'd, no libertine in glowing strains describ'd, [and] no lying chambermaid the rake had bribed."[19] Moral and ethical instruction required suitable roles.

More employed the familiar didactic trope of a frustrating search for happiness. Samuel Johnson, among others, had pop-

---

[15]Hannah More, Preface to *The Search After Happiness*, *The Works of Hannah More* vol.1 (Philadelphia: Woodward, 1832), pp.110-1.

[16]Jane Austen, *Mansfield Park*, 1814, Tony Tanner, ed., (London: Penguin Press, 1985), pp.147-78.

[17]For the circulation figures, see Jones, *Hannah More*, p.15. For the memories of a woman who participated in this play as a girl, see Mary Russell Mitford to Sir William Elford, 3 December 1813, R. Brimley Johnson, ed., *The Letters of Mary Russell Mitford* (New York: The Dial Press, 1925), pp.106-8.

[18]Hannah More, Prologue to *The Search After Happiness*, *The Works of Hannah More* vol.1 (Philadelphia: Woodward, 1831), p.111.

[19]Ibid.

ularized this type of story to underscore the follies of high society.[20] Accordingly, the opening scene depicts four young ladies who have run away "from the gay misery of the thoughtless great, the walks of folly, [and] the disease of state"[21] to seek contentment in the countryside. Like the youthful travelers of Samuel Johnson's *Rasselas*, they find peace of mind elusive. They seek Urania, an elderly shepherdess in "whose sagacious mind" the girls discern that the secrets of bliss lie. On their journey, they meet Florella, a young shepherdess who leads them to Urania and Urania's daughters.[22]

In the next scene, each of the four divulges her various and hapless methods of discovering lasting pleasure. Euphelia has "try'd the pow'r of pomp and costly glare"[23] of aristocratic culture. Yet outdressing competitors for men at court has grown tiresome. Cleora, the Hannah More of this story, believes that the pursuit of knowledge brings gratifying fame. Eschewing "the salique [sic] laws of pedant schools,"[24] she has dabbled in every science and art. Yet quoting learned authorities and using technical jargon do not satisfy her. In contrast, Pastorella has sought fulfillment through fiction, not facts. But reading novels about fashionable frolics has "stole[n] . . . [her] health, and rest, and peace away."[25] Laurinda, on the other hand, has retreated into passive indolence. But her attempt to avoid sorrow through inactivity has made her tired and depressed. In the final scene, Urania recommends the life of a pious, self-disciplined, busy laywoman active in "laborious

---

[20]For a *Search After Happiness* written by a man, see Samuel Johnson, "The Vanity of Human Wishes," 1749 in *Eighteenth-Century English Literature* (New York: Harcourt Brace Jovanovich, 1969), pp.973-8. See also Samuel Johnson, *The History of Rasselas Prince of Abissinia*, 1759, J. P. Hardy, ed., (Oxford: Oxford University Press, 1988); Hester Salusbury (soon-to-be Hester Thrale), "Imagination's Search after Happiness," *St. James' Chronicle*, 8, 9, 10 September 1763.
[21]Hannah More, *The Search After Happiness*, *The Works of Hannah More* vol. 1 (Philadelphia: Woodward, 1832), p.111.
[22]Ibid., pp.111-3; c.f. Johnson, *History of Rasselas*.
[23]More, *Search After Happiness*, *Works*, p.113.
[24]Ibid., p.115.
[25]Ibid., p.115.

schemes" on behalf of other people as the best chance for happiness on earth. An ode to charity ends the play.[26]

In *The Search After Happiness*, More justified institutional education for girls and, at times, adult women. Through the Adamless Eden of Urania's grove, she stressed that young ladies had to escape men at least temporarily in order to become aggressive Christians. The four wanderers lament that "the walks of public life, the toils of wealth, ambition's strife, . . . the crowded city's noisy den, and all the busy haunts of men afford but care and pain." But Urania and her daughters enjoy "the soft, soothing power of calm Reflection's silent hour . . . where Care and Tumult ne'er intrude."[27] Here More seemed to dispute the godly preference for holy matrimony over what ardent protestants saw as unnatural celibacy. Solitude, not the married state, was the "parent of virtue, the nurse of Thought." With solitude "the charm of life shall last," and "shalt prepare . . . [one] for the next life."[28]

Yet More, like the novelists Daniel Defoe and Samuel Richardson,[29] embraced female separatism (at least for adolescents and young adults) to make middling-sort and genteel women ardent protestants, useful subjects, and suitable wives. Accordingly, Urania tells the young travelers to stop roaming the globe for a good time. "For that true peace . . . must be found at home."[30] The reference to "home" meant "in your own breast." Urania does not mean that true peace came from staying at home with a husband and children. Godliness and the resultant inner peace was within one's heart. Female friends

---

[26]Ibid., p.115-9. Coincidentally, this was the lesson of Hester Salusbury (soon-to-be Hester Thrale Piozzi) in her fable "Imagination's Search After Happiness." (*St. James' Chronicle*, 8,9,10 September 1763).

[27]More, *Search After Happiness*, *Works*, p.112.

[28]Ibid., p.113.

[29]In particular, see Daniel Defoe, *An Essay Upon Projects* (London: Cockerill, 1967); Samuel Richardson, *The History of Sir Charles Grandison In a Series of Letters* vol.3, 1754 (Oxford: Blackwell 1931), pp.380-3; Kasbekar, *Power Over Themselves*, pp.104-11. For other proponents of exclusively female seminaries such as Mary Astell, see Katherine M. Rogers, *Feminism in Eighteenth-Century England* (Urbana, Ill.: University of Illinois Press, 1982), pp.71-3; Alice Browne, *The Eighteenth-Century Feminist Mind* (Brighton, Sussex: The Harvester Press, 1987), pp.95-101.

[30]More, *Search After Happiness*, *Works*, p.118.

and relatives, not husband or father, fostered the godly virtues in other women. A self-disciplined and temperate laywoman, bolstered by the support of virtuous female friends, was the best wife, mother, and community caregiver.[31]

The interaction of Urania and her daughters underscores the importance More gave to relationships between females in the promotion of godly living. For Urania, her daughters "bless her growing years, and by their virtues, will repay her cares."[32]

On the other hand, her daughters have benefited from Urania's sound moral and ethical instruction. They are friends and comforts to each other. It is no wonder, then, that this play sold well with the spinsters who nurtured young girls in boarding schools without male intervention. More did not, however, use her own conventional and shadowy mother as the model for Urania, but rather drew upon her father's life and character. The elderly shepherdess' background was the same as Jacob More's. Like Hannah's father, Urania had once had genteel status. "Adverse fortune" had drawn her away from the prosperous estate of her youth. Like Jacob More, she bounces back to educate and advise intelligent and virtuous daughters. Ironically, Hannah More's strong emphasis on the relationship between mother and daughter rested largely on the benevolent patriarchy of Jacob More.[33]

Hannah More's ideal of the godly laywoman both challenged and validated conventional female roles. At times, her protestant emphasis on individual conscience eclipsed her attachment to the traditional gender hierarchy. For example, Urania urges her female admirers to please God and themselves first, and husbands, male friends, and fathers second. The elderly shepherdess tells beautiful Euphelia to redirect her ambition away from pleasing men through fancy dress and artful coquetry toward self-examination and philanthropy. This reorientation

---

[31]Ibid., p.117-9.

[32]Ibid., p.112.

[33]c.f. Kowaleski-Wallace, "Milton's Daughters," pp.284-90. Kowaleski-Wallace suggests that Jacob More's benevolent patriarchy inhibited any emphasis on mother-daughter ties in Hannah More's works. Since More looked to her father for knowledge and advice, according to Kowaleski-Wallace, her works were very man-centered. Obviously, that is not the case here.

would raise her self-esteem and increase her chances for eternal salvation. Invoking the apostle Paul's injunction to obey God rather than man, Urania insists that Euphelia disobey ungodly dictates from a husband or father. To Urania, Euphelia can justify her rebellion by an appeal to the omnipotent authority of the Eternal Father.[34]

Hannah More disguised this challenge to masculine supremacy with a veneer of conformity to the fashionable world. While trying to create virtue in her charges, More did not want to alienate parents and subscribers; hence, Urania guarantees that, in the long term, assertive piety charmed men more than a low-cut bodice or well-turned phrase. A virtuous woman could change the most sinful man into a Christian. Furthermore, unlike Wesleyan preachers, Urania deems fashionable dress and innocent flirtation acceptable if combined with self-control and caregiving. Indeed, a semester budget of a student at the Mores' school indicates a keen interest in expensive clothing and cosmetics. "Coral lips may sure speak common sense."[35]

In a self-revealing passage, Hannah More criticized a young woman for encroaching upon masculine domains. Here Urania tells intelligent Cleora to redirect her ambition to impress men through her display of knowledge into pleasing herself and God through focusing on Scripture. Echoing the Anglican theologian William Law,[36] More contended that virtuous women were better equipped than nearly all men to comprehend the Bible because of their "intuition" and kind ways. Cleora ought to concentrate on learning useful information fit for her gender— "the gentler charms which wait on female life which grace the daughter and adorn the wife" and, most importantly, Bible

---

[34]More, *Search After Happiness, Works*, p.117.
[35]The quotation is from More, *Search After Happiness, Works*, p.117. For the semester budget, see Hopkins, *Hannah More*, pp.20-1.
[36]William Law, "A Serious Call to a Devout and Holy Life," 1726, in *Works of the Reverend William Law* vol.4 (London: n.p., 1893), pp.192-3; Dr. John Gregory, on of the most cited authorities on the education of young ladies, also thought "the natural softness and sensibility" of women "render[ed them] particularly susceptible of the feelings of devotion." (John Gregory, *A Father's Legacy to His Daughters* (London: W. Strahan, T. Cadell, and W. Creech, 1744)[Garland reprint, 1974], p.10.)

study. She should not babble about title page quotations and index citations before men at French-inspired salons, "for a woman shines but in her proper sphere."[37] Since the female sphere involved religion, however, it allowed intelligent women the chance to exercise their minds in satisfying and, at times, independent ways.

Hannah More both followed and defied the traditional gender hierarchy in her own life as well as in her first play. Her close ties to her father fit the close father-daughter relationship idealized by Georgian society, even if Jacob's tutoring of Hannah did not. Her decorous affinity for older, sexually non-threatening men continued into young adulthood. While Urania and her daughters revel in an Adamless Eden, Hannah More and her sisters cultivated prominent, local, and mature men who resembled their father. The Mores were always comfortable dealing with people of both sexes who were either considerably older or younger than themselves. Innovative teachers of children, they had an extraordinary rapport with the middle-aged and elderly, especially men. Their next-door neighbor Dr. James Stonhouse, a physician turned Anglican cleric in his fifties, escorted the Mores about Bristol.[38]

Hannah More entered public and masculine realms through her deferential affinity for older men. The quarters above the school became a meeting place for local elderly savants. The political economist Josiah Tucker and the astronomer James Ferguson asked More to criticize their manuscripts because of her well-known common sense, a quality which contemporaries found elusive in women, particularly schoolmarms. She perfunctorily pleaded that she, as a young woman, knew nothing about trade or the planets. Then, she eagerly took up their offers.[39]

More also became involved in politics, an arena which contemporaries viewed as exclusively masculine, but her involve-

---

[37]More, *Search After Happiness, Works*, p.118.
[38]Hopkins, *Hannah More*, pp.25,41. Kowaleski-Wallace points out More's "fixation with older men," but forgets about her attraction to older women, a pattern that developed after the deaths of older men important in her life (such as her father Jacob in 1783). ("Milton's Daughters," p.285.)
[39]Jones, *Hannah More*, p.14.

ment was largely private and, therefore, within gender standards. The Bristol parliamentary election of 1774 featured the challenge of Edmund Burke and Henry Kruger to the incumbents, Lord Clare and Matthew Brickdale. Hannah More and her sisters were ardent partisans of Burke, having met him in London earlier that year.[40]

Their Park Street school became one of the headquarters for Burke's campaign. Hannah More scribbled casual verse to highlight Burke's virtues, but she praised his personal qualities only. She did not publically endorse his positions on issues; she did not air her private misgivings about his support for the American colonists. This stance adhered to conventional notions of female place. When Burke won an unanticipated victory, a grateful crowd of his supporters publically demonstrated their appreciation of Hannah's contributions in front of the Mores' school on chairing day. The sisters, however, remained properly inside.[41]

Private rapport with established figures could sometimes be as awkward to the sisters as overt participation in politics. In 1774 Burke and Hannah More's close friend Josiah Tucker vilified each other over taxation of the American colonies. One morning, Burke, Tucker, and the historian Catherine Macaulay, who had attacked both Burke and Tucker, visited the sisters, "fortunately in succession."[42]

Failed attempts at marriage to an older man launched Hannah More's career of writing for public audiences in Bath and London. Her first and only *fiancé* was William Turner, a

---

[40]In a letter to an old friend, Burke attributed his victory to "the incredible activity of the best and most spirited friends that ever man had; the faces of many of whom I never saw until this Election." (Edmund Burke to Charles O'Hara, 2 November 1774, George H. Guttridge, ed., *The Correspondence of Edmund Burke* vol.3 (Chicago: University of Chicago Press, 1961), p.72).

[41]c.f. Jones, *Hannah More*, pp.19-20.

[42]Roberts, *Memoirs*, p. 58; Jones, *Hannah More*, p. 19-20. More's support of Burke dimmed after the election. In 1775 she was angry with Burke "over an unhandsome paragraph on the Dean of Gloucester (Josiah Tucker)." Although her new London friends told her that the private and public Burke were two different people, she did not understand "why a person should not be bound to speak the truth in the House of Commons as much as in his own house" (Hannah More to her sisters in Bristol, 1775, Roberts, *Memoirs*, p.58).

local middle-aged notable.[43] In the late 1760s, she met Turner through his young cousins who attended her Park Street school. To More, Turner was the epitome of eighteenth century masculine virtue—an austere country gentleman of moderate estate who avoided the corrupting influence of commerce and fashion. By marrying William Turner, she could recover the gentility denied to her father. But she loved him, not his land. It was a match of similar, not opposite, personalities. Both were earnest and refined; both enjoyed long walks in Turner's Somerset forests. Turner was not a Squire Bramble who swilled liquor and hunted game.

Fragmentary evidence, however, indicates that More loved Turner more like a father than a *fiancé*. Their relationship was akin to what contemporaries viewed as the ideal one between father and daughter. She trusted him and devoted her time to him, giving up her share in the Park Street school upon accepting his marriage proposal. In turn, Turner was tender and condescending toward More. An amateur poet, he was proud of his sweetheart's writings, nailing inscriptions of her work onto trees in his front yard. But there were no outward hints of sexual attraction. It is true that women were not supposed to have erotic feelings. Ladies and gentlemen were not permitted to be explicit in expressing their innermost urges. More, in particular, seemed unusually reserved during this courtship. Turner may have had second thoughts about a woman who approximated the usually unattainable ideal of feminine sexual frigidity.[44]

Whatever the reasons, the engagement lapsed, but not without unforeseen complications. Turner nearly destroyed More with his ambiguous intentions. He jilted her at the church on their wedding day three times. Then, he had the nerve to beg

---

[43]The most detailed (if admittedly antagonistic) account of More's relationship with Turner remains "Recollections of Hannah More," in *The Collected Writings of Thomas de Quincey* vol. 14, David Masson, ed. (London: A. & C. Black, 1897), pp.94-131. de Quincey was an apostate Evangelical whose saintly mother was a close friend of Hannah More in Somerset. In addition, see Hopkins, *Hannah More*, pp.32-7.

[44]Hopkins, *Hannah More*, pp.32-7. For contemporary ideas on courtship and love, see Jean Hagstrum, *Sex and Sensibility: Ideal and Erotic Love from Milton to Mozart* (Chicago: University of Chicago, 1980), pp.1-23.

her for another try at marriage. More was devastated. She suffered "a morbid sensibility of constitution," translated by her last biographer as a full-blown nervous breakdown. But she was much more embarrassed than heartbroken. Concerned about public ridicule, Hannah More understandably worried about the reaction of the school's clientele. Since she let this happen three times, they might have justly questioned her judgment and intelligence! She soon recovered, however. After the last reversal in 1772, William Turner compensated her distress with a lifetime annuity of L200. The local grapevine criticized More for taking the money, chastising "her calculating prudence."[45]

What Bristol did not realize was that Dr. Stonhouse, one of More's father figures, negotiated this settlement without telling her. At any rate, this annuity offered More the financial independence necessary to leave provincial Bristol for the highest literary circles. She never seriously considered marriage again, even if she continued to associate with older men and to advise young ladies to marry.

Older women introduced the newly independent More to London intellectuals, patronizing (or, more appropriately, matronizing) her literary career. She accompanied her sisters Sarah and Martha on a sight-seeing trip to the capital during the winter season of 1773-4. A well-connected subscriber to their school, the venerable Mrs. Edward Lovell Gwatkin, wrote a letter of introduction on their behalf to the portrait painter Frances Reynolds, the sister of the distinguished artist Sir Joshua Reynolds. This "matronizing" was not a real departure, however, from young Hannah's veneration of older men; most of the City's literati were men over forty. Indeed, Reynolds introduced the schoolmistresses to her acquaintances—her brother Sir Joshua, Edmund Burke, Samuel Johnson, and the noted historian of the theater Thomas Percy, among other important men. The Shakespeare scholar Elizabeth Montagu was one of the few learned women on the Mores' itinerary.[46]

---

[45]Charlotte M. Yonge, *Hannah More* (Boston: Roberts Brothers, 1888), p.4.
[46]For Hannah's first impressions of London, see Hannah More to Mrs. Gwatkin, 1773, Roberts, *Memoirs*, pp.38-40.

Hannah More was well-suited and well-prepared to converse with these mature intellectuals. First, she was used to talking with renowned and educated individuals. Second, she embodied the cultural style of Georgian artists and intellectuals who believed in the power of being earnest. More's diligence and moralizing won over the famous Literary Club and Bluestockings in part because nearly all of them had escaped provincial backgrounds similar to hers. For example, the Reynolds were the children of an eccentric schoolteacher in Devonshire. Johnson was the son of a poor bookseller in Lichfield. Burke was the son of an obscure Irish lawyer.

Hannah More also expressed the ambivalence of these self-made men and women toward the fashionable world. Johnson, in particular, excoriated his former patron Lord Chesterfield, "arbiter of taste notoriously identified with the French spirit" of well-mannered dissimulation.[47]

But Johnson cringed and catered to influential ministers for a royal pension. While Burke championed his aristocratic patrons in Parliament, he privately simmered over the necessity of deferring to well-born poltroons.[48]

Although Johnson and Burke prided themselves on their frankness, they indulged in flattery, the core of Francophile politeness. More blandished, too. She laid the compliments on thickly in order to fit in. Johnson once cautioned More that she should "consider what her flattery was worth before she choaked [sic] him with it."[49]

In May of 1774, on her second trip to London, More charmed the eminent actor-manager David Garrick, then 57, whose tolerance for flattery was boundless. It was from Garrick that More learned to make her didactic art entertaining. She admired his moving performances, which had contributed to

---

[47]Newman, *English Nationalism*, p.92; Samuel Shellabarger, *Lord Chesterfield and His World* (Boston: Little, Brown, 1951), pp.287-90, 378-94.

[48]Isaac Kramnick, *The Rage of Edmund Burke: Portrait of an Ambivalent Conservative* (New York: Basic Books, 1977), pp.190-6. c.f. Hannah More's comment—"They (the Reynolds) seem to think that the man and the politician are two different things." (Hannah More to her sisters in Bristol, 1775, Roberts, *Memoirs*, p.58).

[49]Quoted in Jones, *Hannah More*, p.44.

the revival of Shakespeare as the national literary hero. Garrick's acting was natural, in contrast to the stylized official French stage. He played out "the unique and idiosyncratic humors of the roles which he took on."[50] While French actors used the same gestures and movements to show vastly different characters, Garrick stressed the necessity of spontaneity and nuance to adjust to the concept of character. More preferred this type of acting over the mannered and imitative way. She also shared his view that the theater should instruct as well as please. It is true that most of Garrick's patrons at Drury Lane came for a sporting diversion. They were not disappointed, but Garrick, the grandson of a Huguenot refugee, believed that the stage could also be an instrument of public morality. He did much to clean up the acting profession, even if pickpockets and prostitutes continued to swarm to the boxes and galleries. Similarly, he was pious and uxorious off-stage, although frequenting the company of dissipated whigs such as Lord Shelburne and John Wilkes.[51]

More asked Garrick to edit her new play, *The Inflexible Captive*, and to produce it at the patented playhouse in fashionable Bath. He consented. Garrick had helped other budding female playwrights in the past. An uncommon male philogynist who nurtured the ambitions of quite a few intelligent women, he did not discriminate on the basis of sex.[52]

---

[50]George Winchester Stone and George M. Kahrl, *David Garrick: A Critical Biography* (Carbondale: Southern Illinois University Press, 1979), p.36. In addition, see Allardyce Nicoll, *The Garrick Stage: Theatres and Audience in the Eighteenth Century* (Athens, Ga.: University of Georgia Press, 1980), pp.9-15; Cecil Price, *Theatre in the Age of Garrick* (Totowa, N.J.: Rowman and Littlefield, 1973), pp.6-42; A. S. Tuberville, *English Men and Manners in the Eighteenth Century* (New York: Oxford University Press, 1957)[orig. pub. 1926], pp.419-20.

[51]In July of 1772 Lord Shelburne invited to his country estate on the Isle of Wight a number of eminent public figures including his friend David Garrick. Shelburne's guest list that July was "an extraordinary cast" of characters: Benjamin Franklin; John Wilkes; Colonel Isaac Barre, a hero of the fall of Quebec; and the Abbe Andre Morellet, an advocate of constitutional reform in France. For this party and Garrick's friendship with John Wilkes, see Stone and Kahrl, *David Garrick*, pp.373-4.

[52]For Garrick's literary friendships with and patronage of women writers, see Stone and Kahrl, *David Garrick*, pp.403-46.

More grew very close to both David Garrick and his wife Eva, who did not feel the least bit threatened by her husband's latest *protégée*. To More, David Garrick became an invaluable mentor who defended her both as an activist Christian and as a female writer against the barbs of worldly and cynical male critics. The 1760s and 1770s witnessed the appearance of a number of female dramatists such as Frances Sheridan[53] and Elizabeth Griffith. But the theatrical public viewed women playwrights as second-rate aberrations. Garrick's promotion of More helped to pave the way for her unreservedly warm reception. In return, More at first became the dutiful daughter that the childless Garricks had never had and then remained an old friend to Eva Garrick (who died at age 99 in 1822) long after her husband's death.[54]

Thanks to the Garricks, More's *The Inflexible Captive* (published in Bristol in 1774) opened at the Theatre Royal in Bath on 19 April 1775. More based this drama on her own translation of Attilio Regolo by Pietro Metastasio, chief librettist at the court of the Emperor Charles VI during the 1720s and 1730s. The odd voices, foreign speeches, and strange singers necessary for opera made it the diversion of the cosmopolitan and eccentric few. More popularized Metastasio's story, adapting it to the stage.[55]

Here the Carthaginians capture Marcus Attilius Regulus, a Roman general and patrician, during the first Punic War. Carthage hopes to trade Regulus' freedom for a favorable peace with Rome, so they send Regulus and their ambassador to Rome to negotiate a deal. Before Regulus and the ambassador

---

[53]Like More, Sheridan was a successful provincial playwright (in Dublin) before coming to the London stage.

[54]Dr. James Stonhouse paternally recommended Hannah More to the Garricks. See his letter to David Garrick, 21 May 1774, David M. Little and George M Kahrl, eds., *The Letters of David Garrick* (Cambridge, Mass.: Belknap Press, 1963), p. 1956. For the Garricks' consequent invitation to the Mores, see David Garrick to the More sisters, 27 May 1774, Folger Shakespeare Library, Mss, Y. c. 2601 (27).

[55]Although Metastasio was more popular than most librettists with English audiences. See Oliver Goldsmith's assessment of 1773 in *Collected Works of Oliver Goldsmith*, William Friedman, ed. (Oxford: Clarendon Press, 1966), pp.506-8.

leave Carthage, officials make the Roman patrician swear an oath on his impeccable honor. If he fails to persuade the Romans to cease fighting, he has to return to Carthage and face an excruciating execution. Regulus steadfastly refuses to sacrifice his republic's security in order to save his own life. He believes Rome is best served by conflict rather than peace. When he goes home, he exhorts his fellow citizens to continue the war until victory. It is a tough sell. Many Romans want to swap the prominent and popular hostage for peace. In particular, Regulus' family, in conjunction with a rowdy mob, lobby senators and consuls to adhere to Carthaginian preconditions for his freedom. But Regulus remains an inflexible patriot through five acts. He finally convinces his son and, most difficultly, his daughter to accept his self-sacrifice.[56]

   In her choice of a classical story to advance Christian teachings, More displayed the long-standing interchange between civic humanist and zealously protestant thought.[57] She saw no contradiction between classical and Christian views of proper behavior. Regulus shows that active citizenship could be sacrificial in the manner of Jesus. More strongly disagreed with the philosopher Soame Jenyns who claimed that real Christians could not be patriots because governments were inherently evil.[58] More agreed with Samuel Johnson, holding that Christians who withdrew from communal and civic duties were self-

---

[56]Hannah More, *The Inflexible Captive, Tragedies* (London: Cadell & Davies, 1818), pp.335-464.

[57]J. G. A. Pocock, *The Machiavellian Moment: Florentine Political Thought and The Atlantic Republican Tradition* (Princeton: Princeton University Press, 1975), pp.436-61; J. G. A. Pocock, *Virtue, Commerce, and History: Essays on Political Thought and History, Chiefly in the Eighteenth Century* (Cambridge: Cambridge University Press, 1985), pp.37-50, 91-123; Margo Todd, *Christian Humanism and the Puritan Social Order* (Cambridge: Cambridge University Press, 1987), pp.22-52.

[58]Soame Jenyns, *Free Inquiry into the Nature and Origin of Evil*, 1757, *The Works of Soame Jenyns, Esq.* vol. 3 (London: Cadell & Davies, 1790), pp.27-175; Samuel Johnson, "Review of Jenyns' Origin of Evil," The Literary Magazine, 2(1757), p.306; Soame Jenyns, *A View of the Internal Evidence of the Christian Religion*, 1776, *The Works of Soame Jenyns, Esq. vol.4* (London: Cadell & Davies, 1790), pp.1-121; Robert Hole, *Pulpits, Politics, & Public Order in England 1760-1832* (Cambridge: Cambridge University Press, 1989), pp.64-7.

ish, ungodly, and, therefore, only nominal Christians. Three years later, More admitted she liked the octogenarian Jenyns personally, but she thought he was "but a sucking child in Christianity."[59]

More revealingly orchestrated the major action of *The Inflexible Captive* around the relationship between Regulus and his daughter Attilia. This focus was certainly not unique. Relationships between fathers and daughters preoccupied Georgian dramatists. Officially, as Margaret Doody points out in her excellent biography of Frances Burney, playwrights idealized these relationships "as pure and holy, with the strength of heterosexual love, yet delightfully innocent."[60] Women writers "covertly and anxiously" questioned unthinking submission to Father's benevolent will.[61]

In *The Inflexible Captive,* More furtively asked whether father figures always know best. For example, Regulus' daughter Attilia beseeches her suitor Licinius, the tribune, and Manlius, one of two consuls, to work for the ransom of her captive father against Regulus' wishes. She explains to Licinius that she has entered the public and masculine realm of politics to keep policymakers aware of Regulus' fate. "If she be silent who will speak for Regulus?"[62]

To Manlius, Attilia emphasizes the value of her father's "godlike" virtues such as public service and self-discipline to Rome. She has no doubt that her love of her father and the common good coincide. Attilia's advocacy, however, angers Regulus. In the second and third acts, the dialogues between

---

[59]Hannah More to her sisters in Bristol, 1777, Roberts, *Memoirs,* p. 105; for More's appreciation of Jenyns' poetry, see Hannah More to Frances Boscawen, 23 December 1775, Rush Rhees Library, University of Rochester, Mss. Coll. 7, p.3.

[60]Margaret Doody, *Frances Burney: The Life in the Works* (New Brunswick, N.J.: Rutgers University Press, 1988), p.184. Excerpt reprinted by permission of Rutgers University Press. All rights reserved.

[61]Ibid., p. 182; Doody flippantly calls More's tragedies "droopy." She dismisses them as devoid of any objectionable material. Frances Burney, on the other hand, questioned patriarchal authority. My reading of More's tragedies suggests that both Burney and More made barely veiled points about the difficulties faced (and strengths evidenced!) by women. (c.f. Doody, *Frances Burney,* pp.96-7)

[62]More, *Inflexible Captive, Tragedies,* p.340.

Regulus and Attilia underscore the tensions between his Stoic calling to the commonweal, a major ingredient in ardently protestant thought, and her "feminine" appeal to the preeminence of private kinship ties over public obligations to the state. Attilia wants to talk with her father immediately after his arrival. Much to her distress, he shuns her. Regulus feels that Attilia has shamed him through her willingness to compromise Roman security for filial satisfaction. He partially excuses her because she is a female. Devotion to the family instead of the state is typical and, perhaps, appropriate for her sex; however, while he does not want Attilia to be a passive cipher, he thinks she should keep quiet in this situation. Regulus declares that "the present exigence demands far other thoughts, than the soft cares, the fond effusions, the delightful weakness, [and] the dear affections 'twixt the child and parent."[63]

At the same time that More seemed to identify with the sternness of Regulus, she sympathetically portrayed the concern of Attilia. Like Regulus, Attilia is stubborn. The Roman virgin counters that she is a patriot, not a parricide. Her private "vice" of wanting her father back at any price would prevent his execution and then would lead to the public virtue of his renewed leadership. Yet Attilia's arguments only heighten his resolve. Regulus calls his daughter "the worst of his foes—the murderer of his glory." While Attilia admits that she is ready to sacrifice her life to procure his release, he asks with contempt, "Who made a weak and inexperienc'd woman the arbiter of Regulus' fate?"[64]

He, like Hannah More, does not think women were inherently weak. Regulus wants Attilia to be strong and self-denying in his manner. Perseverance, not the pursuit of selfish needs, is necessary and, most important, possible in both sexes. The hapless general laments, "How can she be Regulus' daughter whose coward mind wants fortitude and honour?"[65]

In the fifth act Attilia decides reluctantly "to subdue the woman in . . . [her] soul" and emulate her father's "godlike" rec-

---

[63]Ibid., p.370.
[64]Ibid., p. 390.
[65]Ibid., p.391.

titude. It is a difficult decision for her. Just before Attilia changes her mind, she goes to tell Regulus that she has triumphed over his recalcitrance. While dismissing Carthaginian proposals for peace, the Senate demands that Regulus stay in Rome, vindicating the behind-the-scenes maneuvering of Attilia. Furthermore, plebeian crowds block every escape route accessible to the Carthaginian embassy due to her suitor Licinius' oratory. Regulus stubbornly says farewell to Attilia and begins to leave for Punic ships on the banks of the Tiber. His daughter's trembling detains him. Regulus turns to Attilia and pleads with her to suffer and be still. Here More parroted the traditional view of the fragility and inferiority of women, while she believed that women were capable of exercising the most strenuous aspects of Stoic discipline. According to Regulus, since Attilia could not serve her republic by "fiercely engag[ing] in hardy deeds of arms" due to her sex's "softness," she should "set a bright example of submission, worthy [of] a Roman daughter." Even if "such fortitude . . . [was] a most painful virtue," he reminds Attilia that she is his daughter and, therefore, must be as self-denying as he. She backs down.[66] Their reunion is not the typically blissful one of contemporary drama. It is forced and agonizing for the daughter.[67]

Attilia's acceptance of the values of Regulus resembles Hannah More's acceptance of her own father's values. After Regulus finally departs, Attilia resolves to "dare above her sex's narrow limits," assisted by misery. Attilia would try to be as godly as her father. Yet like More, Attilia also faces an inner struggle between conventional femininity and the unconventional ascetic virtues urged upon her by her father. For More, this stress probably abetted the frequent nervous breakdowns and psychosomatic illnesses which occurred throughout her

[66]Ibid., pp.432-61.

[67]c.f. the father-daughter reunions in the following popular and frequently revived plays . . . Robert Dodsley, *Cleone: A Tragedy*, 1758, (London: John Bell, 1792), Act 5, pp.57-63; David Garrick, *The Guardian*, 1759, in Henry William Pedicord and Fredrick Louis Bergman, ed., *Garrick's Own Plays, 1740-1766* vol.1 (Carbondale, Ill.: Southern Illinois University Press, 1980), Act 2, pp.187-97; Frances Sheridan, *The Discovery*, 1763, in Robert Hogan and Jerry Beasley, ed., *The Plays of Frances Sheridan* (Newark: University of Delaware Press, 1984), Acts 4 and 5, pp.83-101.

long life. It was hard to be "godlike," especially for women because God was male. By means of Regulus and Attilia, More tried to convince herself that the end was worth the pain.[68]

As with Attilia, More juxtaposed the civic-mindedness and self-discipline of Regulus with less "godlike" men. For example, Attilia's suitor Licinius, her brother Publius, and, initially, the consul Manlius support her campaign to keep Regulus in Rome. More made it clear that these men have purely selfish reasons behind their backing of Attilia. Licinius wants to marry Attilia, and her obsession with Regulus' fate cools their courtship. Publius expresses the same filial concerns as Attilia. Manlius hopes to avoid a tumultuous showdown with the Senate which desired Regulus back at any price. The inflexible captive denounces them. Ridiculing their efforts, he calls them unmanly. Here More expressed the conventional association of selfishness with femininity in both sexes. This theme differed from the unconventional message of *The Search After Happiness* in which More presented women peculiarly disposed to ascetic and activist virtues. Sensitive to her vulnerability as a female writer, More adapted to her audience. Whereas she wrote *The Search After Happiness* about females for females, she composed *The Inflexible Captive* for a mixed audience. If More had substituted Urania for Regulus, then she would not have reached as wide a public with her moral about self-sacrifice and self-control. The spread of godliness, not female self-awareness, was her main priority.[69]

David Garrick interceded on behalf of his talented *protégée*. Advertising More's merits, he wrote an epilogue (to be read by a female actress) which launched a preemptive strike against misogynist critics. Garrick characterized men who automatically dismissed women writers as stupid and unmanly. A disciple of Lord Chesterfield's fashionable and woman-hating *Letters* was

---

[68]c.f. Kowaleski-Wallace, "Milton's Daughters," p.289. Kowaleski-Wallace holds that Hannah More's frequent illnesses were symptomatic of psychological uncertainty about how far she sacrificed her identification with her mother in accepting Jacob More's values. I believe that Jacob More's values would be hard to uphold in themselves. In either a son or a daughter, they would cause a degree of stress.

[69]More, *Inflexible Captive*, *Tragedies*, pp.339-57, 361-8, 390.

merely "a sucking fop, thus lounging, straddling, (whose head shows want of ballast by its noddling.)"[70]

Men who sneered at literary ladies projected their own inadequacies on the female sex in general. While scorning women as grown-up children, they were as infantile as the childlike creatures they ridiculed. Most importantly, they lacked the "godlike" virtues of Regulus and, thus, would benefit from imitating the main male character (who unfortunately did not take women seriously either.)

Garrick then mentioned three contemporary women who rivaled the intellectual gifts of any man—Elizabeth Montagu, "who on French wit has made a glorious war, defended Shakespeare, and subdu'd Voltaire;" Elizabeth Carter, "who, rich in knowledge, knows no pride, can boast ten tongues, and yet not satisfied;" and Anna Aiken, "who lately sung the sweetest lay." He challenged any man in the audience to deny the aptitude of these Bluestockings because of their sex, or their personal probity because of their occupation. "What! are you silent? then you are content; silence, the proverb tells us, gives consent." Then, Garrick recounted the merits of *The Inflexible Captive*, hoping to dispel lingering reservations about the gender of its creator.[71]

The play was a hit. *The Inflexible Captive* pleased all the various segments of the theatrical public. For the nobles in their boxes, the neoclassical setting satisfied their taste for cosmopolitan aesthetics. On the opening night, More's sister Sarah observed, "All the world of dukes, lords, and barons were there . . . All expressed the highest approbation of the whole. Never was a piece represented there known to have received so much applause."[72]   For the tradesmen and professionals in the pit and galleries, Regulus probably exemplified the patriot who

---

[70]David Garrick, Epilogue to *The Inflexible Captive*, Folger Shakespeare Library, Mss. 492, fo. 28. Chesterfield's *Letters* came out the same year as *The Inflexible Captive*. Samuel Johnson declared that his book taught "the morals of a whore and the manners of a dancing master." (Quoted in Newman, *English Nationalism*, p.92.)

[71]David Garrick, Epilogue to *The Inflexible Captive*, Folger Shakespeare Library, Mss. 492, fo.28.

[72]Quoted in Henry Thompson, *The Life of Hannah More* (Cadell & Davies, 1838), p.25.

refused to collaborate with the alien influences of an historic enemy.[73] *The Bath Chronicle* noted: "the whole was received with a warmth of applause that reflects great honor on the Authoress and her friends."[74] Even Garrick's potentially controversial epilogue "had a good reception" at the premier.[75] Overall, first-rate actors and Garrick's realistic stage props helped to diminish Regulus' stiffness and to put forth Attilia's anguish. Yet regardless of effusive encouragement from Bath crowds, More depreciated her own work. She refused Garrick's suggestion about bringing the drama to Drury Lane in London because she did not think that it was good enough. Like a dutiful daughter, she attributed its success completely to the reputation of its producer Garrick, not to her skills as a playwright.[76]

Hannah More's poetry, not her *Inflexible Captive*, enraptured London audiences in 1775 and 1776. Sick of the praise and "flattering attentions" in the aftermath of her Bath debut, More told her sisters that she wanted "to venture . . . what is my real value, by writing a slight poem, and offering it to [the London publisher] Thomas Cadell myself."[77] Two weeks later, she finished *Sir Eldred of the Bower*, a ballad set in medieval England. At the same time, More amended *The Bleeding Rock*. She had written this poem a few years before in reference to her humiliation by William Turner. Then, she gave both pieces to Cadell to publish for the enjoyment and edification of her new acquaintances in London. Writing for friends and family was a common practice among eighteenth century poets. Accordingly, since she addressed members of the influential Literary Club,

---

[73]Routine plebeian reactions to similar characters in nearby Bristol suggests this type of plebeian response to Regulus on opening night. (Barry, *Cultural Life of Bristol*, p.198.)

[74]Quoted in Hopkins, *Hannah More*, p.50; the *London Chronicle* lauded the exemplary patriotism of Regulus in a commentary on the published text of More's first tragedy. (Review of *The Inflexible Captive*, by Hannah More., *London Chronicle*, 35(5 April 1774), p.329.

[75]David Garrick to George Coleman, 20 April 1775, Little and Kahrl, *Letters of Garrick*, p.1003. Reprinted by permission of Harvard University Press, Copyright © 1963 by the President and Fellows of Harvard College.

[76]Jones, *Hannah More*, pp.33-4.

[77]Roberts, *Memoirs* vol.1, p.58.

Cadell eagerly anticipated strong sales.[78] He advanced her a hefty forty guineas for her manuscripts, and offered to give her what Oliver Goldsmith had received in 1770 for *The Deserted Village* if she could discover the amount. No records exist to indicate that More claimed Goldsmith's sixty guineas, but she should have. Cadell prospered largely due to the popularity of his new client.[79]

Given the endorsements of Elizabeth Montagu, Richard Burke, and, most importantly, the difficult Samuel Johnson, who despised the reigning fad of old English ballads, *Sir Eldred of the Bower* became "the theme of a conversation in all polite circles."[80] Indeed, after tea one afternoon in 1776, Johnson and More ". . . fell upon *Sir Eldred*. He read both poems through, suggested some little alterations in the first, and did me the honor to write one whole stanza, but in the Rock he has not altered one word."[81]

Drawing upon her friend Thomas Percy's antiquarian research into old English songs, More adorned her favorite ideals of the godly layman and woman with unaccustomed Angevin garb in *Sir Eldred of the Bower*. In the seventeenth and early eighteenth centuries, the centuries between the Norman Conquest of 1066 and Martin Luther were anathema. Ignorance, deceit, and greed flourished during the High Middle Ages. Extravagance and abstraction obscured the mission of the community of Christ. Only the Renaissance and Reformation reversed this decline from the Stoic and patristic ideals of antiquity.[82] Nor were such views restricted to the godly. Alexander Pope, a Catholic, often equated Gothic with barbaric,

---

[78]The Literary Club and the Bluestockings received free copies of More's "little tales." Influential endorsements were priceless to any London publisher or author. For More's appreciation of this marketing strategy, see Hannah More to Frances Boscawen, 23 December 1775, Rush Rhees Library, University of Rochester, Mss. Col. 7, pp.1-2.

[79]For Cadell's enthusiasm, see Hopkins, *Hannah More*, p.63.

[80]Elizabeth Montagu to Hannah More, 26 December 1775, Roberts, *Memoirs*, pp.59-60; Richard Burke to Hannah More, 19 January 1776, Roberts, *Memoirs*, pp.60-1; Sarah More to Martha More, 1776, Roberts, *Memoirs*, pp.61-2.

[81]Hannah More to her sisters in Bristol, 1776, Roberts, *Memoirs*, pp.63-4.

[82]The Christian humanists transmitted these ideas to English protestants. (Todd, *Christian Humanism*, p.22).

looking to ancient Greece and Rome for inspiration in the same way as Dissenting divines.[83]

This antipathy toward the High Middle Ages grew stonger in the 1760s and 1770s. Patriotic historians revived the notion of "the nebulous and ill-documented golden age of the Saxon common man, the age before the coming of the Normans and the establishment of the feudal system."[84] Interest in Saxon language and literature intensified after the publication of Percy's *Relics of Ancient English Poetry* in 1765. The Saxons personified the godly virtues (which is hard to believe, given the self-centered Beowulf!) until the invasion of evil French aristocrats. This idea of the Norman Yoke undergirded contemporary radical critiques of the fashionable worlds, echoing the Levellers and other radicals of the previous century.[85]

While advocating what intellectuals deemed as either godly or Saxon virtues, Hannah More did not want to offend her aristocratic fans unduly with an overt endorsement of the Norman Yoke myth; therefore, she chose an Angevin story from Percy's anthology which passed the literary litmus test posed by classically educated readers. In short, it was simple, clear, and sincere. Most importantly for More, it was didactic. Through conversations with Dr. Percy, she began to recognize that crusading knights could indict current corruption as persuasively as Roman patricians.[86]

Sir Eldred of the Bower exudes More's faith in the instructive power of poetry. The legendary tale begins with a description of Sir Eldred, a twelfth-century knight. Young, rich, and valiant,

---

[83]Alexander Pope, *The Dunciad to Dr. Jonathan Swift, Book the First*, 1728 in *The Complete Poetical Works of Alexander Pope, With Life* (New York: T. Y. Crowell & Co., 1880), pp.390-401.

[84]Newman, *English Nationalism*, p.184.

[85]For the significance of the Norman Yoke concept in the late eighteenth century, see Christopher Hill, "The Norman Yoke," in Christopher Hill, *Puritanism and Revolution* (New York: Schocken, 1964, orig. pub. 1958), pp.75, 94-100, 111-12; Newman, *English Nationalism*, pp.189-91.

[86]Hannah More met Percy on her first trip to London. Frances Reynolds arranged her visit. Sarah More said that she and her sisters found Percy "a sprightly modern, instead of a rusty antique," as the Mores expected. (Sarah More to her sisters in Bristol, 1774, Roberts, *Memoirs*, p.49) See also Hannah More to Dr. Percy, 20 May n.y., Hyde Collection, Firestone Library, Princeton University, Johnson Letters VII, 144.

Sir Eldred is a godly layman who practiced ascetic virtues and discriminate charity. Most critically, he is an Anglo-Norman with an Anglo-Saxon name and character.[87] Yet Sir Eldred has a bad temper which threatens his normally Stoic self-control. After one especially violent rage, he takes a long walk through a nearby forest. There he comes upon the "little, modest mansion" of an aged warrior-sage Adolph and his daughter Birtha. It is love at first sight for Sir Eldred and Birtha. They quickly marry with the blessing of Adolph. Suddenly tragedy strikes when Sir Eldred's spleen gets the best of him. While Birtha embraces her long lost brother Edwy in Sir Eldred's bower, Sir Eldred mistakes Edwy for Birtha's secret lover, and slays him in a fit of anger. Soon after this accident Birtha dies of shock, leaving Sir Eldred and Adolph sad and bitter.[88]

More stressed that Edwy and Birtha are the victims of conventional masculine honor.[89] In shock over her brother's death, "Birtha fainted rais'd her eye/Which long had ceased to stream./On Eldred fix'd, with many a sign/Its dim departing eye."[90] Birtha has loved Sir Eldred single-mindedly, "unlike the dames of modern days/Who court the universal gaze/And pant for public fame."[91] But this emotional dependence kills her. Since the knight plays out his gender role as the jealous husband, he becomes a murderer. If only Sir Eldred had stopped to think before striking, then "his hand ... [would have] never err'd."[92] Once again, More concealed gynocentric tones within a standard construction.

---

[87]"Eldred" meant "old advice" in Anglo-Saxon. (*Webster's New World Dictionary of the American Language*. College Edition. (1957), s.v. "Eldred.").

[88]More, "Sir Eldred of the Bower," *Works*, pp.36-40.

[89]c.f. the common theme of Thomas Chatterton's "Bristowe Tragedy or the Dethe of Syr Charles Bawdin," posthumously published 1772, in *Eighteenth-Century Literature* (New York: Harcourt Brace Jovanich, 1967), pp.1409-14. Syr Charles was based upon Sir Baldwin Fulford whom Edward IV had executed in 1461 for an assassination attempt on the Earl of Warwick. Chatterton portrayed Fulford as a Gothic patriot against the usurpers of the deposed Henry VI. Chatterton glorified Fulford's sense of honor. He celebrated the knight's decision to fight regardless of the possibly bloody consequences.

[90]More, "Sir Eldred," *Works*, p.40.

[91]Ibid., p.39.

[92]Ibid., p.40.

More's other poem of 1775, *The Bleeding Rock*, was not quite as well-received as *Sir Eldred of the Bower*. Here she confessed her humiliation by William Turner in barely veiled language. This piece perhaps was too personal for London literati, even though, as Simon Schama points out, "outward expressions of inner sentiments began, in this period, to be acceptable" in trend-setting France.[93] Like Turner, Ianthe, the main female character, lives on the estate of Belmont close to a hill in Somersetshire called Failand. This sylvan nymph lives during the Roman occupation of Britain. Like Hannah More, she is comfortable with fathers and male friends, not male lovers. Indeed, she thrives because of the intellectual and spiritual companionship of men, the key element of More's relationships and, more generally, godly marriages. Then, young Polydore, "the pride of rural swains," visits Belmont, and steals Ianthe's heart. "Too vain to feel, too selfish to impart," Polydore resembles the sardonic and manipulative Lord Chesterfield more than the indecisive and shy William Turner. But both Turner and Polydore jilt their *fiancée*.[94]

At the same time, *The Bleeding Rock* revealed her skill at appealing to a reader's emotions thorough vivid imagery in a didactic tale, a quality of writing which contemporaries called "sensibility."[95] Like many literati in both Britain and France,[96] More juxtaposed the genuine feelings of Ianthe's heart with the hollow civility of rococo court culture as practiced by Polydore. More thought that this polarity happened in fact as well as fiction. For instance, at a dinner party at Elizabeth Montagu's in 1776, she observed the formation of conversational groups of

---

[93]Simon Schama, *Citizens: A Chronicle of the French Revolution* (New York: Alfred Knopf, 1989), p.149. Excerpt reprinted by permission of Alfred Knopf Incorporated. All rights reserved.

[94]Hannah More, "The Bleeding Rock," *The Works of Hannah More* (Philadelphia: Woodward, 1832), pp.40-1.

[95]For a concise look at "sensibility," see Edward W. Pitcher, "On the Conventions of Eighteenth-Century British Short Fiction: Part Two: 1760-1785," *Studies in Short Fiction*, 12(1975), pp.327-41; Janet Todd, *Sensibility: An Introduction* (London: Methuen, 1986), pp.1-9; Gary Kelly, *English Fiction of the Romantic Period 1789-1830* (London: Longman, 1989), pp.12-3, 42-3.

[96]For the significance of the cult of sensibility in the making of the French Revolution, see Schama, *Citizens*, pp.149-62, 171, 173, 802, 842, 872.

like-minded people. More found several of the clusters less interesting, "as they were more composed of rank than talent." She felt it "amusing to see how **the people of sentiment** singled out each other, and how the fine ladies and pretty gentlemen naturally slid into each other's society."[97]

This polarity, however, was not as rigid as More believed. Bourgeois ambition and aristocratic curiosity produced a degree of cultural fusion. Purveyors of sentiment and talent tried to be fine ladies and, except for the deliberately shabby Dr. Johnson, pretty gentlemen. On the other hand, possession of a "feeling heart" was becoming chic among the great.[98]

In accordance with this "sensibility," More designed the last lines of *The Bleeding Rock* to elicit tears. After Polydore jilts Ianthe, she could not face the public scorn. She begs the gods to change her into stone, making her heart as hard as his. They grant her request. Ianthe's heart dyes red the "flinty adamant" that she became, issuing a constant ribbon of blood. After Polydore hears of Ianthe's transformation, he collapses and, then, commits suicide near the rock, tingeing it with his own "ruddy streams of gore." As a result, "the life-blood issuing from the wounded stone, blend[s] with the crimson current of his own."[99] The rock bleeds forever.

The Garricks helped More to forget her own heartbreak, and to adapt to London society. More stayed with them at their townhouses in the Adelphi and Hampton on her seasonal visits to the capital in the late 1770s. In the lively *Ode to Dragon, Mr. Garrick's House-Dog at Hampton* published in early 1777, she celebrated and honored the domesticity of the Garricks.[100] David and Eva proved that godly morality did not stifle gracious living, intellectual growth, or exquisite feeling for others.[101]

---

[97]Hannah More to her sisters in Bristol, 1776, Roberts, *Memoirs*, p.63.
[98]Schama, *Citizens*, pp.133, 203-5.
[99]More, "The Bleeding Rock," *Works*, p.41.
[100]Hannah More, "Ode to Dragon, Mr. Garrick's House-Dog at Hampton," *The Works of Hannah More* (Philadelphia: Woodward, 1832), pp.42-3.
[101]Revealingly, More urged Dragon (who acted at Drury Lane himself) to be like his master in sheltering "the dog of merit and caress[ing] the cur of broken spirit." (Hannah More, "Ode to Dragon, Mr. Garrick's House-Dog at Hampton," *The Works of Hannah More* (Philadelphia: Woodward, 1832), pp.42-3).

The Garricks eased More's anxiety over the Sunday parties, obscure rituals, and elaborate hairstyles of aristocratic fans. The reputations and incomes of poets, playwrights, actors, and painters depended largely upon the fickle opinions of the notables. Hence, the Garricks counseled their provincial friend to mix propriety with fashion in behavior and dress for acceptability. For instance, David told her to make reasonable exceptions to her refusal to travel or visit on Sundays, while covering for her when she balked at Sunday evening concerts.[102] Eva, a former dancer at the Austrian court, told More about the importance of wearing the right clothes and cosmetics when trying to influence grandees and their wives.

More hated the ridiculous fads of the fashionable world, but she went along with them initially to humor aristocratic hangers-on at literary functions. For example, she wore the current colossal coiffure in London. In the 1770s the prevailing ladies' hairstyle was "as wide as their Hoops and as high in proportion."[103] In a letter to her sisters in Bristol, however, More privately complained that "nothing can be conceived so absurd, extravagant, and fantastical, as the present mode of dressing the head."[104] She said nothing about these concerns publically. Like any middling-sort client in Georgian Britain, More donned "sycophancy's mask,"[105] while advocating truth-telling. The following year she again secretly blasted those ladies who carried on "their heads a large quantity of fruit, . . . [while] dispis[ing] a poor useful member of society, who carried it

---

[102]David Garrick to Martha Hale, 25 July 1777, Little and Kahrl, *Letters of Garrick*, pp.1176-7; Hannah More to her sisters in Bristol, July of 1777, Roberts, *Memoirs*, p.113; Jones, *Hannah More*, p.30.

[103]For this description, see the minor dramatist Mrs. Joel Mendez Pye to David Garrick, 21 November 1774, Folger Shakespeare Library, Mss. W. b. 489, of.35. When Pye got the latest coiffure, she admitted in this letter that she looked "a good deal like one of the Horses in a maiden's Hearse, nodding under Plumes of white Feathers."

[104]Hannah More to her sisters in Bristol, 1775, Roberts, *Memoirs*, p.51; c.f. novelist Tobias Smollett's similar comments on the hairstyles of Parisian men in *Travels Through France and Italy*, Letter VII, 12 October 1763, in *Eighteenth-Century Literature* (New York: Harcourt Brace Jovanich, 1969), p.958.

[105]Roy Porter, *English Society in the Eighteenth Century* (London: Penguin Press, 1982), p.86.

there of the purpose of selling it for bread."[106] Eventually More compromised, with Eva Garrick's blessing. In Frances Reynolds' portrait of 1780, she wore her hair up, but not so high as to prevent her from walking through doorways.[107] But by 1780 the hottest styles in feminine dress were much more simple than 1774. Once again, More adjusted to fashion.

While coaching More on how to please the great, the Garricks worked tirelessly to assist in the production and writing of her most popular play, *Percy*. While More composed Percy in Bristol, David and Eva took the waters at Bath.[108] During their absence, they kept in touch through lengthy and spirited correspondence. Once again, More turned to the Garricks for the alloy of ego boosting and thorough criticism crucial to the development of any young writer. The flattery was, at times, effusive. David Garrick addressed his *protégée* as the personification of the Nine Muses.[109] In turn, More repeated the Duchess of Beaufort's comment that David Garrick was "indisputably the house of lords to Dramatic Poets" because "his fiat preclude[d] all other judgement."[110] The criticisms, on the other hand, were as vigorous as the compliments. On 28 July 1776 David warned that Mrs. Garrick "will criticize you to the bone" because German analysts always "suck an author dry."[111] Although Eva's opinions on the first two acts have not survived, the Garricks showered attention on More's latest project in blunt and perceptive commentaries on the last three acts.

---

[106]Hannah More to her sisters in Bristol, 1776, Roberts, *Memoirs*, p.65. See also Neil McKendrick, "The Commercialization of Fashion," in Neil McKendrick, John Brewer, and J. H. Plumb, eds., *The Birth of a Consumer Society: The Commercialization of Eighteenth-Century England* (Bloomington, Ind.: Indiana University Press, 1982), pp.63-4.

[107]See the second illustration after Hopkins, *Hannah More*, p.18.

[108]For almost a year between June of 1776 and June of 1777, Hannah More did not see the Garricks. (Jones, *Hannah More*, p.34).

[109]Ibid., p.27.

[110]Hannah More to David Garrick, 12 September 1777, Hyde Collection, Firestone Library, Princeton University, Johnson Letters IV, 239.

[111]David Garrick to Hannah More, 28 July 1776, Little and Kahrl, *Letters of Garrick*, p.1120. Reprinted by permission of Harvard University Press, Copyright © 1963 by the President and Fellows of Harvard College.

David Garrick worried that More's godly moralizing tended to interfere unnecessarily with the dramatic action demanded by London audiences weaned on Shakespeare. In rough drafts, her didactic art was as stilted as the mannerist stage in Paris. In reference to the third act, Garrick wrote on 20 August 1776 that the exposure of artifice lacked suspense.[112] By December More's corrections in the third act pleased Garrick, but now her fourth act left him "very cold."[113] The heroine's godliness was stiff and unbelievable. Nevertheless, this increasingly grave and pious actor did not want More to jettison her didactic themes. The Garricks and Hannah More concurred that the stage provided an excellent vehicle to improve the moral standards of the audience. David recognized, however, that her first drafts needed the vibrant sensibility and excitement that disseminated lessons effectively. Accordingly, he and Eva suggested creative ways to enliven More's play without diluting her praise of the godly virtues. In addition, they drafted the best available thespians, costumers, and lighting technicians, and persuaded James Harris, the manager of Covent Garden, the largest patented theater in London, to produce the play in early December of 1777.

Their efforts paid off. Like *Sir Eldred of the Bower*, *Percy* was a literary and commercial success. Almost universally acclaimed, it generated a profit of L750 by March of 1778; it took Lord North's mind off the British debacle at Saratoga; and it was translated into French by Charles de Calonne, Louis XVI's principal minister in late 1780s.[114] Revivals of *Percy* continued to please audiences in the next century.[115]

---

[112]David Garrick to Hannah More, 20 August 1776, Little and Kahrl, *Letters of Garrick*, p.1126.

[113]David Garrick to Hannah More, 17 December 1776, Little and Kahrl, *Letters of Garrick*, p.1148. Reprinted by permission of Harvard University Press, Copyright © 1963 by the President and Fellows of Harvard College.

[114]For reaction to *Percy*, see Elizabeth Montagu to Hannah More, 11 December 1777, Roberts, Memoirs, pp.124-5; David Garrick to the Countess Spencer, 11 December 1777, Little and Kahrl, Letters of David Garrick, p.1203; Hannah More to her sisters, 30 December 1777, Roberts, Memoirs, pp.125-7; Hannah More to Mrs. Gwatkin, 5 March 1778, Roberts, Memoirs, pp.137-40; E. V. Knox, "Percy: the Tale of a Dramatic Success," *London Mercury*, March of 1926, pp.509-14; Jones, *Hannah More*, pp.36-7. Hannah More was apprehensive about bringing out a play right after the surrender of

Like *Sir Eldred of the Bower*, *Percy* recasts a medieval legend from Thomas Percy's *Reliques* into a moral tale. Based on the twelfth-century story of Eudes de Faiel, this drama features the well-known rivalry between the Douglases of southern Scotland and Anglo-Norman Percys of Northumberland (no relation to Dr. Thomas Percy.) Once again, an Anglo-Norman is the tragic hero. *Percy* highlights the dire consequences of well-mannered deception and overweening masculine pride, the primary Chesterfieldian virtues. The Scot is artificial, while the Anglo-Norman Percy is a man of feeling.

As *Percy* opens, dissimulation is destroying the marriage of the Scot Douglas to Elwina, the daughter of Early Raby. In scene one, Birtha and Edric, confidants of Earl Douglas and his wife Elwina, speculate on the causes of the noble couple's unhappiness. Edric notes that Douglas "feign[s] to smile, and by his anxious care to prove himself at ease, betray[s] his pain." Birtha observed that "the canker grief devour[s] Elwina's bloom, and on her brow meek resignation . . . [sits]."[116] Unable to pinpoint the exact reasons for the couple's sadness, Birtha and Edric agree that Douglas and Elwina seem to conceal some painful secrets from each other.

In the next scenes, Douglas and Elwina argue. Douglas wants to know why his marriage was loveless. He thinks that Elwina shows only "cold, ceremonious, and unfeeling duty," not heart-felt love, toward him. On the other hand, Elwina grows defensive, heightening Douglas' suspicions of adultery on her part.

Shaken by her husband's questioning, she turns to Birtha and divulges her predicament. Several years earlier her father Earl

---

General Burgoyne at Saratoga. "What dreadful news from America! we are a disgraced, undone nation. What a sad time to bring out a play in! when, if the country had the least spark of virtue remaining, not a creature would think of going to it." But she reasoned that many, including herself, would benefit from an educational diversion. (Hannah More to her sisters, November of 1777, Roberts, *Memoirs*, p.122).

[115]For instance, see the praise for *Percy* by that friend of Wordsworth and Blake, Henry Crabb Robinson, in his entry of 11 November 1815 in Thomas Sadler, ed., *Diary, Reminiscences, and Correspondence of Henry Crabb Robinson, Barrister-at-Law, F.S.A.* vol.1 (Boston: Fields, Osgood, & Co., 1890), p.323.

[116]Hannah More, *Percy*, *The Works of Hannah More* (Philadelphia: Woodward, 1832), pp.502-3.

Raby had blessed her betrothal to Percy, a knight whom she truly loved. Nevertheless, after Raby's knights received insults from Percy's "churlish foresters," Raby forbade Elwina to see Percy. When Percy left for a crusade, Earl Raby forced Elwina to marry Earl Douglas, Percy's arch-enemy. She suspects Douglas does know that Percy is her true love, but still fears what Douglas would do if he discovered the whole truth. In reality, Douglas does know everything. He only needles Elwina with his inquiries.[117]

Their mutual deceit leads to tragedy. While Douglas and Elwina scheme, Percy returns from the Middle East to see his former *fiancée*. He is dumbstruck by the news of Elwina's marriage to his foe Douglas. In turn, Elwina keeps Percy at arm's length because she wants to preserve her reputation. Then, Douglas stumbles upon Percy, and they clash with Percy disarming his opponent. Yet Douglas' knights and guards intervene, confiscating Percy's sword. Douglas is about to slay Percy, when he notices Elwina's scarf on the Crusader's chest.[118] This public display of his cuckoldry, along with the use of guards to stave off defeat in combat, costs Douglas a considerable loss of face. In order to recoup his tarnished image, Douglas challenges Percy to a second duel without spectators. In the rematch, Douglas kills Percy.

Douglas' victory is pyrrhic, however, because of his hubris. Before the last fight, Douglas arranges to have a cup of poison administered to Elwina in the event of his death. He wants to protect his posthumous image as a good husband. Unfortunately, Elwina hears of Douglas' fall in the first fight, and surmises that he has died. She dutifully drinks the fatal poison, remaining faithful to her wedding vow to obey. Finally, Douglas commits suicide upon seeing his dying wife.[119]

---

[117]Ibid., pp.502-8.

[118]For the 1787 revival of *Percy*, Drury Lane advertised this scene. Douglas wore a combination of medieval and Georgian clothing. He had a sword in one hand, and waved Percy's aquamarine scarf in another. Percy and Douglas' knights did not appear in the print. (William Loftis, "Mr. Wroughton as Douglas," Folger Shakespeare Library, Art Collection, c16, no.1).

[119]More, *Percy*, *Works*, pp.508-16.

Like *The Inflexible Captive*, *Percy* revolves around the strained relationship of a father and his daughter. Regulus orders his daughter Attilia to forgo her filial concerns for the common good. Similarly, Earl Raby dictates his daughter Elwina's choice of a husband to secure his fiefdom. Once again, Hannah More had a daughter subordinate her own feelings to public or family policy. Furthermore, both Earl Raby and Regulus are oblivious to their responsibility for their daughters' despondency. Both Attilia and Elwina "endured it all; and wearied Heaven to bless the father who destroyed . . . [her] peace."[120] Their reconciliations with their fathers are unusually bittersweet for contemporary English dramas.

In contrast to *The Inflexible Captive*, *Percy* pits a relatively godly daughter and her former *fiancé* against a devious father and nominal older husband. More constructed no paragon of virtue in the manner of Regulus, making *Percy* more complex and interesting than her first play. Each character has flaws. Earl Raby and Douglas are manipulative and selfish. Elwina lies. Percy initially would not take no for an answer from a married woman. More stressed that the cunning of the father figures cause the mistakes of Elwina and Percy. At the end of the drama, Raby admits that he has killed the love triangle which he had created. When Raby "snatched the bolt of vengeance" from God, "a righteous God . . . made . . . [his] crime . . . [his] chastisement" in an anti-patriarchal fantasy.[121]

In contrast to the father figures, Percy and Elwina follow the most virtuous path possible in difficult circumstances. More celebrated the rebellion of Elwina and Percy against patriarchal authority in the first three acts.[122] She led her audience to sympathize with the lovers in their struggle against the fathers. Then, in the last two acts, More had Elwina finally submit to her proper duties. But this submission is only outward. Elwina's last

---

[120]More, *The Inflexible Captive*, *Tragedies*, pp.335-464; More, *Percy*, *Works*, p.507.

[121]More, *Percy*, *Works*, p.507.

[122]c.f. the similar rebellion of King Edwy and Elgive against the patriarchal authority of the Council and Dunstan in Frances Burney's *Edwy and Elgive*, 1795, Doody, Burney, pp.180-2.

thoughts are of Percy.[123] Like Samuel Richardson's heroine in
Pamela, Elwina resists her sexual (if not romantic) feelings for
her lover and then reluctantly capitulates to the demands of her
father and husband. Revealingly, More emphasized that Elwina
gains the approval of the powerful and raises her own sense of
self-worth through a superficial surrender to filial concerns and
duties. Stoic self-denial by Elwina requires strength and, at the
same time, diplomatic submission.[124]

In the prologue and epilogue to *Percy*, David Garrick presented a more aggressive woman than the Elwina of the last two
acts. For example, the prologue attacks the custom of female
self-depreciation before the presentation of works of literature
and art. Accordingly, More wrote *Percy* "as the friend and
champion of . . . [her] sex."[125] Women, moreover, could do as
much for their charges, countries, and God as men. In a few
couplets, the tone is half in jest, mentioning the infamous
transvestite Chevalier D'Eon as an example of a female public
servant whose sword by day became a fan by night. But most of
the lines are serious. Garrick reminded the audience that
women were capable of governing. Maria Theresa of Austria
and Catherine of Russia commanded two of the most powerful

---

[123]In Robert Dodsley's conventional *Cleone* (1758), the daughter in trouble
turns to her father and, later, her dying wishes are filial (while she dies in the
arms of her husband). (Dodsley, Cleone, Act 5, pp.57-63). For the making of
Cleone, see Ralph Straus, *Robert Dodsley: Poet, Playwright, and Publisher*
(London: John Lane, 1910, pp.200-51.

[124]Ibid., p.510-6; Samuel Richardson, *Pamela, or Virtue Rewarded: In A Series of
Familiar Letters from a beautiful Young Damsel to her Parents: afterwards in her
Exalted Condition, between her, and Person of Figure and Quality, upon the most
Important and Entertaining Subjects, in Genteel Life*, William M. Sale, ed., (New
York: Norton Press, 1958). c.f. Kasbekar, *Power Over Themselves*, pp.50-1.

[125]David Garrick, Prologue to *Percy*, *Tragedies*, pp.59-60. His first draft was
even bolder than this one.

> Indeed have Men alone the Powre for brains?
> They must rule better, or give us the reins.
> Let us but try our force, and if we fail,
> Men dare not at our bleeding cut and sail, . . .

(David Garrick, Fragment of Rough Draft of Prologue to *Percy*, Folger
Shakespeare Library, Mss. Y. d. 156, of. 42).

polities on earth. Surely, "the sex, without much guilt, may write a play" which urged moral reform.[126]

In the epilogue, Garrick boldly attacked the fashionable world. With More's approval, Garrick juxtaposed the ascetic forbearance of Angevin men and women with the self-indulgence of contemporary Francophile aristocrats. After mocking the macaronis in the audience, he sarcastically admitted that "old vulgar virtue cannot be defended; let the dead rest—the living can't be mended."[127]

Hannah More was more confident in the human ability to change than David Garrick. Nonetheless, she offered the repression of the later Elwina, not her own advocacy, as the role model for schoolgirls in a slim volume of ethical treatises, *Essays on Various Subjects, Principally Designed for Young Ladies*, which she wrote while revising *Percy*. As classroom instruction at boarding schools, these *Essays* were not as popular as *The Search After Happiness*. The lectures were exploratory, tentative, and had no unity. Surprisingly, given the liveliness of *Percy*, they suffered from stilted language (even by eighteenth-century standards) and shopworn platitudes with which no Georgian parent could disagree. Although these *Essays* advance a virtuous alternative to conventional female education, they emphasize the innate inferiority of women. More repeatedly counseled that "girls should be taught to give up their opinions betimes, and not pertinaciously carry on a dispute, even if they should know themselves to be in the right."[128] She did not always take her own advice, however. Hannah More overwhelmed the formidable Samuel Johnson in many literary debates.[129] Yet she insisted that ardently protestant women should obey men even

---

[126]Garrick, Prologue to *Percy, Tragedies*, pp.59-60.

[127]David Garrick, Epilogue to *Percy, Tragedies*, pp.187-8.

[128]Hannah More, *Essays on Various Subjects, Especially for Young Ladies, The Complete Works of Hannah More* vol.2 (New York: Harper and Brothers, 1843), p.377.

[129]For More's literary debates with Dr. Johnson, see Martha More to her sisters in Bristol, 1776, Roberts, *Memoirs*, p. 67; Hannah More to her sisters in Bristol, 1780, Roberts, *Memoirs*, pp.168-9. In the latter letter, More boasted that she was "very bold in combatting some of his darling prejudices: nay, I ventured to defend one or two of the Puritans, whom I forced him to allow to be good men, and good writers." (p.168).

if their consciences conflicted with male dictates. This position seemed to be a clear shift from her first play's invocation of the Pauline injunction to obey God rather than man. Female friends complained about this incongruity between More's actions and essays.[130]

Her actions and essays were not as inconsistent as her friends thought. More held that women "educated" at conventional boarding schools should be silent in male company; these woman had neither the skills nor the tools to challenge men even if these women knew that they were on God's side. She proposed better education for young ladies, nonetheless, to allow them to be able to challenge men. She could take on Samuel Johnson because she had had a good education; conventional women could not. It is true that More severely limited even the learned woman's exemption to dispute a man. More thought that women with a "masculine" education should not either unnecessarily challenge men on mundane points or argue in a way that would question their male opponents' masculinity. Yet through at least acting "feminine," and not "pertinaciously," they had a better chance, More wisely observed from personal experience, to persuade a man to their way of thinking. It is also true that Hannah More held that women were innately inferior to men. But she thought this inferiority was evident only in abstract speculation and physical exercise, irrelevant areas to literary debates and most other intercourse between the sexes. These gynocentric tones were unfortunately lost in the poor organization and pedestrian style of the *Essays*.[131]

---

[130]"Mrs. Walsingham has been reading your *Essays*, and likes them, (especially that on Education) as much as I promised her she would; but on the threshold she stumbled, and wrote me word that Lady Denbigh and she were in the greatest wrath against you for allowing men so much the superiority." (Mrs. Boscawen to Hannah More, 1780, Roberts, *Memoirs*, p.190).

[131]c.f. the error-ridden and superficial discussion of More in Lynne Agress, *The Feminine Irony: Women on Women in Early-Nineteenth-Century English Literature*, (Cranbury, N.J.: Associated University Presses, 1978), pp.48-52, 58-74. Agress stresses that Hannah More was "continually reinforcing women's subordinate role," (p.48) but Agress takes More's lip-service to convention too seriously. Agress also does not comprehend fully that More's derogatory statements about feminine intelligence were part of her critique of female training in contemporary boarding schools and were not necessarily state-

However poorly and provisionally she reiterated her ascetic and activist ideals, More showed uneasiness with her new-found fame and fortune. In her essay "On the Importance of Religion," she criticized herself for the compromises in dress and behavior that she had made in London. She feared that she was not devoting enough time and energy to the community of Christ. After attending Italian operas and dinner parties, it was "a wretched sacrifice to the God of heaven to present Him with the remnants of decayed appetites, and the leavings of extinguished passions."[132] Maybe writing for the stage distracted rather then instructed. In a letter to her sisters, Hannah More wrote that she was ready "to relinquish plays and to live in London without ever setting foot in a public place," especially if Garrick retired.[133]

Given the Garricks' encouragement and the kudos in the wake of *Percy*, however, More went ahead with plans for another tragedy, *The Fatal Falsehood*, in the autumn of 1778. Once again, David and Eva read and edited drafts which More sent them from Bristol. Once again, they recommended enlivening the action without eclipsing the moral. As in her previous plays and poems, More celebrated the plain virtues of rough fathers and mothers, although she placed *The Fatal Falsehood* in Elizabethan, not medieval, England. Like *Percy*, this drama underscores the ill effects of artifice and deceit, the virtues of Chesterfield's *Letters*. Once again, the plot of this tragedy involves a love triangle in which two men love a woman

---

ments about inherent feminine potential. Finally, Agress fails to appreciate the poor quality of eighteenth-century boarding schools for ladies and thus incorrectly considers Hannah More's emphasis on moral and ethical instructions reactionary rather than reformist. This myopic view of More has been echoed (although much more carefully than by Agress) by Sylvia Harcstark Myers who considers Hannah More "the most regressive" of Georgian literary women in "her attitudes toward the advancement of women" in *The Bluestocking Circle: Women, Friendship, and the Life of the Mind in Eighteenth-Century England* (Oxford: Clarendon Press, 1990), p.260.

[132]More, *Essays, Complete Works* vol.2, p.372.

[133]Hannah More to her sisters in Bristol, 1776, Roberts, *Memoirs*, p.72 c.f. Agress, *Feminine Irony*, pp.49-51.

who has pledged herself to one of the men. Once again, the father-daughter relationship is prominent.[134]

But *The Fatal Falsehood* was not a success. Most significantly, when David Garrick died in January of 1779, More lost all interest in this project. She lamented to Garrick's friend Albany Wallis: "Oh Sir! what a friend have I lost! My heart is almost broken! I have neither eaten nor slept since. My tears blind me as I write—. . . I write nonsense—I don't know what I write!" [135] Eva Garrick and other elderly friends convinced her to go on with the production for David's sake and packed the opening night house with paid and armed clappers.[136] Yet without David Garrick's stagecraft and commentary on the last stale acts, it lasted only three nights.[137] This run was considerably shorter than the standard break-even point of nine nights. Hannah More did not care.

Disturbing to her, however, were the claims of Hannah Cowley, a one-time *protégée* of David Garrick. This minor playwright publically charged that More had plagiarized the plot of her *Albina* for *The Fatal Falsehood*. The charges were false, but the publicity damaged More's reputation.[138] In reference to her preparation of a second edition of *The Fatal Falsehood*, her publisher Thomas Cadell told More that she was "too good a Christian for an author."[139]

Hannah More handled the emotional descent from the accolades after *Percy* through religious convictions which deepened after Garrick's death. These activist and ascetic principles had served her well in her transformation from a provincial schoolmistress to an eminent women of letters. Although a

---

[134]Hannah More, *The Fatal Falsehood*, *Tragedies*, pp.193-329. For Garrick's view of this play, see David Garrick to Hannah More, 23 November 1778, Little and Kahrl, *Letters of David Garrick*, p.1254.

[135]Quoted in Hopkins, *Hannah More*, pp.89-90.

[136]Mrs. Boscawen to Hannah More, 1779, Roberts, *Memoirs*, p.165; Jones, *Hannah More*, p.38.

[137]Although the drama had a relatively warm reception. (Review of *The Fatal Falsehood*, by Hannah More, *London Chronicle*, 39(6-8 May 1779), p.436).

[138]For the Cowley controversy, see *The St. James' Chronicle*, 7, 10, 11, 13 August 1779; *The Gentleman's Magazine*, V(49), September of 1779, p. 462; Hopkins, *Hannah More*, p.101-2; Jones, *Hannah More*, pp.38-9.

[139]Hannah More to her sisters in Bristol, 1780, Roberts, *Memoirs*, p.172.

member of London society by 1776, she never lost sight of who she was. It is true that she compromised with the fashionable world in terms of dress, behavior, and literary style, but the alternative to compromise was infeasible to the practical More. There were female writers such as Mary Wollstonecraft and Catherine Macaulay Graham who urged moral reform and, at the same time, openly flouted social rules, but they faced ostracism. The shabby treatment of Wollstonecraft and Macaulay demonstrated the fates of women whom contemporaries thought were too independent. Hannah More was a reformer, not a rebel. She never lost sight of the moral reforms that she wanted to accomplish, despite catering to the quality and their middling-sort imitators. More's identification with entrenched values and beliefs allowed her the freedom to advocate mildly progressive ideas about the education of women. Subtle critiques of aristocracy and patriarchy lay beneath her outward conformity. Understated messages were as far as she could go without enduring another painful public humiliation similar to the William Turner affair.

1779 was a nadir in her life, but it also marked a turning point. Before Garrick's death, More intellectually accepted the ideals of her upbringing. Afterward she embarked on a gradual conversion experience. From a famous literary lady with a didactic streak, she became the personification of the godly laywoman. Therefore, while she still aimed to reform the great and, later, the poor and middling-sort, she never again wrote for the London stage. She gradually realized that the theater was ineffective in propagating godliness. The stage promoted rather than diminished pretense and artifice. In her old age she regretted that she had ever written plays.

Chapter II

Faith and Feeling

Individuals often resent and reject poses and manners required by society. Gerald Newman has noted that eighteenth-century British intellectuals often spurned the cosmopolitan civility imposed by aristocratic patrons. They keenly felt the tensions between inner integrity and external conformity. These artists and intellectuals defined their natural selves as peculiarly English. They scorned polite and imitative behavior because of its French origins. Newman perceives that this embrace of "English Sincerity," in conjunction at times with evangelical faith, dramatically repaired the torn identities and divided psyches of young literati.[1]

As a commercially successful dramatist in the 1770s, Hannah More had wavered between socially acceptable values and the godly "English" virtues. Even though More prospered, she had pondered her decision to accommodate the quality. She wondered whether she had compromised too much with patriarchy and aristocracy. The twin crises of Garrick's death and charges of plagiarism in 1779 sharpened More's awareness of the conflict within herself between the alien fashionable world and the serious and native Christianity of her upbringing. In the early and middle 1780s, More gradually eschewed compromise and experienced spiritual rebirth in part through overt personal identification with the ideal national character. Through periods of introspective study, she shed her ambivalence toward the powerful in her poetry and prose, becoming a prominent social critic on the eve of the French Revolution.

---

[1]Gerald Newman, *The Rise of English Nationalism: A Cultural History 1740-1830* (New York: St. Martin's Press, 1987), pp.139-45; c.f. Marilyn Butler, *Romantics, Rebels, and Reactionaries, English Literature and its Background 1760-1830* (Oxford: Oxford University Press, 1981), p.71-2.

Central to this self-discovery was More's attraction to the Evangelical movement within the Church of England. The label "Evangelical," however, probably hides as much as it conveys about More. "Evangelical" parties, movements, and ideas clutter histories of late Georgian Britain. Accordingly, to understand both More's spiritual pilgrimage and the ways in which she equated "Evangelical" with the English national character requires a brief summary of the most significant beliefs and assumptions of Evangelicals.

Historians usually denote ardently protestant precepts which transcended denominations between 1780 and 1850 as "Evangelical." In turn, they frequently reserve the capitalized Evangelical or Evangelicalism to refer to religious fervor exclusively among Anglicans.[2] Thus in the eye of the semantic hurricane over who was evangelical or Evangelical, most historians agree that Evangelicals (with the capital E) were a self-conscious community of reformers within the Church of England committed to the spiritual and moral regeneration of late Georgian society. In 1785, the year of the parliamentarian William Wilberforce's conversion, there were roughly eighty Evangelicals, including forty to fifty parsons, of whom only two had London livings. They exerted disproportionate influence, however, through the intensity of their convictions and the celebrity of their converts.[3]

Evangelical Anglicans were doctrinely unexacting. They glossed over differences between Calvinist and Arminian soteriology; they cheerfully minimized friction over the meaning of infant baptism.[4]

---

[2]For this semantic convention, see Ian Bradley, *The Call to Seriousness: The Evangelical Impact on the Victorians* (New York: Macmillan, 1976), p.16; Doreen Rosman, *Evangelicals and Culture* (London: Croon Helm, 1984), pp. 5, 15. For a recent refutation of this semantic convention, see D. W. Bebbington, *Evangelicalism in Modern Britain: A History from the 1730s to the 1980s* (London: Unwin Hyman, 1989), pp.1-2. Bebbington applies the capitalized Evangelical to ardently protestant thought, whether inside or outside the Church of England.

[3]Ford K. Brown, *Fathers of the Victorians: The Age of Wilberforce* (Cambridge: Cambridge University Press, 1961), pp.2-6; Bradley, *Call to Seriousness*, pp.16-8; Rosman, *Evangelicals and Culture*, pp.9-10.

[4]In particular, see Brown, *Fathers of the Victorians*, pp.54-6; Michael Hennell, *John Venn and the Clapham Sect* (London: Lutterworth Press, 1958), pp.261-4;

Yet Evangelicals were united both in their pessimistic view of human ability and nature prior to conversion, and their cautiously optimistic view of human ability and nature after conversion. They held that people are innately sinful and doomed to Hell. A sinner could only escape eternal damnation through repentance of sins and acceptance of Christ as Savior. Evangelical Anglicans called this hurling of oneself onto God's good will "conversion." Such doctrines were not unique or original, but rather a reappearance of the emphases of the Reformation.[5]

Mentally distressed, middle-class women were prime candidates for Evangelical transformation. Godly metamorphoses often buoyed and liberated anxious and neurotic individuals in the aftermath of traumatic events, raising self-esteem. There was power in being born again.[6]

Nevertheless, Evangelical leaders tended to target the high and mighty for proselytization. This elitist strategy set them apart from the Methodists. While John Wesley preached to the masses, Evangelicals focused on the affluent. As Ian Bradley notes, "winning the high-born to the cause of Christ had a strong appeal for them, apart from its intrinsic merits; they felt that it would influence those of lowlier station who took their cue in matters of attitude and behavior from their betters."[7]

Evangelical Anglicans were well-suited for their self-appointed mission to the rich. The Evangelical Clapham Sect, a coterie of leaders started in the early 1790s, largely consisted of plutocrats with access to social circles that no Methodist could

---

Standish Meacham, *Henry Thornton of Clapham, 1760-1815* (Cambridge, Mass.: Harvard University Press, 1964), pp.11, 14-25.

[5]For discussions of the Evangelical stance on conversion, see Bradley, *Call to Seriousness*, pp.21-2; Rosman, *Evangelicals and Culture*, pp.11-2; Bebbington, *Evangelicalism*, pp.5-10.

[6]For the frequency of female and middle-class conversions, see Bradley, *Call to Seriousness*, pp.40, 44, 51; For somewhat dated but still useful psychological insights on conversion, see William James, *The Varieties of Religious Experience*, 1902, Joseph Ratner, ed., (New Hyde Park, New York: University Books, 1963), p.189; Robert H. Thouless, *An Introduction to the Psychology of Religion* (New York: Macmillan, 1923), pp.187-224.

[7]Bradley, *Call to Seriousness*, pp.36-7. See also Brown, *Fathers of the Victorians*, pp.4-10, 83-122.

crash.[8] They knew well the social conventions and manners required to persuade aristocrats. This inside information made them well-equipped to present the Gospel to the nominal Christians of the fashionable world. They at times diluted their message in order to win converts. Indeed, Ford K. Brown has accused prominent Evangelicals such as William Wilberforce of possessing "a genius for expediency, opportunism, and 'accommodation.'"[9] Evangelical Anglicans nonetheless indulged in rigorous self-examination and compulsive (yet not gratuitous) charity. This activism could lead to a religion of good works and morals only, but most Evangelicals held that benevolence and propriety were merely the visible measurements, not the necessary preconditions, of a true Evangelical conversion. They maintained the protestant justific-ation by faith alone.[10]

Evangelical Anglicans, once converted, were passionate about their beliefs. They reinvited the emotions into orthodox religion after a century's absence; consequently, their faith tended to be analytically weak. Dogma and speculation paled in comparison to heartfelt commitment and service to the Lord. Yet this preference did not diminish the penchant of Evangelicals for reading and writing.[11]

The Evangelical stress on personal probity and intense feeling validated and complemented contemporary attempts by intellectuals to resurrect what they claimed to be the solely English character of the disciplined and caring layman. The Evangelical philanthropist resembled the mythical Saxon so dear to literati who were active in community affairs and who sought the public good incessantly. The Evangelical mission to

---

[8]David Spring, "The Clapham Sect: Some Social and Political Aspects," *Victorian Studies*, (September, 1961), pp.35-48.

[9]Brown, *Fathers of the Victorians*, p.3. Excerpt reprinted by permission of Cambridge University Press. All rights reserved.

[10]Bradley, *Call to Seriousness*, pp.21-2; Bebbington, *Evangelicalism*, pp. 10-2; Maurice Quinlan, *Victorian Prelude: A History of English Manners 1700-1830* (New York: Columbia University Press, 1941), pp.112-20.

[11]Bradley, *Call to Seriousness*, pp.19-20; c.f. Rosman who cautions that Evangelicals were not intellectual philistines, even if they preferred emotional over speculative religion. (*Evangelicals and Culture*, pp.232-3.)

the Francophile aristocracy fulfilled the nationalistic fantasies of obscure poets who dreamed of censuring the alien mighty.[12]

Hannah More became an Evangelical and evoked nationalist idioms in her efforts to evangelize. During the early and middle 1780s, she became more self-confident and less self-conscious largely because she experienced conversion, however gradual. Accordingly, More withdrew from "immoral" activities that she had previously enjoyed such as writing for the theater. She concentrated on publishing pious poetry for the upper classes. But Hannah More was not one of Brown's alleged opportunists. Evangelical faith made her much less accommodating toward elite protocol. Here More hoped that the Lord would sustain her increasingly caustic crusade against decadent court culture. Her *Sacred Dramas* (meant for private reading only) and *Florio*, for example, censure courtiers who closely resembled the Francophile arbiters of taste in Britain. These pieces also underscore the coincidence of Evangelical and English virtue.

Hannah More became passionate about her creed in the Evangelical manner. Most historians have overlooked the fact that she also drew upon her deepening belief to expose the dangers of misdirected sincerity and passion. Literati who advocated feeling without faith undermined the social order and national character. Only the emotional quality of Evangelicalism, More held, should dictate the intellectuals' search for pure feeling. More became a philanthropist, the most obvious sign of her Evangelical conversion. She here turned to earlier female role models rather than to rich Evangelical males. More presented the conventionally Anglican Bluestockings' combination of individual expression and pious patronage as an example for both men and women. Along with the Blues and others, More sponsored poor geniuses whom she thought could further godly living in England. None of these clients worked out, in part because she ironically assumed the part of the thoroughly aristocratic patron, which she had long criticized.

Hannah More began her metamorphosis with a retreat from society. In the immediate months after David Garrick's death in

---

[12]Newman, *English Nationalism*, pp.123-56, 228-38.

January of 1779, she withdrew from celebrity because she was devastated by the passing of her closest male friend. She temporarily fled the fashionable world, becoming a virtual inmate at Eva Garrick's residences in the Adelphi and at Hampton. For most of 1779 (except for a regular summer trip to the More sisters' home in Bristol), Hannah More and Eva Garrick had few visitors and settled into a reclusive routine. In a letter to her sisters in Bristol, More admitted that her "way of life . . . [was] very different from what it used to be."[13] Needing time and relief for herself, she set aside plans for her project in progress, the tragedy *The Fatal Falsehood*. The controversy over the tragedy's authorship forced her to adopt an even lower profile. At first, More wanted to prepare an affidavit against Hannah Cowley's flimsy (yet irritating) charges of plagiarism, believing that her integrity as a moralist was on the line. But her publisher Thomas Cadell wisely persuaded her to avoid further damaging publicity.[14]

While the Cowley affair raged in the press, More threw herself into a schedule of wide reading, writing letters, and household chores at Eva Garrick's. In the late evening, Garrick and More drowned their sorrows in books, "which . . . [they] read without any restraint, as if . . . [they] were alone, without apologies or speechmaking."[15] It is true that she and Mrs. Garrick were not completely oblivious to outside events. More lamented the firing of her acquaintance General Howe as supreme commander of British forces in North America, the defeat of her

---

[13]Hannah More to her sisters, 1779, William Roberts, ed., *Memoirs of the Life and Correspondence of Mrs. Hannah More* vol.1 (London: R. B. Selley and W. Burnside, 1835), p.160. See also Hannah More to Richard Beringer, 1779, Historical Manuscripts Commission, eds., *The Manuscripts of J. B. Fortescue, Esq., Preserved at Dropmore* vol.1 (London: Eyre & Spottiswoode, 1892), p.162.

[14]For the Cowley affair, see *The St. James Chronicle*, 7, 10, 11, 13 August 1779; *The Gentleman's Magazine*, V(49), September of 1779, p.462; Mary Alden Hopkins, *Hannah More and Her Circle* (New York: Longman, Green, & Co., 1947), pp.101-2; Mary G. Jones, *Hannah More* (Cambridge: Cambridge University Press, 1952), pp.38-9.

[15]Hannah More to her sisters, 1779, Roberts, *Memoirs*, p.160.

friend Edmund Burke in his bid for reelection in 1780, and the violence of the Gordon riots in London.[16]

Yet this negative news only pushed her further into isolation. More acknowledged that she was in deep retirement, although she never considered her stay at Eva Garrick's boring. While mourning, Garrick and More "dress[ed] like a couple of Scaramouches, disput[ed] like a couple of Jesuits, . . . [ate] like a couple of aldermen, walk[ed] like a couple of porters, and read as much as any two doctors of either university."[17] In several ways, More saw seclusion as a blessing in disguise, noting that "as in the annals of states, so in the lives of individuals, those periods are often the safest and best which make the poorest figure."[18] She happily shied away from tedious visits from stupid, if influential, notables. She was tired of catering to the great.

Hannah More's contemplative life from January of 1779 through the spring of 1780 rekindled and focused her commitment to moral reform. She voraciously read puritan authors and works about puritans. During the winter of 1779-80, for example, she pored over the narratives of the godly Matthew Henry and the skeptic David Hume, "two gentlemen of very different ways of thinking on some certain points,"[19] and predictably identified with the saints. This pondering was a common step on the road to Evangelical conversion. Serious study of puritan, dissenting, and even nonjuroring sermons prepared the reprobate to surrender himself to Christ.[20]

More's deepening identity as a serious Christian emboldened her to censure others candidly and publically. In one of her

---

[16]Hannah More to her sisters, 1779, Roberts, *Memoirs*, pp.159-60; Hannah More to Frances Boscawen, 1780, Roberts, *Memoirs*, p.186; Hannah More to her sisters, 1781, Roberts, *Memoirs*, p.199.

[17]Hannah More to her sisters, January, 1780, Roberts, *Memoirs*, p.167; Jones, *Hannah More*, p.39.

[18]Hannah More to her sisters, 1779, Roberts, *Memoirs*, p. 160.

[19]Hannah More to her sisters, 1780, Roberts, *Memoirs*, p.166.

[20]Bradley, *Call to Seriousness*, p.51; Roger Anstey, *The Atlantic Slave Trade and British Abolition 1760-1810* (Atlantic Highlands, N.J.: Humanities Press, 1975), p.168; Jonathan Clark notes the influence of the Nonjuror William Law and the "High Church manual," *The Whole Duty of Man*, on evangelicals. (*English Society 1688-1832* (Cambridge: Cambridge University Press, 1985), p.243.)

rare public forays in early 1780, she felt confident enough to force the suspected Jacobite Samuel Johnson to praise the godliness of the puritan divine Richard Baxter. At a dinner party at Frances Reynolds', Johnson insinuated that Baxter had split with the Anglican hierarchy in 1662 because he no longer possessed the comfortable living of Kidderminster. To Dr. Johnson, Baxter was merely a peeved opportunist. More strongly objected. She correctly pointed out that Charles II had offered Baxter a bishopric which bestowed much more money than Kidderminster. According to More, Baxter turned down this tempting proposition because Charles' ritualistic and intolerant religious policies had disturbed his conscience. She then defended other puritans as good men and excellent writers.[21]

Johnson capitulated, but not for long. He fired back later that same evening when More "alluded rather flippantly . . . to some witty passage in *Tom Jones*." Given her heated defense of Baxter, Johnson could not believe that she could quote from such a racy novel. He angrily warned her that she had made "a confession which no modest lady should ever make." This time More surrendered. Thanking him for his incensed salvo, she assured Johnson that she hated Fielding's bawdiness as much as he did. When More had read *Tom Jones* in her youth, she "was more subject to be caught by the wit, than able to discern the mischief." Her recent diet of Reformed volumes made her recognize that this seemingly innocent diversion was a mistake.[22]

As a stalwart partisan of seventeenth-century saints, More naturally welcomed the first stirrings of the latest revival of heartfelt piety within the Church of England, later known as the Evangelical Movement. A few months after the admonition from Dr. Johnson, her loyal benefactress Frances Boscawen

---

[21]Hannah More to her sisters, 1780, Roberts, *Memoirs*, p.168.

[22]All quotations in this paragraph are from Hannah More to her sisters, 1780, Roberts, *Memoirs*, p.169. c.f. Beth Kowaleski-Wallace, "Milton's Daughters: the Education of Eighteenth-Century Women Writers," *Feminist Studies* 12, 2(Summer, 1986), p.286. Here Kowaleski-Wallace cites More's gratitude for Johnson's correction as evidence of her submissive stance toward older men. Yet she conveniently omits the preceding exchange about Richard Baxter which More decisively won. For additional (if dated) accounts of this incident, see Jones, *Hannah More*, p.46; Hopkins, *Hannah More*, p.61; Quinlan, *Victorian Prelude*, p.59.

sent her a copy of *Cardiphonia* by the Reverend John Newton, a former slave ship captain turned Evangelical cleric. More loved this new book. It is true that she had grave reservations about Newton's attack in Cardiphonia on the Stoic poets and philosophers of ancient Rome. More understood the crucial contribution of classical authors to ardently protestant thought. Yet More loved Newton's use of action-packed stories in the presentation of practical advice in his new book. In general, she found Newton's *Cardiphonia* "full of vital, experimental religion," and "found nothing but rational and consistent piety" in spite of his unfortunate indictments of Seneca, Ovid, Virgil, and Quintilian.[23]

During the next winter social season, More periodically attended Newton's sermons. As one of only two Evangelical incumbents in London, Newton became rector of St. Mary Woolchurch on Lombard Street in January, 1780, due to the patronage of John Thornton, an extremely rich merchant and banker who bought livings and advowsons for Evangelical clergymen on the side.

The reasons for Newton's appeal to More are not immediately apparent. He was a poor public speaker. His unconventional gestures in the pulpit rivaled Samuel Johnson's lack of refinement in the drawing room. Despite his shortcomings, More treasured his message. Newton exhorted Christians to participate in the world in order to improve it. His thesis was neither new nor unique, but his restatement of protestant orthodoxy inspired More to end her self-imposed isolation. Newton gradually became a father confessor to the renowned woman of letters who was weary of the Georgian Babylon around her and who was anxious to emulate seventeenth-century ancestors in spreading the Word and, thus, benefiting the commonweal. Newton liked More (as well as other new prominent friends such as Thornton and his son, the socialite William Wilberforce, and the Vicar of Holy Trinity at Cambridge Charles Simeon) because she respected him. Other

---

[23]Hannah More to Frances Boscawen, 1780, Roberts, *Memoirs*, p.180; Jones, *Hannah More*, p.87.

cosmopolites usually snubbed the Sierra Leone sailor turned Calvinist preacher whom they felt was far below their station.[24]

Hannah More reappeared in London society, now bent on wielding her pen in the moral and ethical instruction of grandees and their families. She appropriated the ancient Christian missionary strategy of first converting the elite for Evangelicals. Throughout the social whirls of 1781 and 1782, she starred at select conversation parties of literati and large yet dull gatherings of magnates and their ladies. At these soirees, aristocratic ignorance of Scripture never failed to astound her. More knew from reading and observation that ignorance fostered vice, hindering the creation of godly laity among the upper orders. She perceived that prominent spiritual illiterates hungered for a lucid introduction to Biblical stories. Accordingly, she dusted off some old dialogues based on Exodus and 1 Samuel that she used to have girls at the Park Street school perform and added several others based on the travails of Daniel and King Hezekiah to comprise skits for private reading, not public performance. Only in this way would there be no sensational distraction from the Word. More then persuaded Thomas Cadell to publish them at the lowest possible price. She wanted to undersell trendy and expensive nontheistic translations from France and the German states.[25]

On the eve of the publication of the *Sacred Dramas*, More confessed to her sisters that she worried about the reaction to her rewriting of Scripture into dialogue form. For the first time in her literary career, she was taking a risk. Samuel Johnson, the most influential of English writers, had recently panned the seventeenth-century poet Abraham Cowley's use of an Old Testament story. In reference to Cowley's *Davideis*, Johnson wrote that "all amplification [of Scripture] is frivolous and vain: all addition to which is already sufficient for the purpose of reli-

---

[24]For Newton's friendships with More and Wilberforce, see Bernard Martin, *John Newton: A Biography* (London: William Heinemann Ltd., 1950), pp.302-21.

[25]Hannah More to her sisters, January, 1781, Roberts, *Memoirs*, pp.192-3; Mrs. Benjamin Kennicott to Hannah More, 1782, Roberts, *Memoirs*, pp.220-1; Hannah More to her sisters, 17 January 1782, Roberts, *Memoirs*, p.223.

gion seems not only useless, but in some degree profane."[26] Clumsy and unauthorized attempts to produce the *Sacred Dramas* in 1793 infuriated godly preachers who objected to Biblical characters on the stage.[27]

More anticipated this turbulence. In the Advertisement published along with the plays, she emphasized that she had kept the original text as much as possible. Only in the trials of Daniel did More invent characters and circumstances. She noted that "the Bible furnishes no more than two persons, Daniel and Darius, and these were not sufficient to carry on the business of this piece."[28] Even there she introduced tropes that did not clash with the existing narrative. More was aware that readers might protest Jewish characters whom she presented as essentially Evangelical. She insisted that she was more interested in "leading [her readers] on to higher religious views, than in securing to myself the reputation of critical exactness." She also pointed out that she "aspired after moral instruction [more] than the purity of dramatic composition."[29] She resisted the temptation to choose more colorful passages in the life of David than his fight with Goliath.

More did not want her dramas to bore "the profane" among the elite, her primary target for edification. In the Advertisement, she appealed to the great's Francophile tendencies, venerating "the excellent Racine [who] in a profligate country and a voluptuous court, ventured to adapt the story of Athelia to the French theatre."[30] In the prologue, she summarized similarities between classical and sacred stories, wooing classically educated sophisticates. Pyrrha and Deucalion parallel Noah's ark; the Aeneid echoes Exodus; and Samson is Herculean. Classical virtues of simplicity, sincerity, and clarity reverberate in

---

[26]Samuel Johnson, *Lives of the English Poets*, 1778, George Birkbeck Hill, ed., (New York: Octagon Books 1967), pp.49-50.

[27]This incident happened at Hull. Yet "a genteel audience" at Doncaster prior to the races applauded the same performance. (Hopkins, *Hannah More*, p.102).

[28]Hannah More, Advertisement to *Sacred Dramas: Chiefly Intended for Young Persons, The Works of Hannah More*, vol.1 (Philadelphia: Woodward, 1832), p.75.

[29]Ibid.

[30]Ibid.

her skits. It was possible to read the following dramas for sheer pleasure. Duty could be delightful.[31]

More's appeasement of the fashionable world, nonetheless, ceased with the prologue. It is true that she remained unsure of herself. She predicted that readers of the *Sacred Dramas* would deem her faith stronger than it actually was. Exhibiting godly apprehension as well as feminine self-depreciation, More thought "sometimes of what Prior . . . [made] Solomon say of himself in his fallen state—'They brought my proverbs to confute my life.'"[32] She compared her belief in God with that of the characters in the *Sacred Dramas* and found herself a hypocrite. Nonetheless, More's selection of stories such as the rescue of Moses, the triumph of David, and the resilience of Daniel foreshadowed her future rather than confuted her present. In each group of verses, God chooses nobly simple outsiders, like Hannah More, to alert royalty and their subjects to the evils of epicene and selfish courtiers.

In *Moses in the Bulrushes*, the Lord empowers female Hebrew slaves to warn a princess of Egypt about the pernicious policies of her father's government. More stuck to the second chapter of Exodus most of the time with a few revealing embellishments. Worried about the number of Israelites in Egypt, the Pharaoh has ordered the deaths of all Jewish male infants. When Jochabed, a Hebrew, gives birth to Moses, she hides him for three months. Since Jochabed can not hide Moses any longer, she desperately places him in a small ark and lets it float down the Nile, hoping for someone to find and help him. Then, while bathing along the Nile's banks, the Pharaoh's daughter saves Moses, disregarding her father's cruel edicts. The princess rescues a prophet who would upbraid her own effete oligarchy.

More's subtle changes from the original story highlight the already substantial role of women as instruments of God against the depraved and powerful. She features the same female characters in the original, but she has Jochabed, her

---

[31]Hannah More, Introduction to *Sacred Dramas: Chiefly Intended for Young Persons, The Works of Hannah More* vol.1 (Philadelphia: Woodward, 1832), p.76.
[32]Hannah More to her sisters, 17 January 1782, Roberts, *Memoirs*, p.223.

daughter Miriam, the princess, and her attendants form an underground female and anachronistically Evangelical network against the abuse of patriarchal authority.[33]

The most self-revealing of her skits, however, are *Belshazzar* and *Daniel*. These dramas deviate considerably from the original text. In her play based on the fifth chapter of Daniel, King Belshazzar of Babylon is a callow and self-indulgent youth. To More, Belshazzar resembled the duc d'Chartres (the older brother of the future Louis Philippe) and Charles James Fox, serving as "Pleasure's slave . . . bound in silken chains, and only tied in flowery fetters, seeming light and loose."[34] Belshazzar arranges "a magnificently impious" feast for "the lewd parasites [which] compose his court," even though Babylon is losing its war with Media and Persia.[35] Unencumbered by inherited wealth and privilege as a Jewish captive in Babylon, Daniel learns from God about the imminent fall of the Babylonian empire. He warns Belshazzar, who haughtily ignores Daniel's divinely inspired insights about the perils of conspicuous consumption to national security. The king perishes in the Median and Persian invasion the next day. More wanted young aristocrats "to read the writing on the wall" before an enervated, luxury-seeking England lost to a coalition of continental powers. More intended to take on Daniel's role.

More clearly delineated the objectives, responsibilities, and limits of the prophetic role in *Daniel*.[36] Here the courtiers, Pharnaces and Soranus, More's own creations, compete with Daniel for the ear of King Darius, the conqueror of Belshazzar's Babylon. Angered by Daniel's influence over the King, Pharnaces and Soranus arrange for the prophet's demise. They persuade the King to decree that petitioners of any being besides

---

[33]Hannah More, *Moses in the Bulrushes: A Sacred Drama, The Works of Hannah More* vol.1 (Philadelphia: Woodward, 1832), p.80.

[34]Hannah More, *Belshazzar: A Sacred Drama, The Works of Hannah More* vol.1 (Philadelphia: Woodward, 1832), p.94. For her views of the Duc d'Chartres and Charles James Fox, see Hannah More to her sister, 1783, Roberts, *Memoirs*, p.286.

[35]More, *Belshazzar, Works*, p.94.

[36]c.f. Christine L. Krueger, *The Reader's Repentance: Women Preachers, Women Writers, and the Victorian Social Discourse*, Princeton University Ph.D. dissertation in English, 1986, pp.100-4.

Darius must face execution in a lions' den. This proclamation
furnishes a pretext to seal Daniel's fate because the prophet,
however loyal to King Darius, prays to Yahweh. The ministers
arrest Daniel. King Darius vainly tries to commute the
prophet's sentence. Astonished by the "artful guile" of his
courtiers, he admits he should have known what Pharnaces and
Soranus were plotting. "When selfish politicians, hackney'd
long in fraud and artifice, affect a glow of patriot fervour, or
fond loyalty, which scorns all show of interest, that's the
moment to watch their crooked projects," according to the
King.[37] But since Persian laws are irrevocable, King Darius has
to throw Daniel into the lions' den.

Araspes, a Persian noble and friend of Daniel, tells the
prophet of the King's dilemma. Araspes pleads that Daniel
should compromise. He suggests that Daniel ought to go
through the motions of obeying this edict, while inwardly pray-
ing to Yahweh. He mentions the precedent of the Syrian
Naaman who had deemed it no violation of his faith to bend
perfunctory to idols if his heart was devoted to the God of
Jacob.[38] Here again More denigrated expedience in the Lord's
service. Daniel rejects Araspes' well-meaning duplicity, presag-
ing the outcome of the tension within More's psyche. He tells
Araspes that he did not quiver before human vengeance
because God would protect him from the lions. Since Daniel
spurns any easy compromise, God would sustain him in his
hour of need.[39]

Daniel, "the people's friend," survives the lions' den with
God's help, and a contrite King Darius appoints him unofficial
prime minister to the throne. The manipulative courtiers are
condemned to death. Unguarded by divine intervention, Pharnaces and Soranus are devoured by the lions, a scene which
anticipates the fates of overly ambitious courtiers during the
French Revolution. Daniel tries to prevent their deaths. He
argues that remorse would supply an appropriate punishment.
As an honorary Evangelical whose authoritative discourse came

[37]Hannah More, *Daniel: A Sacred Drama, The Works of Hannah More* vol.1
(Philadelphia: Woodward, 1832), p.106.
[38]Ibid., p.105.
[39]Ibid.

from God, Daniel reproaches his earthly master for the excessive use of fiduciary prerogative. King Darius retorts that "Fraud's artificer himself shall fall in the deep gulf his wily arts devise[d] to snare the innocent."[40] Reform demands that heads roll.

Serious Christians, however, champion not political reform, but moral regeneration. The spiritual, not the political, state of a kingdom comprised the primary concern of Evangelicals. English society allowed women to be spiritual, but not political. Thus Evangelical women such as More could acceptably assume the oracular role which transcended gender. On the Georgian world-stage, Hannah More could play the prophetess Deborah of the Old Testament. Since morality and politics were in reality inseparable, More in the prophetic role felt free to dispense jeremiads on masculine political topics.

Immediate reaction to the *Sacred Dramas* was mixed. The Quaker philanthropist Jonas Hanway "had set down to read . . . [the Sacred Dramas] with fear and trembling" because he thought the reenaction of Biblical history "was taking an undue liberty with the Scriptures." Yet as soon as Hanway finished reading them, he bought four more copies "and went to a great boarding-school, where he has some little friends." He recommended that the governess make her girls study them "thoroughly."[41] The Bishop of London Robert Lowth, the poet Anna Barbauld, and the educator Sarah Trimmer complimented More's endeavor.[42] But these were the already converted. More had failed to reach her targeted audience, the dissolute among the affluent. Among them, her skits were met with indifference. Most readers, however, were interested in her poem *Sensibility*, published in the same volume.[43]

---

[40]Ibid., p.108.

[41]Hannah More to her sisters, 1782, Roberts, *Memoirs*, p.238.

[42]For Bishop Lowth, see Hannah More to her sisters, 1782, Roberts, *Memoirs*, p.236. For Anna Barbauld, see her letter to Hannah More, November of 1783, Roberts, *Memoirs*, pp.307-8. For Sarah Trimmer, see her letter to Hannah More, 10 May 1787, Roberts, *Memoirs* vol.2, p.60.

[43]Hannah More did complain, however, that the *Sacred Dramas* were "tying a millstone around the neck of Sensibility, which will drown them together [in terms of sales]." (Hannah More to her sisters, 1782, Roberts, *Memoirs*, p.235.)

To explain the popularity of this elegiac tribute to Evangelical passion requires a short detour into sensibility, one of the most sweeping and difficult concepts of the eighteenth century. Sensibility had a variety of related and nuanced meanings as well as several cognates such as "sentiment," "sentimentalism," "sentimentality," and "pathetic." The literary critic Jean H. Hagstrum cites the sixth *Oxford English Dictionary* definition of "sensibility" as the most familiar to the Georgians: "Capacity for refined emotion; delicate sensitiveness of taste; also readiness to feel compassion for suffering, and to be moved by the pathetic in literature and art."[44] Hagstrum adds that "sensibility" also meant tender heterosexual love or any emotion "most amenable to domestic needs and desires."[45]

Janet Todd has noted that sensibility gradually lost its association with sexuality in the late 1760s and 1770s because contemporaries increasingly saw sentiment as a component of the ideal of sexless femininity. The "Man of Feeling" expressed his sensibility physically through the teary eye and the outstretched arm. Sensibility in the fiction of Sterne feminized men, to the alarm of homophobic contemporaries, and gave intellectual and social authority to angelic women whom writers thought had the most power to evince or trigger strong emotions.[46] A leading opponent of this fictional pathos, the angelic Hannah More was ironically its indirect and ungrateful beneficiary.

An asexual yet selfish strain of sensibility attracted a disproportionately young and aristocratic following in the 1770s and 1780s. Using the words of Hagstrum's definition, the "capacity for renewed emotion, delicate sensitivity of taste, and . . . to be moved by the pathetic in literature and art" became much more

---

[44]Jean H. Hagstrum, *Sex and Sensibility: Ideal and Erotic Love from Milton and Mozart* (Chicago: The University of Chicago Press, 1980), p.9. Excerpt reprinted by permission of The University of Chicago Press. All rights reserved.

[45]Ibid., p.10. Excerpt reprinted by permission of The University of Chicago Press. All rights reserved.

[46]Janet Todd, *Sensibility, An Introduction* (London: Methuen, 1986), p.8; Stephen Cox, "Sensibility as Argument" in Syndy McMillen Conger, ed., *Sensibility in Transformation: Creative Resistance to Sentiment from the Augustans to the Romantics* (London and Toronto: Associated University Presses, 1990), p.64.

important to these aristocrats than "the readiness to feel compassion for suffering" or "tender heterosexual love." These genteel men and women of feeling celebrated infantile and mawkish self-indulgence to the detriment of the affection involved in caring about and for others. Before the 1770s, sentiment in fiction had appealed largely to sections of the middle classes in England; this appeal was closely related to the intellectuals' celebration of "English Sincerity." Nobles had looked to the elaborate protocol of Louis XV's France.[47]

The feeling heart, however, became the rage at the court of the new French King Louis XVI, and the Francophile great in Britain soon followed this lead. Thus style seemed to trickle upward for a change. Yet the cult of sensibility tried to shock the bourgeois by taking "bourgeois" sensibility to the extreme. Cult members passionately wallowed in their own feelings and impulses without concern about the consequences. Marie Antoinette and her English admirers swathed themselves with eccentric symbols of the feeling heart, self-consciously rebelling against the polite disguise of their parents.[48]

Critics of this cult such as Hannah More tried to underscore the less narcissistic meanings of sensibility "principally by reducing the scope which it gave to self and self-interest through its emphasis on the individual and his own feelings."[49] These writers stressed the benevolent side of sentiment. To More, Evangelicalism offered the best vehicle to translate emotion into charity.

The first few stanzas of *Sensibility*, however, avoid any mention of Evangelicalism. Desirous of affluent converts, More opened with flattery of her elite and conventionally Anglican

---

[47]For the penchant of the middle classes for sensibility, see Paul Langford, *A Polite and Commercial People: England, 1727-1783* (Oxford: Clarendon Press, 1989), pp.464-5.

[48]In particular, see the trinkets in Simon Schama, *Citizens: A Chronicle of the French Revolution* (New York: Alfred A. Knopf, 1989), pp.145-62. In a recent attack on the narcissistic sensibility of the 1960s in America, George Will asserts that juvenile "cults of self-validating expression" evince "a longing that waxes and wanes like a low-grade infection but never seems to disappear from the temperate, rational bourgeois societies." ("Slamming the Doors," *Newsweek*, 117(25 March 1991), p.65)

[49]Langford, *Polite and Commercial People*, p.481.

friends, presenting them as the cult of compassionate sensibility.[50] She dedicated this poem to Frances Boscawen, her old patroness from Bristol. She portrayed Boscawen as a true woman of feeling who had "deepest felt . . . the deadliest pang which rend the soul have known," after the sudden death of her husband, the naval hero, in 1761. Then tragedy struck Boscawen once again. When her two eldest sons died young, she experienced "the wounds . . . [which] can never heal."[51] Now Boscawen was troubled by her only remaining son's tour of duty in North America. More asked Boscawen if she would trade grief and anxiety for emotional detachment and then answered her own rhetorical question. She guessed that Boscawen, a true woman of feeling, did not strive for an "absence from the pregnant pain." If she repressed or ignored the poignancy in her life, she would be numb to pleasure as well as pain. Frequent mourning helped her to relate to others who knew sorrow, particularly to Hannah More after the death of David Garrick. The need to be part of the sorrow of others compelled Boscawen to reach out to alleviate suffering among the poor and alienated. A "loveless, joyless apathy" or wallowing in her own grief, in contrast, would consign her to a living death.[52]

Similarly, More did not hide her woe over the loss of that true man of feeling, David Garrick. She wrote that Garrick had been a good critic who had "a generous warmth" and "ardent heart." He and Eva had the vigorous heterosexual friendship cherished by earlier purveyors of sentiment. More also listed the poet James Beattie, the bishops of London and Chester, the

---

[50]To her friends and fans, the name dropping of *Sensibility* must have compensated for the leaden lines within the *Sacred Dramas*.

[51]Hannah More, *Sensibility: An Epistle to the Honorable Mrs. Boscawen, The Works of Hannah More* vol.1 (Philadelphia: Woodward, 1832), p.33 More wrote "a few stanzas . . . on the death of Lieutenant John Gwatkin," the grandson of another loyal benefactress Mrs. Edward Gwatkin. For this emotional epitaph, see Hannah More to Martha More, March of 1783, Roberts, *Memoirs*, pp.272-3.

[52]More, *Sensibility, Works*, p33. c.f. The popular poet Frances Greville of the 1750s begged to be relieved of the "feminine" penchant for sensibility. She thought this womanly feeling led to much more sorrow than joy. (Todd, *Sensibility*, p.61, 63.)

artist Sir Joshua Reynolds, Samuel Johnson, the Greek scholar Elizabeth Carter, et. al. as exemplars of "finely wrought spirit" which oozed from every part of their bodies and works.[53] Like Frances Boscawen, they conveyed this spirit through eleemosynary schemes.

More then bitterly attacked the abuse of sensibility by self-centered aristocrats. To her, narcissistic sensibility was as artificial and callous as the cold civility that it was designed to replace. Far from encouraging philanthropy or sympathy, flaunters of tears and handkerchiefs flirted with misanthropy and myopia. More detected the presence of play-acting.[54] Theatergoers sobbed uncontrollably at every cued opportunity. She also discerned that the same people who uninhibitedly and ecstatically wept over the shooting of a poor songbird were oblivious to the homeless. A follower of Jean-Jacques Rousseau, Mr. Sensibility, enjoyed agonizing over "a dying fawn . . . as if a friend, parent, country were no more." Readers of Johann Wolfgang von Goethe winced at the whining of the effeminate Werther, while letting their children starve for affection.[55] These fans of foreigners had no sense of priority. More thus characterized narcissistic sensibility as anti-English, deeming many members of this cult egotistical hypocrites. She observed that "there . . . [were those], whose well-sung plaints each breast inflame, and break all hearts—but his for whom they came!"[56]

More thought, however, that the advocacy of unlimited expression was the most egregious misapplication of sensibility. According to her, sentimental effusions unchecked by Evangelical principles were sociopathic. In a letter to her sisters, More wrote that Lord George Gordon had led a bloody riot in London in June of 1780 because he had "a heated imagination"

---

[53]More, *Sensibility, Works*, p33.
[54]So did others. See the villainous Willoughby in Jane Austen, *Sense and Sensibility*, 1811, Tony Tanner, ed., (Harmondsworth: Penguin, 1986), pp.78-81, 100, 105, 193-202, 324, 341-2. See also Mary Wollstonecraft, *Vindication of the Rights of Woman*, 1792, Miriam Brody, ed., (Harmondsworth: Penguin, 1988), p.193; Thomas Paine, *Rights of Man Part One*, 1791, Eric Foner, ed., (Harmondsworth: Penguin, 1987), pp.49-50; Cox, "Sensibility," pp.63-5.
[55]More, *Sensibility, Works*, p.35. c.f. Todd, *Sensibility*, p.64.
[56]More, *Sensibility, Works*, p.35.

without countervailing morality. Nearly 300 innocents perished because an eccentric pursued his innermost impulses.[57] In *Sensibility*, More professed that excessive emotional vulnerability stimulated "wild, irregular desires, disordered passions and illicit fires."[58] The most extreme men and women of feeling tried to live out their every romantic and sexual fantasy. Insensitivity marked these false prophets of bathos. They did not care what others or God felt.

The Methodists also evinced an overdose of sensibility detrimental to the social order and Christianity. The ranting and raving of field preachers and overnight conversions tapped the disordered passions of the poor, who More snobbishly felt (in this poem at least) were incapable of the exquisite feelings behind the godly and social virtues.[59]

The "right" amount and kind of sensibility, More insisted, complemented belief in God. Anglican commentators usually stressed religion's restraining influence over passion.[60] More mentioned this common observation. But she as an Evangelical emphasized passion's potentially positive contribution to religion. She acknowledged that the meaning of constructive sensibility was nebulous. She wrote that the "subtile essence" of well-directed feelings "elude the chains of Definition, and defeat her pains."[61] but that cloudiness did not stop More. In this poem she characterized positive sensibility as philanthropic and, most interestingly, prophetic impulses.[62] They came from "the secret pow'r" of God "who sheds't . . . gifts upon the natal hour."[63]

---

[57]Hannah More to her sisters, 1781, Roberts, *Memoirs*, p.199.

[58]More, *Sensibility*, *Works*, p.35; c.f. In his introduction to the Penguin edition of Jane Austen's *Sense and Sensibility* (1811), Tony Tanner notes that her characters most afflicted with excessive sensibility are also obsessed with the pursuit of wealth, privilege, and reputation. They seek money and power in order to allow them the opportunity to indulge their impulses. Therefore, their desire to do away with established customs and institutions is very superficial. (p.16).

[59]c.f. Todd, *Sensibility*, p.63.

[60]Robert Hole, *Pulpits, Politics, & Public Order in England 1760-1832* (Cambridge: Cambridge University Press, 1989), pp.89-92.

[61]More, *Sensibility*, *Works*, p.34.

[62]c.f. Cox, "Sensibility," pp.72-4.

[63]More, *Sensibility*, *Works*, p.34.

More versified passionately about the marriage of faith and feeling. If a seriously Christian "bias rules the soul, then sensibility exalts the whole, shed[ding] its sweet sunshine on the moral part."[64] Providentially-granted sensibility created over time a "prompt sense of equity!" It simulated the man or woman of feeling to correct expeditiously "unexamin'd wrongs!"[65] Like the prophets of old, he or she was increasingly "eager to serve, the cause perhaps untried, but always apt to chuse the suff'ring side!" Words were useless to describe the transforming power upon realizing that these Evangelical proclivities lay within oneself. Yet conversation minus the usual "hint malevolent . . . [and] sneer equivocal" was useful in making others aware of their gifts and quality of Evangelical sensibility.[66] More concluded that this kind of social interaction could even supersede the reverent benevolence of her elite friends, overshadowing the gratuitous namedropping of the first few stanzas. As the *Monthly Review* judiciously pointed out, it was no coincidence that she issued witty poetry alongside Scriptural skits.[67]

Elizabeth Montagu, Hester Chapone, and Elizabeth Carter, leading literary ladies, applauded More's critique of "mock feeling and sensibility, . . . at once both the boast and disgrace" of the quality.[68] They were not Evangelicals, but they did pursue a form of sentient philanthropy. They also wrestled with the problem of overwrought expression. More took notice of their efforts. In her next poem, *Bas Bleu*, she offers a tribute to these women. This piece, started in 1783, was passed around in

---

[64]Ibid., p.35; c.f. Todd who incorrectly labels this delineation of Evangelical sensibility "orthodox sentimental fashion" in her *Sensibility*, p.64.

[65]More, *Sensibility, Works*, p.34. c.f. Mary Wollstonecraft thought that sensibility undergirded the traditional social and gender order, providing buzz words and trivial pursuits to distract or ease public opinion. (Wollstonecraft, *Rights of Women*, pp.179-80, 184-5, 193-96).

[66]More, *Sensibility, Works*, p.35; c.f. In Austen's *Sense and Sensibility*, suffering and experience transforms the narcissistic Marianne Dashwood into the patroness Mrs. Brandon. Austen did not allow an Evangelical to darken the doors of the country houses that she wrote about. (p.110-1, 367.)

[67]Review of *Sacred Dramas: Chiefly Intended for Young Persons. The Subjects taken from the Bible. To which is added, Sensibility, a Poem, Monthly Review; or Literary Journal* 67(June, 1782), p.32.

[68]Hannah More to her sisters, 1782, Roberts, *Memoirs*, p.236.

manuscript form among wits and politicians before its publication in 1786.[69] Once again, More developed her ideas on the best relationships between sentiment and religion, while honoring friends.

More dedicated *Bas Bleu* to Elizabeth Vesey, the beloved hostess of the Bluestocking coterie. Vesey exuded other-directed sensibility. She put her guests at ease with her unpretentious sympathy, although she was a bishop's daughter and a member of Parliament's wife. Her childlike naivete, reminiscent of Rousseau's noble savage, lured even the most stuffy and reticent guests into self-revealing and good-humored discussions.[70] By the 1780s this informality began to border on senility as Vesey aged. Yet even the rococo relic Horace Walpole asked approvingly, "What English heart ever excelled hers?"[71]

More could not, nevertheless, characterize Vesey as the ideal woman of feeling. However singularly sincere, Vesey's whimsicality was too much in vogue for More's taste. Elizabeth Vesey probed (or at least seemed to probe) the limits of propriety. In the 1760s gossips had insinuated that she covertly slept with the novelist Laurence Sterne, the spokesman for histrionic intimacy.[72] In the 1770s and 1780s she flirted openly with the Abbé Raynal and, most disturbing to the Bluestockings, absorbed his

---

[69]For the making of *Bas Bleu*, see Hannah More to William W. Pepys, 24 July, 4 August 1783; William W. Pepys to Hannah More, 29 July, 13 August, 21 September, 10 October 1783, Roberts, *Memoirs*, pp.296-306. In the following spring Hannah More was "very busy copying Bas Bleu for the king, who desire[d] to have it." (Hannah More to her sisters, April of 1784, Roberts, *Memoirs*, p.319.

[70]Hannah More, *The Bas Bleu; Or, Conversation. Addressed to Mrs. Vesey, The Works of Hannah More* (Philadelphia: Woodward, 1832), p.16. See also the socialite William W. Pepys' comment in his letter to Hannah More, 29 July of 1783, Roberts, Memoirs, p.298. For a sympathetic view of Vesey as hostess, see Chauncey Brewster Tinker, *The Salon and English Letters: Chapters on the Interrelations of Literature and Society in the Age of Johnson* (New York: Macmillan, 1915), pp.142-51.

[71]Horace Walpole to Hannah More, 15 June 1787, in Paget Toynbee, ed., *The Letters of Horace Walpole, Fourth Earl of Orford* vol.14 (Oxford: Clarendon Press, 1905), p.5.

[72]These rumors about Vesey and Sterne were probably not true. See the fine detective work of Arthur H. Cash, *Laurence Sterne: The Later Years* (London: Methuen, 1986), pp.25-7, 116, 307.

agnostic ideas. She pretentiously read the Abbé only during severe thunderstorms.[73] On the other hand, More thought that Vesey's native passion and energy made up for any orchestrated peculiarity. She facilitated the correct use of sensibility as the amusing hostess or, in the words of More, "enchantress."[74]

Less perplexing than Vesey to More were Elizabeth Montagu, Elizabeth Carter, and Frances Boscawen. They were the ideal women of feeling. Their informed conversation "inspir[ed] and regulat[ed] the rest" of the Blues. Along with Vesey, they "rescued the ravag'd realms of Taste" with cozy symposia or what we would call today support groups, discouraging "Whist, that desolating Hun ... [and] Quadrille ... that vandal of colloquial Wit."[75] Along with Vesey, they replaced imported persiflage and equivoque with tender and empathetic discussion. But Montagu, Carter, and to a lesser extent, Boscawen were much more than sensitive hostesses. They truly appreciated the pathetic in art and literature. Montagu, in particular, vindicated the sentiment of the national hero Shakespeare from the attacks of Voltaire.[76] Carter, although the translator of the callous Stoic Epictetus, painstakingly looked for the "sublime mixture of sentimental emotion and religious awe" in Gothic architecture and English scenery.[77]

---

[73]Tinker, *Salon*, p.151. She also wrote "stream-of-consciousness" letters. For example, see Elizabeth Vesey to Elizabeth Montagu, 1781, R. Brimley Johnson, ed., *Bluestocking Letters* (New York, Dial Press, 1926), pp.120-1.

[74]More, *Bas Bleu, Works*, p.16.

[75]Ibid., p.15.

[76]The resurgent xenophobia of the last half of the eighteenth century guaranteed Montagu's research a warm reception, in spite of its glaring historical errors and slipshod literary criticism. For a penetrating (if harsh) critique of Montagu's defense of Shakespeare, see Tinker, *Salon*, pp.169-72. For sympathetic views of Montagu as literary critic, see Sylvia Harcstark Myers, *The Bluestocking Circle: Women, Friendship, and the Life of the Mind in Eighteenth-Century England* (Oxford: Clarendon Press, 1990), pp.177-206.

[77]Langford, *Polite and Commercial People*, p.473. See also Elizabeth Carter to Elizabeth Vesey, 28 August 1767, *Bluestocking Letters*, pp.275-6. Carter delivered a rendition of Epictetus so faithful to the original that classicists use it today. For Hannah More's praise of Carter, see her *Bas Bleu, Works*, p.15.

Exclusive get-togethers offered rare forums for exceptionally able women such as Montagu, Carter, and More to present and clarify their deepest feelings through poetry and prose. The conversation of the Bluestocking coterie focused on the "natural" sensibility of women, boosting the self-confidence of female writers. Literary ladies no longer "back in a corner slink, distrest; scar'd at the many bowing round, and shock'd at . . . [their] own voices' sound, forgot the thing . . . [they] meant to say, . . . [their] words, half-uttered die away; in sweet oblivion down . . . [they] sink, and of . . . [their] next appointment think."[78] Symposia for and by women provided a vehicle by which sentient feminine "genius toil in Learning's mine not to indulge in idle vision, but . . . [to] strike new light by strong collision."[79]

Yet for all of More's verses about "strong collisions," the Bluestockings frowned upon dialectical skill. They wanted to give women like themselves a chance to express themselves without fear of deeply personal attacks and, consequently, anxieties. Audient kindness, not heated argument, was necessary for women to feel comfortable in traditionally masculine roles. The atmosphere of these gatherings was "void of spleen" with disenfranchised "whigs and tories in alliance."[80] Satiric wit lost out to pleasant consensus. Through praise of intellectual engagement, More subtly pointed out the leading drawback to this absence of rancorous debate. Spreading the Word passionately necessitated the type of confrontation from which the Blues had always shied away. In *Bas Bleu*, More emphasized the importance of "strong collisions" because she had moved beyond the shelter of these symposia.

But then again, so had Montagu, Carter, and Boscawen. It is true that their Christian faith never became as strong as More's. They were conventional members of the Church of England. Yet the sensible sensibility of Montagu, Carter, and Boscawen went beyond subtle shifts in the etiquette of the drawing rooms.

---

[78]More, *Bas Bleu, Works*, p.16.
[79]Ibid., p.17.
[80]Ibid., p.16. For an example of the Bluestockings' avoidance of intellectual conflict, see Hester Chapone to Elizabeth Carter, 11 February [n.y.], *Bluestocking Letters*, pp.177-8.

To the Evangelical More's delight, their philanthropy clearly had a religious bent. Montagu, in particular, nurtured potential geniuses who happened to be poor and pious. More aptly named her "the female Maecenas of Hill Street" because Montagu was intent on discovering and managing talent.[81] The Shakespearean scholar's most prominent *protégé* was James Beattie, a professor of moral philosophy at Aberdeen who wrote poetry.[82] With Montagu's encouragement, Beattie refuted the skeptic David Hume. In turn, Montagu loyally advertised and edited his work. She solicited subscriptions from key allies in the Literary Club. With typical hyperbole, the patroness and her best male author "never failed to make a public display" of their mutual gratitude.[83]

More's initial attempts at playing the role of the religious patroness backfired. More recognized Montagu's tireless efforts on behalf of earnest beginners in *Bas Bleu*.[84] But she understandably did not mention her own *protégés* because of their rebellions against her control. More had hoped that a discriminate and caring Evangelical philanthropy would bond patron and client even closer than Montagu and Beattie. Her *protégés* afforded the first situations in which More took on the role of the sentient Evangelical matron. Yet when in authority, she acted like those insensitive aristocrats whom she had always lambasted.[85] For example, while still confined at Eva Garrick's, she contributed to a common fund for the support of John Henderson, a young, poor philosophy student at Oxford. In conjunction with fellow Bristolites Josiah Tucker and Joseph

---

[81]Hannah More to her sisters, 1776, Roberts, *Memoirs*, p.62.

[82]For Montagu as patroness, see Tinker, *Salon*, pp.189-97; for Beattie as advocate, see Langford, *Polite and Commercial People*, pp.496-71.

[83]Tinker, *Salon*, p.194. c.f. the acerbic comments of Hester Thrale Piozzi concerning Mrs. Montagu and her clients in the entry of 4 May 1808 in Katherine C. Balderston, ed., *Thraliana: The Diary of Hester Lynch Thrale (later Mrs. Piozzi) 1784-1809* vol.2 (Oxford: Claredon Press, 1951), p.1092.

[84]More, *Bas Bleu, Works*, pp.15, 17.

[85]This inconsistent behavior was not restricted to female philanthropists or Evangelicals. When the protofeminist Frances Burney first assumed the role of "advice-giver" to a close female friend, she "[took] on the voice of the world as mediated to her through her [strongly anti-feminist] father's preferences and fears, and her own fears." (Margaret Doody, *Frances Burney: A Life in the Works* [New Brunswick, N.J.: Rutgers University Press, 1987], pp.161-2.)

Cottle, More selected Henderson because of his potential as an apologist for serious Christianity. She wanted to enlist his gift for debate in the rebuttal of what she considered to be blasphemous pundits.[86]

Henderson disappointed More and his other benefactors. He was a dilatory genius whose narcissistic sensibility drifted toward exploring the grotesque and macabre for thrills, not toward love of Christ or of his fellow human beings.[87]

Henderson objurgated More when he learned of his boosters' plans to focus his sentiment on something useful. He especially resented that More had sent an emissary, a Miss Adams,[88] to convey her practical instructions instead of intervening personally. He bitterly pointed out that More had not even bothered to write about her concerns to him. She did not seem to care.

He also deemed More's instructions ill-conceived and puzzling in view of her longstanding distaste for aristocratic etiquette. He could not believe that Miss Adams was cajoling him into becoming a gentleman upon More's orders, in addition to making him translate useful if boring excerpts from Xenophon. In response, Henderson told More: "do not command me to be genteel—it will trouble me—It would be easy to bring many other reasons—*but between us this must be most reasonable*."[89] He appealed to her professed cultural and religious values, noting that his "personage, qualifications, manners, . . . [were] of a clean contrary cast; therefore it would make . . . [him] most foolishly various and inconsistent" if he put on airs.[90] He recoiled from the fashionable world for the same rea-

---

[86]Hopkins, *Hannah More*, p.121.

[87]Josiah Tucker to Hannah More, 3 February 1781, Roberts, *Memoirs*, pp.195-6; Josiah Tucker to Hannah More, 1782, Roberts, *Memoirs*, pp.216-9. c.f. On a trip to Oxford University in the early summer of 1781, More introduced Henderson to Samuel Johnson and did not criticize Henderson in her letter to Eva Garrick, 17 June 1781, Hyde Collection, Firestone Library, Princeton University, Johnson Letters, IX, 328, p.2.

[88]For More's strictures to her emissary, see Hannah More to Miss Adams, 15 June 1782, The Houghton Library, Harvard University, bMS Am. 1631 (298).

[89]John Henderson to Hannah More, 1782, Roberts, *Memoirs*, p.257. Henderson underlined this phrase.

[90]Ibid.

sons and in the same ways, he guessed, that More had. His keen sensibility demanded that he refrain from the conformity of polite disguise which was becoming passé anyway. Yet after receiving this shrill reply, More believed that Henderson was overly touchy and incredibly ungrateful. She dropped him. Henderson's rebellion against rococo civility ironically cost him the patronage of its leading Evangelical critic.[91]

This unpleasant rift with Henderson, however, paled in ferocity and significance beside More's quarrel with the next assertive genius under her sway, the milkwoman and poet Ann Cromarty Yearsley of Bristol. In May and June of 1784 More presided over the construction of her new cottage, Cowslip Green, conveniently located in suburban Bristol. Still unsure of her faith and place, Hannah More wanted a getaway for peace and quiet similar to her extended stay at Eva Garrick's.[92] Then, the cook at the cottage showed her some couplets written by the feeder of Cowslip Green's hogs. After reading these verses, More bubbled over with excitement and energy. She imagined that she had discovered a female Chatterton, a fountain of other-directed sensibility, in this employee, Ann Cromarty Yearsley.

More rushed to aid the milkwoman, her ne'er-do-well husband, and her five malnourished children.[93] More's sudden interest could not have come at a more advantageous time for Yearsley who was struggling to keep her family alive after the

---

[91]Yet she wished him well. See Hannah More to Martha More, 29 March 1783, Roberts, *Memoirs*, p.277.

[92]In particular, Hannah More wrote that she "was quite worn out last week—dined out six days following. It was well Sunday came to my relief, but it is all over now; and now I may very philosophically cry out with Wolsey—Vain pomp and glory of the world! I hate ye!" She feared, however, that she, like Wolsey, did not renounce the fashionable world while visiting its members. (Hannah More to her sisters, 1784, Roberts, *Memoirs*, p.358). For her cottage and her "rambling about the romantic hills and delicious vallies of Somersetshire," see Hannah More to William W. Pepys, 1784, Roberts, *Memoirs*, p.347. For the beautiful scenery around her cottage, see Hannah More to Elizabeth Carter, 1784, Roberts, *Memoirs*, pp.354-6.

[93]Perhaps More was following Eva Garrick's example. A few months earlier, Mrs. Garrick had helped and supervised the rehabilitation of a talented homeless woman in London. (Eva Garrick to Dr. Wright, 11 February 1784, Folger Shakespeare Library, Mss. 486, No.73)

loss of her husband's unearned income and the death of her
mother by starvation.[94] More's help to Yearsley, however, went
beyond food and money. For the next thirteen months, the
education of Ann Yearsley (and family) preoccupied More and
perhaps eased the impact of the deaths of Jacob More and
Samuel Johnson upon her. First, More taught Yearsley basic
rules of grammar and meter and polished her rough drafts.
Second, she brought Yearsley's poetry to the attention of the
Blues and other friends. More then aggressively solicited subscriptions from London authors and aristocrats for the publication of Yearsley's works and the relief of her family. She
attracted roughly 1000 donors. Yearsley's verse particularly
impressed Elizabeth Montagu, "the Maecenas of Hill Street,"
who agreed to manage jointly with More the trust set up for
Yearsley.[95]

More hoped to harness what she considered to be the true
sensibility of Yearsley's poetry for the Evangelical reformation
of patrician society. Yearsley's elegiac thoughts brimmed with
ecstatic "transports." To More, Ann Yearsley needed only to
experience conversion to use wisely her gifts for showing and
eliciting emotion. On the other hand, Yearsley sincerely

---

[94]A minor battle among literary critics has commenced over the social
origins of Ann Cromarty Yearsley. Moira Ferguson and Donna Landry argue
(or rather wish) that Yearsley was always solidly working-class and identified
(correctly in their view) with laborers. (Moira Ferguson, "Resistance and
Power in the Life and Writings of Ann Yearsley," *The Eighteenth Century:
Theory and Interpretation* 27(Fall, 1986), pp.247-68; Donna Landry, *The Muses
of Resistance: Laboring-Class Women's Poetry in Britain, 1739-1796* (Cambridge:
Cambridge University Press, 1990), pp.16-17, 124-5, 285, 303) Mary Waldron
punctures this line by noting that Yearsley married a middling-sort cypher
who had squandered his inheritance. Through this marriage, Waldron writes,
Yearsley knew an exceptional amount about trusts and unearned income
inaccessible to nearly all other milkwomen. To Waldron, Yearsley thus was
not "working-class" at all. ("Ann Yearsley and the Clifton Records" in Paul
Korshin, ed., *The Age of Johnson: A Scholarly Annual* vol.3 (New York: AMS
Press, 1990), pp.7, 10) Synthesizing the insights of Ferguson, Landry, and
Waldron, I see Yearsley as downwardly mobile. I think that Ann Yearsley felt
the pain of poverty acutely because of her previous life as a middling-sort
housewife. This pain informed her poetry and abetted her identification
with the poor and alienated.
[95]Hannah More to Elizabeth Carter, 16 December (1784), Hyde Collection,
Firestone Library, Princeton University, *Johnson Letters*, X, 390, pp.2-3; Jones,
Hannah More, pp.73-4.

appreciated More's compliments and kindness. In *Night. To Stella* and *Mrs. Montagu*, she effusively acknowledged the efforts of More (and Montagu) on her behalf.[96] Her praise was not that "of a sycophant, but of a vehement romantically in love with" her surrogate mother.[97] Yearsley's fast friendship of strong emotional intensity with More had no sexual dimension and thus fit the loving "adoptions" of young women by mature women ubiquitous and accepted throughout the Anglophone world.[98] Indeed, More cherished the true deference and loyalty of Yearsley. Heartfelt gratitude from clients was only too rare in society based on patronage.[99]

More also welcomed Yearsley's fearlessness in challenging the fashionable world's concept of female place. Yearsley's candor paralleled More's newly found Evangelical frankness. In *Clifton Hill, Written in January 1785*, Yearsley blasted the sadomasochism so prized by the alien cult of sensibility but so deadly to feminine spirits.[100]

---

[96]Ann Yearsley, *Poems, On Several Occasions* (London: T. Cadell, 1785); Landry, *The Muses of Resistance*, pp.125-8.

[97]Hopkins, *Hannah More*, p.124. c.f. Moira Ferguson who dismisses the intense if short-lived relationship between More and Yearsley as strictly patron-client in "Resistance and Power," p.255.

[98]For these common female friendships, see Carroll Smith-Rosenberg, "The Female World of Love and Ritual: Relations between Women in Nineteenth-Century America," *Signs: Journal of Women in Culture and Society* vol.1, 1(Autumn, 1975), pp.19-20. For the rich gamut of romantic friendships between Western women in the eighteenth and nineteenth centuries, see Lillian Faderman, *Surpassing the Love of Men: Romantic Friendships and Love Between Women from the Renaissance to the Present* (New York: William Morrow & Co., 1981), pp.74-230; Martha Vicinus, *Independent Women: Work and Community for Single Women 1850-1920* (Chicago: University of Chicago Press, 1985), pp.157-62, 187-210; Sylvia Harcstark Myers, *The Bluestocking Circle: Women, Friendship, and the Life of the Mind in Eighteenth-Century England* (Oxford: Clarendon Press, 1990), pp.16-20.

[99]Hannah More to Elizabeth Montagu, 22 October 1784, Henry E. Huntington Library, Mss., MO 3788, pp.1, 4 as fully reprinted in Mary R. Mahl and Helene Koon, eds., *The Female Spectator: English Women Writers Before 1800* (Bloomington, Ind.: Indiana University Press, 1977), pp.279-81.

[100]Landry, *Muses of Resistance*, pp.130-42; Ferguson, "Resistance and Power," pp.250-1. Clifton Hill is reprinted in George W. Bethune, ed., *Pearls from the British Female Poets* (New York: The World Publishing House, 1876), pp.154-6.

Most assuring to More, the milkwoman's impressive self-knowledge largely came from reading the Bible and John Milton. Even the relatively worldly Montagu "imagin[ed] her mind . . . [had] been enlightened by the study of the scriptures." Montagu further noted that "in the prophets, in Job, and in the Psalms there is a character of thought, and style of expression, between eloquence and poetry, from which a great mind, disposed to either, may be so elevated, and so warmed, as, with little other assistance, to become an orator or poet."[101] To Montagu, Yearsley had this "character of thought." More wholeheartedly agreed. The milkwoman's life and character, More reckoned, posed a formidable foil to ungodly buffoons of high society. She just needed a little Evangelical grooming to prepare her for conversion."[102]

Yet, as Landry notes, More's treatment of Yearsley was confused and was bound to lead to trouble. Through refining Yearsley's sensibility, More tried to civilize the noble savage. Yet she did this "while keeping Yearsley the milk-woman firmly in her place."[103] More was "utterly against taking her out of her Station."[104] Stephen Duck the thresher had killed himself after an unhappy tenure as court poet in the 1730s. More did not want this suicidal fate (made very fashionable by the cult of sensibility) to happen to her dearest Ann. On the other hand, Yearsley also sent mixed signals. In *Night. To Stella*, she endorsed her own current social and economic inferiority, but she warned that she would not let anyone, however friendly, order her around.[105] As Waldron notes, Ann Yearsley was familiar (or thought that she was familiar) with the intricacies of

---

[101]Elizabeth Montagu to Hannah More, 1784, Roberts, *Memoirs*, p.364.

[102]Ann Yearsley thought she had completely identified already with what she perceived to be More's Evangelical principles. She wrote: "Ah, STELLA (her name for Hannah More)! I'm a convert; thou hast tun'd/My rusting powers to the bright strain of joy." (Ann Yearsley, *Night. To Stella*, 1785 as quoted in Landry, *Muses of Resistance*, p.151.)

[103]Landry, *Muses of Resistance*, p.130.

[104]Hannah More to Elizabeth Montagu, 27 September 1784, Henry E. Huntington Library, Mss. Mo 3987, p.4 as quoted in Landry, *Muses of Resistance*, p.20. For a full reprint of this letter, see Mahl and Koon, *Female Spectator*, pp.278-9.

[105]Landry, *Muses of Resistance*, pp.127-8.

unearned income and trust law through her husband's finances and, despite her recent bad luck, saw herself as having been in the same social class as Hannah More.[106] Yearsley thus challenged the exclusive management of her trust by Montagu and More. A bitter fight over the money ensued.[107]

The closeness of their friendship only deepened the acrimony of their quarrel. More promptly resigned from the trust and ordered her publisher Cadell to burn Yearsley's latest manuscripts. To More, Yearsley's new alliance with the Bishop of Derry, a foppish womanizer who treasured Italy over England, confirmed that the milkwoman was merely an opportunist. Ann Yearsley was not a comrade-in-arms against the fashionable world. She was not a fighter for either her sex or Christ.[108]

Yearsley retaliated in kind. She detailed the nuances of their fight in the Bristol press and reminded the public about More's

---

[106]Waldron, "Yearsley and Clifton Records," pp.7, 10.

[107]Here Ann Yearsley's fierce defense of her interests clashed with More's demand for deference. Yearsley had assumed that Montagu and More would hand over the subscriptions totaling L360 to her after publication of her first works. The trustees, however, planned to invest the L360 in five percent securities. David Garrick had invested the profits from *Percy* for More into these stocks. What was good for her was better for Yearsley. The steady if small income from the interest would ease Yearsley's poverty. It would also shield her from the temptations of sudden wealth that More knew firsthand. Yearsley interpreted this sound business practice as an indictment of her ability to care for her family. Yearsley then proposed that she become one of the fund's trustees. She wanted to provide for her family in the way she thought best. More overreacted to Yearsley's technically illegal and rather bold (by contemporary standards) request, thinking the milkwoman had accused her of fraud and venality. For More's side of the story, see Jones, *Hannah More*, p.38, 75; Hannah More to Mrs. Gwatkin, 5 March 1778, Hannah More to Elizabeth Montagu, 1784, Hannah More to Elizabeth Carter, 1785, Roberts, *Memoirs*, pp.138, 368, 391; Mahl and Koon, *Female Spectator*, pp.282-6. For Yearsley's side of the story, see the Preface to the fourth edition of her *Poems on Various Occasions* (1786) as reprinted in Moira Ferguson, ed., *First Feminists: British Women Writers 1578-1799* (Bloomington: Indiana University Press, 1985), pp.382-6.

[108]Hannah More to Elizabeth Montagu, 20 October 1785, Henry E. Huntington Library, Msws. MO 3993, p.2 as quoted in Landry, *Muses of Resistance*, p.155; Montagu cattily predicted that "with . . . [Hervey's] instructions and the dispositions it might inherit from its mother, . . . [Ann Yearsley's newest son] possibly might have risen to some great station—in Botany Bay." (Elizabeth Montagu to Hannah More, 1785, Blunt, *Montagu*, p.185.)

problems with William Turner and Hannah Cowley. She further alleged that More was bilking the trust in order to build yet another country house. She maintained that More envied her writing and was only using her to restart a stalled career. Most irritating to More, she charged her patron with hypocrisy. While a professing Evangelical, More symbolized the moral and ethical problems of the upper classes, according to Yearsley. Drawing upon Old Testament stories, Yearsley made More the focal point of her own campaign against polite propriety.[109]

The Yearsley affair propelled More into another painful period of self-analysis. To the Reverend John Newton, she wondered whether she was too involved in the fashionable world to be able to reform it.[110] To Elizabeth Carter, she confessed that she "was too vain of . . . [her] success [in raising funds]; and, in counting over the money . . ., might be elated, and think—'Is not this great Babylon that *I* have built?'"[111] Yet this time More did not hide. In the immediate aftermath of the Yearsley affair, she concentrated on preserving the reputation of the Bluestocking coterie and finally decided to publish *Bas Bleu*. And Hannah More felt a personal responsibility to enhance the reputation of Horace Walpole, another literary patron lacerated by a stubborn client. Accordingly, she dedicated to Walpole her most direct challenge yet to aristocratic excess, the poem *Florio*, published in the same volume as *Bas Bleu*.

At first glance, Walpole seems an unlikely ally for More. His father had solidified the corrupt oligarchy which ruled Georgian Britain. Horace Walpole dutifully carried on his family's tradi-

[109]Landry, *Muses of Resistance*, pp.158-65. c.f. Ferguson, "Resistance and Power," pp.252-68. Most writers and patrons predictably sided with More, although Yearsley attained a degree of critical respect with later works. Even women writers who were not friends of More contended, however, that Hannah More acted correctly even if they continued to enjoy Yearsley's poetry and plays. See Anna Seward to Helena Maria Williams, 25 December 1787, A. Constable, ed., *Letters of Anna Seward Written Between the Years 1784-1807* vol.1 (Edinburgh: George Ramsay & Co., 1811), pp.295-6; Hester Thrale Piozzi to Penelope Sophia Weston, 2 November 1789 in Edward A. Bloom and Lillian D. Bloom, eds., *The Piozzi Letters* vol.1 (Newark: University of Delaware Press, 1989), p.327.

[110]Hannah More to the Reverend John Newton, 31 May 1787, Roberts, *Memoirs* vol.2, p.65.

[111]Hannah More to Elizabeth Carter, 1785, Roberts, *Memoirs*, p.391.

tion as a parliamentary placeman who vigorously traded in sinecures. He personified the skeptical and cosmopolitan spirit of eighteenth-century aristocratic culture. He was a deist and a non-practicing homosexual. He frequented Parisian salons. His storybook castle Strawberry Hill was far more rococo than Gothic. Like his mansion, his novels and conversations were full of intricate details, detours, and facades.[112]

Accordingly, Horace Walpole disliked quite a few of Hannah More's friends. He hated Garrick's natural style of acting; he hated Johnson's bluntness. He had even archly panned More's *Percy* in 1778[113] The Victorians were to view Walpole as a fussy collector of trivia who was emotionally detached from the rest of humanity.[114] This caricature was not far from the truth.

More, the mother of the Victorians, judged Walpole redeemable for Christ. She overlooked the pretension of his conversation. She saw godly potential beneath his gaudy disguises. Revealingly, her poem *Florio* celebrates the transformation of a worldly and epicene bachelor similar to Walpole into a godly and married layman.[115]

Florio begins with scathing invective against the wealthy and powerful. Here More dropped her usual cryptic recourse to

---

[112]Brian Fothergill, *The Strawberry Hill Set: Horace Walpole and His Circle* (London: Faber & Faber, 1983), pp.15-41.

[113]Jones, *Hannah More*, p.67.

[114]In particular, see Thomas Babington Macaulay, Review of *Walpole's Letters to Horace Mann, Edinburgh Review,* October of 1833, in *Critical and Miscellaneous Essays* vol.2 (New York: Appleton & Co., 1863), pp.214-51. For a kinder, gentler (yet still emotionally detached) Walpole, see R. W. Ketton-Cremer, *Horace Walpole: A Biography* (Ithica, N.Y.: Cornell University Press, 1966), pp.1-7; Fothergill, *Strawberry Set,* pp.15-41.

[115]Similarity of situation may have been another possible reason for their friendship. Both More and Walpole were powerful yet marginal—she because of gender and he because of sexual orientation. Both maintained their power through sexual chastity and neither challenged each other's chastity. Prominent women writers—Mary Wollstonecraft and the historian Catherine Macaulay Graham—and influential male homosexuals—the plutocrat William Beckford, Jr. (the richest man in Georgian Britain) and the dramatist Isaac Bickerstaffe—who violated sexual propriety were vilified by contemporaries. Furthermore, although both More and Walpole were reformers of different sorts—she an Evangelical and he a maverick whig—they identified so strongly with established institutions that their comments are usually taken as quintessentially "conservative."

historical settings and places this poem firmly in her present. In
no way is this rigorous criticism equivocal. Florio, "a youth of
gay renown/ who figur'd much about the town," picks up "with
very moderate reading/ the whole new system of good breed-
ing." As with Walpole, Florio's "native feeling [occasionally]
would intrude, . . . spoil[ing] the vain thing he strove to be."
The indolence stemming from inherited wealth, however,
"warps . . . [Florio's] pliant youth/ from sense, simplicity, and
truth." Along with his friend and philosophe Bellario, Florio
lounges and gossips his days away. Trivia become overly
important to him. Florio, however, never seems to enjoy the
ease and pleasure promised by aristocratic culture. He is
exhausted from doing nothing "at an age/ When youth should
rush on glory's stage/ When life should open fresh and knew
[sic]/ And ardent Hope her schemes pursue."[116]

This slothful atmosphere inhibits any application of the
improving schemes put forth by Bellario, the ersatz and over-
rated philosophe. Indeed, Bellario is as abstract and caustic as
his Tridentine bogeymen. Here More expressed the Evangelical
bias against speculative experts. The mere lip-service of Bellario
and Florio to helping others, according to More, is dangerous
because it has falsely raised sinful expectations among mechanics and merchants and thus has decreased the chances of many
for eternal salvation.[117]

Furthermore, the learning of Bellario and Florio is superficial
and self-serving. Philosophes had charged the godly with intellectual weakness. More showed how this criticism revealed
more about philosophes than about Evangelicals. Bellario and
Florio are as guilty as late medieval bishops in the reliance upon
mistranslated ancient tests. They presume that these dubious
renditions uphold their leisured existence. For example,

---

[116]All quotations in this paragraph come from Hannah More, *Florio. A Tale
for Fine Gentlemen and Fine Ladies. In Two Parts, The Works of Hannah More*
(Philadelphia: Woodward, 1832), pp.19-20. This view of youthful indolence
was not limited to More. Frances Boscawen's connection of inertia and Francophile sentiment was very strong. When Boscawen first heard of the Mont-
golfier brothers and their "air-balloons," she thought that the inventive
Messrs. Charles and Robert "must have had English mothers." (Frances
Boscawen to Hannah More, 1784, Roberts, *Memoirs*, p.334.)
[117]More, *Florio, Works*, p.21.

Bellario and Florio incorrectly think that Epicurus praised glut-
tony as the highest good. More wrote that Epicurus would have
repudiated them if he knew of their misinterpretation of his
writings.[118] Their preference for Edward Gibbon, "Where all is
spangle, glitter, and show/ And the truth is overlaid below,"
further indicates that they do not look to antique sources of
virtue, but rather depend upon skewed commentaries from
their own time and place.[119]

More then contrasted the corrupt milieu of London's elite
with the incorruptible rural squirearchy in the conventional
manner. The best friend of Florio's father is "a cheerful knight
of good estate/ Whose Heart was warm, whose bounty great."
Sir Gilbert's charity and supervision in the village cements the
social hierarchy on the land. He is "a real man," in contrast to
the hermaphroditic Bellario and Florio. More lamented that
"such characters . . . are out of print."[120] She warned that if the
great failed to return to this Tory lifestyle, their "tottering
castles" would "fall," allowing "swarming nabobs" to "seize on
all!"

Sir Gilbert has a daughter named Celia, "whose life is as
lovely as her face/ Each duty mark'd with every grace." Celia is
an Evangelical, unique for a loco-descriptive poem of that era.
On his deathbed, Florio's father had arranged a marriage

---

[118]Ibid,; This part of *Florio* was particularly relished in the rave *Review of
Florio: A Tale for Fine Gentlemen and Fine Ladies; and, the Bas Bleu; or
Conversation, Two Poems, Monthly Review; or Literary Journal* 75(July, 1786),
pp.42-3.

[119]More, *Florio, Works*, p.21; In 1782 Hannah More read "three very thick
quartos of Mr. Gibbon's *History of the Lower Empire*; a fine, but insidious
narrative of a dull period." She "never . . . [rose] from [these] book[s], without feeling sad and disgusted." She judged Gibbon "a malignant painter"
whose "encomiums" of Christian emperors and saints "have so much cold-
ness, and his praises so much sneer, that . . . [she] discover[ed] contempt
where he professes panegyric." (Hannah More to her sisters, 1782, Roberts,
Memoirs, p.236.). In 1788 she refused to buy Gibbon's latest work because
her neighbor had given her a glimpse of "that mass of impiety and bad
taste." She "protest[ed] . . . that if this work were to become the standard of
style and religion, Christianity and the English language would decay pretty
nearly together; and the same period would witness the downfall of sound
principles and of true taste." (Hannah More to William W. Pepys, September
of 1788, Roberts, *Memoirs* vol.2, pp.131-2; Jones, *Hannah More*, p.49).

[120]More, *Florio, Works*, p.21.

between Celia and Florio with Sir Gilbert's consent. But the proposed groom is reluctant. True to form, Florio is most angry over having to miss out on "the mobs polite/ Of three sure balls in one short night" because of his wedding.[121]

Florio's foreign ways upset the harmony of Sir Gilbert's estate. When Florio's "trusty Swiss" bodyguard announces his arrival at Sir Gilbert's gate, "So loud . . . [was] the rap which shook the door/ [that] The hall reecho'd to the roar . . . ,/ The din alarm'd the frighten'd deer/ Who in a corner slunk for fear,/ The butler thought 'twas beat of drum/ [and] The steward swore the French had come." When Florio "muttered" the current slang of the beau monde, he disturbs Sir Gilbert who finds the young man dainty in comparison with the youths of his own "halcyon" days. In turn, Florio yawns "Whene'er Sir Gilbert's sporting guests/ Retail'd old news, or older jests," while humming the latest Italian air. He gags on the castle's English roast beef and beer, while pining for Parisian confectionery.[122]

"Yet, though a disciple of cold art," Florio falls in love with the Evangelical Celia. He tries his best to fight his suddenly heterosexual feelings. Each time he "found his heart to melt" before Celia, "Fashion, with a mother's joy,/ Dipped in her lake the darling boy;/ That lake, whose chilling waves impart/ The gift to freeze the warmest heart." A letter from Bellario temporarily takes him away from Sir Gilbert because it has invited Florio to a party thrown "By Flavia fair, return'd from France."[123] But even as he leaves, he waivers between Celia and the androgynes of the City "for some remains of native truth/ Flush'd his face, and check'd the youth." Later at Flavia's soirée, Celia's godliness continues to haunt Florio as he eats with "the

---

[121]Ibid., p.22.

[122]Ibid., pp.22-3; More declared that she "would rather eat a slice of moonshine with Robin Goodfellow, or sip an acorn full of dew with Oberon, than taste the finest supper that ever Weltjie [the confectioner at the French court] decorate." (Hannah More to Frances Boscawen, 1784, Roberts, *Memoirs*, p.329).

[123]More, *Florio, Works*, p.23.

hogs of Epicurus' sty," More's swinish few at the top.[124] Readers would not find Florio's infatuation singular. Expressing womanly softness and sensibility through faith, according to most writers, titillated both red-blooded and blue-blooded Georgian men. Conventional wisdom held that even rakes, infidels, and fops relished feminine devotion.[125]

But Hannah More added a twist. She emphasized the feminine power to improve men through Evangelical example.[126] At Flavia's party, Florio begins to realize that his taste had changed since his new-found love for the godly Celia. The forced amiability of Flavia starts to grate on his nerves. Suddenly surrounding grand dames look like viragos with satanic faces. Here again More characterized the ungodly as unisexual in the Miltonic way. "Celia! [Florio] murmur'd, and retired.[127]

Florio then experiences conversion. Divided between society and self, Florio becomes consciously right and happy by choosing the seriously Christian ways of Celia. This is not an easy or quick decision. Seated in his chaise on the way back to Sir Gilbert's, Florio "hazards not a single glance/ Nor through the glasses peeps by chance/ Lest some old friend, or haunt well known/ Should melt his resolution down." But once he clears the whig headquarters of Portland Place, his spirits turn ecstatic. He feels "at his inmost soul/ The sweet reward of self-control." He thanks God for his deliverance from the sinful City, praising and serving Christ for unifying his soul and giving direction to his hitherto aimless life. While walking with Celia among the bowers, "Enlighten'd Florio learn[s] to trace/ In Nature's God the God of grace."[128]

---

[124]Ibid., p.24; c.f. a swinish multitude in Edmund Burke, *Reflections on the Revolution in France*, 1790, Conor Cruise O'Brien, ed. (Harmondsworth: Penguin, 1986), p.173.

[125]In particular, see John Gregory, *A Father's Legacy to His Daughters* (London: W. Strahan, T. Cadell, and W. Creech, 1774) [Garland reprint, 1974], pp.22-3.

[126]Ian Bradley points out that "the most important agents in the spread of Evangelical religion among the upper classes seem ... to have been the female members of their families." (*Call to Seriousness*, p.40).

[127]More, *Florio, Works*, p.25; c.f. the superficially different furies that tortured the royal captives in Burke, *Reflections*, p.165. For Milton's influential homophobia, see Hagstrum, *Sex*, pp.24-49.

[128]More, *Florio, Works*, p.26.

Although *Florio* expresses More's hopes for Walpole, it also chronicles her own gradual metamorphosis. As her faith in Christ and herself deepened, her wavering expressed in understated codes disappeared, however slowly. Her native feeling and sense finally overshadowed the facades that she had to construct for herself upon first arriving in London. Her Evangelicalism made it no long necessary to hedge her criticism of the wealthy and powerful. In the 1780s, More confronted the excesses of patriarchy directly. She also ridiculed the pretensions of aristocracy forthrightly. Although a practitioner of practical piety, the mature More was not the expedient and supple chameleon invented by Ford K. Brown. No longer ambivalent, she prepared to outline reforms for both patrician society and plebeian culture.

Chapter III

Piety and Patriotism

Advocates of reform periodically become defenders of incumbent elites. Historians have noted the transformation of Evangelical reformers such as Hannah More into some of the first "conservative" apologists in late-eighteenth-century Britain. Elie Halevy, in particular, maintained that this critical infusion of reformers into loyalist ranks helped to impede the export of the French Revolution to Britain. Evangelical and similar Methodist sermons inculcating obedience and self-denial bolstered popular support for Church and King.[1]

Most studies, however, have strongly suggested that Evangelical reformers borrowed conventional slogans and symbols to further their own culturally subversive agendas. Gerald Newman, among others, has posited that Evangelicals and Methodists masked their campaign for the moral regeneration of the permissive leisured through appeals to national unity in the face of French subversion and aggression. According to Newman, Evangelical writers played on the fears of aristocrats by arguing that rapid moral regeneration among the affluent was the only potent antidote to Jacobinical polemics.[2]

Hannah More's equation of patrician reformation and social peace, however, was much deeper than the effective ploy described by Newman. Prior to the French Revolution, she firmly felt that the extinction of sinful and long-standing tradi-

[1]Elie Halevy, *England in 1815* (New York: Barnes & Noble, 1961) [orig. pub. 1913], pp.424-9, 459.
[2]Gerald Newman, *The Rise of English Nationalism: A Cultural History 1740-1830* (New York: St. Martin's Press, 1987), pp.233-8. See also Geoffrey Best, "Evangelicals and the Victorians," in Anthony Symondson, ed., *The Victorian Crisis of Faith* (London: Society for Promoting Christian Knowledge, 1970), pp.37-56; William Reginald Ward, *Religion and Society in England, 1790-1850* (London: Batsford, 1972), pp.44-54.

tions among the great would both preserve social stability and enhance aristocratic chances for eternal salvation. After the fall of the French monarchy, she held that the Bourbons and their episcopacy deserved defeat and disgrace because of the permissive atmosphere at Versailles. More hoped that the abolition of the African slave trade and the observance of Sabbatarian laws, among other measures, would preempt similar divine retribution against the British ruling classes. Her appeal was largely to lay, not clerical, aristocrats, however. Hannah More did not once mention the many abuses within the Church of England's hierarchy. Rather, she exhorted propertied laypeople to abandon immoral and cosmopolitan tendencies of thought and behavior which Unitarians and deists had seized upon to indict aristocratic and Anglican privilege.

Here More expressed the firm Evangelical belief in the need for elite reformation as a model for the lower orders, rebutting the Unitarian and deist claim of innate aristocratic corruption. Both the Unitarian Joseph Priestley and the deist Thomas Paine argued that the middling classes should lead the country because they were the natural repositories of probity.[3] While she did not deny the bourgeois penchant for rectitude, Hannah More believed in the perfectibility of aristocrats and their poorest dependents. She also realized that sections of the middle and lower classes aped aristocratic behavior and thus their reformation was contingent upon that of the peerage.

To her well-connected readers, Hannah More pointed out the earthly benefits of their own moral regeneration. If the fashionable world returned to what More characterized variously as classical, Saxon, English, or godly qualities of serious simplicity, then British elites could expect deference from their

---

[3]For Priestley, see J. E. Cookson, *The Friends of Peace: Anti-War Liberalism in England, 1793-1815* (Cambridge: Cambridge University Press, 1982), pp.26-7; Isaac Kramnick, *Republicanism and Bourgeois Radicalism: Political Ideology in Late Eighteenth-Century England and America* (Ithaca and London: Cornell University Press, 1990), pp.71-98. For Paine, see E. P. Thompson, *The Making of the English Working Class* (New York: Pantheon Books, 1963), pp.94-6; Albert Goodwin, *The Friends of Liberty: The English Democratic Movement in the Age of the French Revolution* (Cambridge, Mass.: Harvard University Press, 1979), pp.173-6; Gregory Claeys, *Thomas Paine: Social and Political Thought* (Boston: Unwin Hyman, 1989), pp.47-8, 59.

workers. If aristocrats embraced the religion of the heart, then they could expect their laborers to surrender to Christ, not to the siren song of radical corresponding societies. The degree of aristocratic reformation, More wrote, also dictated the survival of peculiarly British tolerance and freedom. She thus proselytized through patriotic appeals that appropriated the usually radical language and imagery of patriotism for the Anglican establishment and portrayed libertarian patriots as alien quislings.[4]

More championed the anti-slavery movement as an endorsement of English and Christian concepts of liberty and virtue. This was not always the case. Born and raised near the many sugar refineries in Bristol, Hannah More was oblivious to the evils of the slave trade until well into the 1780s. She eagerly welcomed the daughters of merchants with West Indian interests at the Park Street school.[5] She portrayed slaveholding favorably in *The Inflexible Captive* (1774), a tragedy which extolled the self-sacrifice of extreme patriotism.[6]

The eye-opening power of Evangelical conversion, however, propelled More to join new like-minded friends such as the Reverend John Newton and William Wilberforce in anti-slavery agitation.[7] In January of 1788, abolitionists asked her to scribble a short poem to influence parliamentarians weighing Wilberforce's resolutions on the slave trade. She agreed. Her only

---

[4]For the radical strain of eighteenth-century patriotism, see Hugh Cunningham, "The Language of Patriotism, 1750-1914," *History Workshop Journal* 12(1981), pp.8-13; c.f. Linda Colley, "The Apotheosis of George III: Loyalty, Royalty, and the British Nation, 1760-1820," *Past and Present* 102(1984), pp.126-9; idem., "Whose Nation? Class and National Consciousness in Britain, 1750-1830," *Past and Present* 113(1986), pp.97-117; F. K. Donnelly, "Levellerism in Eighteenth and Nineteenth-Century Britain," *Albion* 20(1988), pp.261-70.

[5]Mary Alden Hopkins, *Hannah More and Her Circle* (New York: Longman, Green & Co., 1947), pp.17-9.

[6]In particular, see the lines of Barce, the Carthaginian slave, in Hannah More, *The Inflexible Captive, Tragedies* (London: Cadell & Davies, 1818), pp.355-6.

[7]More first met Wilberforce in Bath in the fall of 1787. (Mary G. Jones, *Hannah More* (Cambridge: Cambridge University Press, 1952), p.90). Another scholar, however, maintains that this meeting took place in 1788. (Muriel Jaeger, *Before Victoria* (London: Chatto & Windus, 1956), p.27).

objection was to the short notice of this request. Important and
upcoming votes on slavery's future dictated that she had to
write this piece hastily. But the pressing need for national
redemption via abolition demanded that More publish it without the usual editing and polishing.[8]

The result, *The Slave Trade: A Poem*, urges lawmakers to
emancipate West Indian slaves immediately in order to restore
British rectitude, "clear[ing] the foulest blot that dimmed its
fame."[9] More insisted that extending legal freedoms to Africans
was prudently within the spirit and scope of English laws.
Accordingly, her opening lines distinguish between the liberties
with venerable limits advocated for West Indian bondspeople,
and unrestrained liberty which she identifies with the
"unlicens'd monster" of the Gordon riots of 1780. She percep-
tively noted that these rioters produced what they despised the
most. The mobs "clamour'd for peace, [while] . . . rend[ing] the
air with noise, . . . revil[ing] oppression only to oppress, and in
the act of murder, breath[ing] redress."[10] Significantly, Hannah

---

[8]Hannah More to her sisters in Bristol, January 1788, William Roberts, ed.,
Memoirs of the Life and Correspondence of Mrs. Hannah More vol.2 (London: R.
B. Selley and W. Burnside, 1835), p.97; Wylie Sypher, *Guinea's Captive Kings:
British Anti-Slavery Literature of the Eighteenth Century* (New York: Octagon
Books, 1969)[orig. pub. 1942], p.193; Jones, *Hannah More*, p.84. This haste
did not matter to the already converted. In reference to More's poem, the
Evangelical poet William Cowper loved it "as . . . [he did] all that Miss More
[wrote], as well as for energy of expression as for tendency of design." More,
Cowper suggested, got right to the point of moral reform without "mere
poetic cant." (William Cowper to Lady Heskith, 12 March 1788, Reverend T.
S. Grimshawe, ed., *The Works of William Cowper. His Life, Letters, and Poems*
(Boston: Crosby & Ainsworth, 1866), p.298.)
[9]Hannah More, *The Slave Trade: A Poem, The Works of Hannah More* vol.1
(Philadelphia: Woodward, 1832), p.30; This emphasis on national reputation
was first put forth by the famed lawyer Granville Sharp in the Somerset case
in 1772, and gradually became a commonplace of anti-slavery thought.
(David Brion Davis, *The Problem of Slavery in the Age of Revolution 1775-1823*
(Ithaca: Cornell University Press, 1975), pp.377, 394, 402, 494, 531.) In 1808
Thomas Clarkson, the first historian of the struggle to abolish the slave trade,
stressed this redemptive benefit of emancipation to Britain. (David Brion
Davis, *Slavery and Human Progress* (Oxford: Oxford University Press, 1984),
p.117.)
[10]*More, Slave Trade, Works*, p.27; c.f. Ford K. Brown, *Fathers of the Victorians
The Age of Wilberforce* (Cambridge: Cambridge University Press, 1961), p.109;

More argued that colonial slaveholders were the most vocal proponents of unrestricted liberty, echoing caustic remarks by her mentor Samuel Johnson.[11] She expected to undermine the formidable influence of the West Indian lobby by linking it to disorder and sedition.

More also contended that slaves, however physically alien, were more civilized and, hence, more in tune with British norms than their licentious captors. Stock Negro characters in eighteenth-century fiction either savagely avenge their fate or submissively absorb European pity.[12] More exploited both extremes. She initially praised the African desire for freedom, noting the immeasurable value of liberty to both the English and the Coromantines. Here she referred to Oroonoko, the captive black prince first sketched by the novelist Aphra Behn in 1685.[13] More acclaimed this royal slave's fictional rebellion against his amiable Christian master. However pious or humane, slaveholders were petty despots who ruled without bounds and precedents. Their stewardship of labor and property violated English common law and sense. Oroonoko, in contrast, possesses the attributes of the free-born Englishman ready to fight for his birthright.[14] It is true that More selected this literary reference partly because Oroonoko "served as a prototype for a vast literature depicting African slaves."[15] Her London audience knew this royal bondsman. But she chose Oroonoko partly because he approximates the sincere simplicity that she found in Evangelical laypeople.

More underscored the barbarity of slaveholders and traders *vis-à-vis* the gentility of slaves. She pointed to similarities between the ubiquitous Oroonoko and Greco-Roman heroes equally familiar to her prominent readers. Africans were patri-

---

Roger Anstey, *The Atlantic Slave Trade and British Abolition 1760-1810* (Atlantic Highlands, New Jersey: Humanities Press, 1975), pp.258-9.

[11]For Johnson's bile against West Indians and North Americans, see Davis, *Age of Revolution*, p.398.

[12]David Brion Davis, *The Problem of Slavery in Western Culture* (Ithaca: Cornell University Press, 1966), pp.466, 480.

[13]For Behn and the Oroonoko legend, see Sypher, *Guinea's Captive Kings*, pp.108-21.

[14]*More, Slave Trade, Works*, pp.27, 29.

[15]Davis, *Western Culture*, p.472.

otic. They defended their tribes from European hegemony. Their sense of honor was very strong, "for Pride is virtue in a Pagan soul;/ A sense of worth, a conscience of desert,/ A high, unbroken haughtiness of heart;/ That self-same stuff which erst proud empires sway'd/ Of which the conquerors of the world were made."[16] More thought it ironic that masters idealized Roman republicans for their defiant love of country, while punishing assertive slaves who yearn for their fatherland. She thought it sad that planters pursue their own selfish interests, however gruesome in their effects, without regard to national honor, reputation, or security. West Indian sugar magnates, unlike their heroic chattels, care only about their bottom line.[17]

Africans resemble classical figures in sensibility as well as in patriotism. According to *The Slave Trade*, exquisite feeling is "as keen where Gambia's waters glide,/ as where proud Tiber rolls his classic tide."[18] More rebutted the common argument that Africans felt no pain and, hence, were callous to those in pain. She asked, "When the sharp iron wounds his inmost soul,/ And his strained eyes in burning anguish roll;/ Will the parch'd negro own, ere he expire,/ No pain in hunger, and no heat in fire?"[19] The lack of accounts written by slaves of their ordeals indicated cultural preference, not complacent insensitivity. It is true that More did seem at times to doubt the African ability to reason. She was more sensitive to cultural differences in this poem, however, than Donna Landry allows.[20] To More, reliance on oral storytelling, not the absence of rationality, prevented blacks from composing tragic epics of valor and misery

---

[16]*More, Slave Trade, Works*, p.28; c.f. the similar stylized black in William Cowper's popular ballad, *The Negro's Complaint*, 1788, Grimshawe, *Works of Cowper*, p.300.

[17]More did not go as far as some country ideologues who linked slavery to a mercantilist and scheming court. On the other hand, she also did not share the concerns of those country gentlemen who worried that emancipation expanded the power of the central government to take away property. For a useful discussion of country ideology and anti-slavery agitation, see Davis, *Age of Revolution*, p.259.

[18]*More, Slave Trade, Works*, p.29.

[19]Ibid.; c.f. Sypher, *Guinea's Captive Kings*, pp.194-5; Davis, *Western Culture*, p.411.

[20]Donna Landry, *The Muses of Resistance: Laboring-Class Women's Poetry in Britain, 1739-1796* (Cambridge: Cambridge University Press, 1990), p.239.

in the manner of Homer and Virgil. Illiteracy in Africa, More
contended, impeded European understanding of African pain.
On the other hand, More chastised slavetraders and masters for
their numbness to human suffering. West Indian planters and
merchants were alien barbarians who murdered without
remorse.[21]

More urged unconditional abolition of British involvement in
the slave trade as the best first step to convert master and slave
into devout Anglicans. It is true that pro-slavery apologists and
the Evangelical More agreed that incumbent elites such as West
Indian planters had a mission to civilize from above. Yet More
attacked the prevalent excusing of the slave trade as an unfortunate yet efficient tool for Christian evangelism.[22] She noted
that most slave traders and sugar magnates were not even nom-
inally Christian. Therefore, they could not spread the Word to
Africans. She also noted that the West Indian interest discouraged missionary efforts. Slavers feared the corrosive effects of
Evangelical conversion on the lucrative Atlantic system. More
did not hate West Indian slaveholders personally and spent
much time and effort in an unsuccessful search for a kidnapped
West Indian heiress in the early 1790s.[23] Rather, she thought
they could change through accepting the Word. If planters
became seriously Christian, then they would free their slaves.
Yet More also underscored that if slaves became seriously

---

[21]*More, Slave Trade, Works*, pp.28-9; In her haste for publication, More got
carried away in her praising of Africans. At one point, she claimed that
natives would be saved even if they "had never heard" of the Gospel. This
meant faith, belief, and love of the Christian God were not necessary for
salvation (Brown, *Fathers of the Victorians*, p.110). Yet the silence of Evangelical lawmakers and preachers on this heresy underscores the doctrinally loose
nature of the Evangelical movement.

[22]More's argument was not new. In the 1660s, the puritan cleric Richard
Baxter had condemned the opposition of West Indian masters to the conversion of their slaves. (Davis, *Western Culture*, pp.338-9.)

[23]For the story of the heiress (whose fortune came from kidnapped Africans
and their descendants) kidnapped by a conniving Bristol doctor, see Hopkins, *Hannah More*, pp.129-35. The "good" doctor, who forced the
fifteen-year-old captive (through sexual harassment) to marry him, was represented in court eloquently and successfully by Thomas Erskine, the defense
lawyer of the "Jacobin Twelve" and hero of left-wing male historians.

Christian before emancipation, then they could justify their rebellion.

The gradual amelioration of slavery by missionary societies might seem in line with More's love of social harmony and piecemeal reform at home. Her Evangelical friend, the M.P. Henry Thornton, favored "spreading Christian light and knowledge" within the confines of the peculiar institution, desiring to combine moral progress with social stability and economic growth.[24] But More maintained that missionaries who glossed over the inherent evils of bondage turned Africans against the Word and thus against the one true foundation for social stability and prosperity. She wrote that "Sullen, . . . [the slave] mingles with his kindred dust,/ For he has learn'd to dread the Christian trust;/ To him what mercy can that God display,/ Whose servants murder, and whose sons betray?"[25] If slaves became Christian and free, however, they would then be immediately more tractable and productive than if they remained pagan (or even Christian) bondspeople. Hannah More also predicted that the established Church could gain many new African members if it dropped the impossible goal of reconciling temporal bondage with eternal salvation.

This increased religious fervor would sweep Britain as well as the colonies. More guaranteed that God planned to reward quick and decisive parliamentary action against the slave trade.

---

[24]For Thornton, see Davis, *Slavery and Human Progress*, p.160. Davis claims that Thornton's amelioritivist view was more common among Evangelicals than More's sense of urgency.

[25]*More, Slave Trade, Works*, p.29. c.f. the extremely bitter sense of the Christian betrayal of slaves in Ann Cromarty Yearsley, *A Poem on the Inhumanity of the Slave Trade*, 1788 as reprinted in Moira Ferguson, *First Feminists: British Women Writers 1578-1799* (Bloomington: Indiana University Press, 1985), pp.386-96. Yearsley was More's would-be *protégée* and lingering nemesis; she addressed this piece to the corporation of Bristol a few months after More addressed Parliament, perhaps in a futile attempt to upstage More. (J. M. S. Tompkins, *The Polite Marriage, etc.: Eighteenth-Century Essays* (Cambridge: Cambridge University Press, 1938), p.77; Landry, *Muses of Resistance*, p.238) Anna Seward was jealous of both More and Yearsley. Seward worried that if she wrote a poem on the slave trade, then the critics might compare it unfavorably not only to that of More and Thomas Day's *The Dying Negro*, but also to the work of "the unlettered milkwoman." (Anna Seward to J. Wedgewood, 18 February 1788, A. Constable, ed., *Letters of Anna Seward Written Between the Years 1784 and 1807* vol.2 [Edinburgh: George Ramsay & Co., 1811], p.33)

She asked, "What page of human annals can record/ A deed so bright as human rights restor'd?" By "bid[ding] all be free in earth's extended space," Westminster could assuage divine anger at British domination of trafficking in humans.[26] Slave-trading had stimulated short-sighted selfishness and enervating luxury which disrupted social harmony. Recent violent unrest and military defeat, More maintained, stemmed from this moral decline and portended future disasters sent by Providence. Disinterested abolition, on the other hand, would contribute to a new public-spirited prosperity. A reinvigorated commonweal would complement the spread of ascetic and activist Christianity which, in turn, would enhance civil peace. The colonies would develop like the mother country with a prohibition on perverted commerce. Directed by "a high commission from above," a revitalized and unified Britain would bring faith and freedom to "Afric's suffering clime."[27] Everyone including the misguided slavetraders and planters would benefit from Parliament's first steps toward universal manumission.

Several years later, More galvanized the loyalist reaction against the French Revolution that ironically tended to view the abolition of the slave trade as linked to sedition and disorder. Those working for any kind of change risked the fatal label "Jacobin" or "Paineite" during the cold and, later, hot war with revolutionary France.[28] Hannah More did not adopt this hidebound view, however.[29] Along with fellow Evangelicals and

---

[26]More, *Slave Trade, Works*, p.29.

[27]Ibid., p.30.

[28]Clive Emsley, "The Impact of the French Revolution on British Politics and Society," in Ceri Crossley and Ian Small, eds., *The French Revolution and British Culture* (Oxford: Oxford University Press, 1989), p.38. The successful slave revolution in Saint Domingue also poisoned the air for any parliamentary legislation to abolish the slave trade. c.f. the overly optimistic prospects for abolition given by the Foxite whig Sir Samuel Romilly in his letter to Madame G—, 15 May 1792, *Memoirs of the Life of Sir Samuel Romilly, Written by Himself; With a Selection from his Correspondence* vol.2 (London: John Murray, 1840), p.2.

[29]See her strong endorsement of abolition at the height of apprehension over French revolutionaries in Hannah More to Mrs. Benjamin Kennicott, 23 April 1792, Roberts, *Memoirs* vol.2, pp.330-2; Hannah More to her sisters,

usually hostile Foxite whigs, she courageously lobbied for abolition until her death in 1833, the year of West Indian emancipation.

While addressing MPs, More used forceful and unequivocal
language. In earlier didactic pieces, she had hedged social criticism in cryptic historical allusions. As a provincial female playwright dependent upon the good will of the rich and powerful,
she had expressed her dismay at fashionable behavior and dress
in coded messages. Her deepening reliance on Christ, however,
gradually relieved More of inhibiting self-consciousness. The
sharp tone of her *Slave Trade* confirms More's switch from
accommodation to advocacy, showing her increasing willingness to encounter rejection from the elite. In this poem she
condemned slavery as well as slavetrading. She vehemently
disagreed with those who wanted to ameliorate rather than
to eliminate bondage. Through anti-slavery advocacy, she
celebrated her own individual autonomy from worldly
compromise and from previously felt external constraints on
her conscience.[30]

More was, however, still cautious in censuring sinful practices
closer to home. She published her critical *Thoughts on the Importance of the Manners of the Great, to General Society* anonymously
about the same time as her abolitionist plea to the MPs. This
work had been several years in the making. Dr. George Horne
of Canterbury and Bishop Beilby Porteus of London had
encouraged her. Horne, in particular, felt that God had "led . . .
[More] to associate with" aristocrats and literati in order to
convert them. The Dean compared her calling to that of Esther
in the Old Testament. Like the Jewish prophetess, More
addressed those persons "considerable in reputation, important
by their condition in life, and commendable for the decency of
general conduct" who unwittingly performed acts incompatible
with godly truths.[31] With her recent poem *Florio* (1786), More

---

1792, Roberts, *Memoirs* vol.2, pp.335-6; Sypher, *Guinea's Captive Kings*,
pp.82-3, 195, 311.
[30]Anti-slavery agitation was a liberating experience for many marginal
individuals. In particular, see Davis, *Western Culture*, p.325.
[31]George Horne, Dean of Canterbury to Hannah More, 1786, Roberts,
Memoirs vol.2, p.37.

had hoped to elicit redeemable qualities in Horace Walpole, the epitome of elegant levity. In both her *Slave Trade* and *Thoughts*, she similarly exhorted "the good sort of people" of rank and fortune to comply with Christian principles. Self-revealingly, she warned in both works about the perils of "complaisant conformity" and pleasant decorum to the rich's spirituality.[32]

Yet More worried far more about reactions to her *Thoughts* than to her *Slave Trade*. Indeed, this anxiety contrasted sharply with her fearlessness as an abolitionist, but this apparent inconsistency is quite understandable. Lambasting greedy slave traders was not gauche, but criticizing friends publicly and candidly clashed with typical notions of gentility. More worried about losing her hard-earned social position and, hence, decided to publish her *Thoughts* anonymously. She claimed that anonymity fostered frankness. The unknown writer, she later wrote, "is not restrained from the strongest reprehension, and most pointed censure, of existing errors, by the conscious apprehension that his own faults may be brought forward."[33] Informed readers, however, quickly identified More as the author. Accordingly, Hannah prepared herself for the possibility of "every door shut against . . . [her]."[34]

More especially feared aristocratic anger at her condemnation of quite a few of their most unremarkable customs. Unflappable while rebuking the catastrophe of chattel slavery before the world's finest constituted body, More worried most about responses to her denunciation of minor violations by aristocrats of the fourth commandment. She had always been a strict Sabbatarian. This was due in part to her class and provin-

---

[32]Hannah More, *Thoughts on the Importance of the Manners of the Great, to General Society, The Works of Hannah More* vol.1 (Philadelphia: Woodward, 1832), p.262.

[33]Quoted in Christine L. Krueger, *The Reader's Repentance: Women Preachers, Women Writers, and the Victorian Social Discourse*, Princeton University Ph.D. dissertation in English, 1986, p.103.

[34]Hannah More to her sisters in Bristol, 1788, Roberts, *Memoirs* vol.2, p.103; William Cowper initially thought William Wilberforce was the author. Upon discovering that More did it, Cowper wondered how a woman could write "with a force and energy, and a correctness hitherto arrogated by the men." (William Cowper to Lady Heskith, 31 March 1788, Grimshawe, *Works of Cowper*, p.302.)

cial background. Middling-sort individuals, like More, were the most leery of Sunday recreation in Georgian Britain. And while sporadic in many locales, Sunday sobriety and church attendance were strongly established norms in bourgeois Bristol, More's hometown.[35] But her reverence for the Sabbath was not merely a product of class and place. Centuries of distinctively English theology supported More's deviance from national practice.[36] Thus when she entered the fashionable world in the 1770s, she had balked at participation in socially acceptable activity on the Lord's Day. This singularity had puzzled her new important friends.

But genteel attitudes soon began to change, however slowly. In the 1780s aristocratic Evangelicals had sponsored parliamentary acts and royal proclamations which codified middling-sort distaste for card games and open taverns on Sunday. This did not satisfy More. In *Thoughts*, she went beyond the flagrant infractions covered by existing Sabbatarian legislation and commentary. She exposed the propertied elite's unintentional and habitual neglect of Sabbatarian observance.[37]

More believed that increased Sabbatarian observance had to begin with the great if it was to become common. Appropriate celebrations of the Sabbath by national leaders would renew the special relationship between God and Britain. She strongly endorsed the old commonplace that the English were God's chosen people. Every Sabbatarian observance commemorated this divine preference. In turn, Albion's social peace and economic prosperity depended upon pleasing Him through keeping the Sabbath. Therefore, since corruption trickled down

---

[35]Jonathan Barry, *The Cultural Life of Bristol 1640-1775*, University of Oxford D.Phil. thesis in history, 1985, pp.136, 313.

[36]For English Sabbatarianism, see R.J. Bauckham, "Sabbath and Sunday in the Protestant Tradition," in D.A. Carson, ed., *From Sabbath to Lord's Day* (Grand Rapids, Mich.: Zondervan, 1982), pp.321-9; Kenneth L. Parker, *The English Sabbath: A Study of Doctrine and Discipline from the Reformation to the Civil War* (Cambridge: Cambridge University Press, 1988), pp.8-91; David S. Katz, *Sabbath and Sectarianism in Seventeenth-Century England* (Leiden: E. J. Brill, 1988), pp.1-20.

[37]*More, Thoughts, Works*, pp.265, 267-9. For royal and parliamentary codification of the Fourth Commandment, see Maurice J. Quinlan, *Victorian Prelude: A History of English Manners 1700-1830* (New York: Columbia University Press, 1941), pp.54-5.

the social order, even small lapses by the quality on Sunday strained the special relationship between God and His chosen people.[38]

This elitism was why More dwelt upon the sins of Sunday coiffures and concerts. For example, she lamented that the same well-meaning souls "who would gladly contribute to a mission of Christianity to Japan or Otaheite" had their hair done on the Sabbath. The reasons for More's concentration on Sunday hairdressing are not readily apparent. At first glance, she appears both to mock and to match the triviality of aristocratic civility with criticism of a relatively petty domestic "evil." But More was serious. She demanded pharisaical consistency in abstention from Sunday employment and entertainment. She complained that the great adapted Sabbatarian strictures to their routines.[39] More observed that ladies usually did not send for milliners or masons on Sundays. Yet these same women thought nothing of sending for their hairdresser after church in order to dress for hastily arranged parties later that afternoon.[40]

---

[38]More, *Thoughts, Works*, pp.265-6; In contrast, the late Dissenting divine Philip Doddridge (1702-1751) had condemned this superficial transfer of the Mosaic covenant to Britain, and felt that Sabbatarian observance was merely an artificial human convention. Usually More cited the Rev. Doddridge with pleasure. He strongly influenced the Evangelicals. But she strongly disagreed with him here. (Philip Doddridge, *A Course of Lectures on the Principal Subjects in Pneumatology, Ethics, and Divinity with Reference to the most considerable Authors on each Subject* (London: J. Rivington, 1763), pp.534-6.)

[39]So would antisabbatarian radicals in the nineteenth century. See Brian Harrison, *Peaceful Kingdom: Stability and Change in Modern Britain* (Oxford: Clarendon Press, 1982), pp.138-9.

[40]Lady Eleanor Butler had her hair cut, styled, and powdered on a Sunday even after she had read More's *Thoughts* four months before. See the entries of 17 April, 20 April, and 10 August 1788 in Lady Butler's diary as reprinted in Eva Mary Bell, ed., *The Hamwood Papers of the Ladies of Llangollen and Caroline Hamilton* (London: Macmillan, 1930), pp.89-90, 122. John Byng hated Frenchified frippery as much as More did, but he thought nothing of having his hair combed and powdered on a Sunday. See the entries of 13 June and 4 July 1790 in his travelogue through the Midlands as reprinted in C. Bruyn Andrews, ed., *The Torrington Diaries* vol.2 (London: Eyre & Spottiswoode, 1935), pp.175, 229. For another example of preparing for a party after church, see Harriet Francis to Mary Johnson, 27 October 1797, *Francis Letters* vol.2, p.421.

To More, expedient exemptions such as Sunday hairdressing inflicted spiritual hardships on hapless servants who "dare[d] not remonstrate, for fear . . . [they] should be deprived of . . . [their] employment for the rest of the week."[41] Working on Sunday simply for their ladies' convenience robbed laborers of their time for rest and devotion and, thus, poisoned ties between peeress and servant.[42] More also worried about dependents, creating their own exemptions in imitation of their employers. Small faults by the privileged few could become national apostasy, infuriating the Lord.

Certain devotional events such as Sunday concerts of sacred music number among the forbidden aristocratic amusements on More's list. She conceded "the innocence and even piety of Sunday concerts." Their lyrics came from the Bible; their music was "the divine Handel's." She admitted that "some attend[ed] these concerts with a view to cultivate devout affections."[43] Nevertheless, the good intentions of these audiences did not mitigate the "invincible objection of an evil example . . . [to] minds less enlightened, and to faith less confirmed."[44] Here she dreaded the consequences of fashionable behavior, however harmless, on the poor. The lower orders, More observed, considered concerts a secular diversion. Since servants accompanied their lord and lady to oratorios, they knew that their employers broke the fourth commandment without penalty. Domestics and artisans, More reported, expected local authorities to indulge their amusements on Sunday because magis-

---

[41]More, *Thoughts, Works*, p.265; c.f. the similar, although less picayune, argument of fellow Evangelical William Wilberforce in *A Practical View of the Prevailing Religious System of Professed Christians in the Higher and Middle Classes in this Country Contrasted with Real Christianity* (Boston: Ebenezer Larkin, 1799) (orig. pub. 1797), pp.123-4.

[42]c.f. the exegesis of Ford K. Brown who ignores More's genuine concern for the poor here in his *Fathers of the Victorians*, pp.99-100. More's apprehension over domestic resentment of the fashionable Sunday is overstated, but even the worldly Jack MacDonald, a footman and hairdresser, felt put upon by a French lady who wanted to play cards with him on a Sunday. See John MacDonald, *Memoirs of an Eighteenth Century Footman 1745-1779*, John Beresford, ed., (London: George Routledge & Sons, 1927) (orig. pub. 1790), pp.229-30.

[43]More, *Thoughts, Works*, p.267.

[44]Ibid., p.268.

trates tolerated Sunday concerts. Indeed, most recreational entertainments for the rich during the eighteenth century were customarily holidays for their servants.[45]

More perceived that the poor resented the legal double standard of new vigorous enforcement of Sabbatarian statutes and continued genteel violation of the same laws. Like Sunday hairdressing, Sunday concerts injured social relations between the estates. Most distressingly, the Sunday concert itself inadvertently provided lewd recreation for charges. While the great contemplated "the hallelujahs of heaven," their servants loitered "in the street, exposed to every temptation; engaged, perhaps, in profane swearing, and idle, if not dissolute conversation."[46] Sunday concerts were inimical to both civil peace and the reformation of the poor.

More insisted that legal privilege did not insulate aristocrats from divine precepts during weekdays as well as on the Sabbath. In particular, the quality had no exclusive right to lie, or no special liberty to convey lies by proxy. She abhorred the convention whereby masters forced their servants to tell unwanted guests that milords were not at home. False denials expediently saved one from the "idle invader." This convenience, however, "induc[ed] a general spirit of lying" because domestics closely imitated their employers[47] and, as Elisabeth

---

[45]E. P. Thompson, "Patrician Society, Plebeian Culture," *Journal of Social History*, 7(1974), p.394.

[46]More, *Thoughts, Works*, p.267; Other Evangelicals shared More's concern over the adverse effects of Sunday concerts on servants. In particular, see Thomas Gisborne, *An Enquiry into the Duties of Men in the Higher and Middle Classes of Society* vol.1, (London: B.& J. White, 1793), p.167.

[47]More, *Thoughts, Works*, p.267. Five years later in his celebrated *Political Justice*, the radical (and atheist) William Godwin also dwelt upon "the accumulation of moral damage which occurs if you ask your servant to tell an unwelcome visitor that you are not at home when in fact you are." (William St. Clair, *The Godwins and Shelleys: The Biography of a Family* (New York: W. W. Norton, 1989), p.74) In the early nineteenth century, however, the second Mrs. Godwin lied repeatedly through her servants. (St. Clair, *Godwins and Shelleys*, p.245) See also the relatively tolerant view of this practice in the radical Thomas Holcroft's first novel, *Anna St. Ives*, Peter Faulkner, ed., (London: Oxford University Press, 1970)[orig. pub. 1792], pp.22-3, 426-7. Holcroft was Godwin's best friend. For the emulation of masters and mistresses by their servants, see J. Jean Hecht, *The Domestic Servant Class in Eighteenth-Century England* (London: Routledge & Kegan Paul, 1956),

Jay translates this passage, because employers' children imitated prevaricating domestics.[48]

More's commentary qualified the old stereotype of inherently dishonest servants, placing most of the blame for domestic dissimulation on masters.[49] She pointed to the "gradual initiation" of fresh rural servants into the cesspool of London society, noting one new butler's distress at shifting "truths." His lady had ordered him to lie to visitors indiscriminately. Frequently, his lady invited guests without informing him. On these occasions, she ordered him to fetch those visitors to whom he had lied a few minutes before. This about-face placed the honest butler in an awkward position. More sensed the "suppressed indignation" of this former farmhand at the deceit of his lady. In general, tensions within genteel households flared with the number of vicarious falsehoods.[50]

Servants, nevertheless, learned to dissimulate, receiving rewards for poker faces and steady voices. More discerned that this type of obedience ironically eroded deference. Jaded servants lied for their own convenience as well as for their master's. They pragmatically choreographed deferential behavior for treats. These same servants periodically rebelled because they had no real respect for duplicitous employers. Aristocratic veracity, More argued, determined aristocratic power.[51]

Inappropriate perquisites for domestics such as tips also weakened hierarchical authority. More wanted to extend the "economic rationalization" of the eighteenth century inside the country house and urban mansion in order to increase the rec-

---

pp.200-28; Cissie Fairchilds, *Domestic Enemies: Servants and Their Masters in Old Regime France* (Baltimore: The John Hopkins University Press, 1984), pp.107-19.

[48]Elisabeth Jay, *The Religion of the Heart: Anglican Evangelicalism and the Nineteenth-Century Novel* (Oxford: Clarendon Press, 1979), p.135.

[49]c.f. the conventional "Rules for Servants," *The Town and Country Magazine; or, Universal Repository of Knowledge, Instruction, and Entertainment*, 24(January, 1792), p.20.

[50]More, *Thoughts, Works*, p.267.

[51]Ibid. More exposed here the self-interest behind most displays of servile loyalty and affection. Cissie Fairchilds has suggested that such a revelation dismayed and scared French masters of the late eighteenth century. (*Domestic Enemies*, pp.155-6)

titude of both master and servant.[52] Her hatred of "vails," the contemporary term for tips in private households, was not unique. Georgian masters habitually complained that gratuities from guests made servants autonomous and impertinent. Lord Chesterfield, the quintessential Francophile aristocrat, had successfully worked to eliminate many obligatory gratuities in the 1760s. He had argued that vails offended foreign guests unaccustomed to giving money for service in private homes.[53]

Hannah More's attack on "vails" was gravely moral and less cosmopolitan than Chesterfield's, focusing on the gratuity of "card money" left untouched by his efforts. She viewed the tipping of servants by guests during card games "as a worm which is feeding on the vitals of domestic virtue."[54] Leaving "card-money" at the table, More suggested, decreased the number of scrupulous servants. Sober families hosted considerably fewer games of faro and whist than the most fashionable. Consequently, servants quit pious households for the most fashionable since Evangelicals offered little opportunity for card-money. More complained that "the advantage of dependents . . . increas[ed] in a direct ratio to the dissipation of . . . [their] employer."[55] She found it ludicrous that domestics had begun to levy additional "excise taxes" for pouring wines, serving foods, and checking coats. With card-money, they already made more money than rural curates. She wrote that their insolence increased with their income. More bitterly suggested that abolition of customary gratuities would put the City's servants in their proper place. The best butlers, chefs, and head gardeners could make up to a comfortable 100 guineas annually with numerous gratuities, perquisites, and allowances; many eighteenth-century rural curates starved on a measly forty pounds per year.[56] No tipping at private homes would greatly

---

[52]Thompson, "Patrician Society," p.384-5.

[53]For an excellent discussion of vails and the aristocratic reaction against them, see Hecht, *Domestic Servant Class*, pp.89-90, 158-73.

[54]More, *Thoughts, Works*, p.265.

[55]Ibid., p.266.

[56]Ibid.; For the salaries of curates and servants, see Harold Perkin, *The Origins of Modern English Society* (Toronto: University of Toronto Press, 1969), pp.23-4. Commentators complained about overpaid and overweening servants throughout the eighteenth century. In particular, see the excerpts

lessen the disparity in wealth between London menials and country clergymen.[57] More's exclusive focus on male domestic servants seems a bit antique and limited for the late eighteenth century. It is true that the number of domestics was increasing during these years. Yet most new domestics were female and this type of personal service had diminishing social relevance as a model with the dominance of waged labor in urban and industrial areas.[58] More was strangely silent on the pernicious and widespread effects of masterly amorality on either female or salaried dependents.

Nevertheless, More predicted that the scrapping of disruptive traditions within genteel households would buttress national identity as well as social hierarchy. She traced these troubling ways to continental, especially French, influence. She shuddered at those aristocrats who justified their frivolous Sundays with examples drawn from papist countries. She acknowledged that cosmopolites had amused themselves on the Sabbath with imported diversions for the last hundred years. Nevertheless, More repudiated prescription. The passage of time did not cleanse error. This was especially true in Britain. More believed that the French and Spanish could "at least, plead the sanction of custom, and the connivance of the law."[59] In contrast, England, God's favorite, had godly artisans and merchants who had long followed Sabbatarian statutes.

---

from documents in Bridget Hill, ed., *Eighteenth-Century Women: An Anthology* (London: George Allen & Unwin, 1984), pp.238-9; the entry of 11 January 1789 in Hester Thrale Piozzi, *Thraliana: The Diary of Mrs. Hester Lynch Thrale (Later Mrs. Piozzi) 1784-1809* vol.2, Katherine C. Balderston, ed., (Oxford: Clarendon Press, 1951), p.725; Hecht, *Domestic Servant Class*, pp.77-124.

[57] Fellow Evangelical Thomas Gisborne, in contrast, encouraged his rich readers to give their servants "little presents of books or of money for particular deserts, and premiums for long service." He did not, however, discuss card-money. (*Duties of Men* vol.2, p.474.)

[58] For the feminization of domestic service in the late 1700s, see Bridget Hill, *Women, Work, and Sexual Politics in Eighteenth-Century England* (Oxford: Basil Blackwell, 1989), pp.125-9; Fairchilds, *Domestic Enemies*, pp.15-6, 51, 158, 241. For possible reasons behind feminization, see also Sir Walter Scott, *The Antiquary*, William Parker, ed. (London: J.M. Dent & Sons, 1969) (orig. pub. 1816), pp.56-7.

[59] More, *Thoughts, Works*, p.268.

Thus the great's Sunday amusements were evil and imported innovations. To More, equally alien and pernicious was the manipulation of servants through lies and tips. Here she inverted the usual argument that the distinctively English custom of "vails" angered French and German guests.[60] More urged the quality to return to what she considered native practices because Church and King depended upon their godly patriotism. Since sections of the laboring poor, particularly domestics, aped aristocratic disdain for indigenous virtue, "Reformation must begin with the great."[61] Her admonitions about genteel behavior extend far beyond the mundane rituals of the drawing room. The rest of her *Thoughts* condemns the narcissistic cult of sensibility which had captured many young aristocratic minds. More had touched upon this topic before. In her poem *Sensibility*, she had briefly commented on the abuse of lachrymose sympathy. Her *Thoughts* translates into prose many of her earlier verses. She repeated that even an other-directed sensibility uninformed by Evangelicalism was a casual, precarious instrument of good. Feeling for others without Scripture ceased to operate if the distressed were out of sight. It also lacked priority. Overwrought socialites blubbered over the health of housepets, but were indifferent to the plight of houseboys.[62] Her *Thoughts* expand on these themes of social irresponsibility. More upbraided those who helped others only for fun. She conceded that giving felt better than receiving. But charitable efforts required perseverance. Hannah More had learned patience from her turbulent patronage of John Hen-

---

[60]c.f. novelist Maria Edgeworth who associated refusal to tip servants with a Jewish and, to contemporaries, alien character in *Castle Rackrent*, George Watson, ed., (London: Oxford University Press, 1964)[orig. pub. 1800], p.36.
[61]More, *Thoughts, Works*, p.274. c.f. William Stafford who argues that the Evangelicals' "sense of sin works for obedience but against nationalism: because of man's wickedness the state is essential; but characteristically their pride in their native land is reduced by their sense of its depravity." ("Religion and the Doctrine of Nationalism in England at the Time of the French Revolution and Napoleonic Wars" in Stuart Mews, ed., *Religion and National Identity* (Oxford: Basil Blackwood, 1982), p.388) Stafford echoes uncritically the rather dated insights of V. G. Kiernan in his "Evangelicalism and the French Revolution," *Past and Present*, 1(1952), pp.44-56.
[62]More, *Thoughts, Works*, pp.270-1; c.f. the similar arguments of William Wilberforce, *Practical View*, p.238.

derson and Ann Yearsley. She had discovered that "nothing short of such a courageous piety growing on the stock of Christian principle" could withstand difficult clients. Too often philanthropy became misanthropy because of "the disappointments which benevolence encounters in the failure of her best concerted projects and the frequent depravity of the most chosen objects of her bounty." Diffident and self-interested attempts at charity soured hierarchical relationships, constructing a "cumbersome and impenetrable armour of distrust" between rich and poor. The great needed to draw strength and wisdom from Scripture in order to be sturdy stewards of national wealth.[63]

More, nevertheless, remained optimistic about prospects for moral renewal from above. She saw the 1780s as an age of aristocratic improvement. It is true that the bulk of her *Thoughts* snap at mundane details of genteel routines. Yet she was "willing to flatter . . . [herself] that the moral and intellectual scene about us . . . [has begun] to brighten." Parliamentary support of anti-slavery petitions augured the transformation of the Hanoverian kingdom into a government "of our God and His Christ."[64] Most critically, collaboration between Anglican bishops and Dissenting preachers over abolition diffused "a catholic temper" in the clergy. Liberal toleration amongst ardent protestants, More wrote, blossomed in the same ratio as informed philanthropic efforts. Civility between Anglicans and Dissenters gelled social harmony and national solidarity, the earthly signs of divine approval. King George and Queen Charlotte, although staunch defenders of Anglican privilege, encouraged godly living and unity, setting a good example for London society.[65] The royal proclamation of 1787 sanctioned serious

---

[63]More, *Thoughts, Works*, p.270. c.f. the defense of benevolence without faith in Robert Bage, *Hermsprong; or, Man As He Is Not* vol.1, Stuart Tave, ed., (University Park, Pa.: Pennsylvania State University Press, 1982)[orig. pub. 1796], pp.208-13, 223-9. Bage was a Unitarian papermaker turned novelist and was a friend of Joseph Priestley and Richard Price.

[64]More, *Thoughts, Works*, p.273.

[65]Evangelicals particularly loved the staid royal couple. Indirectly praising George III, Thomas Gisborne stressed the importance of a monarch's piety for the moral state of a kingdom. (*Duties of Men* vol.1, pp.66-75.) For the general groundswell of support for the previously unlovable George III in

and ecumenical endeavors "to instruct the poor, to inform the ignorant, and to reclaim the vicious." This growing intolerance of both patrician and plebeian depravity left hope that the British "shall more and more become 'that happy people who have the Lord for their God.'"[66]

This united godly front was, however, a mere figment of Hannah More's imagination. Typical of Dissenters, the Unitarian Richard Price in 1787 shared with More an almost millenarian optimism, but for very different reasons. He was much more excited over the first signs of the separation of church and state in Europe and America than over the royal sanction of parochial Sabbatarianism. He lobbied much harder for the repeal of discriminatory legislation against fellow dissenters than for Wilberforce's campaign to abolish the slave trade. Anti-aristocratic to the core, Price held much more faith in the ability of the middling classes than in landed parasites to lead Britain in an age of moral improvement.[67] More, in contrast, endorsed the ancient marriage of religion and civil policy, snubbed the campaign for removal of sectarian disabilities, and looked to incumbent elites for moral guidance. Accordingly, affluent Anglicans warmly received More's *Thoughts* over those of Price, calming her fears of ostracism. The essay sold out very quickly, forcing the pleasantly surprised Thomas Cadell to publish seven editions in four months. Mary G. Jones has correctly

---

the last forty years of his reign, see Colley, "Apotheosis of George III," pp.94-129. The Evangelical love of George III was not always mutual; after being told Henry Thornton was nearby, the King said, "I hate such canting Methodists," and then sang aloud, "Youth's a season fit for joy, Love then is our duty," before lapsing into his periodic madness. (Sylvester Douglas, *The Diaries of Sylvester Douglas (Lord Glenbervie)* vol.1, Francis Bickley, ed., (London: Constable & Co., 1928), p. 181.)

[66]More, *Thoughts, Works*, p.274.

[67]Richard Price, *The Evidence for a Future Period of Improvement in the State of Mankind, With the Means and Duty of Promoting It, Represented in a Discourse, Delivered on Wednesday, 25 April 1787, at the Meeting-House in Old Jewry, London, to the Supporters of a New Academical Institution among Protestant Dissenters* (London: T. Cadell, 1787), pp.5, 21-5. For Price's lukewarm anti-slavery position, see Sypher, *Guinea's Captive Kings*, p.62. For the unsuccessful campaign of 1787-90 to end sectarian discrimination in employment, see Goodwin, *Friends of Liberty*, pp.65-98; Cookson, *Friends of Peace*, pp.10-2; J. C. D. Clark, *English Society 1688-1832* (Cambridge: Cambridge University Press, 1985), pp.340-4.

attributed "some of its success ... to Miss More's fame as a writer, which was well established by 1788; some to her inside knowledge of the stately homes of England, which titillated the palate of the middling classes who had not the entree and entertained those who had."[68] The nature of More's recommendations and assumptions also contributed to the essay's popularity. Some influential readers such as Queen Charlotte adopted the simple and minor adjustments put forth by More. They shared her faith in the aristocratic power to solve complex national problems. Even the Unitarian *Analytical Review* praised More's section on the unhappy side effects of Sunday hairdressing, although deploring that "the great, as they are called, are treated with a deference, to which, from an author, they are not entitled."[69] It is true that a few notables such as Horace Walpole ridiculed the "puritanical strictness" of More's allegiance to the fourth commandment.[70] But most felt comfortable with More's assessment of the manners of the propertied elite. Her essay reflects genteel culture, while criticizing it. Her *Thoughts* lack passion, and call for tolerance. They discuss trivialities and list painless ways to exact deference and to establish stability.

The outbreak of the French Revolution in 1789 prompted More to amplify her calls for the return of English grandees to native virtues. Like most British observers, Hannah More initially welcomed the storming of the Bastille. She characterized the fall of French absolutism as the demolition of one of Satan's "great engines." She hoped yet to witness "the utter extinction" of popery and slavery, the intact vehicles of the Devil. To More, the Vatican, Versailles, and the West Indies were "stupendous and elaborate inventions ... [which] aggravat[ed] the misery of mankind by mountains of sin, and masses of calamity."[71] Nevertheless, the victory of "the lawless rabble"

---

[68]Jones, *Hannah More*, p.107. Excerpt reprinted by permission of Cambridge University Press. All rights reserved.

[69]Review of *Thoughts on the Importance of the Manners of the Great to General Society, Analytical Review*, 1(August, 1788), p.469.

[70]Jones, *Hannah More*, p.109.

[71]Hannah More to Horace Walpole, September 1789, Roberts, *Memoirs* vol.2, pp.170-1; c.f. the similar contentions of the Evangelical Granville Sharp in

in Paris troubled her. More soon considered despotism and popery lesser evils compared to what she saw as the anarchy and atheism across the Channel.[72] She claimed, however, that the sins of the French nobility caused the horrors of the Parisian crowd. More feared similar convulsions from both overt and hidden declines of faith among the highest ranks at home. Developing her previous arguments about the correlations between aristocratic behavior and social cohesion, she published *An Estimate of the Religion of the Fashionable World* in 1790.

More's *Estimate* initially traces declension to the abuse of civil and religious liberties enshrined in the unwritten constitution. Absent from the *Estimate* is the rosy view of universal toleration which Hannah More had held two years before. She pointed out that serious Christianity in England "decreased in . . . proportion to . . . having secured the means of enjoying it."[73] She extolled the political arrangements of 1688. But she perceived that the recent moral revolution inspired by alien socialites both manipulated and contravened the spirit of William and Mary's restoration of British rights. Law and privilege unfortunately protected free-thinking dissipation. Many ladies and gentlemen abused cherished expressive freedoms through opinion and activity contrary to the Word.[74]

1797 as quoted in Anstey, *Slave Trade*, p.160. More also initially advocated increased grain exports to famine-stricken France to help "in this their dreadful extremity." (Hannah More to Eva Garrick, 23 June 1789, Folger Shakespeare Library, Mss. 487, fo. 64.)

[72]Hannah More to Horace Walpole, September 1789, Roberts, *Memoirs* vol.2, pp.188-9. c.f. her acquaintance Hester Thrale Piozzi who felt that the unrest in France "will end in Air; because Anarchy naturally finishes in Despotism, and Despotism in a Country long accustomed to Monarchical Government, naturally drops into the hands of a King." (Piozzi to Samuel Lysons, 8 July 1789, Edward A. Bloom and Lillian D. Bloom, eds., *The Piozzi Letters* vol.1 (Newark: University of Delaware Press, 1989), p.298.) Excerpt reprinted by permission of Associated University Presses. All rights reserved.

[73]Hannah More, *An Estimate of the Religion of the Fashionable World*, *The Works of Hannah More* (Philadelphia: Woodward, 1832), p.278.

[74]References to 1688 quickly disappeared from Anglican commentaries after 1790. The Terror in France tarnished the legitimacy of any revolution, however glorious. (Robert Hole, *Pulpits, Politics, and Public Order in England, 1760-1832* (Cambridge: Cambridge University Press, 1989), p.110.)

More cautioned readers about those "under the beautiful mask of an enlightened philosophy."[75] While professing tolerance, drawing-room philosophes were intolerant. Fashionable skepticism dictated exclusion of Evangelical principles in high society. Libertarians, More reported, substituted new satanic prejudices for the old godly precepts behind constitutional guarantees. This perversion of native ideals threatened social harmony in addition to the tradition of tolerance peculiar to Britain. Bigoted infidelity spread downward through example, poisoning the minds of the poor against divine and human authority.[76]

More primarily blamed, however, casual benevolence and worldly prudence for elite decadence. She stressed that a Christian commonwealth required much more than charitable works and reasonable ethics. More lauded the tremendous explosion of generosity during the eighteenth century, funding a bevy of causes from her own commercial success. To More, "the many striking acts of public bounty . . . justly entitl[ed] the present age to be called . . . the Age of Benevolence."[77] Nevertheless, most patrons regrettably thought that almsgiving reduced the need for religion of the heart. More noted that munificence had replaced Christianity among the great. Charity unwittingly contributed to ungodly luxury and dissipation which, in turn, promoted private distresses far greater in number than philanthropists could combat. She wrote that "though more objects are relieved by our money, yet incomparably more are debauched by our licentiousness."[78] Works without faith led to social disorder, while sending well-meaning donors to Hell.

Faith without works and morality without piety, More discerned, also made Britain ripe for French turbulence. Hypocrisy, in particular, inflamed class tensions. Magnates and peeresses frequently "professe[d] to believe like an apostle, and yet . . . [led] the life of a sensualist."[79] This inconsistency

---

[75]More, *Estimate, Works*, p.279.

[76]Ibid., pp.279-80, 286-7.

[77]Ibid., p.280.

[78]Ibid.; c.f. Quinlan, *Victorian Prelude*, pp.57-8; Brown, *Fathers of the Victorians*, pp.104-5.

[79]More, *Estimate, Works*, p.293.

disgraced Christian institutions in the eyes of other aristocrats and, most ominous, the middling and lower orders. Here More failed to notice that domestic service in fashionable households often sparked godliness among the best servants as a way for the menials to show up their employer's family in the eyes of the Lord.[80] As an elitist Evangelical, More insisted that the deferential always copied their betters' dubious lead. The rebellious, on the other hand, resented aristocratic immunity from prosecution for immoral or blasphemous acts. They understandably wondered why magistrates enforced statutes that concerned their diversions, but not those of the rich. More argued that abandonment of this double standard would quiet divisive arguments about legal privilege.[81]

But More also realized that serious Christianity among the great had to be more than an ascetic code of self-denial to form the basis of a healthy body politic. Well-heeled Anglicans favored the secular benefits of religion to the detriment of their spirituality, measuring the utility of faith solely by its restraint on the human will.[82] Drawing-room philosophes, on the other hand, desired to filter morality from the so-called "superstition" of revealed religion. They thought only this separation would allow good ethics to produce good governors.[83] More as an Evangelical disagreed with both positions. She urged aristocrats to obey and worship God fully. Then, their dependents would

---

[80]Deborah M. Valenze, *Prophetic Sons and Daughters: Female Preaching and Popular Religion in Industrial England* (Princeton: Princeton University Press, 1985), pp.68, 124-32, 182, 202.

[81]More, *Estimate, Works*, pp.288-91.

[82]This utilitarian view of religion became dominant in Anglican circles during the 1790s. The French Revolution underscored to the British establishment that the Bible set down rules of proper conduct and induced believers to follow these rules. (Hole, *Pulpits*, pp.134-5.) See also Thomas Philip Schofield, "Conservative Political Thought in Britain in Response to the French Revolution," *Historical Journal*, 29(1986), pp.605-11.

[83]In the next few years, Thomas Paine was the most prominent defender of morality without piety. For example, see his *The Age of Reason: Being an Investigation of True and Fabulous Theology*, 1794, in William D. Van der Weyde, ed., *The Life and Works of Thomas Paine* vol.8 (New Rochelle, N.Y.: Thomas Paine National Historical Association, 1925), pp.3-6, 11-4, 277-86. For the similar arguments of William Godwin and James Mackintosh, see Hole, *Pulpits*, pp.135-6.

do the same. In contrast, where the quality maintained a sterile propriety for reputation's sake only, many observant artisans and servants did the same. Like their posturing patrons, workers rejected Christ as irrelevant. This social emulation, More reported, weakened deference. No longer could leaders automatically attribute to the Lord inexplicable things such as inequality. Only faith in "the Supreme Disposer" could reconcile the ambitious to the political and social status quo.[84]

More predictably prescribed godly education for elite youth to preempt radical unrest. She and her sisters had run an excellent school for well-to do girls in Bristol. There the Mores had offered a marketable mix of snobbery and scholarship. In her latest recommendations for young aristocrats of both sexes, Hannah More stressed only religious instruction, dropping the training in polish and charm. She pointed out that the standard curriculum of the previous century had introduced the youngest scholars to patristic texts as soon as possible and had continued to emphasize those texts to adolescents over mannered alternatives. Here More once again yearned for a return by the ruling classes to what she considered an old English norm, vilifying the cosmopolitan coaching of the recent past.[85] Revived commitments by distinguished families to rigorous religious education from cradle through adolescence were necessary to counteract the foreign airs and philosophies which had sapped the moral fortitude of Britain's future oligarchs. The corrective power of Christian instruction would purify downward through social imitation, rendering attendance at Sunday schools fashionable.[86]

The rich and powerful avidly read More's *Estimate*, despite its angry invective and preachy tone. Thomas Cadell published five editions in five years. Praise was nearly universal and typically effusive. Predictably, the Reverend John Newton "hope[d] that

---

[84]More, *Estimate, Works*, pp.288-91, 300-1; Fellow Evangelical William Wilberforce and the Baptist Robert Hall echoed More's concern over the reduction of religion to morality by both Anglicans and deists. (Wilberforce, *Practical View*, pp.12-3, 76-7, 113, 142-3, 227, 230; Hole, *Pulpits*, p.137.)

[85]More, *Estimate, Works*, pp.282-5.

[86]Ibid., pp.285-8. For a developed Evangelical program for elite education, see Gisborne, *Duties of Men*, pp.447-60.

'the Estimate,' if it comes in their way, will prove to them, 'as a light shining in a dark place,' for which they will have reason to praise God, and to thank the writer."[87] Less predictably, Bishop Barrington of Salisbury and Durham, a long-time yet conventionally aristocratic friend of More, hoped that the *Estimate* would "produce reformation in those for whose benefit it is professedly written."[88]

Some of her most unlikely readers greeted More's criticism of the affluent in a different way than she had intended. The so-called "Republican" Bishop of Llandaff, who strongly sympathized with Mirabeau and Talleyrand, believed that her *Estimate* would "do much good, if any writing can do much good in a country which is debauched by its riches and prosperity."[89] An anonymous cartoonist published by the Paineite William Holland depicted More as a staunch defender of radical advocacy against a particularly sour outburst from Queen Charlotte (in reality, one of More's biggest fans) in a cheap print."[90]

But her *Estimate* left most readers more indifferent than persuaded. Rabid followers such as the Duchess of Gloucester ignored suggestions in the essay which interfered unduly with their lives.[91] In 1795 More admitted to her Evangelical friend

---

[87]Reverend John Newton to Hannah More, February 1791, Roberts, *Memoirs* vol.2, pp.244-5.

[88]Shute Barrington, the Bishop of Salisbury to Hannah More, 23 February 1791, Roberts, *Memoirs* vol.2, p.247. Barrington had been a friend of More since at least 1781. For their meetings, see Hannah More to Eva Garrick, 17 June 1781, Hyde Collection, Firestone Library, Princeton University, Johnson Letters IX, 328, p.3; Hannah More to an unidentified correspondent, 18 June 1782, Beinecke Rare Book and Manuscript Library, Yale University, Osborn Collection, Files 85.11.1; Hannah More to Martha More, 1783, Roberts, *Memoirs* vol.1, p.275. For Barrington as a key contributor to the trust for Ann Yearsley, see Hannah More to Elizabeth Carter, 16 December (1784), Hyde Collection, Firestone Library, Princeton University, Johnson Letters X, 390, p.3.

[89]Richard Watson, the Bishop of Llandaff to Hannah More, February 1791, Roberts, *Memoirs* vol.2, p.242. For the most useful look at Watson, see John Gascoigne, "Anglican Latitudinarianism and Political Radicalism in the Late Eighteenth Century," *History*, 71(February, 1986), pp.34-6.

[90]For a reproduction and discussion of this very interesting print, *Contrasting Opinions of Paine's Pamphlets* (published 26 May 1791), see David Bindman, *The Shadow of the French Revolution: Britain and the French Revolution* (London: British Museum Publications Ltd., 1989), p.108.

[91]Jones, *Hannah More*, p.114.

Zachary Macaulay that the genteel did not heed her warnings, despite strong sales and rave reviews. She began to realize that reformation of the great would take a long time.[92]

More, however, still worried about the deleterious effects of aristocratic corruption such as social disorder. Her fears intensified with unprecedented political events. She felt with some justification that apostate magnates and bureaucrats were terrorizing defenders of hierarchy and religion in France. These innovators, More claimed, incited impressionable artisans and servants to murder anyone who spoke up for the old regime. Most worrisomely, these self-proclaimed tribunes of the people hoped to export their horrors to the Dutch Republic, the German states, and Britain. Sadly to More, demagogic and ungodly posturing appealed to an influential handful of Foxite parliamentarians (admirers of anything French, whether the ancien-regime or the National Assembly) and ambitious literati. Of the latter group, the most dangerous was Thomas Paine whose pro-French *Rights of Man* sold over 200,000 copies in two parts by 1793. Widespread distribution of Paine's flippant attacks on the constitution and Church required a vigorous response. Accordingly, the Pitt ministry formed local loyalist organizations which handed out pamphlets full of patriotic bromides.[93]

---

[92]Hannah More to Zachary Macaulay, 1795, Roberts, *Memoirs* vol.2, pp.454-5. See also Hannah More to William Wilberforce, 1795, in William Wilberforce Papers, Special Collections Department, Duke University Library, Durham, North Carolina.

[93]For the content of loyalist propaganda, see Maurice Quinlan, "Anti-Jacobin Propaganda in England, 1792-1794," *Journalism Quarterly*, 16(1943), pp.9-15; Donald E. Ginter, "The Loyalist Association Movement of 1792-3 and British Public Opinion," *The Historical Journal*, IX, 2(1966), pp.179-90; Robert R. Dozier, *For King, Constitution, and Country: The English Loyalists and the French Revolution* (Lexington: University of Kentucky Press, 1983), pp.76-102; Robert Hole, "British Counter-revolutionary Popular Propaganda in the 1790s," in Colin Jones, ed., *Britain and Revolutionary France: Conflict, Subversion, and Propaganda* (Exeter: University of Exeter Press, 1983), pp.53-69; Trevor McGovern, "Conservative Ideology in Britain in the 1790s," *History*, 73(1988), pp.238-47; Harry T. Dickenson, "Popular Conservatism and Militant Loyalism 1789-1815" in Harry T. Dickenson, ed., *Britain and the French Revolution* (New York: St. Martin's Press, 1989), pp.104-10.

The Bishop of London beseeched Hannah More to scribble casual prose for loyalist circulation. "More sympathetic to the Evangelical revival than most of the bench," Bishop Porteus agreed with her that the French Revolution was the result of the depravity and unbelief that had first infected the French aristocracy and clergy and then went on to corrupt the masses.[94] He thought, however, that a direct didactic appeal to the poor would be far more appropriate in this emergency than the slow dissemination of virtue downward through initial reformation of the peerage. Thus Porteus wanted the versatile More to translate genteel apologies for the constitution and the Church into streetwise vernacular. He maintained that More's unusual knowledge of the poor gained from her face-to-face philanthropy placed her in a special position to produce literature accessible to a "low" or popular audience. He wanted her to write "some little thing tending to open . . . [the lower ranks'] eyes under their present wild impression of liberty and equality."[95]

More initially said no to her old friend. She understood the risks of this extraordinary request. Writing explicitly about politics was inappropriate for a woman. Working on this pamphlet would distract her from her charities. Most critically, her recent essays held that moral reformation ought to begin with the great. Genteel dissipation made efforts to reform and control dependents ineffective, according to More. Porteus, nevertheless, persisted. Finally, "on one sick day" in the summer of 1792, Hannah More reluctantly churned out an earthy dialogue entitled *Village Politics by Will Chip, a Country Carpenter*.[96]

In this famous tract, More developed and clarified elitist and xenophobic themes she had explored in earlier works. Here the

---

[94]For Porteus, see R. A. Soloway, *Prelates and People: Ecclesiastical Social Thought in England 1783-1852* (Toronto: University of Toronto Press, 1969), pp.35-6. Reprinted by permission of the University of Toronto Press. All rights reserved.

[95]Hannah More to Frances Boscawen, 1793, Roberts, *Memoirs* vol.2, p.345. See also Hannah More to Eva Garrick, 8 January 1793, Folger Shakespeare Library, Mss. 487, fo. 81; Quinlan, *Victorian Prelude*, p.74; A. G. Newell, "Early Evangelical Fiction," *Evangelical Quarterly*, 38(1966), p.14; Jay, *Religion of the Heart*, pp.151-2.

[96]Hannah More to Frances Boscawen, 1793, Roberts, *Memoirs* vol.2, p.345.

loyalist blacksmith Jack Anvil persuades the Paineite mason Tom Hod to reject the fashionably French ideas and ways of social superiors. An ungrateful exciseman, "like many others who take the king's money and betray him," has preached the libertarian gospels to Tom, among other impressionable artisans, at the local tavern.[97] This was a personal attack on Thomas Paine because Paine had been an exciseman in the 1760s and early 1770s. Tom suddenly becomes miserable after discussing the second part of *Rights of Man* with this cagey placeman. The mason had never known how unhappy he is supposed to be until he "had the good luck to meet with this book."[98]

More repeatedly emphasized that corruption cascaded from literate to illiterate. She belittled popularizers of natural rights theories and Enlightenment cant.[99] When Jack asks Tom what is wrong, Tom spouts glittering phrases gleaned from Paine who, to More, has drawn upon the musings of traitors to their own noble estate across the Channel. Tom the mason has no idea what liberty, equality or general reform means, although Jack the smith makes it clear that he knows these words to mean expropriation of property (including his own) for rapacious alehouse politicians. Tom does not listen to Jack initially and simply yearns for the mirage of "freedom and happiness" allegedly enjoyed by Parisian sans-culottes and their powerhungry patrons.[100] In this opening exchange, More misrepresented the Saxon bluntness of Paine as full of alien abstractions and mistranslated the radical call for legal equality as an apology for social levelling. She underscored, however, the inability of

---

[97]Hannah More, *Village Politics. Addressed to All the Mechanics, Journeymen, and Labourers, in Great Britain. By Will Chip, a Country Carpenter, The Works of Hannah More* (Philadelphia: Woodward, 1832), p.62.

[98]Ibid., p.58; c.f. the argument of "Tam Thrum, an auld weaver" of Edinburgh who insinuated that well-off Paineites manufactured popular dissatisfaction solely for their own aggrandizement in the anonymous *Look before ye Loup* (1793) as quoted in Hole, "Popular Propaganda," p.62.

[99]c.f. the Foxite whig James Mackintosh, *Vindiciae Gallicae: Defense of the French Revolution* (London: G. G. J. and J. Robinson, 1791)[Woodstock reprint, 1989], pp.122-5.

[100]More, *Village Politics, Works,* pp.58-9, 61-2. For Paine as a "radically chic" fop speaking to easily persuaded monkeys, see William Kent's drawing of 1793 in Bindman, *Shadow of the Guillotine,* p.113.

would-be tribunes to direct revolutionary enthusiasm into coherent channels.[101]

More championed the English constitution, the invaluable legacy of gradual reform from above, over what she crudely characterized as "French" natural rights. Jack points out that the capture and demolition of the Bastille had briefly introduced long-standing English liberties to France, but natural rights proponents had ruined this glorious moment. They had legitimized the undeferential license of hack writers and third-rate doctors and had rationalized indiscriminate slayings. In contrast, Britons in 1792 lived under those true friends of liberty—George III and William Pitt—who had eschewed the use of force against their own people. Indeed, the Pitt administration refrained from violent roundups of suspects in the 1790s, relying instead on exemplary prosecution and harassment that had worked to quell malcontents so well in the previous decades.[102] As Jack says, it made no sense to regress to the level of a brutal despotism which shed blood gratuitously.[103]

More's caricature of ruthless French revolutionaries was all too true, but she unfairly linked the Jacobin view of natural rights to the whole diverse spectrum of artisanal radicals. Most "members unlimited" of the radical corresponding societies revered the English constitution as much as More did and were as leery as she was of the Parisian clique.[104] On the other hand, a significant minority of the urban loyalist associations committed to the defense of the constitution (and the distribu-

---

[101]c.f. Claeys, *Thomas Paine*, p.151.

[102]For Pitt's savvy constitutional restraint, see Clive Emsley, "An Aspect of Pitt's 'Terror': Prosecutions for Sedition During the 1790s," *Social History*, 6(May, 1981), pp.155-75; idem, "Repression, 'Terror' and the Rule of Law in England During the Decade of the French Revolution," *English Historical Review*, 100(October, 1985), pp.801-25.

[103]The contrast between British and French liberty was a commonplace of loyalist literature and art. For prints making *The Contrast*, see Bindman, *Shadow of the Guillotine*, pp.42-4, 63, 117-22, 126-7. c.f. the radical whig Samuel Parr, who classified the denigration of other countries (namely France) in the glorification of one's homeland as false patriotism and unchristian chauvinism in a sermon of 1803 reprinted in William Field, ed., *Memoirs of the Life, Writings, and Opinions of the Rev. Samuel Parr, LL.D* (London: Henry Colborn, 1828), pp.415-20.

[104]Goodwin, *Friends of Liberty*, pp.174-9, 194-200.

tion of *Village Politics*) embraced parliamentary and fiscal reforms that Hannah More and the Pitt ministry abhorred. To these loyal and patriotic subjects, the organic body politic did not stop growing in 1688.[105] It was also a mistake for More to assume that aristocratic defenders of the French Revolution in England were betraying their ancestors' legacy. Fox and Grey were building upon that tradition of gradual change, even if their machinations and morals justifiably led More and Paine alike to question their motives and qualifications as tribunes for the people. The Foxites continued to invoke imagery from the Glorious Revolution long after the unfolding events in France had tarnished all revolutions, however glorious, to most loyalists. For instance, James Mackintosh, the able spokesman for the parliamentary opposition, admired the revolutionaries of 1688 "not in contending for what they then DID, but for what they now WOULD DO" about extending civil and political rights through existing institutions.[106]

To More's credit, however, Jack does not belabor the grisly September Massacres commonly recounted by loyalist mouthpieces.[107] Rather this smith dwells upon the perversion of expressive freedoms wrought by the revolution. Gallic crowds executed innocents on trivial or trumped-up accusations with impunity. More stressed to her mass audience that the majority of these victims of mob violence were not pampered scions. Jack observes that "they're all so free that nobody's safe."[108] Tom, then, reminds Jack of the *lettre de cachet* which the Bourbons had used to arrest suspects arbitrarily and indefinitely. Jack admits the sins of the ancien-regime, noting the French proclivity for centralized repression. But casual incarcerations in Paris had increased since the Declaration of the Rights of Man and Citizen. Jack also notes that similar detentions were

---

[105]Ginter, "Loyalist Association Movement," pp.179-90.

[106]Mackintosh, *Vindiciae Gallicae*, p.346. See also Lionel McKenzie, "The French Revolution and English Parliamentary Reform: James Mackintosh and the Vindicae Gallicae," *Eighteenth-Century Studies*, 15(1980), pp.264-82.

[107]For pamphlets with graphic depictions of the atrocities, see Hole, "Popular Propaganda," p.60.

[108]More, *Village Politics, Works*, p.58.

rare in Georgian England due to twelfth-century precedents.[109] Of course, Jack fails to mention the forbidding bastilles and aristocratic privileges of the twelfth century still embedded in English justice and so prominent in radical propaganda.[110]

Although oblivious to the inconsistencies of her own government, Hannah More exposed the hypocrisy of the French Reign of Virtue. Unitarians such as Richard Price had hoped that the fall of the Bastille would usher in a "reformation of manners and virtuous practice" in both France and Britain.[111] To Price and other Rational Dissenters, the emerging middle-class vanguard in both countries would bring bourgeois probity to government, setting a shining example to the rest of society.[112] More correctly pointed out that the new bosses in Paris were as vicious as the old ones. The vague doublespeak of natural rights stemmed directly from the artifice and equivoque of the ancien-regime. Like Madame du Barry, revolutionary leaders meant exactly the opposite of what they said. For example, "an enlightened people" according to the new duplicity "put out the light of the Gospel, confound[ed] right and wrong, and grop[ed] about in pitch darkness."[113]

The rights of the free-born Englishman, however, were not based on fashionable deceits, but rather on historical events. The civil wars ensured that no one, however privileged, was

---

[109]Ibid., p.59; This difference in due process between English and French justice was a common comparison in loyalist propaganda. See Dickinson, "Popular Conservatism," pp.107-8.

[110]For a scathing attack on the legal system, see William Godwin, *Caleb Williams*, David McCracken, ed., (London: Oxford University Press, 1970)[orig. pub. 1794], pp.71-9, 138-206, 239-53.

[111]Quoted in Soloway, *Prelates and People*, p.28.

[112]Cookson, *Friends of Peace*, pp.26-7, 121-3.

[113]More, *Village Politics*, *Works*, p.62; c.f. Barbara Taylor, *Eve and the New Jerusalem: Socialism and Feminism* (New York: Pantheon Books, 1983), p.13. The loyalist linkage of Bourbon and Jacobin France has been overlooked by historians fixated on the extraordinary events of 1789 and its aftermath. This has been rectified somewhat by Gerald Newman who suggests that loyalists opportunistically tarred the Jacobins with Bourbon duplicity, a specter that had energized popular opinion for the previous half century. (*English Nationalism*, pp.233-8.) Yet Harry T. Dickinson, the most recent commentator on popular conservatism, still restricts loyalist pique at "French principles" to ideological hatred of the post-Bastille governments. ("Popular Conservatism," pp.104-10.)

above the law. No exclusive rights shielded friends of the Crown from justice. The blacksmith cites the familiar and exceptional case of Lord Ferrers whom the state had executed in 1760 for the murder of his steward. Both peers and peasants had no natural license to kill in Albion. The National Assembly, on the other hand, reserved privileges to murder to the politically correct. Girondins and Jacobins who fought for expressive freedoms sanctioned the slaughter of refractory priests and court functionaries with whom they differed.[114]

While deploring the inconsistencies of revolutionary virtue, More encased her own advocacy of moral regeneration in hoary constitutional idioms. This is most evident in Jack's stories about his lord and lady. Sir John and wife have moved into Sir John's ancestral castle shortly after their marriage. The smith recalls that Sir John's wife, an admirer of rococo architecture, wanted to raze "this noble building," and remodel it "in her frippery way." Sir John, the paragon of probity, disagreed. His Gothic home, an allegory for the unwritten constitution, "outstood the civil wars, and only underwent a little needful repair at the revolution" in 1688. It served as a pattern for neighbors. Sir John refused to tear it down simply because of "a dark closet, or an awkward passage, or an inconvenient room or two in it."[115] Jack praises Sir John for his moral fortitude against faddish innovation. More clearly wanted to encourage Sir John's heroic qualities among the rich and powerful. If newly pious aristocrats rallied around hallowed institutions, then the middling sort and poor would close ranks behind their leaders. After all, Jack idealizes Sir John.[116]

---

[114]More, *Village Politics, Works*, p.59, 61-2; For the uses of Lord Ferrers' execution (including those of Hannah More), see Douglas Hay, "Property, Authority, and the Criminal Law," in the compilation *Albion's Fatal Tree: Crime and Society in Eighteenth-Century England* (New York: Pantheon Books, 1975), pp.34, 37.

[115]More, *Village Politics, Works*, p.59; c.f. Edmund Burke, *Reflections on the Revolution in France*, 1790, Conor Cruise O'Brien, ed. (Harmondsworth: Penguin, 1986), pp.117-122. Mary G. Jones aptly describes More's allegorical defense of the constitution as "Burke for Beginners." (*Hannah More*, p.134.)

[116]c.f. Philip Anthony Brown, *The French Revolution in English History* (New York: Barnes & Noble, 1965)[orig. pub. 1918], pp.92-3.

Later in the tract, More dressed a call to serious Christianity in a plea for the restoration of British tolerance. However loyalist, she wanted to discourage Church-and-King violence against dissenters and radicals.[117] Even if the Pitt ministry had largely forsworn armed coercion against the "seditious," there was an "unofficial terror of beatings, inquisitions, sackings, and ostracism, which went on during" the 1790s.[118] Gentlemen at times manipulated drunken brawlers to settle petty scores in the name of the Church and the King, but laborers were quite capable of vigilante action against dissenters and radicals on their own.[119] Mob violence against mainly middle-class, dissenting gentlemen, More (and other rich Anglicans) perceived, was a loose cannon of working-class anger that could turn or be turned by wealthy Paineites against the rich and powerful regardless of sect or faction.[120]

---

[117]So did More's friends. In particular, see Beilby Porteus, the Bishop of London to Hannah More, 1791, Roberts, Memoirs vol.2, p.289; Frances Boscawen to Hannah More, 1791, Roberts, *Memoirs* vol.2, pp.290-1. See also Anna Seward to Lady Gresley, 30 July 1791, *Letters of Anna Seward* vol.3, pp.93-4.

[118]Emsley, "Repression, 'Terror' and Rule of Law," p.802.

[119]More was not alone in seeing unscrupulous gentlemen behind all "Church-and-King" hooligans. See the radical whig Sir Samuel Romilly to a Madame G—, 2 August 1791, *Memoirs* vol.1, p.431; the equally radical whig Samuel Parr in his own *Memoirs* vol.1, pp.305-6. Pioneering accounts of "Church-and-King" by left-wing historians ironically tended to echo More's view that shadowy social superiors always bribed and coached "Church-and-King" toughs—R. B. Rose, "The Priestley Riots of 1791," *Past and Present*, 18(November, 1960), pp.68-88; Thompson, *The Making*, pp.19, 27, 73-5, 78, 104-5, 112-3, 116, 132-3, 182, 184, 279, 473, 567, 735. Yet see the completely independent action of working-class conservatives in Alan Booth, "Popular Loyalism and Violence in the North-West of England, 1790-1800," *Social History*, 8(October, 1983), pp.295-313.

[120]Putting guns into the hands of drunken laborers or condoning their vigilante actions were regarded as dangerous by none other than William Pitt himself, since bearing arms indicated true citizenship in English political thought. For genteel concerns about "making the people more politically conscious" through even nonviolent loyalism, see J.R. Western, "The Volunteer Movement as an Anti-Revolutionary Force, 1793-1801," *Historical Journal*, 71(1956), pp.603, 610-1. c.f. The British ambassador to the Hague, Lord Auckland, thought that loyalist violence strengthened "the hands of executive government" against dissenters, disagreeing with the Foreign Secretary Lord Grenville's hatred of all popular riots. (Lord Auckland to Lord Grenville, 26 July 1791, Historical Manuscripts Commission, eds., *The*

Thus Jack tells Tom that true Britons, unlike Frenchmen, refrained from liquidating or dehumanizing political and religious opponents. The smith hopes that "even republicans and levellers . . . will always enjoy the protection of our laws." As much as he hates libertarian polemics, Jack would hate to live in a kingdom without freedom of conscience. The smith goes on to condemn widespread bigotry against the godly. He knows of many patriotic (in its pro-government sense) dissenters and many nominal churchmen who sympathize with the French. "A good man [that is, one who supports the Pitt ministry] is a good man," the smith holds, "whether his church has got a steeple to it or not."[121] Serious Anglicans did not hate papists or presbyterians, but rather attempted to convince them of their errors through example. Serious Anglicans did not burn the homes and businesses of well-to-do Dissenters, but rather showed their love to king and country by reading their Bibles and "minding their own business." Nevertheless, More did not go as far as her friend, the Evangelical poet William Cowper, who advocated repeal of discriminatory legislation against Dissenters and Catholics.[122]

More also partially retreated from her previous linkage of social disorder and aristocratic dissipation. In particular, Jack hopes that the affluent would "set us a better example about going to church, and those things; but still hoarding's not the sin of the age; they don't lock up their money—away it goes, and every body's the better for it." The smith speculates that he would chastise the fashionable world for spending too much on "feastings and fandingoes," if he was a parson. Since Jack is only a poor tradesman, however, he welcomes conspicuous consumption because of the resultant jobs. The smith notes that "their coaches and their furniture, and their buildings, and

---

Manuscripts of J. B. Fortescue, Esq., Preserved at Dropmore vol.2 (London: Eyre & Spottiswoode, 1892), p.140); Hester Thrale Piozzi thought that "one Loyal Riot is worth twenty legal punishments [of radicals.]" (See her *Thraliana* vol.2, p.813)

[121]More, *Village Politics, Works*, p.61; c.f. the similar argument of the loyalist mouthpiece "Jobb Nott" as quoted in Hole, *Pulpits*, p.107.

[122]More, *Village Politics, Works*, p.63; William Cowper to Joseph Hill, 16 December 1792, Grimshawe, *Works of Cowper*, p.425.

their planting" employed many workers in luxury trades and service industries.[123]

Here More even excused the genteel substitution of benevolence for Christianity. Jack reminds Tom that the English poor relief system was unique in Europe. Indeed, the privileged funded infirmaries, hospitals, and schools for the poor. If leveling occurred, Jack contends that this philanthropy would cease and the needy would suffer.[124] More's shift in emphasis was clearly the consequence of serving a popular, not elite, audience. Strident anti-aristocratic criticism in a vulgar tract would have played into the hands of enemies of the constitution such as Tom Paine and William Vaughan who urged rule by the virtuous regardless of birth or sect.[125]

Official dechristianization in France quickly dispelled More's expedient moderation on genteel levity. She expressed the common revulsion at the sacking of churches, the burning of hymnals, and the decapitation of nonjuring priests (and of the Most Christian King) during the turbulent winter of 1792-3.[126] The indifference of key English lords and bishops to these grave events, however, particularly infuriated her. The fashionable world had winked at unbelief for the previous half-century. Consequently, blasphemous rhetoric now circulated unchal-

---

[123]The indispensability of the big spender was a common argument of loyalist apologists. See Hole, "Popular Propaganda," pp.58, 60-1. In the early nineteenth century, the Reverend Thomas Malthus gave this conventional assumption about consumer demand clinical respectability. For a summary of Malthus' views on conspicuous consumption, see Paul K. Conkin, *Prophets of Prosperity: America's First Political Economists* (Bloomington: Indiana University Press, 1980), pp.39-40.

[124]More, *Village Politics, Works*, p.61; c.f. Soloway, *Prelates and People*, pp.73-4.

[125]This is the only instance that seems to corroborate the "cunning" attributed to the Evangelical More by Newman and Brown. But here More certainly did not embrace the amoral credo of "private vices, public benefits" as alleged by Brown. c.f. Brown, *Fathers of the Victorians*, pp.127-8. For Paine and Vaughan, see Soloway, *Prelates and People*, p.29.

[126]Hannah More to Horace Walpole, 7 January 1793, Roberts, *Memoirs* vol.2, pp.354-5; William Cowper succinctly characterized this widespread sense of outrage. In a letter to the Reverend Walter Bagot, he wrote: "Though you are a Tory, I believe, and I am a Whig, our sentiments concerning the madcaps of France are much the same. They are a terrible race, and I have a horror both of them and their principles." (4 March 1793, Grimshawe, *Works of Cowper*, p.430.)

lenged in this unprecedented crisis, falling upon receptive ears throughout the social spectrum. While writing and publishing *Village Politics* in late 1792, More had looked to the Anglican clergy for decisive support. Yet their relatively languid response disappointed her.[127] Reluctantly, in April of 1793, Hannah More published a didactic open letter to Jacob Dupont, an atheist firebrand in the National Convention.[128] Writing off the completely depraved once again, she hoped to reach "a good many religious people, both in the church and among the different sects, whose fondness for French politics entirely blind[ed] them to the horrors of French impiety."[129] Appropriately, she donated proceeds from this "shilling pamphlet . . . sold for a half-crown" to the aid of *émigré* Catholic priests, combining moral exhortation with a public (and controversial) display of British tolerance.[130]

---

[127]More's perception of indifferent prelates and parsons was incorrect. R. A. Soloway notes that most Anglican clerics were dispassionate toward the French Revolution until the September Massacres. But after that bloody fall, they were the cheerleaders for the Pitt ministry's jihad against the Great Satan across the Channel. (*Prelates and People*, pp.29-33.)

[128]Later that year, this animosity toward Dupont took on a hauntingly personal dimension. In a letter to an old friend, More wrote about two young female French teachers who had worked at her sisters' school. These "fierce, ambitious, romantic, and irreligious" women had brothers who had worked closely with Louis-Philippe-Joseph, Duc d'Orleans, the radically chic and regicidal cousin of Louis XVI. More "cut the story short by saying—that we have heard of the catastrophe of the whole family—The brother proves to be Dupont, the famous atheist—one sister is married to Brissot who was guillotined last week—the Wife and Mother followed him to his execution." The other teacher and her surviving brother escaped to Philadelphia "where they just died of the plague." More closed by writing (perhaps with both sadness and satisfaction) that "So Egalite [nickname for Duc d'Orleans] with whom the brother lived, Villery with whom the sister lived, brother, sister & whole family are wiped out from the face of the Earth at once!" (Hannah More to Eva Garrick, 21 November 1793, Folger Shakespeare Library, Mss. 487, fo. 87.)

[129]Hannah More to Horace Walpole, April 1793, Roberts, *Memoirs* vol.2, pp.358-9.

[130]Ibid., p.359; Some Dissenters blasted More for her assistance to foreign papists. For example, see the anonymous *Gideon's Cake of Barley Meal: A Letter to the Rev. Wm. Romaine on his preaching for the Emigrant Popish Clergy, with Some Strictures on Mrs. Hannah More's Remarks, published for their Benefit* (London: n.p., 1793). Radical cartoonists such as Richard Newton and Isaac Cruikshank satirised help for formerly well-to-do "parasites." See their prints

While helping royalist refugees, More ridiculed nostalgia for the ancien-regime. In her *Remarks on the Speech of Mr. Dupont*, she did not parrot Burke's flowery praise for rococo manners. Nor did she construct "a nobler France" of the Regency or of Cardinal de Fleury in the manner of Burke and, later, Samuel Taylor Coleridge, William Cobbett, and William Hazlitt.[131] While personally upstanding, Louis XVI had surrounded himself with "despotic ministers" and "superstitious and corrupt" priests like all Bourbons, according to More. The French court and church had always needed reform. Thus More had initially welcomed the new constitutional monarchy in Paris, which seemed to place the French on the same lofty level of revolutionary England a century before. In this pamphlet, she regretted the lost opportunity for the establishment in another country of "the Patriot's fair idea of well-understood liberty, the politician's view of a perfect constitution together with . . . a pure and reasonable, a sublime and rectified Christianity."[132]

In hindsight, she felt that she should have known better. Her regrets reflect the struggle of English writers in 1790s and beyond, as Barton R. Friedman discerns, "to reconcile two worlds: one, the world of the old regime, seemingly dead; the other, Orc-like, announcing its enraged right not merely to life but to power."[133] Unlike most loyalists and radicals who viewed

in Bindman, *Shadow of the Guillotine*, pp.207-8. Most wealthy Anglicans, however, applauded More's efforts. More raised nearly L250 from the sales of her open letter. For an overview of British help to the priests, see Dominic Bellenger, "The Emigre Clergy and the English Church, 1789-1815," *Journal of Ecclesiastical History*, 34(1983), pp.392-410.

[131]For Edmund Burke's glorification of the ancien regime and its chivalry, see his *Reflections*, p.168-71. By 1796, however, Burke had changed his mind, blaming "the most licentious, prostitute and abandoned . . . and at the same time the most coarse, rude, savage, and ferocious" protocol at the court of Louis XVI for the fall of the monarchy. (Quoted in Soloway, *Prelates and People*, p.28.) For this "nobler France" invented by British pundits, see Seamus Deane, *The French Revolution and Enlightenment in England 1789-1832* (Cambridge, Mass.: Harvard University Press, 1988), pp.13-4, 169-70.

[132]Hannah More, *Remarks of the Speech of M. Dupont, Made in the National Convention of France. On the Subjects of Religion and public Education, The Works of Hannah More* (Philadelphia: Woodward, 1832), p.304.

[133]Barton R. Friedman, *Fabricating History: English Writers on the French Revolution* (Princeton: Princeton University Press, 1988), p.37. Excerpt reprinted by permission of Princeton University Press. All rights reserved.

the old and new regimes as fundamentally different, however, More anticipated the themes of Charles Dickens' *A Tale of Two Cities* (1859) whereby "revolution proves to be repression by another name."[134] The intolerant dictatorship of 1793, More wrote, was merely a horrific permutation of the "enlightened" absolutism of the 1780s. "Extravagant mischiefs" naturally produced equally egregious errors, however superficially different. Thus the authoritarian and cosmopolitan atmosphere at Versailles unwittingly created the Jacobin regicides whose arrogance rivalled that of the Sun King's. This causal relationship confirmed to More that leisured corruption could have apocalyptic results because of the ironic and unintended effects of social emulation and deference. The servants had overheard Voltaire.[135]

More worried that the English elite risked similar surprises if they continued to resist or to criticize native virtues and institutions. She laughed at those "well-meaning but mistaken" pundits who "conjured up fancied evils" in discussion of the unwritten constitution. The Foxites, in particular, attacked the chimeras of torture, superstition, and arbitrary executive power in England, equating Pitt and George III with continental leaders. These imaginary grievances became real for many because of "cheap poison" from the pens of collaborators. More exhorted her well-heeled readers not to listen to "the whimsical

---

[134]Ibid., p.171. Excerpt reprinted by permission of Princeton University Press. All rights reserved. Sir Samuel Romilly, a Foxite and a strong supporter of the Revolution until the September massacres, seemed to approach More's position in his letter to M. Dumont, 10 September 1792, *Memoirs* vol.2, p.4. Here he wrote bitterly: "How could we ever be so deceived in the character of the French nation as to think them capable of liberty!"

[135]More, *Remarks, Works*, p.308; c.f. McGovern, "Conservative Idealogy," p.244. By the late 1790s commentators attributed this downward spread of corruption to elaborate conspiracy, not careless stupidity. Hole, *Pulpits*, pp.153-6; Soloway, *Prelates and People*, pp.34-45; Deane, *French Revolution and Enlightenment*, pp.6-11, 14, 23-5, 38, 166-7, 170) In a letter to an old friend, Hannah More predictably relished the conspiracy theory in "Barruel's *Historie du Jacobinisme* which throws all of the blame of the Revolution on Voltaire, the King of Prussia and the other Philosophes." (Hannah More to Eva Garrick, 16 November 1797, Folger Shakespeare Library, Mss. 488, of. 9.)

knights of La Mancha" chasing windmills, but rather to appreciate their hard-won liberties envied by the rest of Europe.[136]

She was confident, however, that the Terror had finally turned the British aristocracy away from blind sympathy for France. Genteel participation in loyalist organizations gladdened Hannah More, although she confessed that she had always known that the British aristocracy was fundamentally different from continental nobles because its ancestors had long ago learned to reconcile freedom with social responsibility.[137]

Serious Christianity among the affluent, nevertheless, was necessary to husband their revived patriotism. The most crucial lesson of the French revolution, More wrote, was "that no degree of wit and learning, no progress in commerce, no advance in the knowledge of nature, or in the embellishments of art, can every thoroughly tame that savage, *the natural human heart*, without RELIGION."[138] Young aristocrats had bestowed intellectual and social power on those who showed heartfelt emotions throughout the 1770s and 1780s. At the same time, they had continued to mock the Word along with older devotees of arid rationalism. In France, this dangerous combination of intense feeling and overt atheism exploded (sometimes literally) in the faces of histrionic dilettantes. Accordingly, More wanted to harness feeling for faith in the name of social order and national security. She prayed that "a temperate and well-regulated zeal" for Jesus would replace revolutionary and unrestrained sensibilities.

Most importantly, this redirection had to begin with the influential quality who had popularized heated skepticism in the first place.[139] It was not enough for the propertied classes to

---

[136]More, *Remarks, Works*, pp.305-6.

[137]Ibid, pp.310-1 c.f. the similar confidence that the French revolution could not happen in Britain because of its "principles of the protestant religion—the toleration laws, and the trials by juries" in Anna Seward to J. Johnson, 20 September 1794, *Letters of Anna Seward* vol.4, p.4.

[138]More, *Remarks, Works*, p.308.

[139]Ibid., pp.308-9; Other Evangelicals made similar yet Scriptural arguments. See Gisborne, *Duties of Men* vol.1, pp.110-21; Wilberforce, *Practical View*, pp.243-8. See also the similar positions of conventional Anglican moralists such as the Earl of Carlisle and the Prebendary of St. Paul's Cathedral as discussed in Richard A Soloway, "Reform or Ruin: English Moral Thought

rally politically on the side of the Pitt administration. At the very least, the most effective benevolence on behalf of the emigres required the accountability of Christian virtue. Secular appeals for the refugees such as those by Frances Burney and Edmund Burke were not sufficient.[140] In a wider sense, genuine patriotism demanded the Evangelical religion of the heart.

More closed her pamphlet with a ringing endorsement of the war against revolutionary France. She pointed out that conquest and revenge, the usual ends of dynastic conflict, were not the war aims this time. To More and most conventional Anglicans, this conflict was an ideological defense of constitutional guarantees against a crusade to subvert them. She hoped that the dark clouds of war might even bring about the end of "licentious and irreligious principles" among the affluent.[141]

Here More parted company, however, with the majority of the godly, who wanted to stick with secret diplomacy and economic sanctions to contain French aggression without the sin of war. Unitarians predictably characterized wars, especially this one, as the most egregious expression of aristocratic arrogance and avarice. Widely rumored to be secretly Unitarian, the Anglican reformer Christopher Wyvill viewed the war as a way to maintain both the moral and political corruption of the aristocracy. Opposition to the use of force, however, was not restricted to rational Dissenters and the corresponding handful

---

during the First French Republic," *Review of Politics*, 25(January, 1963), pp. 114-6, 119-21.

[140]Hannah More to John Eardley-Wilmot, 27 January 1794, Beinecke Rare Book and Manuscript Library, Yale University, Osborn Collection, Shelves c.42. c.f. Edmund Burke, "Case of the Suffering Clergy of France, Refugees in the British Dominions," a contemporary reprint from *The Evening Mail*, 19 September 1792, Beinecke Rare Book and Manuscript Library, Yale University, Osborn Collection, Shelves c.42; Frances Burney, *Brief Reflections Relative to the Emigrant French Clergy: Earnestly Submitted to the Humane Consideration of the Ladies of Great Britain*, 1793 as printed in R. Brimley Johnson, ed., *Fanny Burney and the Burneys* (New York: Frederick A. Stokes, 1926), pp.108-10. Burney had just married the *émigré* solder Alexandre d'Arblay.

[141]More, *Remarks, Works*, p.310. See also Hannah More to Eva Garrick, 19 March 1793, Folger Shakespeare Library, Mss. 487, of. 84. c.f. the similar prowar apologies in Bishop Porteus to Hannah More, (Late Summer?) 1793, Roberts, *Memoirs* vol.2, p.366; Bishop Porteus to Hannah More, 11 November 1793, Roberts *Memoirs* vol.2, pp.380-1.

of Anglican fellow travelers. The Baptist Robert Hall, in particular, was adamant that all wars contradicted "all the rules of morality," considering this conflict no exception to this rule.[142]

Evangelical MPs Wilberforce and Thornton were not pacifists like Hall, but rather feared that the war would sidetrack pet Evangelical projects such as the reformation of genteel manners and the abolition of the slave trade.[143] On abolition, they were right, the House of Commons repeatedly defeated antislavery legislation in the paranoid atmosphere of 1792-93. On reformation of manners, however, they were wrong and More was right; the invasion scares eventually energized a new seriousness (if not godliness) among previously hedonistic ladies and gentlemen determined to avoid the grim fate of the Second Estate in France.[144] Unreconstructed aristocrats like Charles James Fox complained that this new seriousness "contributed much to remove the barriers between them and the vulgar and to propagate levelling and equalising notions."[145]

It is a truistic understatement to say that the French Revolution engendered many strains and tensions. But the fall of the French monarchy remarkably did not change the thought of Hannah More, but rather justified it. Her warnings about the disorderly effects of aristocratic dissipation seemed to come all too true. Events confirmed to her that the British great needed to purify their lives from alien practices such as slavery, Sunday diversions, and intolerance. It was not opportunistic "cunning,"

---

[142]Cookson, *Friends of Peace*, p.42. Excerpt reprinted with the permission of Cambridge University Press. All rights reserved. For Wyvill, see Gascoigne, "Latitudinarianism and Radicalism," pp.32-5.

[143]In a clearly strained letter to Wilberforce, Hannah More sympathized with Bristol merchants who claimed the war had caused a depression, but still begged to differ with her esteemed friend on the merits of the war. (Hannah More to William Wilberforce, 1794, Roberts, *Memoirs* vol.2, p.410) Yet when the end of the Terror diminished the ideological justification for the war, More confided to an old friend that "she hoped for the return of peace without . . . [to restore] tranquility at home. (Hannah More to Eva Garrick, 29 December 1795, Folger Shakespeare Library, Mss 488, fo.4.)

[144]John Pollock, *Wilberforce* (New York: St. Martin's Press, 1977), pp.121-3; Standish Meacham, *Henry Thornton of Clapham, 1760-1815* (Cambridge, Mass.: Harvard University Press, 1964), pp.80, 88.

[145]See the entry for 15 January 1794 in Lord Glenbervie, *Diaries* vol.1, p.39.

as Gerald Newman has suggested,[146] when More wrapped her sermonettes in the Union Jack. It was, rather, deep conviction in the religious underpinnings of elite status and sound politics. Indeed, this strong Evangelical belief would soon lead More to consider the relationship between faith and paternalism in her famous *Cheap Repository* tracts.

---

[146]c.f. Newman, *English Nationalism*, pp.233-8.

Chapter IV

Charity and Character

Between 1795 and 1798 Hannah More wrote at least 49 of the 114 ballads, allegories, and short stories collectively known as the *Cheap Repository*.[1] Unlike her tragedies and essays of the 1770s and 1780s, these pamphlets addressed the middling and lower estates of British society. As with her *Village Politics* (1792), she hoped "to improve the habits and raise the principles of the common people . . . and abate their relish . . ." for the critiques of monarchy and aristocracy by radical reformers such as Thomas Paine.[2] In a letter to her old friend Eva Garrick, she complained that the "wickedness" of mechanics and laborers had grown so alarming that "if there is not a little pains taken with them I really think we shall soon be in the situation of France."[3]

In order to reach both country gentlemen and their clients, More used a variety of methods in the making of the *Cheap Repository*. Extolling the parsimony of dour schoolmistresses and the ingenuity of stern artisans, she catered to a mass audi-

---

[1]Hannah More was the chief author, editor, and organizer of the *Cheap Repository*. Other contributors included Sarah More, Hannah's sister; the Reverend John Newton, the famous slave trader turned Evangelical cleric; Selina Mills, the future wife of Zachary Macaulay and mother of Thomas Macaulay; Henry Thornton, Evangelical MP and banker; and William Mason, a noted poet. Authors signed their tracts with a pseudonym or a single initial. Hannah More signed her stories with the letter "Z." (G. H. Spinney, "Cheap Repository Tracts: Hazard and Marshall Edition," *The Library*, 20(1939-40), pp.310-11.)

[2]Hannah More, *The Works of Hannah More* vol.1 (Philadelphia: Woodward, 1832), p.190. In addition, see Hannah More to the Reverend John Newton, 1794, in William Roberts, *Memoirs of the Life and Correspondence of Mrs. Hannah More* vol. 2 (London: R. B. Selley and W. Burnside, 1835), pp.427-8.

[3]Hannah More to Eva Garrick, 27 December 1794, Folger Shakespeare Library, Mss. 488, fo.1.

ence by imitating the vibrant and simple language of conventionally racy chapbooks and broadsides.[4] Consequently, her stories advised and amused.

They were deliberately inexpensive thanks to aristocratic patronage and commercial success. While lords and ladies bountiful gave away large numbers of tracts at charity schools, prisons, workhouses, and hospitals, laborers could also afford to buy More's didactic tales. At a half-penny to one and one-half penny per installment, the *Cheap Repository* cost far less than books (including Thomas Paine's *Rights of Man*), periodicals, newspapers, and membership fees in lending libraries.[5]

Funding by prominent subscribers such as William Wilberforce and William Pitt initially defrayed the expenses of printing and distribution, helping More to compete with the cheap-

---

[4]More collected popular literature in order to write popular literature. (Richard D. Altick, *The English Common Reader: A Social History of the Mass Reading Public 1800-1900* (Chicago: University of Chicago, 1957), p.75; Mary Alden Hopkins, *Hannah More and Her Circle* (New York: Longmans, Green, and Co., 1947), p.212) The Bishop of London Beilby Porteus, who had encouraged More to write the *Cheap Repository*, noted late in 1794 that "I should also be much gratified with the sight of those invaluable original productions, both in prose and verse, which you have collected together from your friends the village hawkers and peddlers; they would form the best sans culotte library in Europe, and will, I dare say, some day or other be visited by travelers, as we now do the Vatican or the Museum." (Porteus to Hannah More, 1794, Roberts, *Memoirs* vol. 2, pp.425-6.) For an excellent comparison of More's tracts and popular literature, see Susan Pedersen, "Hannah More Meets Simple Simon: Tracts, Chapbooks, and Popular Culture in Late Eighteenth-Century England," *Journal of British Studies*, 25(1986), pp.84-113.

[5]Altick, *English Common Reader*, pp.48-66 ; More had problems with the hawkers and booksellers who complained about their profit margins. During 1795 the gentry bought tracts at the rate of 25 for 1s. 6d. to give away at institutions. Hawkers bought tracts at the rate of 25 for 10d. to sell to customers for 1/2d. to 1d. Disputes began when many genteel distributors wanted to buy the tracts for themselves on expensive paper, while hawkers wanted to buy them even cheaper from More and the other authors. (Spinney,"Cheap Repository Tracts," p.303.) In January of 1796, she told her friend Zachary Macaulay that "we were mistaken in believing them cheap enough for the hawkers. I find they have been used to get three hundred percent on their old trash; of course, they will not sell ours, but declare they have no objection to goodness, if it were but profitable." (Hannah More to Zachary Macauley, 6 January 1796, Roberts, ed., *Memoirs* vol. 2, p.460.) Resolution of this trouble came with two qualities of paper and a bargain rate of 24 for 6d. for hawkers. (Spinney, "Cheap Repository Tracts," p.303.)

est publications.[6] The strong sales of annually collected volumes on expensive paper and with handsome binding in 1796, 1797, and 1798 eliminated the need for subscriptions.[7] Nevertheless, between March of 1795 and February of 1796 (when the deluxe versions were unavailable), the Cheap Repository Tract Society sold and distributed nearly two million leaflets.[8]

In these tracts More championed virtues such as sobriety, thrift, and serious Christianity, virtues often associated with dissenters and some middling-sort Anglicans (like herself). At the same time, she celebrated the customary ideal of paternalist hierarchy as the best vehicle to promote godly behavior. Aiming to reform the morals and manners of rural artisans and laborers through the *Cheap Repository*, More echoed the humanist and puritan reformers of preceding centuries who made the self-discipline of activist and ascetic Christianity the key prerequisite for charity and patronage. In contrast to the relaxed, theatrical, and convivial nature of conventional eighteenth-century paternalism, More's paternalism was serious, disciplinary, and intrusive.

Such a comparison immediately begs for a definition of the multi-faceted phenomenon which scholars since the late nineteenth century have called "paternalism." Accordingly, paternalism is the use of power by those with economic and cultural authority to comfort and control dependents in order to ensure social stability and, thus, to reinforce what the powerful see as the common good. Paternalistic relationships are designed to resemble traditional ties between parents and children. (Indeed, the root of paternalism is *pater*, the Latin word for

---

[6]More did not expect the tracts to be commercially successful and, therefore, opted for subscriptions. (*Bristol Journal*, 18 April 1795 as quoted in Spinney, "Cheap Repository Tracts," p.301.) The gossiping connoisseur Horace Walpole was a close friend who chided More for her seriousness. Ironically, he was one of the first subscribers in January of 1795. (Horace Walpole to Hannah More, 24 January 1795, *Letters of Horace Walpole* vol. 15, Paget Toynbee, ed., (Oxford: Clarendon Press, 1905), p.336.)

[7]Subscriptions totaled a little over L1000 in the first year. (Spinney, "Cheap Repository Tracts," p.302.)

[8]Hannah More, diary entry, 22 September 1798, Roberts, ed., *Memoirs* vol.3, p.61; Spinney, "Cheap Repository Tracts," pp.301-2. In 1796 the Society sent 40,000 tracts to the United States. (Hannah More to Martha More, 1796, Roberts, ed., *Memoirs* vol. 2, p.475.)

father.) Like familial relationships, paternalist ones are highly personal and particularistic. Thus the most vigorous and effective forms of paternalism are conducted face-to-face, not through impersonal or indirect means.[9]

Paternalism changes with time and place. To compare More's ideal of paternalism with orthodox paternalistic relationships in eighteenth-century England requires a detour through the contours and gestures of Georgian paternalism. The gentry and aristocracy in Georgian Britain certainly used their economic and cultural authority to comfort and control their dependents in the interests of social stability. They were paternalists. Familial analogies abound in genteel discussion and praise of British society with its long-standing vertical alignments of patronage and clientage.[10] But such relationships weakened in the eighteenth century largely because many gentlemen shunned frequent face-to-face contact with their dependents. The construction of exclusive parks with high fences and intricate gardens with iron gates highlighted residential segregation of the great from their workers. Landowners usually did not farm and, thus, rural laborers did not meet their lord in the field as an employer. The relationship between lord and laborer become more "a cash nexus" than a filial friendship. Magnates delegated direct control of their work force to tenant farmers and village tradesmen. These elements of the rural middling-sort, not the

---

[9]For this definition of paternalism, see John Kleinig, *Paternalism* (Totowa, N.J.: Rowman & Allanheld, 1983), pp.3-17, 200-17. c.f. Gerald Dworkin, a philosopher, sees paternalism as fundamentally coercive. Paternalistic relationships, according to Dworkin, inherently interfere with an individual's liberty of action. But Dworkin forgets that paternalists can be persuasive as well as coercive. (Gerald Dworkin, "Paternalism," in Richard A. Wasserstrom, ed. *Morality and Law* (Belmont, Calif.: Wadsworth, 1971), pp.107-26.) For the efficacy of face-to-face paternalism, see Howard Newby, *The Deferential Worker: A Study of Farm Workers in East Anglia* (Madison: University of Wisconsin, 1979), p.51, 374, 422-3.

[10]For the frequency of familial analogies, see J.C.D. Clark, *English Society 1688-1832* (Cambridge: Cambridge University Press, 1985), pp.74-7, 81-8. For the standard survey of eighteenth-century British patronage and clientage, see Harold Perkin, *The Origins of Modern English Society* (Toronto: University of Toronto Press, 1969), pp.17-62.

gentry, directly administered the Poor Laws.[11] But even farmers partially withdrew from the lives of laborers in the last quarter of the century. Temporary day laborers replaced farmhands who had lived with the farmer's family for at least a year.[12] But face-to-face contact between lord and laborer occurred "on calculated occasions of popular patronage."[13]

The reasons for these events lay in the very nature of paternalism. The sociologist Howard Newby has suggested that paternalistic relationships "necessarily consist of two opposing and contradictory elements."[14] On one hand, a hierarchical relationship requires the recognition of common interests which bind both parties in a friendship. The powerful want their dependents to celebrate these common interests with them periodically and publicly. In eighteenth-century Britain, magnates sponsored festivities in which everyone in the local community participated. Squires, for example, provided feasts for laborers after the completion of important agricultural tasks such as the wheat harvest. They presided over the laden table and excessive drinking. Some gentlemen, furthermore, donated animals and pounds for popular matches of bull-baiting and cock-fighting. Along with their servants at ringside, they wagered on a winner.[15] Their wives conspicuously and indiscriminately gave relief to the poor on ceremonial occasions such as coronations, jubilees, and funerals.[16]

On the other hand, in any paternalistic relationship, the powerful want to keep some distance, or preserve hierarchical differentiation, between themselves and their dependents.[17] Deliberate aloofness on the part of the Georgian great coin-

---

[11]E.P. Thompson, "Patrician Society, Plebeian Culture," *Journal of Social History*, 7(1974), pp.388-9.

[12]For the replacement of permanent workers with temporary ones, see K.D.M. Snell, *Annals of the Laboring Poor: Social Change and Agrarian England 1660-1900* (Cambridge: Cambridge University Press, 1985.)

[13]Thompson, "Patrician Society," p.389. Excerpt reprinted by permission of the *Journal of Social History*. All rights reserved.

[14]Newby, *Deferential Worker*, p.422.

[15]Robert W. Malcolmson, *Popular Recreations in English Society 1700-1850* (Cambridge: Cambridge University Press, 1973), pp.56-74.

[16]Ibid., pp.64-7.

[17]Newby, *Deferential Worker*, p.422.

cided with their congenial sociability at harvest home dinners, betting pastimes, and patriotic illuminations. At these gatherings aristocrats donned elegant wigs and coats which set them apart from their laborers and tenants. They spoke and acted differently. Both their pompous clothing and their bearing were meant to intimidate dependents.[18]

Similarly, the middling orders eagerly imitated the aristocratic style in order to lord it over their journeymen and servants. This social emulation prompted the quality "to devise modes more exclusive."[19] It is true that the gentry and aristocracy resorted to naked exhibitions of legal and economic power such as the game laws and turnpike statutes in order to show that they were in charge. Nevertheless, squires and their middling-sort imitators preferred to use a combination of conspicuous display and benevolence in the cultivation of deference.[20]

The gentry also used the Church to underscore both communal solidarity and hierarchical differentiation. Many gentlemen forced their laborers to attend Sunday services. The orders seemingly worshiped together. The major concern of the gentry, however, was not the spiritual well-being of their charges. The great wanted another chance to display publicly the differences between the orders. Every Sunday dependents observed the haughty late arrival and early exit of magnates and ladies who sat in exclusive and padded pews.[21]

During the eighteenth century, deference was as ritualistic and theatrical as its obverse, paternalism. According to Newby, deference is the acceptance or endorsement by the powerless of their economic and social inferiority. Newby distinguishes

---

[18]Thompson, "Patrician Society," p.389.
[19]Quoted in Gerald Newman, *The Rise of English Nationalism: A Cultural History 1740-1830* (New York: St. Martin's Press, 1987), p.44. See also the essays in Neil McKendrick, John Brewer, and J.H. Plumb, *The Birth of a Consumer Society: The Commercialization of Eighteenth-Century England* (Bloomington, Ind.: University of Indiana Press, 1982.)
[20]Thompson, "Patrician Society," pp.387-8.
[21]Ibid., p.389; Malcolmson, *Popular Recreations*, p.74. See also the entry of 28 July 1793 in John Byng's travelogue through north Wales as reprinted in C. Bruyn Andrews, ed., *The Torrington Diaries* vol.3 (London: Eyre & Spottiswoode, 1936), p.251.

between deferential attitudes and deferential behavior. He points out that deferential behavior is "more apparent than real."[22] In reference to anonymous threats addressed to Georgian gentlemen, E. P. Thompson suggests that "deference could be very brittle indeed, and made up of one part of self-interest, one part of dissimulation, and only one part of the awe of authority."[23] Dependents posed deferentially in order to curry favor with their masters. Then, in the anonymity of the crowd, these same men and women ridiculed and menaced their benefactors. On the other hand, Newby writes that a dependent expresses deferential attitudes when he defends the social hierarchy in a heartfelt way, not for some type of reward.[24] But in the eighteenth century a dependent's expression of true deference was provisional, hinging on the person in charge. The degree of real or staged deference was contingent upon the lord's skill at the give-and-take dialectic of paternalism.

Serious challenges to the balancing acts of paternalism and deference came from dependents who wanted their customary perquisites and treats preserved from economic rationalization. According to Newby, in any paternalistic relationship, dependents occasionally take their identification with the social hierarchy too far for the paternalist businessman. If employers hand out gifts and privileges, then workers may come to consider them rights over a number of years. Then, the paternalistic relationship "becomes entirely inflexible, making it incapable of surviving changed economic circumstances."[25] If employers rescind gifts and privileges, then workers become very bitter and angry. The personal nature of paternalism intensifies the bad feelings of mistrust.[26] In eighteenth-century Britain, labor unrest stemmed from the workers' reassertion of traditional rights which their employers ignored or scrapped in

---

[22]Newby, *Deferential Worker*, p.406.
[23]Thompson, "Patrician Society," pp.399-400. Excerpt reprinted by permission of the *Journal of Social History*. All rights reserved.
[24]Newby, *Deferential Worker*, pp.110-18, 397.
[25]Ibid., p.432.
[26]Ibid., p.183.

pursuit of profits. Food rioters grew resentful because the magistracy no longer intervened on their behalf. [27]

Another threat to eighteenth-century paternalism was the godly who lived mainly in urban and industrial areas. Largely outside the alignments of patronage and clientage on the land, dissenters and, later, Evangelical Anglicans objected to the rituals, ceremonies, and sports which conventional paternalists used to exact deference. The godly fixation on self-discipline, in particular, clashed with the bawdy mirth of communal conviviality. The descendants of humanists and puritans lobbied gentlemen and clergy to cease tolerating and even underwriting popular recreations. For most of the century their campaigns for the moral reformation of play fell on deaf ears. But after 1780 their concern for popular self-discipline became fashionable. By the end of the century many sports and rituals were no longer completely acceptable to the gentry as a way of displaying organic ties. [28] In addition, inspired by the Bible as well as by revolutionary France, some artisanal radicals wanted to eliminate hierarchy altogether in the 1790s.

In seven representative pamphlets, [29] Hannah More reconciled the virtues of the godly layperson with the traditional ideal of an organic society based on patronage and clientage. More was certainly not alone among elite commentators in attempting such a reconciliation during the 1790s. The theologian

---

[27]Thompson, "Patrician Society," pp.384-7.

[28]Malcolmson, *Popular Recreations*, pp.158-71.

[29]I selected the following seven of More's pamphlets—*The Shepherd of Salisbury Plain, The Two Shoemakers, The History of Tom White, the Post Boy, Black Giles the Poacher, The Sunday School, A Cure for Melancholy*, and *The History of Mr. Fantom, the New-Fashioned Philosopher*. Each one presented characters which repeat throughout the rest of the leaflets. At the same time, each addressed different segments of More's audience. *The Shepherd of Salisbury Plain* displayed the ideal rural laborer, while *Black Giles the Poacher* pitted the stereotypical petty thief against the model magistrate. *The Two Shoemakers* and *The History of Tom White, the Post Boy* showed the upward social mobility of ideal juvenile workers. *Mr. Fantom, the New-Fashioned Philosopher, A Cure for Melancholy*, and *The Sunday School* were examples of the late tracts designed for consumers of the elegant annual volumes. *Mr. Fantom* contrasted the ideal merchant with a selfish bourgeois who tried to be a savant. In *A Cure for Melancholy*, a middling-sort widow gave her time and money for the public good, and emerged from a depression. In *The Sunday School*, this widow offered the ideal institute for teaching poor children to read the Bible.

William Paley and the parliamentarian Edmund Burke, among others, tried, too. Hannah More, however, was particularly well-suited to construct a detailed godly paternalism. As an Evangelical Anglican, she reflected the godly crusade for moral reform. As a fixture of London society, she cherished the social hierarchy. In an age of unprecedented political and economic change, More wanted to place paternalist hierarchy on a firmer foundation than rehearsed gestures and theatrical poses; therefore, she made self-disciplined and serious Christianity, not sociability, the centerpiece of paternalism. To More, only if the poor adopted the inner spirituality and strength of Evangelical Anglicanism could they merit the charity and patronage of their social superiors. Significantly, she urged face-to-face contacts between laborers and employers on a regular basis, not at occasional gatherings. She hoped intrusive surveillance in the form of true Christian fellowship would increase real deference and productivity. In addition, she condemned the conspicuous consumption which gentlemen and master craftsmen used to impress their dependents. She advised them to spend their discretionary income on the deserving poor and endeavored to make discriminate charity as appealing as possible to both sexes.

Finally, More characterized both participants in customary festivities and advocates of legal equality as self-indulgent solvents which dissolved social cohesion. They were not worthy of the kindness of the rich, according to More. Reminiscent of both the letter and intent of Elizabethan regulation, her restrictions on charity and patronage would have made it more difficult for the distressed to get relief allowed by the practices of conventional justices or by the provisions of the new generous Speenhamland system. While she maintained that discriminate charity and patronage would bridge cultural and social differences between the haves and have-nots of late Georgian Britain, her relegation of alehouse haunters, bull baiters, food rioters, and Paineite politicians into the ranks of the undeserving underscored social and cultural polarization.

The most famous of Hannah More's tracts, *The Shepherd of Salisbury Plain*, presents her ideal of the poor family deserving charity and patronage from their social betters.[30] The model drew upon the real experiences of the shepherd David Saunders of West Lavington. In part one of this story, published in March of 1795, Mr. Johnson, "a very worthy gentleman walking across Wiltshire," meets the shepherd, "a clean, well-looking, poor man, near fifty years of age."[31] After an enlightening and lively conversation about the shepherd's life, Mr. Johnson commends the shepherd's earnest piety and cheerful contentment with a half-crown. He then promises to meet the shepherd and his family soon. In part two of this story, published in June of 1795, Mr. Johnson visits the shepherd's family at home. Impressed by the heartfelt religion of the shepherd, his wife, and their eight children, he joins with the local curate and gentry to reward the shepherd and his wife with better housing and employment. The poor laborer is overjoyed, creeping with his wife "into one corner of the room, where they thought that they could not be seen, and fell on their knees, devoutly blessing and praising God for His mercies."[32]

The Shepherd of Salisbury Plain reflects entrenched beliefs about the role of patronage in society. To Mr. Johnson, the shepherd, and Hannah More, the best social order was authoritarian, hierarchical, organic, and local.[33]

No eighteenth-century paternalist disagreed.[34] For instance, the relationship between Mr. Johnson and the shepherd ap-

---

[30]For the best-to-date discussions of *The Shepherd of Salisbury Plain*, see Ford K. Brown, *Fathers of the Victorians* (London: Cambridge University Press, 1961), pp. 129-55 and Marlene Alice Hess, *The Didactic Art of Hannah More* (Michigan State University Ph.D. dissertation in English, 1982), pp.115-17.

[31]More, *Works, The Shepherd of Salisbury Plain*, p.191.

[32]Ibid., p.200.

[33]For contemporary Evangelical Anglican defenses of paternalist hierarchy, see William Wilberforce, *A Practical View of the Prevailing Religious System* (Boston: Ebenezer Larkin, 1799)[orig. pub. 1797], pp.240-4; Thomas Gisborne, *An Enquiry into Duties of Men in the Higher and Middle Classes of Society*, vol.1 (London: B.& J. White, 1793), pp.120, 131, 167-8; Robert Hole, *Pulpits, Politics, and Public Order in England, 1760-1832* (Cambridge: Cambridge University Press, 1989), pp.128-9. For Evangelical paternalism in the 1830s and 1840s, see David Roberts, *Paternalism in Early Victorian England* (New Brunswick, N.J.: Rutgers University Press, 1979), pp.8, 62, 153, 218, 237, 263.

[34]There is an exception. Joseph Priestley, the Unitarian victim of a loyalist mob in Birmingham in 1791, advocated a less authoritarian form of paternal-

proximates that between father and son, even though both are in their fifties. Mr. Johnson dominates and directs the conversations. He talks, while the shepherd listens. He questions and, then, the shepherd answers. Mr. Johnson's manner, like any good JP, combines friendliness with condescension.

Most critically, the imperious father aids the deferential son and his family. Here More made it clear that her story's real shepherd, a Biblical synonym for master or leader,[35] is Mr. Johnson whose personal intervention, in conjunction with local officials (other shepherds), saves human sheep from malnutrition. In turn, the poor laborer and his wife gratefully obey their well-dressed "shepherd" or "father" and even tolerate his rude intrusion on their Sunday family prayers. All of More's characters know and fulfill their duties, obligations, and places.[36]

To More, everyone benefited from paternalism. Mr. Johnson and the Reverend Jenkins gain spiritually, while the shepherd improves materially. Like Edmund Burke's *Reflections on the Revolution in France* (1790) and William Paley's *Reasons for Contentment* (1791), *The Shepherd of Salisbury Plain* maintains that the organic society, not the legal equality of revolutionary France, fostered the greatest possible degree of human perfectibility. If More's readers learned their proper places from these tracts, then they would achieve their potential as defined by God. She thought that these hierarchical friendships ought to outlast a century which had witnessed social and cultural polarization between the gentry and their laborers. A renewed commitment to traditional bonds between unequals would reduce the resentment of the poor. Just and righteous shepherding would thwart the hopes of supporters of the French Revolution such as the poet William Wordsworth whose own unpublished "Adventures on Salisbury Plain" claimed that

---

ist hierarchy. (Margaret Canovan, "Paternalistic Liberalism: Joseph Priestley on Rank and Inequality," *Enlightenment and Dissent*, 2(1983), pp.23-37.)
[35]For examples, see Psalm 23, Jeremiah 23:1-6, and Mark 6:30-4.
[36]More, *Works, The Shepherd of Salisbury Plain*, pp.191-200.

a healthy, unified body politic depended upon the overthrow of inherently corrupt gentlemen.[37]

More's ideal laborer and his family fit traditional definitions of the deserving poor. Since the sixteenth century, law and custom had designated the physically infirm, untrained children, the seasonally unemployed, and severely underemployed as worthy recipients of private charity and public relief.[38] More agreed. For example, the shepherd's wife suffers from rheumatism, which renders her unable to work outdoors. Mr. Johnson proposes "to endow a small weekly school of which . . . the Shepherd's wife shall be the mistress, . . . teaching ten or a dozen girls to knit, sew, spin, card, or any other useful way of getting their bread."[39] Similarly, he and the Reverend Jenkins agree to set up the severely underemployed shepherd (raising eight children on eight shillings per week) as the parish clerk and Sunday schoolmaster. They also decide to subsidize the shepherd's children in the vacant house of the late clerk, a larger and sturdier resident than his current hut. Several months earlier, when the shepherd was unemployed because of heavy snow, he had welcomed the timely blankets and food donated by the Reverend Jenkins and Farmer Jones.[40]

Reflecting the enduring spirit of the Elizabethan Poor Laws, More clarified and restricted the relatively unexacting criteria by which most eighteenth-century justices discriminated between the deserving and undeserving poor. Like the sixteenth-century framers of public poor relief but unlike most Georgian magistrates, More felt that the deserving poor had to be neat, sober, frugal, orderly, and God-fearing. In other words, the young, handicapped, seasonally unemployed or severely

---

[37]For Wordsworth, see Stephen C. Gill, "'Adventures on Salisbury Plain' and Wordsworth's Poetry of Protest 1795-97," *Studies in Romanticism*, 11 (1972), pp.48-65.

[38]A. L. Beier, *The Problem of the Poor in Tudor and Early Stuart England* (London: n.p, 1983); Paul Slack, "Books of Orders: The Making of English Social Policy 1577-1631," *Transactions of the Royal Historical Society*, 30(1980), pp.1-22; J.D. Marshall, *The Old Poor Law 1795-1834* (London: Macmillan, 1968); Peter Dunkley, *The Crisis of the Old Poor Law in England, 1795-1834* (New York: Garland, 1982).

[39]More, *Works*, p. 200.

[40]More, *Works, The Shepherd of Salisbury Plain*, pp.199-200.

underemployed had to exercise the godly virtues before their social superiors should aid them through private charity and public relief.[41] For example, when Mr. Johnson first meets the shepherd, the neatness of the shepherd's clothing most impresses "the very worthly gentleman walking across Wiltshire." While the faded and patched coat of the shepherd indicates his poverty, the darned socks and mended shirt of the shepherd displays his merit (and his wife's diligence!). To Mr. Johnson, the shepherd's neatness suggests that he is sober and frugal, and therefore, is a poor person to whom a gentleman could talk.[42] After a brief exchange about the weather, Mr. Johnson likes the shepherd because "he always accustomed himself to judge favorably of those who had a serious deportment and solid manner of speaking."[43] The gentleman begins to want to help the shepherd. In contrast, he notes that "if a man accosts me with an idle, dissolute, vulgar, indecent, or profane expression, his character is as bad as his language gave me to expect."[44] To Johnson, such behavior forfeits any claim to the benefits of an organic society. However deserving by traditional standards, such a man does not receive any charity from Mr. Johnson. More's call for a renewed paternalism was selective and disciplinary.

The *Cheap Repository* recommends the employment of very young children, the saving of income, and the renunciation of communal festivities as important ways to become or stay deserving. She most persuasively praised manual training, thrift, and self-denial in tracts which presented a dichotomy of saintly and pernicious characters. In these stories, no shades of

---

[41]Other Evangelicals were far more vague in their concepts of the deserving and undeserving poor. For example, see Gisborne, *Duties of Men*, p.120; Wilberforce, *Practical View*, p.258.

[42]Cleanliness was an indicator of godliness and, to More, it was missing among her poor neighbors in "the little beggarly buildings" which surrounded her cottage in Somerset. In a letter to Mrs. Garrick, she wrote that "honeysuckles are all in bloom and will help smell down the stink of the Pig-sty and other savory smells with which our neighbors treat us." (Hannah More to Mrs. Garrick, 26 June 1797, Folger Shakespeare Library, Mss. 488, of.8)

[43]More, *Works, The Shepherd of Salisbury Plain*, p.191.

[44]Ibid.

gray exist. For example, in *The Two Shoemakers*, published in five parts between March of 1795 and March of 1796, the good apprentice James Stock overcomes the stigma of dependence on the parish through hard work and Evangelical Anglicanism, becoming the most prominent cobbler in his county. The bad apprentice Jack Brown, on the other hand, squanders the advantages of a yeoman's background through indolence, profligacy, and blasphemy. Like the famous engravings by William Hogarth in the 1750s, *The Two Shoemakers* lays down simple and clear rules of business rectitude by means of the juxtaposition of a diligent, ascetic hero and a lazy, self-indulgent villain.[45]

Similarly, in *The History of Tom White, The Post Boy*, published in two parts in March and September of 1795, the title character has his good and bad sides. No matter how much Tom gives in to the ubiquitous temptations of traditional festivities and consumer goods, he returns to the frugal guidelines of his atypical upbringing. At first, Tom is the "good" character, pinching pennies and praising God. "The son of a honest laborer at a little village in Wiltshire," he learns to save as a servant for Farmer Hodges who "would have turned him out of his service if he had ever gone to the ale-house." Then, the "bad" or conventional side of Tom temporarily eclipses his "good" or Evangelical Anglican education. Like nearly all Hanoverians, he is seized by an inordinate love of money and material things. Unsatisfied with saving the measly wages of a servant, Tom leaves Farmer Hodges "to drive a chaise, to get money, and to see the world."[46] Soon a typically convivial post boy who profited from the eighteenth-century boom in domestic tourism, Tom wastes his profits on flashy clothes and useless trinkets, and spends his spare time at fives, cards, cudgel-playing, laying wages, and drinking.[47]

---

[45]*The Two Shoemakers* is found in More, *Works*, pp.201-23. For a discussion of Hogarth's prints, see Ronald Paulson, *Popular and Polite Art in the Age of Hogarth and Fielaing* (Notre Dame: University of Notre Dame Press, 1979).

[46]More, *Works, The History of Tom White, the Post Boy*, p.244.

[47]For the boom in tourism, see Roy Porter, *English Society in the Eighteenth Century* (New York: Penguin Press, 1982), pp.245-7. Irresponsible postboys were obviously a plague to the genteel traveler. In particular, see the entries

Nevertheless, the "good" Tom inevitably reappears. Sober and diligent once again, he saves money, drawing upon the ardent protestantism of his youth. When Tom does spend, he invests in secure linchpins, tight harnesses, clean windows, and comfortable upholstery for his carriage. Consequently, his business prospers because of his reputation as a safe and reliable driver on the road to Bath. A few years later, he reconciles with Farmer Hodges, who deems him worthy of further patronage. Tom's thriftiness, in particular, delights the stern yeoman who "offer[s] to let him a small farm at an easy rate, and promise[s] him assistance in the first year, with the loan of a small sum of money."[48] Catering to the materialism of Georgian Britain, More insisted that juvenile industry developed personal economy which attracted patrons. In turn, these patrons had a "natural tendency" to make someone rich, the elusive goals of many erstwhile entrepreneurs who read the *Cheap Repository*.[49]

The easiest way for James Stock and Tom White to save is to avoid the festivities of communal leisure. In *The Two Shoemakers* and *The History of Tom White, the Post Boy*, Hannah More repeatedly stressed the monetary costs of traditional recreational activities such as drinking at alehouses and attendance at fairs, particularly in terms of lost work time. Rough conviviality encouraged the vices which doomed the poor in the "sink-or-swim" economy of Georgian Britain—idleness, promiscuity, inebriation, and profligacy.[50]

---

of 21 August 1790, 10 and 12 July 1793 in John Byng's travelogues as reprinted in *Torrington Diaries* vol.2, p. 275; vol. 3, pp.192, 201.

[48]More, *Works, The History of Tom White, the Post Boy*, p.266.

[49]More failed to acknowledge that universal thrift would slow down commercial transactions, making no one rich.

[50]More, *Works, The History of Tom White, The Post Boy*, pp.228, 230; This is similar to the argument of the Reverend William Adams, *The Duties of Industry, Frugality and Sobriety. A Sermon Preached before a Society of Tradesmen and Artificers, in the Parish Church of S. Chad, Salop, on Easter Monday, 1766.* 3rd. edn., Shrewsbury, 1770, pp.21-2 as quoted in Malcolmson, *Popular Recreations*, p.93. c.f. the Reverend David Davies who could not ascribe the extreme poverty that he witnessed in Berkshire in 1787 to "sloth or wastefullness" as reprinted in M. Dorothy George, ed., *English Social Life in the Eighteenth Century: Illustrated from Contemporary Sources* (London: Sheldon Press, 1923), p.21.

She warned that sinful recreations weakened the moral and physical state of male laborers. This charge rebutted defenders of customary recreations who viewed these events as builders of manhood. The poet and cleric George Crabbe,[51] among others, lamented the success of Evangelicals in the making of what he considered effeminate laborers who enjoyed the private pleasures of middling-sort women. More knew that she had to break the popular connection between masculinity and conviviality in order to increase the number of the deserving among the poor. Hence, in *The Two Shoemakers* she presented the marbles player, fairgoer, and alehouse denizen Jack Brown as an effeminate coward dominated by his mother. On the other hand, More presented the godly James Stock as the masculine foil to the effeminate Jack. James maturely and manfully meets the test of life through prayer and Bible-reading.[52] Her use of "effeminate" as negative and "masculine" as positive may seem strange, coming as it does from a female author who preferred sexually non-threatening men. Yet More here once again appropriated a conventional construct for an unconventional agenda against convivial paternalism.

In general, More underscored the perils of communal leisure to all rural laborers, whether male or female. In these stories, whenever workers congregate to play, something terrible always happens to individual workers. For example, Jack Brown ends up in a debtors' jail after he loses his rent money to a band of strollers at a roadhouse called the Blue Posts. Since these performers of "that sing-song ribaldry by which our villages are corrupted" disappear, the JPs imprison Jack.[53] Rejected by his family, he catches the jail fever and nearly dies.

Public diversions threatened the very social stability and cohesion that the powerful thought they fostered. Here More struck at the heart of eighteenth-century paternalism. In *The History of Tom White, the Post Boy*, she contrasted the disorderly

---

[51]George Crabbe, "The Village," (1783) in Geoffrey Tillotson, Paul Fussell, and Marshall Waingrow, eds., *Eighteenth-Century English Literature* (New York: Harcourt, Brace, and Janovich, 1969), pp.1423-30. In addition, see *The Sporting Magazine*, vol. 28, no. 168 (September, 1806), pp.261-2.
[52]More, *Works, The Two Shoemakers*, pp.201-5.
[53]Ibid., p.213.

effects of bad old customs with the pleasant unity caused by discriminate charity. Several years after Farmer White becomes a prosperous tenant, he builds a large barn. The carpenters and thatchers expect White to sponsor the usual holiday of roof-raising. On this occasion, employers supply their workmen with a large quantity of liquor. The workmen do not ordinarily return to their construction site for a couple of days. Farmer White balks at this wasteful practice. He gives his laborers a plenteous mid-day dinner with one mug of beer each to reward their skill at roof-raising. He refuses to give them any more spirits because he expects them to go back to work for the afternoon. Heavy drinking at roof-raising celebrations robs bread from laborers' families because of the lost wages. Most critically to Farmer White, inebriation transforms deferential "reasonably creatures" into saucy "brute beasts." White's way of prudent paternalism leads to contented workers who "all went merrily" back to carpentry and masonry, "fortified by a good dinner."[54]

Similarly, Farmer White and the neighborhood parson reform the autumnal sheep-shearing feast. On this occasion Farmer White orders his wife cook a nourishing supper of meat and puddings for the Christians of the village community. He sets up two tables according to local status. He sits at the head of one, consisting of the godly among his neighbors and laborers. His wife sits at the head of the other one, consisting of the old and infirm poor who were self-disciplined. Before the dinner, the laborers' children gather flowers to adorn the horns of the ram. Then, White's children give plenty of pudding to the flower gatherers. Discriminate charity to the deserving begins young. During the dinner, the vicar talks to each guest, getting "acquainted with their several characters, their spiritual wants, their individual sins, dangers, and temptations." The poor seem touched by the genuine interest shown by the cleric. After the dinner, they all sing the sixty-fifty psalm in unison and return home "happy and not drunk."[55]

---

[54]More, *Works, The History of Tom White, the Post Boy*, p.288.

[55]Ibid., Pp.229-30; c.f. "Evangelicalism could not accommodate itself to the traditions of popular leisure without abandoning its basic presuppositions; indeed, there was virtually no room for compromise." (Malcolmson, *Popular Recreations*, p.101) Richard Arkwright designed similar yet secular ceremonies

In contrast, Farmer White notes that the ribaldry of traditional sheep-sheering dinners is leveling. If the farmer's family is tipsy, then boozy intimacy dissolves hierarchical difference. If the workers are drunk, then riot against authority is a strong possibility.[56]

Unlike the standard patronage of cockfights and cudgels by gentlemen, More's selective paternalism disqualified gamblers, fighters, and drunkards from charity and patronage. Farmer White, in particular, fires the sole carpenter who insists on the customary allotment of liquor at the roof-raising and tells other farmers in the parish about the carpenter's insolence. Consequently, this laborer does not get work.[57] This limitation, coupled with the awful fates awaiting the "bad" poor, goads the stubborn to change their behavior.

Not everyone was pleased with More's reconciliation of the godly virtues with paternalism. In 1795 Horace Walpole, one of her subscribers, complained to More about "the cruelty of making the poor [in her tracts] spend so much time in reading books, and depriving them of their pleasure on Sundays."[58] Traditional tories had grave reservations.[59] Conservative periodicals remembered the puritan drive against popular culture in the early seventeenth century. They believed that the puritan abandonment of festivities and sports angered the usually deferential poor and thus sparked rebellion against the social

---

to increase the virtue of his cotton operatives. For a discussion of these festivities, see the entry of 28 October 1781 in Sylas Neville, *The Diary of Sylas Neville 1767-1788*, Basil Cozens-Hardy, ed., (London: Oxford University Press, 1950), p.279.

[56]More, *Works, The History of Tom White, the Post Boy*, p.229.

[57]Ibid., pp.228-9.

[58]In a letter to one of her sisters, More reported Walpole's comment and her response. (Hannah More to her sister, 1795, Roberts, *Memoirs* vol.2, p.432.)

[59]William Cobbett, the loyalist journalist, initially praised the tracts. Upon returning to England from Philadelphia in 1800, he promised to visit More as soon as possible. (Mary G. Jones, *Hannah More* (New York: Greenwood Press, 1968), p.145.) Yet the Evangelical drive against popular culture eventually changed Cobbett's mind about More. For his celebration of ancient, manly pastimes, see *Cobbett's Weekly Political Register*, 5 June 1802, pp.652-7; 29 January 1803, pp.99; 14 January 1804, pp.54-5. For Cobbett's conversion from loyalism back to radicalism, see Ian Dyck, "from 'Rabble' to 'Chopsticks': The Radicalism of William Cobbett", *Albion*, vol. 21 1(Spring, 1989), pp.56-87.

hierarchy in the 1640s. With typical hyperbole, they concluded that renewed crusades against harmless play would lead to disorder and, eventually, regicide. Moral reformers played into the hands of Jacobins who wanted to abolish privilege and to destroy paternalism.[60]

On the other hand, leading dissenters such as the historian David Bogue dismissed More's attack on popular culture as window dressing from a venal hireling of the Pitt ministry. Bogue noted that the prime minister was a subscriber to the *Cheap Repository*. At the same time, Pitt had suspended civil liberties such as habeas corpus and had quashed moves to end civil disabilities against the godly outside the Church of England. While agreeing with More on the evils of communal conviviality, Bogue questioned the timing of the tracts. He alleged that they were smokescreens to distract dissenters from abhorrent policies. Consequently, he thought Hannah More, the chief author, had sold out to Old Corruption.[61]

In a letter to Zachary Macaulay, More said that "attacks on the supposed violence of my aristocratic principles" did not bother her, but she admitted to him that

> you know how much more I have had to sustain from
> my supposed attachment to democrats and dissenters.
> My episcopal and other friends suspect me
> of leaning too strongly to that side.[62]

Proud of her middle way between hidebound tories and radical dissenters, More hoped that "all pretty names of party and sect shall be done away, and charity shall be all in all!"[63] She

---

[60]*Anti-Jacobin Review and Magazine*, V, 1799, p.80, 314, 340, 359; *The British Critic*, 17(May, 1801), p.444. On the eve of the Blagdon Controversy, More complained to William Wilberforce that "*The Anti-Jacobin* is spreading more mischief over the land than almost any other book because it is doing it under the mask of loyalty. It is representing all serious men as hostile to the Government." (Roberts, *Memoirs* vol. 3, p.102)

[61]Forster Papers, Henry Thornton to Zachary Macaulay, 20 February 1796 as quoted in Jones, *Hannah More*, p.149.

[62]Hannah More to Zachary Macaulay, 19 February 1796, Roberts, *Memoirs* vol. 2, p.463.

[63]Ibid.

meant both disciplinary benevolence and loving accord here since, to More, disciplinary benevolence insured loving accord.

More designed her paternalism to make the poor sincere Christians and, then, to check on their spiritual progress regularly. Farmer White's reformation of existing festivities was only a first step. For More, the primary ways to instill both popular godliness and deference were the sponsorship of Sunday schools, persistent face-to-face inspections of dependents' lives, and the responsible stewardship (shepherding) of wealth by gentlemen and their middling-sort imitators.

Hannah More believed in the corrective power of education. As a schoolmistress in the 1760s and 1770s, she had instructed rich girls in order to preserve their self-esteem and enable their salvation from aristocratic culture. As a philanthropist in the 1790's, she established several Sunday schools in remote areas of Somerset in order to counter any danger posed by popular culture to the social order.[64] She preached what she practiced. In *The Sunday School*, published in May of 1797, a middling-sort widow explains how to set up and run an institute for teaching reading skills to poor children.

The administration of this ideal school depends upon hierarchical differentiation. Everyone has his or her proper place. For instance, the founder, Mrs. Jones, dictates policy and procedure at the school. Mrs. Jones determines the curriculum to insure respect for authority. The pupils read only the Bible and simple devotional books. It is true that many philanthropists allowed their pupils a much wider variety of subjects than More,[65] but

---

[64]For More's involvement in the Sunday schools, see Arthur Roberts, ed., *The Mendips Annals, or a Narrative of the Charitable Labours of Hannah and Martha More in their neighborhood, being the Journal of Martha More. Fourth Edition.* (London: James Nisbet and Co. 1861); Jones, *Hannah More*, pp.151-71.

[65]Thomas Walter Laqueur, *Religion and Respectability Sunday Schools and Working Class Culture 1780-1850* (New Haven: Yale University Press, 1976), pp.128-34; Political economists advocated a national educational system which taught both reading and writing to the poor. (Adam Smith, *An Inquiry into the Nature and Causes of the Wealth of Nations*, 1776, Edwin Cannon, ed., (New York: The Modern Library, 1937), pp.730-40; Frederick Morton Eden, *The State of the Poor* (London: Cass, 1966)[orig. pub. 1797], p.27; Gertrude Himmelfarb, *The Idea of Poverty: England in the Early Industrial Age* (New York: Knopf, 1984), pp.58-63.)

Hannah More thought that the teaching of writing and arithmetic might give poor children ideas above their station.[66]

Mrs. Jones also shames pranksters and rewards achievers at special ceremonies, but she does not teach and, thus, does not attend every Sunday session. Her role at the school resembles that of a large landowner on an estate. Accordingly, Mrs. Jones delegates her authority, picking her housekeeper Betty Crews to be the chief teacher. Although Betty has no experience or formal training, she is "a real Christian," has "excellent sense" in carrying out Mrs. Jones' orders, and has received a vocational education. Betty communicates with poor children more easily than Mrs. Jones because of her lowly background.[67] In turn, Betty creates her own hierarchy of students based on age, aptitude, and, most critically, attitude. The older, more literate, and more tractable a scholar becomes, the more status that scholar attains within the confines of the school.[68]

Christianity binds together the school's hierarchy. Mrs. Jones declares to Betty and her charges that they have common interests in spreading the Word and attracting additional students. At an early and impressionable age, the students become partners in a cooperative enterprise toward their salvation. The school becomes a godly family to counter the influence of parents who follow the bad old customs.

Material rewards induce reluctant recruits to read the Bible, to obey their superiors, and to join the family. Mrs. Jones and Betty dispense encouraging words and little gratuities after correct completion of drills. The prizes of food and clothing to the deserving temporarily ease the hardships of toiling in the fields, helping at least the best students to identify with Mrs.

---

[66]So did Jonas Hanway, one of the founders of the Sunday School Society. (Laqueur, *Religion and Respectability*, p.126); c.f. *The British Critic*, the organ of the Anglican hierarchy, praised those schools which imparted only vocational training to poor children. (Review of *Sketch of State of the Children of the poor in the Year 1756, and of the present State and Management of all the Poor in the Parish of St. James, Westminster in January, 1797, The British Critic*, 9(June, 1797), p.686-7.)

[67]c.f. Sarah Trimmer, *The Economy of Charity* (London: Cadell & Davies, 1787), pp.40-1. Trimmer believed that genteel ladies should directly teach their charges in their Sunday schools.

[68]More, *Works, The Sunday School*, pp.172-4.

Jones and her agenda. Like traditional festivities, the award rituals at Sunday schools are used by the powerful to validate their control.[69]

More stressed that the establishment of Sunday schools aided the individual patron as well as the social hierarchy. Most significantly, Mrs. Jones pleases God by her evangelical efforts. More cited God's pleasure as more important than the act of ameliorating human misery.[70] If he did not approve of one's almsgiving, one should not bother.

In addition, More stressed the earthly benefits of discriminate charity to female givers such as Mrs. Jones. In the 1790s well-to-do women were judged by their outward appearance, not their inner beauty, and were trained to be dilettantes practiced at flower arranging, French, and dance. Their adult roles as wives and mothers went unnoticed and unappreciated. In contrast, More's Evangelicalism elevated the home into a spiritual unit, and the mother-wife into a spiritual leader. Her activist Christianity and holy virtues transcended gender and thus pushed her genteel female characters into the world to help the deserving poor, letting old maids and young mothers use their skills in socially acceptable and personally satisfying ways.

In the *Cure for Melancholy*, published in January of 1797 (as the preface to *The Sunday School*), Mrs. Jones is a widow of a rich merchant who leaves her with a modest annuity. She is

---

[69]For the award ceremonies, see More, *Works, The History of Hester Wilmot*, pp.236-9. Published in June of 1797., this tract was the sequel to *The Sunday School*. More and her sisters held annual feast days for their schools and the Mendips. She invited both scholars and gentlemen. Sometimes the gentlemen waited on the scholars. This "king-for-a-day" role reversal was part of the theatre of old paternalism. (Roberts, *Mendip Annals*, pp.64-5, 116) She also set up female friendly societies in the villages of Shipham and Cheddar which held periodic godly feasts. (Hannah More to Eva Garrick, 4 August 1795, Folger Shakespeare Library, Mss. 488, of.2) At these dinners she noticed unprecedented communal cooperation. (Hannah More to the Reverend John Newton, 15 September 1796, Roberts, *Memoirs* vol.3, p.465.)

[70]More, *Works, The Sunday School*, p.172; c.f. William Paley, *Moral and Political Philosophy*, 1785 in *The Works of William Paley* (Philadelphia: Woodward, 1831), pp.66-71; Boyd Hilton, *The Age of Atonement: The Influence of Evangelicalism on Social and Economic Thought 1785-1865* (Oxford: Clarendon Press, 1988), pp.100-6.

inactive and broods on her tiresome existence. She shops in a vain attempt to break up the ennui which has beleaguered her. It does not work. Fortunately, Mr. Simpson, the godly vicar of her parish, tells her that she is "as much concerned in the duties inculcated in my sermon [on the good Samaritan] as Sir John with his great estate." In a revealing plot twist, More has Mrs. Jones become Evangelical and set up a Sunday school. Mrs. Jones' melancholy disappears and she advances the public good by increasing the number of the deserving among the poor.[71]

More agreed with a wide range of female commentators including the radical and feminist Mary Wollstonecraft. Middling-sort and genteel women could help their country as serious and informed philanthropists and, in the words of Gary Kelly, "could perhaps effect what men, working through politics at the local or national level, could not."[72] Unlike Wollstonecraft, however, More upheld paternalist hierarchy, not legal equality, as the best way to foster discriminate charities run by both genders.[73]

Several of More's characters question the benefits of Sunday schools. Farmer Hoskins, for instance, believes that educated servants are uppity, sedentary, and radical in spite of the best intentions of Mrs. Jones. Laborers and carpenters who can read the Bible can also read Paineite polemics. The farmer predicts that Mrs. Jones' discriminate charity will produce exactly the opposite of what she wants to happen. Mrs. Jones retorts that the purpose of Sunday schools is to interest the poor in godly literature. Since the Bible is far more lively than any radical piece, the poor will not stray from the moral and ethical instruction in the scriptures.[74]

---

[71]More, *Works, Cure for Melancholy*, pp.167-72.

[72]Gary Kelly, *English Fiction of the Romantic Period 1789-1830* (New York: Longman, 1989), p.91.

[73]Mary Wollstonecraft, *Vindication of the Rights of Woman* (Harmondsworth: Penguin Press, 1988)[orig. pub.,1792]; For a suggestive comparison of More and Wollstonecraft, see Mitzi Myers, "Reform or Ruin: a Revolution in Female Manners," in Henry Payne, ed., *Studies in Eighteenth-Century Culture*, vol. 11, 1982, pp.199-216. She finds striking similarities between More and Wollstonecraft.

[74]More, *Works, The Sunday School*, pp.174-6.

Although most bishops and parsons agreed with Mrs. Jones, quite a few gentlemen shared Farmer Hoskins' reservations. On a tour through north Wales, John Byng bitterly complained that Sunday schools allowed even the lowliest to enjoy "Amours, or Paine's Pamphlets." Byng yearned for an ill-defined past when the illiterate masses had looked to their superiors for guidance and comfort. He blamed Sunday schools for turning the people against their Church and King.[75] Byng never visited the Mendips, but he resembled the Somerset notables who feared More's own schools would erode deference.

Even Mrs. Jones admits problems in exacting true deference at her school. She complains that meeting one day per week is inadequate to change the innermost feelings and desires of many of her students. Indeed, the displayed deference at her school is as tenuous as at traditional events. Mrs. Jones and Betty worry that some students parrot verses in order to get new socks or a piece of bread. These same students have no intention of applying what they had memorized to their lives during the work week.[76] Finally, Mrs. Jones can not guarantee what her students read and though outside of class. While she insists that the Bible was the most potent antidote to Paine,[77]

---

[75]See Byng's entry for 15 July 1793 in *Torrington Diaries* vol.3, p.211. See also his entries of 22 June 1789 and 13 June of 1790 in *Torrington Diaries* vol.2, pp.80, 178. For the stodgy opposition to More's schools, see Hannah More to an unknown correspondent, 1792, R. Brimley Johnson, ed., *The Letters of Hannah More*, pp.154-5. c.f. the Rector of Lincoln College, Oxford, who also worried about how Jacobins and Dissenters would exploit newly literate laborers. (Edward Tatham, *Letters to the Right Honourable Edmund Burke on Politics* (Oxford: Oxford University Press, 1791), pp.94-5; Hole, *Pulpits*, p. 138.) At first, *The British Critic* welcomed "the advantages of an early systematic education [for the poor], having religion for its basis and an eternity for its object." (Review of *Remarks on the Speech of M. Dupont, Made in the National Convention of France, on the Subjects of Religion and Publication. By Hannah More.*, *The British Critic*, 1(May, 1793), p.32) Five years later, it linked popular literacy to the growth of radicalism. (*The British Critic*, 11(March 1798), p.266)

[76]More *Works, The History of Hester Wilmot*, pp.236-9.

[77]Like Hannah More, Thomas Paine viewed Sunday schools as an obstacle to popular revolution. In an attack on the restoration of Catholic privileges by the Directory, Paine suggested that both the Directory and its British sympathizers should "devise means to establish schools of instruction, that we may banish the ignorance of that ancien-regime of kings and priests had spread among the people." Sunday schools only perpetuated this ignorance. He

Thomas Laqueur has noted that radical "working-class politics was largely the creation of people steeped in religion and the Bible."[78] Scripture is full of marginal people who challenge the social order at God's behest. Mrs. Jones enables her pupils to read about the prophets as well as to grasp texts which call for obedience such as Romans 13 and 1 Peter 2:13-17.

In order to monitor and guide the spiritual progress of both poor children and their parents adequately, More urged personal and, at times, unannounced inspections by lord and lady bountifuls. In *The Shepherd of Salisbury Plain*, More urged careful consideration of possible candidates for private charity, especially of those who claimed to be Christian. The paternalism of Mr. Johnson is more intrusive than that of Fielding's Squire Allworthy, or that of Paley's instructions to the rich. It had to be. Paternalist relationships in the countryside weakened due to the proliferation of temporary day laborers such as the shepherd in the last quarter of the eighteenth century.[79] The close scrutiny of the shepherd by Mr Johnson expresses the gentry's concern. Even after Mr. Johnson gives the shepherd a half-crown at the end of part one, he is not convinced of the shepherd's worthiness for further charity and patronage. He wonders if the shepherd acts like a Christian in order to get money. He wants to observe how a poor man who carried such an appearance of regularity, piety, and obedience spent the Sabbath.

Accordingly, Mr. Johnson stops by the shepherd's cottage in part two. Although troubled by traveling on the Sabbath, Mr. Johnson feels that Sunday is "the only time in which the shep-

---

wanted policymakers in France and Britain "to propagate morality, unfettered by superstition." (Thomas Paine, *Worship and Church Bells, A Letter to Camille Jordan*, 1797 in William M. Van der Weyde, ed., *The Life and Works of Thomas Paine* (New Rochelle, N.Y.: Thomas Paine National Historical Association, 1925), p.31) William Godwin, the utopian theorist, also saw Sunday schools as new and unfortunate creators of unthinking deference. (William Godwin, *Enquiry Concerning Political Justice* (Oxford: Clarendon Press, 1971)[orig. pub., 1793], pp.33-8, 235-9; Hole *Pulpits*, pp.139-40.)

[78]Laqueur, *Religion and Respectability*, p.244. Excerpt reprinted by permission of Yale University Press. All rights reserved.

[79]Henry Fielding, *The History of Tom Jones: A Foundling* (New York: Barnes & Nobles, 1967); Paley, *Works*, pp.496-9; Thompson, "Patrician Society," pp.384-7.

herd's employment allowed him to be at home with his family.[80] Since Mr. Johnson is "not above entering very closely into . . . [the shepherd's] character," he "wishe[s] to take the family by surprise." Hence, the gentleman eavesdrops outside the half-open front door of the shepherd's cottage. After a few minutes, the barking of the shepherd's dog draws the attention of the family to the well-dressed stranger at the door. Mr. Johnson steps right into the house without any apologies and starts to quiz the shepherd on spiritual matters. More wanted her genteel readers to follow Mr. Johnson's example in order to stem the decline of face-to-face control of the poor by the rich. She advised the gentry to scrutinize the growing number of free and mobile laborers and to set stringent expectations for their behaviors before restoring or establishing reciprocal relationships of obligation.[81] In contrast, Squire Allworthy never tells the gentry to follow up on recipients of their benevolence.[82]

Home visits by the landlord were critical in the assessment of the spiritual state of dependents. To More, possible adult candidates for continual charity and patronage had to maintain a spiritualized household. Her advocacy of religious discipline and instruction at home was certainly not new. Continental humanists in the sixteenth century disseminated the idea of the family as a spiritual unit among English protestants. It became a commonplace of puritan and, later, Evangelical Anglican thought. Yet strikingly, More made private charity conditional upon the fulfillment of domestic religious duties which implanted sobriety, thrift, punctuality, and industry, among other virtues. For instance, after Mr. Johnson arrives at the shepherd's cottage, he heartily approves of the shepherd's spiritualized household. In a plain and clean room, the shepherd catechizes his wife and family. The father examines his family

---

[80]More, *Works, The Shepherd of Salisbury Plain*, p.195.

[81]William Wilberforce agreed. "True Charity is wakeful, fervent, full of solicitude, full of good offices, not easily satisfied, not so readily to believe that everything is going on well as a matter of course, but jealous of mischief, apt to suspect danger, and prompt to extend relief." (Wilberforce, *Practical View*, p.258.)

[82]Fielding, *Tom Jones*; Paley, *Works*, pp.496-9.

on what they have learned in church that morning and how they can apply the lesson to their lives.[83]

The gentleman notes that the shepherd appropriately considers his wife a spiritual equal and key priority. Mr. Johnson praises the shepherd's wife's important role in daily prayer, reading sessions, and vocational training of the children and especially likes the fact that the shepherd has sacrificed his own needs to care for his ailing spouse. Here Mr. Johnson makes it clear that the shepherd is the shepherd or master of his family and correctly wears the breeches in this spiritualized household. Echoing seventeenth-century puritans, More viewed the ideal conjugal relationship as a reciprocal and patriarchal friendship.[84]

Mr. Johnson dresses plainly in his visits to the shepherd's home. Squires usually dressed to overawe the lowly, but Mr. Johnson feels he can spend his money better on the shepherd. Discriminate and creative charity, not conspicuous consumption, engendered gratitude and respect. Since the couple's practical piety dispels the lingering doubts about the shepherd and his wife in Mr. Johnson's mind, the gentleman joins with the local curate to give the recently vacant parish clerk's job to the shepherd, and to establish the shepherd and his wife as the teachers.[85]

---

[83]More, *Works, The Shepherd of Salisbury Plain*, pp.198-9; Paley, *Works*, pp.496-9. For the humanist origins of the spiritualized household, see Margo Todd, *Christian Humanism and the Puritan Social Order* (Cambridge: Cambridge University Press, 1987), pp.96-117. For the spiritualized household in Evangelical Anglican thought, see Elizabeth Jay, *The Religion of the Heart: Anglican Evangelicism and the Nineteenth-Century Novel* (Oxford: Claredon Press, 1979).

[84]More, *Works, The Shepherd of Salisbury Plain*, pp.195-9. For excellent discussions of Evangelical marriages, see Earnest M. Howse, *Saints in Politics* (Toronto: University of Toronto Press, 1952), pp.168-71; Leonore Davidoff and Catherine Hall, *Family Fortunes: Men and Women of the English Middle Class, 1780-1850* (London: Hutchinson, 1987). For excellent discussions of puritan marriages, see Kathleen Davies, "The Sacred Condition of Equality—How Original Were Puritan Doctrines of Marriage?," *Social History*, 5(1977), pp.563-78; Edmund Leites, "The Duty to Desire: Love, Friendship, and Sexuality in Some Puritan Theories of Marriage," *Journal of Social History*, 15(1982), pp.384-408.

[85]More, *Works, The Shepherd of Salisbury Plain*, pp.199-200.

Mr. Johnson also agrees to pay the difference in rent between the shepherd's cottage and the late clerk's residence. Here More suggested a private and discriminate alternative to subsidies granted to laborers by various parishes to tide them over the depressions and dearths of the 1790s. Southern counties, in particular, supplemented earned wages to keep up with rising bread prices, increasingly large families, and the replacement of "living-in" farmhands hired by the year with temporary day laborers. In 1795, the same year in which More published *The Shepherd of Salisbury Plain*, the Speenhamland system of supplemental allowances to the needy began.[86] More disliked these adaptions of the Old Poor Law. Her idea of almsgiving was more discriminate than that of the Berkshire justices. In order for the gentry to help the poor help themselves, the poor, according to More, had to help themselves beforehand by practicing the virtues of a godly layman such as sobriety, thrift, and industry. Only then should private individuals or local officials supplement low incomes. Indeed, even customary economic obligations should rest upon the recipient's character and deference. To More, personal probity as well as circumstance made one deserving of the obligations of the organic society.

While condemning the Speenhamland solution, More disagreed with Edmund Burke and the Reverend Malthus who wanted to let the poor shift for themselves without any help from the bench. In particular, inspired by the bad wheat harvests and rising grain prices of the 1790s, Burke in *Thoughts and Details on Scarcity* (1795) argued that workers should depend solely upon their sobriety, frugality, industry, and ingenuity without any help from local government authorities. Here Burke drew upon the dogma of those moral philosophers who sought universal truths for applications in a national economy. He admired Adam Smith. Like Smith, Burke firmly upheld free trade in commodities, not special privileges for any one sector of an economy. Both Smith and Burke saw labor as the mother

---

[86]For the replacement of permanent workers with temporary ones, see Snell, *Annals of the Laboring Poor*, p.102. For the Speenhamland system, see J. R. Poynter, *Society and Pauperism: English Ideas on Poor Relief 1795-1834* (Toronto: University of Toronto, 1969), pp.45-52.

of all commodities, but Burke concluded from this truism that the government ought not to grant privileges to human commodities such as unemployed and underemployed workers. Even sickness and age did not oblige magistrates to bestow public poor relief, a traditional right of the impotent impoverished since the sixteenth century.[87] In any case, the poor were to blame for their poverty because they failed to exercise sobriety, frugality, and regularity and, as Malthus added in 1798, because they multiplied too rapidly.

Political economists thought that laborers should make every attempt to become competitive by practicing the godly virtues. "All the rest [Including local poor relief] is downright fraud."[88] Poor rates subsidized crime and disorder because they removed the incentives to become sober, thrifty, and regular.[89] As for the inherently uncompetitive, Burke left only private and discriminate charity which rewarded good behavior. While he eloquently lamented the abolition of aristocratic privilege in revolutionary France, he was only too willing to facilitate the abolition of the few "privileges" on which the poor in England counted. Similarly, although Malthus defended the preferential tariffs of the Navigation Acts in contrast to Smith and Burke, he was only too willing to let along disease, famine, and war in order to reduce the poor's drag on the national economy.

William Paley and Hannah More disagreed with Burke and Malthus. Unencumbered with the laws of political economy (at least with regard to public relief), they expressed the long-standing view that local government had a duty to relieve deserving poor people. In *Moral and Political Philosophy* (1785), Paley celebrated the local collection and distribution of alms by magis-

---

[87]Edmund Burke, "Thoughts and Details on Scarcity," 1795, in *The Works of Edmund Burke* (London: Bohn, 1909-12), vol.5, p.84; Gertrude Himmelfarb, *The Idea of Poverty: England in the Early Industrial Age* (New York: Knopf, 1984), pp.66-73; J.G.A. Poçock, "The Political Economy of Burke's Analysis of the French Revolution," *Historical Journal* 25(1982), pp.331-49.

[88]Burke, "Thoughts and Details," p.84.

[89]This was an increasingly common complaint. The Unitarian reformer Joseph Priestly as well as the Anglican Bishop Buller agreed with Burke that the Poor Laws inhibited popular self-discipline. (Hole, *Pulpits*, p.131; Isaac Kramnick, "Religion and Radicalism: English Political Theory in the Age of Revolution," *Political Theory*, 5(1977), pp.511-2.)

trates. He boasted that no knowledge of political economy was necessary to an overseer of the Poor Law. "A country gentle-man of very moderate education, and who has little to spare from his fortune, by learning so much of the poor-law as is to be found in Dr. Burn's *Justice*, and by furnishing himself with a knowledge of the prices of labor and provision" would suffice.[90] Like the humanists of late medieval Italy and the tory opposi-tion to the Walpole ministry in the 1720s and 1730s,[91] Paley viewed the ideal magistrate as an austere, small landowner who would always look out for the public good rather than for his selfish interests. The pragmatic archdeacon understood that the public good and the gentry's interests coincided in the Poor Laws. Hence, Paley repeated the standard descriptions of deserving and undeserving recipients while permitting the relief of vagrants with believable stories of woe. Unlike More, he saw no need to coerce the poor to be sober, frugal, and industrious by means of withholding charity and patronage from the idle and drunk. It was more expedient to humor the laboring poor rather than to antagonize them and, as Paley observed, "whatever is expedient is right."[92]

Furthermore, in *Reasons for Contentment* (1791) Paley, unlike Burke, Malthus, and More, wrote that the godly virtues were most common among rural laborers. The lower orders had no choice but to be sober, frugal, and industrious. Insulated from the enervating evils of luxury, many laborers led satisfactory lives. And when they became ill, old, handicapped, or under-

---

[90]Paley, *Works*, p.67. For a general discussion of Paley's views on poverty, see Martin Lowther Clarke, *Paley: Evidences of the Man* (Toronto: University of Toronto Press, 1974), pp.63-8. For Paley as an out-of-step defender of the old paternalism, see Thomas A. Horne, "'The Poor Have a Claim Founded in the Law of Nature': William Paley and the Rights of the Poor," *Journal of the History of Philosophy*, 23(1985), pp.51-70. For Paley as a latent radical, see Hole, *Pulpits*, pp.73-82.

[91]J.G.A. Pocock, *Virtue, Commerce, and History: Essays on Political Thought and History, Chiefly in the Eighteenth Century* (Cambridge: Cambridge University Press, 1985), pp.48-50.

[92]Paley, *Moral and Political Philosophy* Book 2, Section vi, 1785 in *The Works of William Paley–A New Edition* (London: W. S. Orr, 1849), p.505. c.f. Horne, "Paley and the Poor," p.56.

employed, the organic society ought to rescue them regardless of their morality.[93]

More trusted the charity of local magistrates, too. This confidence in JPs managing the persistent problems of poverty is most evident in *Black Giles the Poacher*, published in two parts in November and December of 1796. In part one, it seems if the magistrate has errored. Here Giles lives off the game and crops of neighboring farms, and his children's begging at the gate to the common. He is "bad," an abuser of the customary rights of villagers and tenant. "The pious clergyman and upright justice," Mr. Wilson, tries to redeem Giles' children by giving "the least hackneyed in knavery," Dick, a job planting beans.[94] Like the ideal citizen of both eighteenth-century commonwealth men and the old "country" opposition to whig oligarchy,[95] Mr. Wilson is austere, masculine, selfless, independent, and versatile. After Giles sees the boy working, he scolds Dick for accepting the job, and sabotages the gentleman's planting by putting twelve seeds in one hole instead of one at a time. Part one ends with an unfair situation. Giles informs on the "good" Jack Weston. Jack has killed a hare to thank Mr. Wilson for outdoor relief the JP gave him and his family during the previous spring. Jack does not know that "game was private property."[96] Knowing that "he did not sit on that bench to indulge pity, but to administer justice," Mr. Wilson punishes the "good" Jack, while Giles continues to poach and steal with impunity.[97]

Nevertheless, the law catches up with Giles in the second part of the serial. Giles harasses old widow Brown, pulling up her onion bed. Then, he orders his son Dick to strip her apple tree on a Sunday morning when everyone is in church. In order to deflect suspicion from himself and his family, Giles plants a hatful of apples on the ledge of the casement window of Tom Price, "the best boy in the Sunday school."[98] Mr. Wilson sees

---

[93]Paley, *Works*, pp.496-9; Trevor McGovern, "Conservative Ideology in Britain in the 1790s," *History* 73(1988), pp.241-2.
[94]More, *Works, Black Giles the Poacher*, p.252.
[95]Pocock, *Virtue, Commerce, and History*, pp.48-50.
[96]More *Works, Black Giles the Poacher*, p.253
[97]Ibid.
[98]Ibid., p.256 .

through this deception and declines to move against Tom without full proof. A guilty conscience leads Dick to the Sunday school the following week. He makes a dramatic confession before the class and the ubiquitous Mr. Wilson. Just as the magistrate goes to apprehend him for stripping the apple tree, a decayed brick wall falls on Giles during his weekly poaching for partridges, killing him. In the meantime, Mr. Wilson arranges for several farmers to pitch in and pay off the "good" Jack Weston's fine, and binds out Giles' children as apprentices to guide them from their father's "bad" example. Combining politic maneuvering with Evangelical virtue, Mr. Wilson displays the selective disciplinary nature of More's paternalism in his enforcement of property and Poor Laws.[99]

While discriminate relief by JPs constituted responsible stewardship to More, magisterial tolerance for the price-fixing of food rioters was irresponsible. Since the fifteenth century, normally law-abiding elements of the working population had coerced merchants and millers to lower their food prices in dearth times. Artisans stopped shipments, burned mills and warehouses, and sold food themselves at so-called just prices, usually in times of scarcity.[100] Colliers and clothworkers rioted the most because they relied upon market towns and ports for their food. In well-established and close-knit market towns and villages, the "stable and intimate community life provided memberships that enabled . . . [rioters] to act coherently and

---

[99]Ibid., pp.254-8.

[100]E. P. Thompson has discovered a set ideology of bread rioters, which held that no one should profit egregiously at their expense. Therefore, in times of acute shortages, mobs and magistrates should regulate prices. (Edward P. Thompson, "The Moral Economy of the English Crowd in the Eighteenth Century," *Past and Present*, 50(February, 1971), pp.76-136.) More recently, John Bohstedt and John Stevenson have cautioned that Thompson's concept of a moral economy is too rigid and simple to describe the complex motives and preconditions behind food rioting. (John Bohstedt, *Riots and Community Politics in England and Wales 1790-1810* (Cambridge, Mass.: Harvard University Press, 1983); John Stevenson, "The Moral Economy of the English Crowd: Myth and Reality," in Anthony Fletcher and John Stevenson, eds., *Order and Disorder in Early Modern England* (London: Cambridge University Press, 1985), pp.218-38) In particular, Bohstedt notes regional variations in food rioting, pointing out the urban or protoindustrial proclivity for these disturbances.

purposively to carry out shared moral and political objectives."[101] In contrast, temporary agricultural laborers were too dependent on their distant masters to participate.

Food rioters were remarkably disciplined, returning money to factors after the sale of produce at the just price. At least after 1700, no merchant or miller died as a result of assaults by mobs on their workplaces. Furthermore, most food disturbances were intricate rituals. In almost a parade formation, rioters spoke all the paternalist pieties to please JPs, beseeching their tacit cooperation. But their deference was only situational. If rioters were outside the sight of squarsons, they justified their behavior in terms of self-interest.

In turn, if the food riot did not exceed community standards for pilfering and violence, the gentry might go easy on the rioters, at times actively cooperating with the rioters to set the "fairest" price. Justices tailored their benevolence on these ceremonial occasions to deflect popular anger toward acceptable targets such as scheming middlemen. In close-knit market towns, "the durable bonds between authorities allowed each to calculate and to influence the actions of the other."[102] Food rioting and the permissive genteel response were part of the theatre of traditional paternalism.

In the eighteenth century, statutes against forestallers and engrossers lapsed, as magistrates welcomed the self-regulating market in food. Consequently, JPs were less sympathetic than their seventeenth-century ancestors to the grievances for food rioters. At the same time, food rioting was frequent in the late eighteenth century, particularly in the crises of 1766, 1795-96, and 1800-01. Once again, the most disturbed areas were insular entrepots, while the countryside was quiescent.

More reflected the growing antipathy among the gentry toward food rioting. In November of 1793 the Cheap Repository Tract Society distributed a test run of a ballad, "The Riot," before deciding on nationwide sales and distribution. "The Riot" predictably reviles rioters. More heard that distribution of

---

[101]Bohstedt, *Riots and Community*, p.68.
[102]Ibid. Reprinted by permission of Harvard University Press, Copyright © 1983 by the President and Fellows of Harvard College.

this ballad stopped "a very formidable riot among colliers in the
vicinity of Bath . . . [who] resolved to work no more, but to
attack first the mills, and then the gentry."[103] Colliers, the most
likely group to riot, lived in villages surrounding More's cottage
in Somerset.

In 1795-96, a winter which witnessed widespread disturbances
in nearby Devon, More strongly condemned mob action
against suspected forestallers and engrossers. In *The History of
Tom White, the Post Boy, Part 2*, printed for the harvest of 1795,
the parson tells Mrs. White, the wife of Tom, that food rioting
is bad. An Evangelical, the parson maintains that God usually
let humans alone, allowing physical and natural laws to shape
events. Most of the time, More's God was the watchmaker of
the Enlightenment, but occasionally her God intervened in the
material world. Sometimes He sent inclement weather such as
the rainy summers of 1794 and 1795 for some unknowable
propose. Christians should welcome natural disasters such as
successive crop failures because they reminded Christians of
God's awesome power.[104]

Nevertheless, in More's view, food rioters welcomed bad harvests for selfish reasons. She saw through their phony deference. While professing loyalty to local authorities, food rioters
were extortioners who would do away with the gentry if it were
in their interest. Unruly colliers and clothworkers waited for
shortages to reap profits from public disorder. Unlike farmers
and dealers, they took what did not belong to them. Unfortunately, riot exacerbated misery by interfering with the natural
or providential supply of food. Selling at the just price could cut

---

[103]Hannah More to Mrs. Boscawen, November of 1793, Roberts, *Memoirs*
vol.2, p.384.
[104]More, *Works, The History of Tom White, the Post Boy*, pp.231. See also
McGovern, "Conservative Ideology," p.246. In general, Christian commentaries on poverty in the 1790s were distanced from want. The dearths of
1794 and 1795 did not stop More from describing the nation as "flourishing"
with "L600,000 in the treasury . . . Such national wealth!" (Hannah More to
Martha More, 1795, Roberts, *Memoirs* vol.2, p.434). For a recent look at the
grim impact of depression and dearth in the 1790s, see Roger Wells, *Wretched
Faces: Famine in Wartime England, 1793-1801* (London: St. Martin's Press,
1988).

off future shipments of grain to a disturbed area. In fear of mob reprisals and low prices, farmers could keep their produce. Dealers and factors could flee disturbed areas with their inventories, making food distribution difficult. The deserving and truly deferential poor could starve because of this greed of food rioters.[105]

More believed that God ultimately knew what was best. A proponent of limited intervention with regard to prices Himself, God expected humans to cease tampering with His natural laws such as that of supply and demand. It was the height of human folly to stand up to God and His national self-regulating market in food. Thus, justices should carry out legal and judicial action against those who circumvented God's natural order. These villains were outrageous profiteers as well as food rioters. In December of 1790, More told Mrs. Garrick that she went "about to all the justices in the County to obtain redress for the poor in the important article of bread; the laws were shamefully neglected, that the poor had more than two pounds less bread for a shilling in our County of Somerset, than [in] Bristol, Bath, and other towns." She thanked God that she traveled to forty parishes to point out this fraud.[106]

Yet five years later, in view of widespread unrest, she aimed her criticism at opportunistic troublemakers, not negligent justices in the countryside. Her attacks were in the name of helping the deserving rural poor against undeserving urban predators such as food rioters. Misguided and perfunctory intervention by JPs in the marketplace would deprive the deferential worthy of the finite resources available to them, and would help the "bad." In general, magistrates should not regulate prices and wages in contradiction to God's natural order. Foreshadowing the arguments of landlords in favor of the New Poor Law of 1834, More's paternalism justified the

---

[105]More, *Works, The History of Tom White, the Post Boy*, pp.230-3. For an excellent treatment of Evangelical attitudes toward the marketplace, see Boyd Hilton, *The Age of Atonement: The Influence of Evangelicalism on Social and Economic Thought 1785-1865* (Oxford: Clarendon Press, 1988).

[106]Hannah More to Eva Garrick, 11 December 1790, Folger Shakespeare Library, Mss. 487, of. 69.

protection of providentially ordained property rights over the maintenance of arbitrary and, therefore, humanly inspired customary rights. Using secular explanations, Paley and Burke agreed with More than only the market can dictate price.[107]

According to More, people could best reduce the sting of dearth by practicing the godly virtues. Here More's view of occasional providential intervention exposes her disdain for the starving and undeserving poor. To More, suffering may be a device used by God to transform the reprobate into the Christian. Perhaps God sent the fear and pain of hunger to induce sobriety, thrift, regularity, and ardent protestantism, and, therefore, to transform superficial deferential behavior into really deferential attitudes. In contrast, indiscriminate charity as prompted by sympathetic magistrates encouraged those who clung stubbornly to old deceptive and disruptive ways. Therefore, the recalcitrant should starve. Like God, one should be cruel to be kind. Accordingly, More excluded food rioters from the benefits of the organic society. Those who tried to circumvent His natural laws were undeserving of private charity and public relief. The parson declares to Mrs. White that "those who have been seen aiding, abetting any riot, any attack on butchers, bakers, wheat-mows, milk, or millers, we will not relieve; but with the quiet, contented, hard-working man, I will share my last morsel of bread."[108] Food rioters who seemingly looked

---

[107]More, *Works, the History of Tom White, the Post Boy*, pp.230-33; Burke, *Works*, pp.82-6; Paley *Works*, pp.496-99; Hilton, *Age of Atonement*, pp.7-26. For a look at the "for the landlords" ethos behind the New Poor Law of 1834, see Peter Mandler, "The Making of the New Poor Law Redivivus," *Past and Present*, 117(1987), pp.131-57.

[108]More, *Works, The History of Tom White, the Post Boy*, p.233; c.f. the similar if secular sermon against food riots by the hero in the Unitarian Robert Bage's novel, *Hermsprong; Or Man as He Is Not* vol.3, Stuart Tave, ed., (University Park, Pa.,: Pennsylvania State University Press, 1982), pp.195-9. In the same letter that More talks about the Bath riot, she noted the "real" reason for the colliers' distress: "their own bad management." Then, she resolved to work on the recipes for cheap dishes which she eventually inserted at the end of *The History of Tom White, the Post Boy, Part 2*. She declared that she would get more satisfaction from telling the poor how to cope than "from having written the Iliad." (Hannah More to Mrs. Boscawen, November of 1793, *Roberts Memoirs* vol.2, p.384)

to paternalist relationships for redress were primary targets of More's selective and disciplinary organic ties.

More also relegated those laborers swayed by radical reformers to the ranks of the undeserving. Many radical reformers such as Thomas Paine shared More's desire to train the poor to be self-disciplined.[109] But they also wanted to dispose of the institutions of paternalist hierarchy, while More wanted to strengthen paternalism.

More argues that the quest for expressive freedoms and representative government aimed to maximize individual well-being and liberty at the expense of the interests of the community of Christ. It is true that More concentrated much more vitriol on popular culture than on radicalism.[110] But in her mind, radical advocacy was part of popular culture and, thus, a particularly perilous manifestation of ignorant self-indulgence, as indicated by the revolutionary events across the Channel. Radicals were individualist and, therefore, selfish. In contrast, the organic society was communitarian; therefore, in More's paternalism, it was liberal to deserving Christians. She obviously overlooked Paine's proposals of old age pensions, public works projects, and free public schools which would have helped many more deserving Christians than her selective and disciplinary organic ties.[111]

In general, More thought that utopian schemes driven by abstract French philosophy dissolved the links between the gentry, the middling orders and the poor. More did not spearhead the attack against the philosophes for their contribution to the fall of the ancien-regime. Several years before, Edmund

---

ten the Iliad." (Hannah More to Mrs. Boscawen, November of 1793, Roberts *Memoirs* vol.2, p.384)

[109]For example, see Francis Place, *The Autobiography of Francis Place*, Mary Thale, ed., (Cambridge: Cambridge University Press, 1972); Wollstonecraft, *Rights of Woman*.

[110]Susan Pederson correctly notes that More's tracts fought Simple Simon more than Thomas Paine. But she fails to see that More in the tracts characterized libertarian, radical advocacy as the ultimate result of an ignorant, self-indulgent popular culture, which Pedersen (like so many late twentieth-century historians) celebrates. (Pedersen, "Hannah More Meets Simple Simon.")

[111]Thomas Paine, *Rights of Man Part Two* (Harmondsworth: Penguin Press, 1987)[orig. pub. 1792], pp.210-73; Gregory Claeys, *Thomas Paine: Social and Political Thought* (Boston: Unwin Hyman, 1989), pp.80-2.

Burke had connected the Enlightenment to the Revolution.[112] During and after the bloodshed of the Terror, revulsion at the works of Voltaire and Diderot became fashionable in Britain. In her hatred of natural rights theorists, More was not exceptional. She put forth a penetrating indictment of libertarian ideas for social and cultural polarization between rich and poor in *The History of Mr. Fantom, the New-Fashioned Philosopher* published in July of 1797.

Here Mr. Fantom, a rich retail trader from London, is "reckoned a sober, decent man, but he . . . [is] covetous and proud, selfish, and conceited."[113] He endeavors to distinguish himself by becoming a philosophe in the countryside, "devoting his time to his new plans, schemes, theories, and projects for the public good." Although he mouths the fine words of the Enlightenment such as liberality, love of mankind, and benevolence, he unfortunately does not know their meaning. He only cares about other people if they live at a convenient distance. He laments the partitions of Poland, seeks independence for the Latin American colonies, and contrives a scheme to liberate Europe from religious bigotry. The more Fantom talks about helping others, however, the more selfish he becomes. He overworks and underpays his servants, forbidding them to go to church. He ignores "the petty sorrows or workhouses and parish apprentices" and even refuses to help a poor family during a fire at their house.[114]

"A honest, plain, simple-hearted tradesman of the old cut," Mr. Trueman is the "good" foil to the "bad" Mr. Fantom. Like the heroes of "country" ideology earlier in the century, Mr.

---

[112]Edmund Burke, *Reflections of the Revolution in France* (Harmondsworth: Penguin Press, 1988)[orig. pub. 1790], pp.211-5; Seamus Deane, *The French Revolution and Enlightenment in England 1789-1832* (Cambridge, Mass.: Harvard University Press, 1988), pp.4-14.

[113]More, *Works, The History of Mr. Fantom, The New-Fashioned Philosopher*, p.120; c.f. Hole, *Pulpits*, pp.158-9.

[114]c.f. the similar anecdotes for MPs a year later in the playfully conservative *Anti-Jacobin or Weekly Examiner*, 36(9 July 1798) as quoted in Wendy Hinde, *George Canning* (London: Collins, 1973), p.61. For the full poem *New Morality* from which this selection of Hinde comes, see John Hookham Frere, *The Works of John Hookham Frere* vol.1, W. E. and Sir Bartle Frere, eds., (London: Basil Montagu Pickering, 1872), pp.137-31.

Trueman resists the commercial corruption and factional speculation of London. As Mr. Fantom discusses public-spiritedness,
Mr. Trueman is public-spirited.[115] While Mr. Fantom dismisses
a poor neighbor's fire as a trifle in comparison to the contem-
plation of universal benevolence, Mr. Trueman risks his life to
whisk away an infant from an upper room which the fire has
not yet reached.[116] While Mr. Fantom is cowardly, greedy, and
affected, Mr. Trueman is a "True Man" whose godliness under-
pins his masculinity. The practical efforts of Mr. Trueman, an
Evangelical, to fulfill parish offices and to increase literacy
contrasts favorably with the impractical musings of a crabbed
intellectual. More skillfully rebutted here the radical charge that
Evangelicals cared only about distant problems such as West
Indian slavery.

Most importantly, unlike Mr. Trueman, Mr. Fantom sets a
bad example for his servants. It is true that Mr. Fantom, like
Mr. Trueman, is sober, thrifty, and industrious. Yet unlike Mr.
Trueman, he ridicules Christianity and rejects paternalism
because he has learned bits of truistic jargon from the
philosophes. Indeed, he denounces hierarchy and the Lord in
front of his servants. Consequently, Mr. Fantom transforms his
butler William into a thieving murderer, an outcast from
society.[117]

More thought it critical to transmit paternalist ideas to the
upwardly mobile such as Mr. Fantom. She saw this social group
as the most susceptible to radicalism. This concern is very
evident in *The Two Shoemakers* and *The History of Tom White, the*

---

[115]More, *Works, The History of Mr. Fantom, the New-Fashioned Philosopher*, p.121;
Pocock, *Virtue and Commerce*, pp.28-50.

[116]c.f. the rescue of a girl from a fire by a Frenchified intellectual contrasted
with the petulant selfishness of a tory squire in William Godwin, *Caleb
Williams*, David McCracken, ed., (London: Oxford University Press, 1979)
[orig. pub. 1794], pp.42-6.

[117]More, *Works, The History of Mr. Fantom, the New-Fashioned Philosopher*,
pp.126-9; for a similar reflection on "those vicious practices that disgrace
every rank and description of the community," see Review of *A Sermon,
preached before the association for discountenancing Vice, and promoting the Practice
of Religion and Virtue, in St. Ann's Church, Dublin, on Thursday, the 5th of May,
1796. By the Rev. William Magee, B. D. Junior Fellow of Trinity College, Dublin,
Member of the Royal Irish Academy, and Cor. Member of the Literary and Philosophical Society of Manchester*, The British Critic, 11(March 1798), p.267.

Post Boy. A tiny minority among the deserving poor such as James Stock and Tom White rose socially by means of a fragile combination of merit, patronage, and grace. In *The Two Shoemakers*, after James Stock becomes one of the parish apprentices of the cobbler Mr. Williams, he handles most of Williams' customers due to the drinking problem of his master. Williams then dies suddenly of alcohol poisoning in an alehouse. The creditors of Mr. Williams establish James in business through low-interest loans, recognizing his industry and sobriety. James takes over Mr. Williams' store and increases sales.[118]

A devout Evangelical, James now faces the many perils which material success poses to his eternal salvation. He could have followed the paths of many new masters who abused their power over employees. These tradesmen tended to give no charity to the deserving poor and to mistreat their apprentices.[119] Rich artisans felt that the personal bonds of the organic society were superfluous because they as artisans had become commercially successful. Tragically, they forgot that they were once downtrodden and dependent. They bragged about their success, sobriety, industry, and struggle. They coveted the material possessions and political power of rich neighbors and were attracted to radicalism. They thought that they were sinless because God had blessed them. More condemned the smug complacency of such artisans. Having left hell on earth, these social climbers, according to More, seemed destined for eternal perdition. But she, like most Christians, held that material prosperity was not inherently evil.[120]

More specified methods of overcoming these obstacles to divine blessing. Most significantly, James Stock transforms his shop into a spiritualized household. He incorporates Christianity into his business decisions and the lives of his apprentices. James thus does not mistreat his apprentices because he knows that his celestial master is omniscient. He relies on the personal bonds of the organic society. He treats his apprentices as if they

---

[118]More, *Works, The Two Shoemakers*, pp.205-6.

[119]M. Dorothy George suggests that abusive masters were not always new or upwardly mobile. See her *London Life in the Eighteenth Century* (New York: Harper & Row, 1965)[orig. pub. 1925], pp.215-67.

[120]More, *Works, The Two Shoemakers*, p.206.

are his own children. Consequently, his apprentices confide in Stock. They consider their master their friend in the sense of both the patron and the intimate.[121] Stock's paternal kindness also brings paternal concern over the spiritual and moral state of his apprentices. James uses personal ties to train his youth in regularity and religion. For example, he makes his apprentices write out six texts of Scripture in "a neat copybook with gilt covers" every Sunday evening. The notebooks cost only four pence, and last one year. When the boys show their work to Stock, he praises the boy who has the most legible handwriting. Then, Stock teaches them how to apply the Biblical lessons that they have copied to situations in their own lives. He picks texts appropriate for their place in society. In particular, while quoting Scripture, he gently admonishes an apprentice who played on the job if Stock left the shop. In reference to Ephesians 6, a favorite chapter of Old World magnates and New World slave-owners, he explains what the apostle Paul meant by sincere obedience to your earthly master. The apprentice heeds the message.[122] In *The History of Tom White the Post Boy Part 2*, Farmer White, a former stagecoach driver, treats his adult laborers in the same manner.[123]

In accordance with her distaste for traditional indulgence in mindless consumption, More counseled rising farmers, tradesmen, and merchants about the most cost-effective ways of giving relief to the distressed. First, she told them that if they were in debt, then they should never give. If an artisan gave away money need for interest payments, he placed himself at risk of becoming poor. Second, if he were in debt, then he should work longer hours than usual to afford eleemosynary schemes without default. The extra money earned would go to

---

[121]Christianity intensified the already familial atmosphere at small shops. A working master with at most five employees fosters a workplace "highly favorable to the paternal, filial, and fraternal happiness—and to the cultivation of good moral and civil habits—the sources of public tranquility," according to one observer of Manchester's clothworkers. (John Aiken, *A Description of the Country from Thirty to Forty Miles round Manchester*, 1795, p.573 as quoted in John Rule, *The Experiences of Labour in Eighteenth-Century Industry* (New York: St. Martin's Press, 1981), p.38.)

[122]More, *Works, The Two Shoemakers*, pp.206-7.

[123]More, *Works, The History of Tom White, the Post Boy*, pp.228-9.

charity, creating more deference than impressive Adamesque furniture or Wedgewood ware. When his debt from Mr. Williams' creditors still stands, James Stock decides to add one to two hours to his twelve-hour day in order to take his former master's son out of the "care" of his mother at the poorhouse. By showing an example, Stock gets his other employees to pitch in. Will Simpson, a journeyman, helps his master until well into the night. Working together doubles the profits, allowing charity for others besides Tommy Williams. Third, artisans should discriminate. Stock helps Tommy because he is an untrained youth who believes in punctuality and Christ. He does not assist the lazy and selfish Mrs. Williams. On the contrary, she loses custody of her son to Stock. The shoemaker stipulates that Tommy can never return to the poorhouse and its "railing and swearing," if he stays at Stock's. Giving up Tommy for nothing, Mrs. Williams remains undaunted and undeserving.[124]

If all employers from the Crown to James Stock followed More's intolerant, meddlesome, and earnest paternalism, then she thought she could strengthen relationships between members of the orders. Her God and paternalism were selective and disciplinary. Her poor heroes had to be ascetic and caring Christians. If they refused, they faced the prospect of no charity and patronage from their betters. Although More did not want the poor to become seriously Christian simply because of the expected earthly benefits, the primary message of *The Shepherd of Salisbury Plain* was that the recitation and application of Biblical lessons could prove valuable both spiritually and materially to those who could not make ends meet.[125] Like her poor characters, her poor readers would choose the best course in spiritual and material terms if penalties existed for the "bad" and incentives encouraged the "good." More was certain that her tracts would make her poor readers seriously Christian without upsetting the political dominance of landed wealth.

But no rapid changes in the behavior of the poor happened after many of them read the *Cheap Repository*. However large the approximate number of rural laborers who read the tracts,

---

[124]More, *Works, The Two Shoemakers*, p.208.
[125]More, *Works, The Shepherd of Salisbury Plain*, pp.197-8.

More's stories had no discernible influence on her poorest readers. Indeed, no one could have been as frugal as James Stock, or as persevering as the shepherd during the depressions and dearths of the 1790s. The commentators on poverty including Hannah More did not understand this cold fact. Like Burke's advocacy of genteel abdication of public responsibility for poor relief, More's paternalism would have made it more difficult for the distressed to live by limiting charity and patronage to the self-disciplined who shunned food riots and Paineite pamphlets. As successive crop failures and rising food prices worsened conditions for the poor in the countryside in the 1790s, poaching and thievery increased as men stole to feed their families. Crowds rioted for food. The poor continued to forget their troubles through festive indulgences, even if they read the didactic message of the *Cheap Repository*.

At the same time, the tracts' influence on justices, masters, and their wives is hard to determine.[126] More offered sound counsel for the gentry and middling orders to comfort and control their dependents, putting old nostrums of paternalism and public-spiritedness on a more watchful basis than seasonal bread and circuses. The best way to instill deferential attitudes and thus to insure social stability was to sponsor face-to-face schemes of discriminate charity. Eschewing the new laws of political economy, the ideal paternalist ceased supporting traditional festivities and pursuing new luxuries. The ideal gentleman fulfilled his public responsibility as a godly magistrate who punished the idle and drunk and helped the sober and thrifty. In a village shop, the model master watched over his apprentices in the spiritualized workplace. Proper ladies ended their indolent frivolity and gave their time and money to help the deserving and the social hierarchy via the Sunday school.

Yet the subtle qualifications and different conclusions of commentators on paternalism left doubts in the minds of

---

[126]In the next century, Lawrence and Jeanne Stone have noted that a much higher proportion of landowners (than in the eighteenth century) lived on their estates year round, and took a personal interest in their laborers. They asserted that Evangelical sermons and tracts were one of the causes of this more vigorous paternalism. (Lawrence and Jeanne C. Fawtier Stone, *An Open Elite? England 1540-1880* [Oxford: Oxford University Press, 1984], p.327.)

genteel readers about the writers' references to an immutable natural or providential order. Aware of the differences among commentators, readers selectively chose the advice which best fit their situations or confirmed to their own inclinations. [127] Most well-to-do people already left the destitute to their fate, buttressed by More's insistence on disciplinary organic ties which left no room for the majority of rural and urban workers. The line she drew between the deserving and undeserving made it easy for the privileged to ignore most laborers and apprentices. More's stories were popular among the gentry and middling orders because she expressed the increasingly stern attitude of the rich toward the poor which eventually would form the basis of the rigidly discriminate New Poor Law of 1834.

The printer's desire for big profits over godly principles caused the Cheap Repository Tract Society to stop distributing and selling new tracts in September of 1798. In a bitter letter to Zachary Macaulay in September of 1797, More wrote that "Mr. M. [John Marshall, the printer] has never belied my first opinion of him, selfish, tricking, disobliging from the first to last."[128] William Cobbett, a distributor of the tracts in far-off Philadelphia, agreed, calling Marshall a "rascal . . . [who] wished to turn the whole work to his own private advantage; or to suppress it altogether."[129] Indeed, Marshall wanted to dilute the prim lessons of the stories, and to promote tales in tune with conventional morality. Buoyed by the twin successes of sales and distribution, he tempted More with an offer to achieve even greater commercial success. More balked. She was already

---

[127]c.f. Mandler, "New Poor Law," pp.138-9; Mark Blaug argues that local considerations, not set ideologies or Whitehall directives, determined poor relief practice. (Mark Blaug, "The Myth of the Old Poor Law and the Making of the New," *Journal of Economic History*, 23(1963), pp.151-84.)

[128]Hannah More to Zachary Macaulay, September 1797 in *Letters of Hannah More to Zachary Macaulay, Esq.* (London: n.p., 1860), p.10.

[129]William Cobbett to Edward Thornton (the British chargé d'affaires in Washington and no relation to More's friend Henry Thornton), 27 August 1798, G. D. H. Cole, ed., *Letters from William Cobbett to Edward Thornton written in the years 1797 to 1800* (London: Oxford University Press, 1937), p.5. The reference to Marshall and More in this letter stumped Cole because he assumed that Cadell & Davies had published the tracts. (pp.7-8)

weary from writing tracts. Marshall's audacity gave her the excuse to cease production of new leaflets, and to declare the *Cheap Repository* a victory for the godly.[130] She then sold the right to issue reprints of the stories to Evans, Hazard, and Rivington, a troika of virtuous businessmen.[131] Although More had catered to a mass audience through popular language and style, she and her Evangelical friends in the Society held that enough was enough. The godly virtues were too important to compromise with the dictates of a market economy.

---

[130]Sarah More to Eva Garrick, 12 December 1799, Folger Shakespeare Library, Mss. 488, fo.32.

[131]Spinney, *Cheap Repository*, p. 307. See Chapter 7 for the renewed *Cheap Repository* between 1817 and 1819.

Chapter V

Power and Propriety

In 1798 the Reverend Thomas Bere, the curate of Blagdon and local magistrate, exhorted his parishioners against the nearby Sunday school set up by Hannah More. Although the number of pupils at the Blagdon school then temporarily decreased, Bere's diatribe seemed small and harmless to More and the inhabitants of Blagdon, a mining village in the Mendip mountains southwest of Bristol. After a quick public apology from Bere, few in Blagdon remembered it, but for More it was the harbinger of a grueling trial. In April of 1800 Bere demanded that More fire a suspected Methodist on her staff, sparking a long and bitter controversy. For the next three years, pamphleteers and prelates assailed each other over the merits of More's Sunday schools. Friends of Bere slandered More as a Methodist and a Jacobin; friends of More, in turn, made Bere out to be a flaming Socinian. The blistering personal attacks on both More and Bere nearly destroyed their public careers.

In 1961 Ford K. Brown published what has become the definitive account of the Blagdon Controversy. Earlier biographers of Hannah More (nearly all women) had taken her part, portraying her as a helpless victim of male powerplays who took no direct part in her own defense. Brown dispelled this myth with new evidence clearly showing More as "the field commander of her forces, planning, scheming and directing, leading . . . [her male supporters] along with intelligent flattery, instructing [them] in the smallest details and . . . even if necessary revising [their] compositions."[1] Brown, however, condemned More's public maintenance of the victim image while plotting retalia-

---

[1]Ford K. Brown, *Fathers of the Victorians: The Age of Wilberforce* (Cambridge: Cambridge University Press, 1961), p.201.

tory moves in secret. He judged that this deft maneuvering "can hardly be thought of as showing her in a very good light."[2] Reflecting rather than reflecting upon Georgian propriety, Brown faults More for not being as passive and gentle in private as she was in public. In doing so, he ignores the shackles that her sex placed upon Hannah More and how she used these fetters to her advantage. He also leaves out the difficulty men had in publically attacking a woman who seemed to adhere to gender standards and how men in this pamphlet war postured back and forth between chivalrous and scurrilous.

Beset by the crippling *cause célèbre* that she had always feared, More rode out the storm by following in public the roles women had customarily performed in the family. She respected and at least seemed to play by the rules of feminine conduct when she skirted the impermissible as a female Christian educator in an impoverished backwater. In private, she took on the traditionally feminine part of the power behind the throne. She knew that if she were to keep her schools open, then she would have to use subtly her well-connected male contacts in London to stymie Bere's attack. She followed this strategy even if it left her open to charges of bossiness and manipulation.[3]

From the founding of her first school in Cheddar village in 1789, Hannah More realized that a ladylike surface could disarm adversaries or reassure friends dismayed by the steely determination beneath the affectation of delicacy and helplessness. She adopted this stance even in her correspondence with William Wilberforce, the young Evangelical friend and M.P. who had suggested to the More sisters that they set up Sunday schools. For instance, in a letter of September, 1789, Hannah

---

[2]Ibid., p.226. Excerpt reprinted by permission of Cambridge University Press. All rights reserved.

[3]Both before and after legal equality, ambitious and practical women of diverse backgrounds have practiced a similar political artistry. For the most lucid discussion of this kind of political artistry, see Elisabeth Israels Perry, *Belle Moskowitz: Feminine Politics and the Exercise of Power in the Age of Alfred E. Smith* (New York: Oxford University Press, 1987), pp.xi-xiii, 152-60, 217-8. See also Rebecca E. Klatch, *Women of the New Right* (Philadelphia: Temple University Press, 1987), pp.205-8; Arlene Elowe MacLeod, *Accommodating Protest: Working Women, the New Veiling, and Change in Cairo* (New York: Columbia University Press, 1991), pp.142-63.

More diplomatically made it clear to Wilberforce that the More sisters would directly run the schools, although they deeply appreciated the financial help from male benefactors such as himself. She effusively thanked him for his "liberality" and attributed saving "starving and half-naked multitudes" from ignorance to their friendship. Yet she also directed Wilberforce and their mutual friend Henry Thornton to distribute "necessitous villages with Books etc." She formally asked for their approval of her list of materials, but she expected them to send the requisition promptly to her sisters' home at Park Street. Most revealingly, she felt guilty about talking shop while "lying under" the guise "of being sentimental and corresponding," but she thought Wilberforce would understand.[4]

Wilberforce did understand and quickly sent the books that More wanted. He was very comfortable with the More sisters' leadership and described it with masculine imagery. He endorsed the fact that Hannah More and her sister Martha were, in the words of Dr. Arthur Roberts, "the Atlasses who [bore] the burden on their shoulders; or, to use, Mr. Wilberforce's simile, were the mainspring of the machine."[5] Wilberforce appreciated the difficulty of the Mores' undertaking, comparing them to Spencer's lady-knights fighting numerous ogres. Sensitive yet not beholden to conventions of gender, he found it quite acceptable for her to ask frankly for additional funds, noting that "not to do so would be to give way either to pride or to false delicacy."[6] More knew that local notables in Somerset would be harder to handle than Wilberforce. Callous farmers, minor gentlemen, and officials of dying market towns in Somersetshire worried that More, a well-connected and sophisticated outsider, would siphon some of their own faltering authority and meager status. These hard-working and long-

---

[4]Hannah More to William Wilberforce, September of 1789, in William Wilberforce Papers, Special Collections Department, Duke University Library, Durham, North Carolina. William Roberts incorrectly dates this letter as "1795" in *Memoirs* vol.3, pp.445-6.
[5]Arthur Roberts, ed., *Mendip Annals: or, A Narrative of the Charitable Labours of Hannah and Martha More in Their Neighbourhood. Being the Journal of Martha More. Fourth Edition.* (London: James Nisbet and Co., 1861), p.2.
[6]Ibid., p.21.

suffering men on the fringes of gentility resented a famous
woman writer and a life-long urban resident telling them what
to do or what to change. They also bristled at the potential for
widespread social disorder caused by More's schools. Literate
laborers would spurn agriculture and mining for sectarian politics, a threatening trend to these petty squires "as insolent aristocrats as any ci-devant nobles of France."[7]

To smooth over local ruffled feathers More strictly preferred
what contemporaries considered feminine techniques of persuasion to outright confrontation. In a meeting with a Farmer
C. who linked religion to "the ruin of agriculture," the More
sisters endured his open hostility to their school at Cheddar
until they began to "talk of the excellency of his wine, as though
. . . [they] had been soliciting a vote at an election." Farmer C.
immediately smiled and his "good humour . . . was considerably
heightened by" the Mores' insistence that they were not asking
for a donation from him.[8] He then went on to give the sisters
what they were looking for—priceless information about his
parish and its other leaders. Only "after artfully weeding out of
him, by slow degrees, all the material outline of Cheddar, and
feeling . . . [that they] had gained ground with him" did the
sisters leave "this ignorant, cold, unfeeling rich farmer."[9]

Hannah More and her sisters improved at "the art of canvass-
ing" with practice. The Mores visited the eleven farmhouses
mentioned by Farmer C. and catered to the social pretensions
of these yeomen. At each house, they "fondled" the "ugly children," hugged the "pointers and spaniels," and quaffed liquor.
"After these irresistible flatteries," the Mores then stressed the
worldly benefits of their schools to small landowners, promising
fewer poachers and low poor rates. Assuaged by the irresistible
charm and earthy logic of London's smartest female wit, the
eleven farmers entrusted their own children and laborers to the
Mores for at least a few hours each Sunday.[10]

---

[7]Quoted in Mary G. Jones, *Hannah More* (Cambridge: Cambridge University
Press, 1952), p.155.
[8]Roberts, *Mendip Annals*, p.14.
[9]Ibid., p.15.
[10]Hannah More to William Wilberforce, 1789 as reprinted in Roberts,
Mendip Annals, p.17. For the secular arguments used by Hannah More and

The sense of intimacy and sympathy that endeared the sisters to Farmer C. heartened conscientious if unimaginative curates and mellowed the jealousy of less able clergy. Cultivation of the sporting curate of Wells shaped their feminine brand of political artistry toward clerics of all stripes. The curate of Wells had covered or at least played at covering the pastoral duties for the vicar of Cheddar who resided at Oxford University and who had never set foot in his parish. This all-too-common arrangement made little or no difference to the negligible spirituality of Cheddar parishioners. The curate of Wells was a conventionally sociable drunk who boxed religiously and who used the Bible as a stand for his flowerpot. This alcoholic athlete who had never shown any affinity for books was naturally not amused at the sisters' plan to transform "his" drinking and pugilistic companions into literate Christians. [11]

Hannah More turned to Wilberforce for advice. Through cryptic astronomical allusions, Wilberforce suggested that the sisters invite Methodist preachers to Cheddar and then present themselves to the curate as the only viable alternative to these enthusiasts. [12]

Wary of any attachment to Methodism, More rejected Wilberforce's confrontational and unnecessarily devious politics. She instead banked on the curate's vanity and lethargy, honoring him with home-cooked dinners, copious drinks, and the invitation to deliver the inaugural address at their school. The curate caved into the sisters' orchestrated respect, but in his speech pointedly reminded them and their students not to subvert the Erastian establishment. The Mores seemed to listen intently to the sportsman's discourse on the divine right of kings, but privately noted that "the Divine right of the king of Kings seemed to be a law above his comprehension." [13] More and her

---

others for Sunday schools, see Thomas Walter Laqueur, *Religion and Respectability: Sunday Schools and Working Class Culture 1780-1850* (New Haven: Yale University Press, 1976), p.231.

[11] Hannah More to William Wilberforce, 1791, Roberts, *Memoirs* vol.3, pp.295-301; Roberts, *Mendip Annals*, p.19.

[12] Roberts, *Mendip Annals*, p.20.

[13] Ibid., p.23.

sisters continued to give only obligatory lip-service to the non-resident incumbent's verities throughout the 1790s.

The Mores' relationship with clergymen was not always one of barely veiled contempt. The ladies' social cachet and philanthropic zeal energized the handful of serious parsons in Somersetshire. Horribly ill-paid and unappreciated, these dutiful servants of God were resigned to their insignificance until fed, flattered, and empowered by the Mores. In turn, the Mores benefitted politically from these cooperative clerics, however small in number and stature. The support of "truly Evangelical" curates such as Jones of Shipham lessened lingering suspicions that the organizations built by the Mores within the Church were ultimately responsible not to the licensed priests, but to Hannah More.[14]

Restricting their work among adults to women's clubs also let the Mores run their schools without threatening the masculinity or authority of nominal supervisors. Male clerics could hardly organize their female parishioners into friendly societies without charges of impropriety or effeminacy from male parishioners. The Mores could directly evangelize women without controversy, playing the acceptable role of asexual and angelic "big" sisters to poor women. Noblesse oblige for and by women was "indeed received with much pleasure by the women, and many smiles by the men." The clergy graced the feasts hosted by club members and did little more than to encourage their wives to subscribe. Taking full advantage of clerical abdication, the Mores made it clear that the dairymaids and miners' wives were to answer to Hannah More, "the legislator of these new societ[ies]," for any heresy or irregularity. The clubs were "subservient to the schools, the rules of the club restraining the women to such . . . points of conduct respecting the schools."[15]

To conceal her immense local power Hannah More conformed to tradition by underscoring her feminine delicacy and indifferent health. This conformity went beyond staged gestures and ladylike postures. Hannah More was frequently ill

---

[14]c.f. Jones, *Hannah More*, p.164.
[15]Roberts, *Mendip Annals*, p.64. See also Hannah More to an unnamed female correspondent, 1792, Roberts, *Memoirs* vol.3, pp.313-4; the Evangelical *Christian Observer*, 3(March, 1802), pp.180-1.

throughout her long life. Incapacitating headaches plagued her during the 1790s. Her physical weakness makes her weekly galloping on horseback along mountain trails between schools seem quite remarkable. As Dr. Roberts noted, these isolated paths were "scarcely, indeed, safe places for a traveller to pass, much less for unprotected females to be resorting to continually."[16]

Equally astounding in view of her "feeble constitution" was her limitless energy. Hannah More and her Victorian admirers validated this unusual zeal in a lady by pointing out its providential origin. Dr. Roberts noted that faith in Christ carried Hannah More and her sisters through "stormy waves" of local opposition and underpinned their perseverance. The Mores were "Christian heroes" who "adventured into places where even stout men feared to follow them." Their auspicious, poised initiative came not from what contemporaries considered masculine "self-confidence—far from it, for [the Mores were] . . . great self-distruster[s]—but rather from the assurance . . . that . . . it was a work which God had apparently put into their hands by providential leanings."[17] God allowed Herculean weakness in women to triumph over ungodly rodomontade in men. God used Hannah More "whose frame was the weak and languid vehicle of a strong and warm heart" to transform "the most hard and rugged natures . . . into tenderness." God employed the Mores' political aplomb to change "rough workers in the coal-pits" into "gentle-hearted, philanthropic Christians."[18]

It would be a mistake to assume that the Mores' finessing the border between the conventional and subversive was free of intense frustration. Staying just within the soothing perspectives of an undoubted Christ and a unquestioned femininity could overcome most, but not all, of the pitfalls associated with the exercise of womanly power in a man's world. Eccentric teachers proved to be the most chronic and intractable problem. Although finding qualified personnel,

[16]Roberts, *Mendip Annals*, p.3.
[17]Ibid., pp.3-4.
[18]Ibid., p.4.

Hannah More was unable to hire teachers who had the political savvy that she and her sisters had. Unfortunately for the Mores, the most dedicated preceptors tended to be evangelicals outside the established Church who had fewer qualms than Hannah More about antagonizing the Anglican clergy.

These tactless teachers also tended to be men. The first Cheddar schoolmistress was a self-described Methodist, but she followed the Mores' uneasy accommodation with the curate of Wells. Mrs. Baber, her successor, even surpassed the Mores at public relations. She converted old Farmer C. into a financial supporter and undercut a genteel boycott of the Cheddar school in the early 1790s through bribes of free gin to poor parents. Although a formidable figure to students, Mrs. Baber made it clear that she had no interest in outshining or embarrassing the Mores and, after 1794, the new Evangelical curate of Cheddar, Mr. Boak.[19] After Baber's death in 1795, the same people who had "thrown stones at her on her first coming, attended her to the grave in deep mourning, self-invited."[20]

Male teachers such as Harvard, Turner, and Younge equalled Baber's zeal, but lacked either her political skills or her gender restraints. In particular, the Nailsea master Mr. Younge did not suffer fools gladly. Probably a Methodist, he was abrasive and abrupt. He insulted patrons of his school in 1795 and, in turn, the farmers of Nailsea "begged [the Mores] to be so good as to remove him."[21]

Handling this difficult situation tested the Mores' mastery of the art of politics. At first, they rejected the posture of modest self-effacement that they had often employed successfully. The sisters refused to cashier Younge and thus risked a rare confrontation with the surrounding community. The Mores admitted that pride was Mr. Younge's besetting sin, but "his subsequent conduct [after the latest insults] was so perfectly that of a Christian, that [they] were led to hope, should a reconciliation take place, he would yet be greatly blessed to the poor people

---

[19]Jones, *Hannah More*, p.161.
[20]Hannah More to Henry Hoare, 17 August 1795, Roberts, *Memoirs* vol.3, p.444.
[21]Quoted in Jones, *Hannah More*, p.166.

here."[22] To the Mores, Younge no longer seemed a petulant defender of his own masculine honor, and the farmers appeared to be insolent and malicious. The sisters listened to "these unreasonable men a long time to no purpose," but stressed that they would close the school if the farmers harassed Mr. Younge.[23]

The farmers called their bluff and continued to clamor that Mr. Younge be fired. As usual, the Mores, Hannah especially, wanted to moderate the farmers' position and eventually to win as many converts as they could without discord. The sisters partially retreated. They did close the day-school, but they replaced Younge with a poor, amiable collier as master of the Nailsea Sunday school. As Patty More noted, "it is our own business to swallow great doses and go on."[24] The Mores' compromise eased tensions; the farmers loved the collier and even offered to underwrite his wages as master of a reopened day-school. The sisters were privately astonished that "these sages who persecuted a very able master should now consent to a poor collier as the instructor of their children," but also noted a few years later that Nailsea had become their most harmonious and effective school.[25]

Although pleased with the happy ending in Nailsea, Hannah More did not want to lose Younge's pedagogical talents, so she transferred him to their new school at Blagdon. Initially, this switch seemed to be a good move. In 1795, the curate and JP of Blagdon, Mr. Bere, and his churchwardens had begged Hannah More to set up a school partly in order to reduce the high local incidence of theft and riot. These officials were desperate and were willing to accept any help from the Mores, even if that help included the grating Younge. Bere and company were not disappointed by the Mores and their abrasive schoolmaster. The Blagdon school, coupled with the Sunday reading set up by the curate, "prospered beyond [the Mores'] hopes." Petty crime

---

[22]Roberts, *Mendip Annals*, p.128.
[23]Ibid., p.130.
[24]Jones, *Hannah More*, p.166.
[25]Roberts, *Mendip Annals*, p.178; Hannah More's diary entry of 10 June 1798, Roberts, *Memoirs* vol.3, pp.59-60.

miraculously subsided.[26] The Mores were too successful, and
the curate felt threatened by their achievement. To Bere, unde-
sirable reversals of authority were happening under Younge's
tenure. Most irritatingly, the parish notables were confessing
their sins to Younge, not the Reverend Bere. In his capacity as
justice of peace, Bere notified the sisters in early 1798 about the
"extraordinary decorum of the men on that day" of a mass confession before Younge.[27] The sisters thought Bere approved of
this irregularity, but they were wrong. A few months later Bere
blasted the school in a sermon.

In the face of this sneak attack, the Mores stood firm. Bere's
ungentlemanly betrayal allowed the sisters to bypass feminine
propriety. As Patty More wrote, "it was now time to rouse a
little."[28] The sisters called an impromptu meeting of the
villagers and farmers of Blagdon at which Hannah More
exhaustively exhorted "the people" to support the school. She
also threatened to close the school if Bere did not apologize
publically. She countered Bere's charges of irregularity at the
school with his own alleged heterodoxy. To the sisters'
advantage, Bere had left himself vulnerable to a counterattack
by Hannah More with a denial of the divinity of Christ in that
same sermon.

The parish was "thrown into confusion" with the rift between
More and Bere. Parishioners felt intimidated and "fear[ed] to
offend the justice, as he ruled them with a rod of iron." Yet in
Blagdon the toughest party was Hannah More as Bere wavered
in his opposition "and came to [the Mores'] house in great
agitation."[29] The sisters confronted Bere with his letters of
praise for the school and its curriculum. Bere started to feel
guilty, and was "brought again to confess before witnesses the
extraordinary benefit the school had been of to the parish." The
sisters accepted this rather humiliating admission. No longer
afraid of the magistrate's wrath, "the people" returned to the
school and Sunday reading.[30]

---

[26]Jones, *Hannah More*, pp.170-1.
[27]Roberts, *Mendip Annals*, p.204.
[28]Ibid., p.215.
[29]Ibid. c.f. Jones, *Hannah More*, p.171.
[30]Roberts, *Mendip Annals*, pp.215-6.

Bere had only begun to fight, however. He eventually decided to forgo closing the school in favor of getting rid of the schoolmaster. To develop this new strategy he must have known about the brouhaha at Nailsea, and he must have watched very closely the controversy that rocked neighboring Wedmore and its school in the summer of 1798. At Wedmore, although laborers and the curate supported opening of the school, the farmers were not appeased by the Mores' soothing promises. They worried that the school would undermine deference for the propertied and predicted that "the day the school was opened there would be the beginning of such rebellion in England as had taken place in Ireland and France."[31] Ironically to forestall a violent reaction by disappointed laborers against their stubborn employers, Hannah More defied the farmers and set up a school under Mr. Harvard, a dedicated and forceful Methodist. Harvard was as indiscreet as Younge, however, and quickly inflamed the already tense situation with his heterodox opinions. After a long, hot summer, the farmers complained directly to the Dean of Wells about Harvard's derogatory remarks about bishops, his fire-and-brimstone rhetoric, and his distribution of Methodist brochures. To stem this offensive "Hannah was obliged to write letters to Dr. Moss and other high powers, and use all her influence" to keep the school open.[32]

In the meantime, the farmers set up an alternative school and told the Mores' clientele to send their children to this school if they wanted to keep their jobs. To attract their students back the sisters replaced Harvard with a schoolmistress in the hope that a seemingly self-effacing woman "might soften these barbarians."[33] Harvard's dismissal pleased the farmers, but did nothing for the school, which the sisters considered moribund by 1800.

To get rid of Younge and to debilitate the Blagdon school, Bere followed the farmers of Wedmore. He at first spread "malicious tales" which tarred Younge as an enthusiast and

---

[31]Roberts, *Mendip Annals*, p.212; Jones, *Hannah More*, p.169.
[32]Roberts, *Mendip Annals*, p.225; Jones, *Hannah More*, pp.169-70.
[33]Roberts, *Mendip Annals*, p.226; Jones, *Hannah More*, p.170.

then bribed parishioners to spy on their dour teacher. By April of 1800, Bere had enough evidence of unlicensed preaching to bury Younge and tersely told the Mores that he would publish the charges if the Mores retained Younge. Patty More portrayed the curate in Satanic terms, writing that "the curate and justice no longer concealed the cloven foot, but broke out in great fury against poor Younge, our schoolmaster, by getting a loose, silly lad to swear a false oath to the prejudice of his character."[34]

The Mores were ready to play rough, although with chivalrous knights-errant. Hannah More and her sister Patty were in London when Bere launched his second attack in April.[35] They found Bere's complaint against Younge "short and impudent" because it demanded Younge's dismissal before the schoolmaster could "plead his own case, or relate his own tale." To put Bere in his proper place Hannah turned to her male friends among London's elite, "both Members of Parliament and Bishops . . . [who] were . . . disgusted with the haughty proceedings of the Somersetshire justice."[36]

Upon returning from London, Hannah More selected a male champion, the Reverend Sir Abraham Elton, a Evangelical clergyman, local JP, and large mineowner. Ostensibly, Elton was to investigate the charges against Younge and to mediate the dispute with Bere. He was to be an objective judge, but More knew that he would vindicate Younge.[37]

Bere was not mollified by Elton's stalling mission and sent to the rector of Blagdon, Dr. Crossman, thirteen depositions charging Younge with unlicensed preaching. Crossman characteristically shrank from any fracas, and it came as no surprise that the spineless rector passed the buck to the elderly Bishop of Bath and Wells whose son, Dr. Moss, handled most of his

---

[34]Roberts, *Mendip Annals*, p.227.

[35]The surviving evidence indicates that the Mores stayed in London through at least the middle of May. See the letter mailed from London from Hannah More to Hester Thrale Piozzi, 15 May 1800, The John Rylands University Library of Manchester, English Mss. 556, fo.153. There is no mention of Hannah More's problems in Blagdon in this letter.

[36]Roberts, *Mendip Annals*, p.228.

[37]Ibid.; *Brown, Fathers of the Victorians*, p.196.

business. Both Mosses knew and liked the Mores,[38] but the Bishop and his son did not like the behavior of Younge as portrayed in the depositions. They advised Hannah More to transfer Younge somewhere else to defuse this crisis, a decision which had satisfied the Bishop in Wedmore.[39]

The Mores knew that Bere would not stop at Younge's dismissal and, while conversing with the Mosses, decided to turn up the pressure on their adversary. Eager to silence Bere once and for all, Hannah More understood that spirited engagement was more persuasive coming from a man than a woman. She thus enlisted the Reverend Sir Abraham to deliver a damning polemic against Bere at the Shipham school before, among others, her womens' clubs and twelve Anglican clergymen. In his sermon, Elton portrayed Bere as a Socinian and declared that Bere, not Younge, ought to be charged with "penal statutes." Elton's speech swayed "the people" once again against the curate of Blagdon. To Patty More, "it was Sir A.'s talents and rank in life, . . . which produced the change, not genuine conviction that their own credulity had been produced by secret enmity to the cause of religion."[40] Elton's greatest and most popular talent was acting as an aggressive protector of aggrieved female victims. Elton's posturing in a familiar heroic role probably attracted many nominal Christians who would otherwise have supported Bere.

Bolstered by Elton's success,[41] Hannah More secretly relayed the mineowner's case against Bere to the Mosses in June of 1800. Her temporary switch from victim to victimizer, however, cost her some momentum from Elton's triumph. The bombshell of Bere's potential Unitarianism only made the hierarchy dither; Crossman and the Mosses kept shuffling More's secret file on Bere back and forth between their offices. Hannah More also overplayed her hand with the covert offensive of June.

---

[38]Hannah More to her sisters, 1800, Roberts, *Memoirs* vol.3, p.107.

[39]Brown, *Fathers of the Victorians*, p.197.

[40]Roberts, *Mendip Annals*, p.229.

[41]The unconditional support of male friends such as Henry Thornton also raised her spirits. For an example of this support, see the letter excerpted in Standish Meacham, *Henry Thornton of Clapham, 1760-1815* (Cambridge, Mass.: Harvard University Press, 1964), p.48.

Amazed by her unexpected audacity and alarmed by the strong evidence against Younge, the Mosses finally pressured the Mores to transfer the schoolmaster to tutoring the children of a rich Evangelical family in Ireland.[42]

To rebound from this loss of face, More turned again to her champion the Reverend Sir Abraham. The mineowner demanded that Bere make his charges against Younge public, although Elton said nothing (or knew nothing as Ford K. Brown suggests) about More's clandestine transmission of the case against Bere. In response, Bere pointed to the recent diocesan decision and reiterated that he had forgiven his enemies. Infuriated by Bere's smugness, Elton, not More this time, petitioned Crossman and the Mosses to order the formal publication by the curate of the charges against Younge. The hierarchy endorsed Elton's petition, feeling that any further publicity was moot with Younge safely in Ireland.[43]

The Mosses' endorsement was reasonable; it also inad-vertantly led to the most vindictive spectacle of this entire affair. On 12 November 1800, Bere obeyed the episcopal order to publish the charges and convened a meeting of locally promi-nent friends at the George Inn in Blagdon to weigh the accusa-tions and testimonies against Younge. The participants in this kangaroo court were long-time opponents of Sunday schools, and its chair was Colonel Francis Whalley, an unregenerate Squire Western. The Mores were troubled by the presence of Hilary Addington, the brother of the soon-to-be prime minister, on this "court" and immediately began to cultivate him. The Mores were ultimately successful in wooing Addington through dinners and conversations,[44] but at this meeting he joined the other "judges" in finding Younge guilty of extempore prayer and unlicensed preaching. The "judges" urged the Mores to guarantee that Younge would never work at Blagdon again.[45]

Hannah More privately exploded and then closed the Blag-don school on 16 November. This move was perhaps a petulant

---

[42]Brown, *Fathers of the Victorians*, p.197-8.

[43]Ibid.

[44]Hannah More to Eva Garrick, 31 January 1803, The Pierpont Morgan Library, New York, R-V Autographs Misc. English, MA 3751.

[45]Brown, *Fathers of the Victorians*, pp.197-8.

overreaction, but it crafted the diocesan perception that Hannah More was the put-upon victim who promptly needed the Bishop's help. Bere inadvertantly abetted the Mores' injured image with a garish celebration of his victory replete with pealing church bells and ebullient illuminations. News of Hannah More's plight and Bere's arrogance reached the Mosses, who happened to be in London that December. The messengers of this information, no doubt, were the prominent Bishops and MPs who had lined up with the Mores in April. The representation of Hannah More as prey seemed to stick among aristocrats and literati. Even Hester Thrale Piozzi, hardly a friend of Hannah More, wondered: "What can have inspired any countryman of mine to debase his Profession And Birthplace by an Endeavour to traduce that admirable creature Hannah More?" Piozzi warned that if Bere's "vile detractions should injure her feeble health, the mischief done would be past . . . [her] computation."[46]

Self-interest at the highest levels complemented sympathy for Hannah More and her sisters. Ford K. Brown suggests that Wilberforce, Porteus, Barrington, *et al.* also bribed the Mosses, notorious yet not unconventional for their cupidity, with promises of patronage if they would help the Mores. The Evangelical interest emphasized to their guests that disciplining Bere could be both lucrative and just.[47]

The sisters as perceived victims thus gave cover to the naked venality of the Mosses. In January of 1801, the Mosses had Dr. Crossman first reprimand Bere for his ungentlemanly gloating and then insist upon Bere's resignation because of his allegedly anti-trinitarian views. The Bishop and his son also encouraged Hannah to reopen the school, which she did on 25 January. Bere was astonished by this change in fortune and refused to resign. Crossman then formally fired him on 2 February. Bere still refused to resign or accept Crossman's decision and appealed to the Mosses, who were unexpectedly obdurate.[48]

[46]Hester Thrale Piozzi to the Reverend Thomas Sedgwick Whalley, 30 December 1800, The Henry W. and Albert A. Berg Collection, The New York Public Library, Astor, Lenox and Tilden Foundations.
[47]c.f. Jones, *Hannah More*, p.174; Brown, *Fathers of the Victorians*, pp.198-9.
[48]c.f. Brown, *Fathers of the Victorians*, p.200.

After the Mosses seconded Crossman, the embattled curate turned to public opinion. He portrayed himself as the victim of a shadowy puritanical faction at court, pointing out the behind-the-scenes, feminine nature of the conspiracy against him. Ford K. Brown sympathizes with Bere here, noting that "he had never been confronted with his accusers or seen the charges against him."[49] Brown fails to realize, however, that if More barked her case in a public forum, she would have breached the rules of feminine conduct and thus would have been politically incorrect. In contrast, Bere's posturing as victim compromised his masculinity and probably cost him support in the short term. In a particularly egregious breach of gentlemanly etiquette, Bere published the letters between himself and the diocesan officials and further angered Crossman and the Mosses.

Yet Bere's exposure of a powerful, shadowy interest with a woman leader engaged and enraged the populist and vituperative writers for the *Anti-Jacobin Magazine* who could never countenance a "Bishop in Petticoats."[50] From its first issue in 1798, the *Anti-Jacobin Magazine* had never liked the idea of educating the poor and had routinely warned that the Church was in danger from what it labelled puritan fanatics or, in reality, Evangelical Anglicans.[51] Its contributors had exempted Hannah More, however, from criticism before her second fight with Bere became public. Indeed, it warmly received her latest work on female educational reform.[52] This kudo came from the pen of the exiled American loyalist Jonathan Boucher, who had set up similar schools to the Mores' for slaves in Virginia in the 1760s.[53]

In June and July of 1801, however, the *Anti-Jacobin* turned against More explicitly. The unnamed reviewer of Bere's first

---

[49]Ibid.

[50]A moniker coined by William Cobbett.

[51]In particular, see *Anti-Jacobin Review and Magazine*, 1(October, 1798), pp.398-402; 1(November, 1798), pp.550-60; 2(April, 1799), pp.361-71; 3(June, 1799), pp.177-80; 3(July, 1799), pp.319-22; 4(September, 1799), pp.33-5; Brown, *Fathers of the Victorians*, pp.157-8, 168-83.

[52]*Anti-Jacobin Review and Magazine*, 4(September, 1799), pp.190-99.

[53]For Boucher's schools, see Anne Y. Zimmer, *Jonathan Boucher: Loyalist in Exile* (Detroit: Wayne State University Press, 1978), p.57.

and second pamphlets (and of a hasty rebuttal by the Reverend Sir Abraham) identified the rabidly patriotic Hannah More with domestic and foreign treason. Her sex made the most inviting target. The reviewer was most uncomfortable with a woman defying a clergyman. More's stubbornness lowered Bere "to the state of a competitor or opponent, of a man [!] greatly beneath him, in the scale of society."[54] In other words, Bere was struggling with a woman who should have shown her deference for the Church and its clergymen by dismissing the schoolmaster immediately and without comment. To the reviewer, the diocesan officials disgraced themselves both as men and as priests by catering to this laywoman and her Methodist teacher. Crossman, in particular, shared More's "feminine" guile, whereas Bere was "a real man" who eschewed secrecy and manipulation.[55]

Elton, nevertheless, was the most ridiculous and duped man in the entire drama, according to the *Anti-Jacobin*. The reviewer ridiculed Elton's characterization of More as "a female Scipio." He found the mineowner's "adulation of Mrs. More . . . gross, fulsome, and offensive; it removes no imputation; it rebuts no argument; it confutes no fact; . . . it disgraces alike the object of it, and the person by whom it is lavished."[56] Elton's chivalry was "Quixotic," and the *Anti-Jacobin*, in a parody of feminism, thought More "ought not to have employed a champion, but to have manfully fought her own battle."[57] The reviewer must have known that More would have never left Bristol a generation ago if she had followed his dubious advice.

In its issue of August, 1801, the "cunning" of Hannah More became the focus of the *Anti-Jacobin's* fire. A review of two pamphlets favorable to Bere excerpts passages that suggest the Mores were fooling influential men through womanly gestures. Hannah More was really not the "pattern of female excellence and Christian charity" that she wanted the world to believe she was.[58] She was not an angelic virgin, but a dragon lady. Her

---

[54]*Anti-Jacobin Review and Magazine*, 9(July, 1801), p.280.
[55]Ibid., pp.278-82. c.f. Brown, *Fathers of the Victorians*, p.211.
[56]*Anti-Jacobin Review and Magazine*, 9(July, 1801), p.291.
[57]Ibid., p.295. c.f. Brown, *Fathers of the Victorians*, p.212.
[58]*Anti-Jacobin Review and Magazine*, 9(August, 1801), p.392.

duplicity, the reviewer argued, was most evident in her selection of the Reverend Sir Abraham as an allegedly impartial arbitrator. More knew that Elton and Bere had long been enemies. As the curate enforced the law, "she pushes Sir Abraham forward, without one blush of shame on her cheek, for having mentioned him as a common friend and a fair referee before, to be her pleading, her writing advocate, her very strenuous champion, her very zealous votary." With typical hyperbole, the *Anti-Jacobin* also noted that her ruthless chicanery violated the uniquely British right of due process by "the accusations clandestine in their production, concealed in their operation, even still concealed, and still clandestine to the very clergyman accused."[59]

Very disturbing to the *Anti-Jacobin* was the petticoat influence over the "reptilian" Dr. Crossman, the senile Bishop, and his opportunistic son. Hannah More had engineered "a most paradoxical union of prelacy with disunion." She was an evil witch who could "conjure up even good spirits, even the very angels of the church, to do her work of mischief for her." She posed "in all the glory of a good angel" yet an unlikely alliance with Satan enabled her "to . . . direct the storm upon the head of opposing worthiness itself."[60]

These public charges of undue feminine power forced the Mosses to reinstate Bere as the curate of Blagdon in September of 1801. Hannah More was not severely damaged by the *Anti-Jacobin*, since she was acting as a woman, whether angelic or demonic. The Mosses and their lackey Crossman, however, were weakened by the periodical's revelations which suggested to contemporaries that they were not acting as men. To control damage to his image the Bishop subtly admitted that he had been misled by More and Elton and ordered the restoration of Bere. In response, Hannah More once again closed her school and hoped that the crisis would pass.[61]

Her hopes were unfounded. Newly confident of episcopal support or, at least, indifference, Bere and his malicious allies

---

[59]Ibid., p.393.
[60]Ibid., p.394.
[61]c.f. Brown, *Fathers of the Victorians*, p.209.

intensified their misogynist barbs against the Mores, "the Weird Sisters." It is true that Hannah More's supporters underscored the low Welsh origins and youthful republican sentiments of Bere in a shrill and shabby manner,[62] but they did not stoop as low as the ribald humor of the pro-Bere camp. In one of the latest apologies of the curate, Miss More became a whore who drew "within the vortex of her petticoat, numerous bodies of the regular Clergy of the land."[63] "Sir Abraham's Amazon" had always been a whore, "having not in her youth kept her mind in temperance, soberness, and chastity." The William Turner affair and the fortuitous annuity resurfaced in pro-Bere polemics as prime examples of the financial prostitution of "the renowned Scipio in petticoats."[64] To the defenders of Bere, Hannah More's alleged lewdness was not limited to her youth. "The Imperial Juno of Literature and Methodism"[65] was covertly yet not formally married to Dr. Crossman, a passive milksop who loved domineering women.[66] A secretly loose woman herself, "the Semiramis of the day" winked at fornication at her schools and remained silent about her male teachers molesting female students.[67]

Here the pro-Bere camp turned the shocking images of gender inversion associated with both Bourbon and revolutionary France against a woman who had helped to link gender inversion with both Bourbon and revolutionary France.[68] Dur-

---

[62]William Cobbett, the master of scurrility, ironically whimpered that "Bere and all his friends are abused without measure and without mercy; his relations, his wife, and even his parents are ridiculed." See Cobbett's *Weekly Political Register*, vol.1, 10(27 March 1802), p.301.

[63]Edward Spencer, *Truths, Respecting Mrs. Hannah More's Meeting-Houses, and the Conduct of Her Followers; Addressed to the Curate of Blagdon* (Bath: W. Meyler, 1802), p.48.

[64]Ibid., pp.6, 18.

[65]*Anti-Jacobin Review and Magazine*, 11(April, 1802), p.425.

[66]Rumors reached the highest circles in London that More had illegitimate children, either by Crossman or her old fiance William Turner. In particular, see the lemony entry of 15 February 1802 in Sylvester Douglas, *The Diaries of Sylvester Douglas* (Lord Glenbervie) vol.1, Francis Bickley, ed., (London: Constable & Co., 1928), p.316.

[67]Spencer, *Truths*, pp.6, 53-8.

[68]For a particularly lucid discussion of these images, see Joanne Schrader Chambliss, *The French Revolution, Gender, and the British Response: Toward a*

ing the 1780s, More and most writers had created images of effeminate socialites manipulated by salon hostesses who looked to Paris. During the 1790s, More and most loyalists had concocted odious images of politically active women who wanted to imitate the perceived sexual promiscuity and ambiguity of the new French republic. Hannah More had joined male loyalists in questioning the masculinity of radicals who could not control their women. The *Anti-Jacobin et al.* cynically made More the politically and sexually active virago and the Mosses and Crossman her mincing minions.

To defend her reputation against these outrageous assertions More once again relied upon influential male champions and kept quiet publically. She understood the power of at least the semblance of propriety. Thus Hannah More turned down the advice of the Lord Chancellor and the Bishop of London to take legal action and to reply personally to the pro-Bere onslaught.[69] She wanted to show everyone that she was not a virago, but a victim. Privately, she had no intention of being a real victim and encouraged the rebuttal of the *Anti-Jacobin* by the *British Critic*, the authoritative organ of the Anglican episcopacy.[70] She orchestrated the publication of friendly pamphlets written by others, directing the influential publishers Cadell and Davies to circulate uncritical testimonials by nine local parsons "as widely as" they could.[71]

Hannah More flattered the wavering with letters that underscored both the intensity of her philanthropy and the precariousness of her health.[72] She appreciated help from any quarter

---

More Complex Understanding of the Early Origins of Victorian Domesticity, Vanderbilt University M. A. thesis in history, 1989, pp.5-57.

[69]Wilberforce agreed with More's refusal to consult a lawyer and her abstention "altogether from publishing." See William Wilberforce to Hannah More, 11 December 1801, *The Correspondence of William Wilberforce* vol.1, Robert Issac and Samuel Wilberforce, eds., (London: J. Murray, 1840), p.234.

[70]See *British Critic*, 18(August, 1801), p.216; 19(January, 1802), pp.90-4; 19(April, 1802), p.439; 19(June, 1802), pp.663-4; 20(August, 1802), p.203. See also the Evangelical *Christian Observer*, 3(March, 1802), pp.180-5.

[71]Hannah More to Cadell and Davies, 27 July 1801, The Houghton Library, Harvard University, Autograph File. Excerpt reprinted by permission of the Houghton Library, Harvard University.

[72]For example, see Hannah More to the Reverend J. Stubbs,

and even entertained the Italian husband of Hester Thrale Piozzi whom she had tastelessly shunned twenty years before.[73] Although shaken and sickened by the stream of defamation, Hannah More felt sure she would prevail with well-connected male friends on her side.[74]

More was right to keep quiet and let her enemies hang themselves with excesses. The coarse misogyny of Bere and company was so outrageous that it backfired. The abuse crested in the summer of 1802 as the Reverend William Shaw, Rector of Chelvey, had More cavorting with two soldiers and an actor at the same time. The bawdy Rector himself presented an inviting target to the More camp; his ties to radicals and Unitarians revived concerns about Bere's anti-trinitarian sermons.[75] Yet it was his fictional pornography about the epitome of a proper lady that was politically untenable. Even the *Anti-Jacobin* in August, 1802 distanced itself from the gross invective of Shaw. The *Anti-Jacobin* felt sure that the Reverend Bere disapproved of these attacks on More's unimpeachable propriety, although no firm evidence suggests that he did.[76] With its acknowledgement of Hannah More as the victim, the conservative periodical's negative campaign petered out[77] and, in December of 1803, turned positive with a surprisingly upbeat report on

---

3 February 1802, Gratz Mss., R.L.S., The Historical Society of Pennsylvania, Philadelphia, Pennsylvania.

[73]Hester Thrale Piozzi to the Reverend Thomas Sedgwick Whalley, 23 April 1801, The Henry W. and Albert A. Berg Collection, The New York Public Library, Astor, Lenox and Tilden Foundations.

[74]For the poor state of Hannah's health, see Hannah More to William Wilberforce, 1801, Roberts, *Memoirs* vol.3, p.148; Hannah More to Mrs. Charles Grant, 19 January 1803, Gratz Mss., Case 11, Box 16, A.L.S., The Historical Society of Pennsylvania, Philadelphia, Pennsylvania. c.f. Jones, *Hannah More*, p.176.

[75]Brown, *Fathers of the Victorians*, pp.218, 220. Revealingly, radical and Unitarian periodicals took Bere's part. In particular, see *Monthly Review*, 35(June, 1801), pp.214-5; 35(August, 1801), pp.445-7; 37(February, 1802), pp.203-4. The Evangelical *Christian Observer* pointed out that the irony of the *Anti-Jacobin* championing a Jacobin. (3(March, 1802), p.184)

[76]*Anti-Jacobin Review and Magazine*, 12(August, 1802), p.444; Brown, *Fathers of the Victorians*, p.220.

[77]See the attenuated tone of *Anti-Jacobin Review and Magazine*, 15(May, 1803), pp.90-2. Although it was briefly joined by Cobbett's *Weekly Political Register*, vol.2, 4(31 July 1802), pp.119-22.

activities at one of the Mores' schools. According to the *Anti-Jacobin's* eyewitness, "here was no methodism.'"[78]

Hannah More also benefited from the death of the elder Moss in April of 1802 and the subsequent appointment of Dr. Richard Beadon to the see of Bath and Wells. She charmed the new Bishop with a self-effacing vindication of her schools and, in the words of her last biographer, "with becoming restraint she dealt briefly with the charges directed against herself."[79] She showed both maternal concern for the poor in her charge and resignation to anything the Bishop decided. Flattered by her obedience, Beadon graciously told Hannah More that she obviously had no need to defend her character before him. He told her that if she was "not a sincere and zealous friend to the constitutional establishment both in Church and State . . . [she was] one of the greatest hypocrites as well as one of the best writers in His Majesty's dominions."[80] Unlike the Mosses, Beadon was not threatened by public charges of undue feminine power and officially blessed her schools, although he wisely recommended that she not reopen the one in Blagdon.

Hannah More was the winner in the Blagdon Controversy even if she no longer operated a school in Blagdon. She weathered this storm largely because the public sympathized with her carefully crafted image as a lady in distress.[81] She went on to write the most popular works of a commercially successful career and ironically carried out her own Bere-like campaign in 1805-06 against the dissenting schools of Joseph Lancaster.[82]

---

[78]*Anti-Jacobin Review and Magazine*, 16(December, 1803), p.532; Brown, *Fathers of the Victorians*, p.221.

[79]Jones, *Hannah More*, p.177. Excerpt reprinted by permission of Cambridge University Press. All rights reserved. For More's lengthy vindication, see her letter to the Bishop of Bath and Wells, 1802, Roberts, *Memoirs* vol.3, pp.123-39. Roberts incorrectly dates this letter as "1801."

[80]The Bishop of Bath and Wells to Hannah More, 1802, Roberts, *Memoirs* vol.3, p.140; Jones, *Hannah More*, p.178.

[81]See also the suggestive words of Robin Reed Davis, *Anglican Evangelicalism and the Feminine Literary Tradition: From Hannah More to Charlotte Bronte*, Duke University Ph.D. in English, 1982, pp.67-8.

[82]For a concise summary of this campaign, see Jeremy Bentham to Samuel Bentham, 18 September 1806, *The Correspondence of Jeremy Bentham: January, 1802 to December, 1808*, vol.7, J.R. Dinwiddy, ed., (Oxford: Clarendon Press, 1988), pp.379-81.

In contrast, Bere relapsed into obscurity and remained a mere curate until his unnoticed death in 1814. Hannah More's success as a politician did not please Ford K. Brown, who thought her public posturing and private maneuvering did not place her "in a very good light."[83] One can only accept Brown's verdict if one disapproves of successful female politicians who finesse the social limitations placed upon women. Similarly, Hannah More's struggle as a prominent woman under fire is curiously overlooked by Mary G. Jones, who thinks she drew attacks largely because of her religion and her schools.[84] More knew that she was also attacked because of her sex, and her triumphant strategy took this reality into account.

---

[83]Brown, *Fathers of the Victorians*, p.226.
[84]Jones, *Hannah More*, p.179. See also Thomas Laqueur who contends that "the underlying question [in the Blagdon Controversy] remained the degree to which laymen might participate in certain aspects of the Church's work." (*Religion and Respectability*, p.75) The boldface and underline are mine.

Chapter VI

Firmness and Femininity

The bugbears of late Georgian treatises on female education were conventionally masculine attributes in women and conventionally feminine attributes in men. For most of the eighteenth century, commentators had lambasted the growing emphasis on teaching girls trivial accomplishments. Hannah More was foremost among those Jeremiahs and Esthers who held that fashionable curricula consisting of musical scales, dance steps, and floral arrangements stunted the intellectual and moral development of women. Such superficial training, pundits charged, rendered women incapable of performing their traditional roles of daughter, wife, and mother.[1]

Most disturbing to its critics, the cultivated artifice of female
· education blurred gender attributes and ruined native virtues. Feminine influence in the fashionable world encouraged what literati claimed to be alien and feminine traits in gentlemen. Writers observed firsthand that duplicitous conformity and infantile sentiment imported from France had reduced the free-born Englishman into a mincing dilettante.[2] Mary Wollstonecraft lampooned Bourbon monarchs and British soldiers who outdid their ladies in splendor of dress and poverty of discourse.[3] Partly in order to restore a serious and public-spirited

---

[1]For example, see Henry Mackenzie, *The Mirror* vol.2, 1779-80, (London: Parsons reprint, 1794), p.47; Thomas Day, *The History of Sandford and Merton: a Work intended for the Use of Children*, 1785, (New York: Evert Duyckinck, 1818), pp.126-7, 202-30; Veena P. Kasbekar, *Power Over Themselves: The Controversy about Female Education in England 1660-1820*, University of Cincinnati Ph.D. in English, 1980, pp.31, 70, 100, 103.

[2]Gerald Newman, *The Rise of English Nationalism: A Cultural History 1740-1830* (New York: St. Martin's Press, 1987), pp.80-4, 100-9.

[3]Mary Wollstonecraft, *Vindication of the Rights of Woman*, Miriam Brody, ed. (Harmondsworth: Penguin, 1986)[orig. pub. 1792], pp.97-9, 104-7, 145-7. See

manliness, both Wollstonecraft and More, her professed opponent, prescribed academic subjects and ethical instruction for girls. Only with mental exercise and inner discipline could women competently raise children and constructively converse with their fathers and husbands. Most critically, feminine influence informed by study would encourage "masculine" attributes such as rationality, intelligence, and patriotism in male patricians. Nevertheless, most reformers worried that "masculine" women were not an antidote to "effeminate" men. They shuddered at those female autodidacts such as Wollstonecraft who publically called for sexual equality under the law. They unfairly linked advocates of full citizenship for women to the Jacobins of Paris who ironically had beheaded overly assertive women during the Terror.[4]

Hannah More shared this common desire to enrich the education of young ladies without (at least publically) questioning masculine supremacy. Using the perceived extremism and personal foibles of Wollstonecraft for cover, she summarized in entertaining and marketable ways the usual criticisms of boarding schools for girls. Unlike most pundits, however, More eschewed glittering generalizations in favor of specific remedies. In three popular works published between 1799 and 1808, she not only explained the pedagogical causes for confusion over the definitions of female and male, but she also distinguished the ways in which children of both sexes could assume what she claimed to be ideal and separate gender attributes and roles.

---

also Mary Ann Radcliffe's bitter complaints about the displacement of women in traditionally female trades such as hatmaking and hairdressing by "effeminate" men. (*The Female Advocate, Or an Attempt to Recover the Rights of Woman from Male Usurpation,* 1799 in *The Memoirs of Mrs. Mary Ann Radcliffe; Familiar Letters to Her Female Friend* (Edinburgh: Manners & Miller, 1810)[Garland reprint, 1974], pp.405-7, 426, 428, 466-7)

[4]For example, see the Reverend Richard Polwhele, *The Unsex'd Females, A Poem* (London: Cadell & Davies, 1798)[Garland reprint, 1974], pp.7-14. This animus against aggressive, radical females had a visual dimension in vituperative prints and cartoons. See the furies, viragoes and she-males of loyalist artists as reproduced in David Bindman, *The Shadow of the Guillotine: Britain and the French Revolution* (London: British Museum Publications Ltd., 1989), pp.93, 103, 128-9, 158-9.

Most critically, the principles of Evangelical Anglicanism informed More's realistic reform agenda, one also necessarily adjusted to the anti-French hysteria during the Napoleonic Wars. According to More, if parents raised their daughters with the precepts of the religion of the heart, then women could complement and improve the lives of men as loyal subordinates, not as disloyal competitors. Such women could also expect a higher degree of respect and autonomy from newly converted husbands and fathers whom female example had influenced. In contrast, devotees of French permissiveness such as Madame de Stael, More wrote, disturbed male lives and, thus, decreased male respect for the dignity and independence of women.

More, nevertheless, minimized sexual differences in these mature works. She recommended ascetic and godly virtues regardless of gender. She defended ancient models of Christian androgyny. Through conventional appeals to gender differences, however, More tried to make consistent her often contradictory views of sexual ambiguity. But the stronger she wanted to sunder sex roles and characteristics, the stronger she seemed to erode the rationale for the gender hierarchy. More attempted to disinfect female education reform of androgyny, but she unintentionally blurred distinctions between the sexes. [5]

In the early spring of 1799, Hannah More published her *Strictures on the Modern System of Female Education with a View to the Principles and Conduct of Women of Rank and Fortune*. She had been writing this book for some time. The *Cheap Repository* and Sunday schools had distracted her, delaying the date of publication. [6] In a sense, her *Strictures* is an overdue sequel to her *Thoughts* and *Estimate*. The stated goal of her *Strictures* matches those of her previous essays directed to the wealthy and powerful. Typical of Evangelicals, More garrulously reiterated that the privileged must restore the religious basis of English society

---

[5]This chapter in particular answers Mitzi Myers' indirect call for a study of Hannah More's "complex rhetorical counterpoint." ("Reform or Ruin: A Revolution in Female Manners," in Henry Payne, ed., *Studies in Eighteenth Century Culture*, vol.11, 1982, p.209.)

[6]For the making of More's *Strictures*, see Mary G. Jones, *Hannah More* (Cambridge: Cambridge University Press, 1952), p.114.

through setting an example of godly living for their dependents to follow. Her *Strictures* do more than beat a dead horse, however. Unlike male Evangelicals, More identified women of leisure as the prime catalysts for beneficial change, vigorously appealing to debutantes and dowagers alike to commence the process of moral reform.

More stressed the extensive effects of female influence on society. This emphasis was confused and rambling. She never precisely defined the elusive word influence. Her inquiry seems to assume, nonetheless, that influence was the power of individuals to produce results without the exertion of physical force or authority and, thus, was well-suited for what eighteenth-century Europeans thought was the physically weaker sex. The origins of this power lay in birth, wealth, or ability. When More wrote "female" and discussed female influence, she referred exclusively to privileged ladies who she thought could dictate male behavior.[7] In contrast, advocates for legal equality for women such as Mary Wollstonecraft and Mary Hays tended to depreciate female influence on male-dominated society and to lament the baleful influence of male authority on female minds.[8]

More did not deny that men often abused their powers over women, but she was not as blind as Wollstonecraft and Hays to the innovative and covert ways that well-to-do women influenced powerful men. In Chippendale chairs and behind Oriental screens, ladies helped to shape male reputations and careers. Wielding real yet never institutional powers, the society matron

---

[7]c.f. the similar yet less cluttered stress on female influence by the anonymous "writer" of *The Female Aegis; or, The Duties of Women from Childhood to Old Age and in Most Situations of Life Exemplified* (London: Sampson Low, 1798)[Garland reprint, 1974] on pp. 1-4, 38-43. "Writer" is in ironical quotes because the *Aegis* is an almost literal plagiarism of the Evangelical Thomas Gisborne's *Enquiry into the Duties of the Female Sex* (1797); See also the Evangelical Elizabeth Hamilton's discussion of influence in her *Letters Addressed to the Daughter of Nobleman on the Formation of the Religious and Moral Principle* vol.1 (London: Cadell & Davies, 1806)[Garland reprint, 1974], pp.106-19.

[8]For example, see the Unitarian Mary Hays (a close friend of Wollstonecraft and Godwin) in her *Letters and Essays, Moral and Miscellaneous* (London: T. Knott, 1793)[Garland reprint, 1974], pp.19-30.

could humiliate those men who violated the rules of proper behavior in mixed company.

More thought that ladies often misused their subtle power to influence young gentlemen through encouraging the artifice and immorality that contemporaries associated with femininity in both sexes. Her blame of rich women for male effeminacy was a variation on the ancient theme in Christian and classical thought about luxury, "this vice of women," according to Tertullian.[9] To Christians and Jews, luxury, defined in Genesis 2-3 as anything unneeded, began when Eve ate a fruit which was unnecessary for nourishment and relief. In Christian writings, "Dame Luxury," a rich and subtly powerful daughter of Eve, tempts young male pilgrims with things unnecessary for nourishment and relief such as "the delights of the flesh" and, in extreme cases, with "unnatural crimes . . . in opposition to God" such as bestiality and sodomy.[10]

More did not worry about those homosexual men who, in molly-houses and urban parks, imitated affected and loose women,[11] but she was extremely concerned about young heterosexual men who, in mixed company, were only too willing to please affected and loose women. More complained that conventional hostesses gradually weakened the character of impressionable male adolescents, rendering them as yielding and superficial as their female counterparts. The nominal Christianity of most peeresses set the light and impious tone in the fashionable world. In conversations touching upon religion,

---

[9]Quoted in John Sekora, *Luxury: The Concept in Western Thought, Eden to Smollett* (Baltimore: The Johns Hopkins University Press, 1977), p.40.
[10]Sekora, *Luxury*, pp.43, 46. This view was not restricted to Christians in the eighteenth century. Jean Jacques Rousseau also blamed the ladies of Paris for luxury and subsequent moral decline. (Judith N. Shklar, *Men and Citizens* (Cambridge: Cambridge University Press, 1969), pp.144-5; Jean Bethke Elshtain, *Public Man, Private Woman: Women in Social and Political Thought* (Princeton: Princeton University Press, 1981), p.163)
[11]For homosexual effeminacy in Georgian Britain, see Randolph Trumbach, "London's Sodomites: Homosexual Behavior and Western Culture in the 18th Century," *Journal of Social History*, 11(1977), pp.12-3, 17-8, 22-4. Trumbach suggests that, contrary to popular contemporary opinion, most sodomites in eighteenth-century London did not imitate loose and affected women and were conventionally masculine.

the conventional lady frequently undercut her male guests' professed creed with "a faint tone, a studied ambiguity of phrase, and a certain expression in her countenance." [12]

Male Evangelicals in the drawing room usually encountered this subtle ridicule which tormented would-be suitors brought up as serious Christians. Especially mortifying to these gentleman, according to More, were young ladies who flirted with depraved duelists and, in turn, contemptuously dismissed Evangelical objectors to dueling. [13] More judged that female ridicule of male seriousness was far more damaging to the faith of young heterosexual men than nontheistic books or their own male friends. These young fellows resisted adverse masculine influence, but always succumbed to harmful female magnetism. A womanly smirk at a male expression of Evangelical religion "put all his resolution to flight." [14] Feminine sneers at religion were "light, keen, missile weapon[s which] the irresolute, unconfirmed Christian will find it harder to withstand, than the whole heavy artillery of infidelity united." [15] Since women determined male reputation in the fashionable world, then the hitherto Christian bachelor quickly jettisoned his principles for popularity.

More overestimated female power over male behavior here. Heterosexual men in Georgian Britain socialized primarily with other heterosexual men, not with women. Young bucks regularly dispensed (at least temporarily) with the moral and religious precepts of their childhood to please male friends. They

---

[12]Hannah More, *Strictures on the Modern System of Female Education with a View to the Principles and Conduct of Women of Rank and Fortune, The Works of Hannah More* vol.1 (Philadelphia: Woodward, 1832), p.314. c.f. the case of the young Henry Thornton whose uncomfortable evenings in 1782 spent with fashionable rich women strengthened his faith. (Standish Meacham, *Henry Thornton of Clapham, 1760-1815* (Cambridge, Mass.: Harvard University Press, 1964, pp.26-7)

[13]For a fictional example of a reluctant duelist (but not Evangelical) who goes along with the bloody game in order to please a woman, see Sir Walter Scott, *The Antiquary*, William Parker, ed., (London: J.M. Dent, 1969)[orig. pub. 1816], pp.184-5, 192.

[14]More, *Strictures, Works*, p.315.

[15]Ibid., p.314.

whored, gambled, and blasphemed usually without the slightest regard for what a dowager or debutante thought.[16]

Yet More was right to point out that both hostesses and rakes had deemed male piety as "effeminate," dissuading insecure youths from religion. She had helped to disseminate the increasingly conventional idea that women were more religious than men, but she contended that this contrast did not imply that religious men were petty milquetoasts who withdrew from the world. Her male friends of the Clapham Sect possessed the conventional attributes of masculinity; they "were patriotic, generous, broad-minded [within the confines of protestantism], decent, chivalrous, and free-spirited [again, within protestant limits!]."[17] Women of rank and influence were wrong to call persistently Christian men (and women) "mighty harmless good creature[s]," whispered in a mocking manner. More observed that this humiliation commonly persuaded boys (and probably quite a few tomboys) "secretly to vow, that . . . [they] will never be a good harmless creature."[18]

Through rewarding artifice and immorality, rich women fostered male effeminacy. The loss of aristocratic virility, according to More, came not through the Word, but through the preference of rich women for aristocratic men who were not "patriotic, generous, broad-minded, decent, chivalrous, and free-spirited."[19] This attack on the poor choice of men by ladies appears to be not unique at first glance. Alice Browne notes that "women's bad taste in men was sometimes blamed [in the eighteenth century] for encouraging male effeminacy; effeminate men who spend their time drinking tea with women are stock comic characters in the period," most notably in the frequently revived drama *Miss In Her Teens* (1747) by Hannah

---

[16]For examples of young men encouraging each other in licentious behavior, see the entries of 3 March 1772 and 12 January 1783 in Sylas Neville, *The Diary of Sylas Neville (1767-1788)*, Basil Cozens-Hardy, ed., (London: Oxford University Press, 1950), pp.151, 300.

[17]Norman Vance, *The Sinews of the Spirit: The Ideal of Christian Manliness in Victorian Literature and Religious Thought* (Cambridge: Cambridge University Press, 1985), p.8. Excerpt reprinted by permission of Cambridge University Press. All rights reserved.

[18]More, *Strictures, Works*, p.314.

[19]Vance, *Sinews of the Spirit*, p.8.

More's mentor David Garrick.[20] More did not see the humor, however, and cleverly projected the old argument that virtue in one sex was vice in the other against those who considered religious men effeminate. The *salonières* preferred blasphemous men who were passive, gullible, fussy, diplomatic, and who were "more disposed to expect attentions than to make advances."[21]

Related to this abuse of feminine influence, More argued, was the nonsensical slang used by aristocrats of both sexes. Eighteenth-century writers had long equated correct grammar with moral probity, high birth, and classically educated gentlemen.[22] To More, the fashionable, particularly gentlemen, lost caste when they repeated the hyperbolic metaphors and portmanteau nouns of society matrons. More repeatedly blamed rich women for the vacuous discourse of the fashionable world. Hampered by poor education, matrons lacked a wide or discriminating vocabulary. Limited by gender expectations, the rare literary lady "affected to talk below [her] natural and acquired powers of mind," hoping to please men.[23] In order to talk to rich women, men tried to outdo them in silly babble and behavior. More lamented that men "were too apt to consider the society of ladies as a scene in which they are rather to rest their understandings, than to exercise them."[24]

This masculine prattle was a commonplace of heterosexual courting. Those who dispensed with this foolish type of wooing suffered through questioning of their gender identities. More reported that most female arbiters of taste considered men who displayed their intellectual and religious interests in the company of women epicene, while characterizing a lady who

[20]Alice Browne, *The Eighteenth-Century Feminist Mind* (Brighton, Sussex: The Harvester Press, 1987), p.47.

[21]More, *Strictures, Works*, p.390.

[22]Olivia Smith, *The Politics of Language, 1791-1817* (Oxford: Clarendon Press, 1984), p.9. With her rooting for the straightforward vernacular of middling-sort male radicals, Smith overlooks the slang of fashionable ladies which elite grammarians such as Lord Monboddo had found as vulgar as that of tradesmen.

[23]More, *Strictures, Works*, p.370; c.f. *The Female Aegis*, pp.38-43, which blamed men for favoring and encouraging the most frivolous females. For examples of this feminine slang from the middle decades of the eighteenth century still common at its close, see Browne, *Feminist Mind*, p.105-6.

[24]More, *Strictures, Works*, p.369-70.

discussed books with men as unfeminine. Despite the Blue-stockings' mixed literary parties from the middle of the eighteenth century onward, malignant female influence contin-ued to create a dearth of intellectual conversation between affluent men and women at the turn of the century. Society matrons discouraged their guests from understanding them-selves or others.[25]

More did not think, however, that womanly influence was inherently bad. If used wisely, it was indispensable for any com-plex culture. She held the increasingly conventional idea that the degree of civilization, especially among men, depended upon female sentiments and habits. In turn, a society's treat-ment of women determined its degree of civilization.[26] More did not elaborate on these rather commonplace generaliza-tions. She did not specify the kind of treatment of women or the female sentiments and habits that spawned civilization. She did discern that few commentators realized the influence of female principles on male character even if most acknowledged the power of female elegance on the manners of men. More noted that most rich women were sufficiently conscious of their power to influence male manners and were "not backward in turning it to account."[27] She contended that they should use this power for proselytizing men rather than to refine dress and protocol. Radicals also wanted women to help facilitate the spread of ethics among men,[28] but More differed from them in

---

[25]c.f. Browne, *Feminist Mind*, pp.117-8; Katherine M. Rogers, *Feminism in Eighteenth-Century England* (Urbana, Ill.: University of Illinois Press, 1982), pp.31-2, 211.

[26]For Georgian writers who viewed women as a civilizing influence, see Browne, *Feminist Mind*, pp.28-9; Sylvana Tomaselli, "The Enlightenment Debate on Women," *History Workshop Journal*, 19(Autumn, 1985), pp.101-24.

[27]More, *Strictures, Works*, p.313; Nancy Armstrong, "The Rise of the Domestic Woman" in Nancy Armstrong and Leonard Tennenhouse, eds., *The Ideology of Conduct: Essays on Literature and the History of Sexuality* (London and New York: Methuen Press, 1987), p.130.

[28]See the radical Thomas Holcroft's strong heroine who almost goes through with a marriage to a rake in order to reform his morals and manners in *Anna St. Ives*, Peter Faulkner, ed., (London: Oxford University Press, 1970), p.137, 153-5, 185-9, 259-65. Anna finds it very difficult to reform the despicable Coke Clifton and leaves it to her true love Frank Henley to finally turn

hoping that women would spearhead a Christian, not merely secular, morality. She observed that those ladies who were often arrogant in worldly stratagems, however ethically prudent, were often diffident in their true Christian duties.

More wanted to transfer feminine confidence to godly matters. She thought that a switch to discriminate charity and heartfelt devotion would increase female influence in the long-term. In contrast, the current use of feminine power over men for levity and vanity, More contended, would lead eventually to the "Turkish" suppression of women. In Islamic countries, the moral and intellectual degradation of women was the greatest in the world because men paid adoration to the mere external charms of a woman. Muslim society enslaved women, and feminine influence in the Ottoman Empire had waned over the centuries.[29] More insisted that females in Britain enjoyed (or could enjoy) unprecedented blessings of education, protestant religion, and the delightful pleasures of relatively, if not legally, equal intercourse between the sexes. But women misemployed, More wrote, their peculiar privileges of living in England. Peeresses knew only too well how they determined sumptuary displays and tea-party manners. More held that "this [was] not enough." Dictating style only demeaned their high and holy calling as rich English women. More hoped that "women thus richly endowed with the bounties of Providence, will not

---

Clifton around. The reform that Anna and Frank had in mind for Clifton was purely a reasonable secular morality with little mention of Christianity.

[29]Islamic culture was "a traditional figure for otherness within British culture, perhaps as old as the crusades, but one that recurs with peculiar intensity in the late eighteenth and early nineteenth centuries," especially among women writers. (Donna Landry, *The Muses of Resistance: Laboring-Class Women's Poetry in Britain, 1739-1796* (Cambridge: Cambridge University Press, 1990), pp.267-8) See also the entry of October, 1797 about the Saracens and women in Elizabeth Lady Holland, *The Journal of Elizabeth Lady Holland (1791-1811)* vol.1, Earl of Ilchester, ed., (London: Longmans, Green, & Co., 1908), pp.157-8; Rogers, *Feminism*, pp.4, 93-4. On the other hand, More was tolerant, like most affluent Britons, of Turks that she met in person. In particular, see her extremely cordial meeting with the Porte's ambassador and his entourage in Hannah More to her sisters, 10 May 1786, Roberts, *Memoirs* vol.2, pp.21-2; c.f. the similarly comfortable chat between British aristocrats and senior officials at the Turkish Embassy in late December of 1793 in Sylvester Douglas, *The Diaries of Sylvester Douglas (Lord Glenbervie)* vol.1, Francis Bickley, ed., (London: Constable & Co., 1928), pp.31-2.

content themselves with polishing when they are able to reform; with entertaining when they may awaken; and with captivating for a day, when they may bring into action powers of which the effects may be commensurate with eternity."[30]

More stressed that this beneficial female influence was especially needed "in this moment of alarm and peril" during the fight with successive French dictatorships. She cautioned her readers that polemics "of infidelity in Great Britain [were] at this moment principally directed against the female breast." Although the Terror had finally discredited "the doctrines of Voltaire and their associates," the purveyors of disbelief were "now attempting to attain their object under the close and more artificial veil of German literature."[31]

More was reacting here to a late flowering of narcissistic sensibility in the German states popularized and promoted in Britain by the radical novelist Elizabeth Inchbald and, to a lesser extent, the young Walter Scott. German writers of the late 1790s hated the French (and their invasion of the Rhineland) as much as Hannah did, but reflected the prerevolutionary cult of sensibility based in Paris. The dramas of August von Kotzebue, in particular, celebrated the selfish neglect of duty and glorified adultery as self-expression. More's disdain for Kotzebue and revivals of Goethe's *Sorrows of Werther* was not unique. The Unitarian Mary Hays attacked the Germans for reflecting the vapidity of the conversation of the old regime. Anglicans Maria Edgeworth and Jane Austen satirized the extreme individualism of German sentiment in their novels. Uniquely vehement, nevertheless, was More's insistence on the power of these German writers to sway feminine minds against established institutions.[32]

---

[30]More, *Strictures, Works,* p.313; c.f. Lynne Agress, *The Feminine Irony: Women on Women in Early-Nineteenth-Century English Literature* (Cranbury, N.J: Associated University Presses, 1978), pp.61, 67.

[31]More, *Strictures, Works,* p.319.

[32]Gary Kelly, *The English Jacobin Novel 1780-1805* (Oxford: Clarendon Press, 1976), pp.65, 113; idem., *English Fiction of the Romantic Period 1789-1830* (London: Longman, 1989), pp.77, 129; Marilyn Butler, *Romantics, Rebels, and Revolutionaries: English Literature and Its Background 1760-1830* (Oxford: Oxford University Press, 1981), pp.4, 72-5, 107, 157; idem., *Jane Austen and the War of Ideas* (Oxford: Clarendon Press, 1975), pp.92-3, 114-20, 229-36;

Hannah More linked the alleged tolerance of adultery by fashionable ladies in part to the "German school," agreeing with the observations of John Bowles, the token High Church-man of the Clapham Sect.[33] This link was at best tenuous. Lady Elizabeth Holland, a notorious adulteress and divorcee, hated German plays as much as More did and felt that their hyper-bolic egoism merely compensated for the dullness of Teutonic town life. No one with any taste, Lady Holland wrote, would be influenced by such "harlequin farce."[34] Since More did not overestimate the taste of female aristocrats, however, she did not dismiss the threat of these plays to genteel minds so readily. Ever the prophetess, she called upon aristocratic women "in a warning voice" to quit reading this trash and to "contribute their full and fair proportion towards the saving of their country."[35]

More called aristocratic women to come forward without losing their privileges of class and qualities of sex. She exhorted them to use the most appropriate way of their power—that is, to increase public morals and to lead a religious revival. More characterized these callings as customary and almost constitu-tional. Female influence determined the health of exclusively British institutions and attributes. At war now with "the tremendous confederacies against religion, and order, and

Ernest A. Baker, *The History of the English Novel, Volume V: The Novels of Senti-ment and the Gothic Romance* (New York: Barnes & Noble, 1961)[orig. pub. 1929], p.152; idem, *The History of the English Novel, Volume VI: Edgeworth, Austen, and Scott* (New York: Barnes & Noble, 1961)[orig. pub. 1929], p.126; Hays, *Letters and Essays*, pp.93-4; Maria Edgeworth, *Castle Rackrent*, George Watson, ed., (London: Oxford University Press, 1964)[orig. pub. 1800], pp.65-6; Jane Austen, *Mansfield Park*, Tony Tanner, ed., (Harmondsworth: Penguin Press, 1985)[orig. pub. 1814], pp.147-218.

[33]John Bowles, *Reflections at the Conclusion of the War* (London: F. & C. Riving-ton, 1800, p.72. Ironically, Bowles wrapped his call for feminine morality in a well-received appeal for the restoration of the Bourbons, a dynasty that nearly all English intellectuals had associated with the most egregious vices prior to the war. Other moralists besides Bowles and More linked the perceived rise in adultery to the general increase in accessible fiction, not only to the German imports. (Kelly, *English Fiction*, p.8.)

[34]See the entry for 20 November 1798 in Lady Holland, *Journal* vol.1, pp.211-2. See also the entries for 11 May and 27 June 1792, 1 November 1797, idem., pp.6-7, 11, 166-7.

[35]More, *Strictures, Works*, p.313.

governments, which the world ever saw," what England needed was for rich women to exert themselves with a "patriotism both firm and feminine, for the general good!"[36]

More emphasized that she was not calling for Amazonian warriors or politicians. She wanted British women to serve their country in natural and customary ways. More underscored that her ideology asserted sexual differences while she alleged (incorrectly!) that Mary Wollstonecraft wanted women to become men with full citizenship. According to More, to maximize their influence women ought to adopt the salutary aspects of their gender role. For instance, she wrote that they should not be as carnal as men. It should be noted that More as an Evangelical certainly did not countenance male promiscuity, but she accepted the commonplace (at least here) that "real" women were asexual and "real" men were not. Indeed, this stress on "feminine" chastity was certainly not a new or atypical idea; most conduct books "equated 'natural' femininity with passive asexual virtue."[37] Unlike John Bowles and most other male commentators who celebrated a self-effacing womanly modesty,[38] however, More viewed feminine chastity or, for wives, fidelity as a springboard for the exercise of feminine power. To her, sexual propriety bestowed to women the moral authority and legitimacy to censor the wicked, especially evil men. She did not go on to note that virginity freed single women such as herself from the encumbrances of a husband, children, and venereal and puerperal disease, but she did emphasize that asexuality or, secondarily, a companionate marriage was to powerful women as action was to the orator—"it is the first, the second, the third requisite."[39]

---

[36]Ibid, p.313; c.f. Mary Poovey, *The Proper Lady and the Woman Writer: Ideology as Style in the Works of Mary Wollstonecraft, Mary Shelly, and Jane Austen* (Chicago: University of Chicago Press, 1984), p.33.

[37]Vivien Jones, ed., *Women in the Eighteenth Century; Construction of Femininity* (London: Routledge, 1990), p.57. See also Rogers, *Feminism*, p.9, 240-2; Armstrong, "Domestic Women," p.104.

[38]For example, see Bowles, *Reflections*, pp.71-4. For the general stress on this type of modesty in conduct books, see William St. Clair, *The Godwins and the Shelleys: The Biography of a Family* (New York: W. W. Norton, 1989), p.506.

[39]More, *Strictures, Works*, p.313; c.f. Bonnie S. Anderson and Judith P. Zinsser, *A History of Their Own: Women In Europe from Prehistory to the Present,*

More contrasted this empowering prudery with the debilitating "lust" of Mary Wollstonecraft, judging that unlimited sexuality demeaned women in general. This unflattering allusion to Wollstonecraft, "a professed admirer and imitator of the German suicide Werter," was not singular; in the late 1790s her stormy personal life posed an inviting target for most opponents of legal equality for women. Nothing was off limits to Wollstonecraft's detractors—her close (yet platonic) friendship with the married artist Fuseli; her living with the American adventurer Gilbert Imlay without benefit of clergy (she wanted marriage even if he did not); her suicide attempts (after Imlay vacillated on a possible wedding); and even her recent death in 1797 of childbirth.[40]

More did not mention these unfortunate events, but she did shudder at Wollstonecraft's allegedly "direct vindication" of adultery in *The Wrongs of Woman: or, Maria*. In this novel published posthumously in 1798, the heroine Maria suffers through a horrific marriage full of sexual, physical, and verbal abuse. Maria leaves her husband George only to find that he hunts her down wherever she goes. George finally imprisons Maria in a mental institution and takes into custody their infant daughter who eventually dies from the lack of maternal care. Maria befriends Henry Darnford (and her prison guard Jemima) and they help Maria to escape from the private madhouse and George's control. Maria comes to consider Darnford her husband and "he solemnly pledge[s] himself as her protector—and

---

vol.2 (New York: Harper & Row, 1989), p.126-7. Proponents of legal equality for women also did not want women to pick up the bad habits that contemporaries thought were peculiar to men. For instance, Mary Hays condemned "masculine women" who "ape[d] ... the unrestrained passions, and the numberless improprieties of men," noting that "such are masculine in the worst sense of the word." (*Appeal to the Men of Great Britain in Behalf of Women* (London: J. Johnson & J. Bell, 1798[Garland reprint, 1984], pp.34-5.)

[40]More, *Strictures, Works*, pp.319-22. For an example of these philippics on Wollstonecraft's personal life, see Polwhele, *Unsex'd Females*, pp.24-31. Wollstonecraft was actually quite shy about sexual intimacy for most of her life. For her sexuality, see Eleanor Flexner, *Mary Wollstonecraft: A Biography* (New York: Coward, McCann & Geoghegan, 1972), pp.27, 54, 134, 136-9, 141-2, 185-202, 232-7; Claire Tomalin, *The Life and Death of Mary Wollstonecraft* (New York: Harcourt Brace Jovanovich, 1974), pp.13-20, 36-7, 56-62, 83, 85-6, 89-91, 118-22, 131, 145-50, 188, 205-13.

eternal friend." Defending her relationship with Darnford before a tribunal, Maria expresses Wollstonecraft's hope that both men and women could legally end bad marriages without difficulty.[41]

More bristled at this suggestion that women should imitate men who left, divorced, or simply cheated on unlovable spouses. She characterized any attempt to end the double standard as levelling the high moral standards of women to those of men. More did allow that women could and should borrow what she considered "good" masculine characteristics such as rationality and love of country, but she contended that the true taste and right principle in a woman came from instinctive knowledge of what a women was or could do. Adultery was not an option for a woman, even if men violated the conjugal vow with impunity. She wanted women to have authentic lives where they evinced passive asexuality. Ironically, so did Wollstonecraft before meeting Gilbert Imlay in revolutionary Paris.[42] More never met or wanted to meet an Imlay.

Buoyed by feminine sexual virtue, More wanted women to be feminine in their public advocacy of Evangelicalism. She wanted ladies especially to proselytize with " discretion," although in private she recommended this way to both men and women.[43] A fierce sectarian spirit in a woman was an unauthentic as a "female Machiavel" or a "warlike Thalestris," the mythical Amazon queen. More contended that "fierceness has made as few converts as the sword, and both are peculiarly ungraceful in a female."[44] The male profligate, she maintained, easily

---

[41]Mary Wollstonecraft, *The Wrongs of Women: or, Maria*, Janet Todd and Marilyn Butler, eds., *The Works of Mary Wollstonecraft* vol.1 (London: William Pickering, 1989), pp.75-184; Rogers, *Feminism*, pp.190-3; Jane Spencer, *The Rise of the Woman Novelist: From Aphra Behn to Jane Austen* (Oxford: Basil Blackwell, 1986), pp.132-7.

[42]c.f. Spencer, *Woman Novelist*, p.99-100.

[43]For instance, see Hannah More to William Wilberforce, 1795, in William Wilberforce Papers, Special Collections Department, Duke University Library, Durham, North Carolina.

[44]More, *Strictures, Works*, p.314; This was a point ironically echoed by the radical Mary Hays. She wrote that "know, however, that I come not in the garb of Amazon, to dispute the field right or wrong; but rather in the humble attire of a petitioner, willing to submit the cause, to him who is both judge and jury." *Appeal*, p.v.). The equally radical William Godwin had his

defeated the arguments of androgynous women by drawing attention to their unauthentic aspects. Such a rake was always disconcerted, however, by Evangelical ladies acting within their gender roles. Defend Christianity, More argues to rich women, always with a feminine spirit.

More stressed, nonetheless, that women should not be afraid to avow their faith publically. It is true that More worked within the system for gradual natural change. Yet she knew from personal experience in the 1770s that there were unsatisfactory ways of accommodation. Indeed, the nominal Christianity of ladies of rank hurt more than outright masculine depravity.

By what means could women become both feminine and influential? By which means could ladies learn to influence gentleman in a positive way? More's *Strictures* held out the promise of a comprehensive liberal and Christian education beginning in infancy for both sexes. She acknowledged that errors in the current way of education were not gender specific. She admitted that she had to talk about boys in reference to the training of girls, comparing herself to a geographer who canvassed the air, soil, and produce of one's country that a neighboring kingdom shared. For the purposes of this book, however, she had decided to limit her discussion mostly to the special nuances of female education.[45]

An Evangelical head-start for affluent girls would determine womanly potential and influence. More condemned Rousseau and the radical historian Catherine Macaulay Graham who had "decried the practice of early instilling religious knowledge into the minds of children," underscoring the importance of Christian education from cradle to grave.[46] She understood that the naive young "who [were] just launching on the ocean of life,

---

hero bedeviled by an "infernal Thalestris" in *Caleb Williams*, David McCracken, ed., (London: Oxford University Press, 1970), p.214. The "conservative" Mary Radcliffe, however, eagerly took off "the gentle garb of a female, and assuming some more masculine appearance" in order to draw attention to the plight of London prostitutes. (*Female Advocate*, p.399).

[45]More, *Strictures, Works*, p.311.

[46]Ibid., p.351; So did the *Female Aegis*, p.16. c.f. Agress, *Feminine Irony*, p.61. For Ms. Macaulay Graham, see her *Letter on Education with Observations on Religious and Metaphysical Subjects* (London: C. Dilly, 1790)[Garland reprint, 1974], pp.136-9.

[were] just about to lose their own right convictions."[47] Although soon immersed in fashionable or popular practices, properly educated teens were redeemable for Christ. As adults, they usually returned to the teachings of their childhood after tiring of the levity of the beau monde. If girls were not trained early, then they would learn through interaction with high society to reject serious Christianity permanently. If they had a inadequate or late education, then they would influence their brothers improperly.

Like nearly all writers of conduct books for young ladies, More glorified the mother's role in the early instruction of both daughters and sons. She wrote that "the great object to which YOU, who are or may be mothers, are more especially called, is the education of your children."[48] More maintained the commonplace that the cultivation of suitable gender behavior should form a large part of maternal inheritance. While even unbreeched, boys should be encouraged by their mothers to do those things deemed traditionally masculine. Girls, on the other hand, should look up to their mother as a role model.[49]

Yet God had delegated to mothers the primary responsibility for imparting the one thing needful to both their boys and girls. More lamented that too few aristocratic women exercised this maternal duty well, chastising maternal sponsorship of baby balls. Premature conspicuous consumption fostered by mothers precipitated a lasting love of luxury which enervated young ladies and emasculated young men. Hence, mothers had to become Evangelical; they had to undergo conversion. Only then could they instill in both sons and daughters that "religion

---

[47]More, *Strictures, Works*, p.312.

[48]Ibid., p.322 Poovey, *The Proper Lady*, p.29-30. This elevation of mothers' status was typical of Evangelicals. For example, see *The Female Aegis*, p.16. More, however, was unique in giving specific recommendations to mothers.

[49]c.f. the Quaker Priscilla Wakefield who maintained that there was "no reason for maintaining any sexual distinctions in the bodily exercises of [very young] children." To Wakefield, confining girls from infancy to sedentary activities was criminal. (*Reflections on the Present Condition of the Female Sex, with Suggestions for its Improvement* (J. Johnson, Darton, & Harvey, 1798) [Garland reprint, 1974], p.20.); the historian Catherine Macaulay Graham who also thought that "the sports and studies" of boys and girls should "be the same" in her *Letters on Education*, p.50.

[was] the only sure ground of morals; that private principle [was] the only solid basis of public virtue."[50] This maternal calling exceeded mere memorization of set prayers and doctrines at the family dinner table. More wanted the Evangelical mother to monitor closely the application of these precepts by her boys and girls in their separate (if overlapping) spheres.

More preferred converted mothers over hired teachers for children under eight, blaming tutors for later androgyny. She contended that Evangelical mothers were far less likely to emphasize trivial accomplishments than masters or governesses. Teachers made a girl learn easy or showy drivel because it was in their selfish interest. Comparing teachers to tenants at rack-rent, More perceived that they wanted "to bring an immediate revenue of praise and profit."[51] These teachers were all too common. Mary Russell Mitford recalled that her governess Miss Rowden made her and classmates perform "a play interspersed with songs, at the breaking-up time, to conclude with a grand ballet; so the specimens might be afforded of the vast improvement of her pupils to parents, uncles, guardians, grandmammas, and second cousins." Ironically, Miss Rowden's selection was *The Search After Happiness*, Hannah More's first play.[52]

Hannah More was far more alarmed by cynically ambitious teachers than Miss Mitford or most contemporaries and recommended prompt maternal intervention. To More, the conventional governess did not consider the permanent damage of their spurious curricula on their female pupils, let alone, on English masculinity. Most revealingly, many of them were foreign papists who naturally valued "a correct pronunciation and an elegant phraseology over piety and principle." More concluded that "the labours of a wise mother, anxious for her daughter's best interests," clashed with those of the teachers. She admitted that most women cherished their daughters' triumphs, however small. Unlike the teachers, nonetheless, their vested interest was the preemption of both "the vanity that

---

[50]More, *Strictures, Works*, p.322. c.f. Agress, *Feminine Irony*, pp.173-4.
[51]More, *Strictures, Works*, p.327.
[52]Mary Russell Mitford to Sir William Elford, 3 December 1813, R. Brimley Johnson, ed., *The Letters of Mary Russell Mitford* (New York: The Dial Press, 1925), pp.104-5.

admiration [for inconsequential feats] may excite," and the misbegotten appreciation of female influence that such vanity kindled.[53]

She told parents, "who [were] the lords of the soil," to fire these time-servers. Mother knew best. Maternal instruction for young children was crucial because "the best efforts of a careful education are often very remote; they are to be discovered in future scenes, and exhibited in as yet untried connexions." Mothers had the inclination to nurture over a long time; strangers on the make did not. Mothers could guide girls to the less glamorous but more central aspects of their gender roles. They could choke off the scourge of fashionable androgyny at its source. They could even reestablish the ability of authority figures to impose their will successfully in this age of revolutions. No longer would daughters unnaturally show "something of that spirit of independence, and disdain of control, which characteriz[ed] the times."[54] Mothers understood that female education could only build upon Evangelical principles taught early in life.

For older girls, More proposed a core of moral and religious subjects as the best route to equip them for marriage and motherhood. For adolescents, she evaded the controversy over whether home or school education was most conducive to learning, offering instead detailed practical hints about the selection and presentation of academic courses. Here More once again finessed the boundary between the conventional and the subversive. Her suggested topics—history, geography, philology, and religion—were standard feminine fare. Yet More

---

[53]More, *Strictures, Works*, p.327; c.f. *The Female Aegis* was not as harsh on teachers, and only told parents to be careful in their selection of teachers. (pp.145-6); c.f. the Quaker Priscilla Wakefield who urged parents to be especially careful of penniless refugees from revolutionary France who had flooded the teaching profession in her *Reflections*, pp.48-9. More does not share explicitly the evangelical horror at dance classes taught by ambitious teachers. For a typical revulsion at dancing tutorials, see the letter to the editor excerpted from *Evangelical Magazine and Missionary Chronicle* in *The Beauties of the Evangelical Magazine* vol.1. (Philadelphia: William Woodward, 1803), p.169.
[54]More, *Strictures, Works*, p.338.

wanted these disciplines taught in a most unladylike manner in order to ensure separate gender behavior in adulthood.[55]

More wished to make classes aimed at self-understanding demanding. She believed this raising of expectations for girls required not the usual abridgements and novels, but rather an undiluted diet of "great" books written by men. Mastery of simplified extracts gave women false pride in their achievements and made them gratuitously challenge better-educated men. She lamented that this type of teaching only seemed to confirm Swift's misogynist aphorism: "that after all her boasted acquirements, a women will, generally speaking, be found, to possess less of what is called learning than a common school boy."[56] Even ghastlier to More, the reign of compendiums at female boarding schools had cheapened the discourse of the privileged, regardless of sex.

More reserved, however, her most scorching criticism for the use of novels in the classroom. She pointedly echoed the standard Evangelical view that reading fiction inherently encouraged the artifice associated with femininity in both sexes. She worried about limiting girls to a genre dominated by women.[57] To More, girls who read only romance novels with nasty male villains and anti-patriarchal fantasies tended to have an inflated degree of self-worth. Even though More had written about strong women struggling with arrogant men in her own fiction and drama, her *Strictures* suggest that women novelists with their gynocentric plots were leading young ladies to advocate the fiction of sexual equality.[58]

---

[55]For the standard curriculum at female boarding schools, see Browne, *Feminists Minds*, pp.41-2.

[56]Ibid., p.345; c.f. Miriam Leranbaum, "'Mistresses of Orthodoxy:' Education in the Lives and Writings of Late Eighteenth-Century English Women Writers," *Proceedings of the American Philosophical Society*, 121(August, 1977), p.295.

[57]For the remarkable quantity and quality of eighteenth-century novels by women, see Dale Spender, *Mothers of the Novel: 100 Good Women Writers Before Jane Austen* (London: Pandora Press, 1986), pp.116-37; Spencer, *Woman Novelist*, pp.viii-xii, 3-22; F. G. Black, *The Epistolary Novel in the Late Eighteenth Century: A Descriptive and Bibliographical Study* (Eugene, Ore.: University of Oregon Press, 1940), p.8.

[58]See also the excepts from Maria Edgeworth, *Practical Education*, 1798, pp.296-7, 332-3 in Bridget Hill, *Eighteenth-Century Women: An Anthology* (London: George Allen & Unwin, 1984), pp.60-1. Nevertheless, More did not

More's *Strictures* prescribe a list of male classics to puncture these female illusions, "for showing them the possible powers of the human mind, you will bring them to see the littleness of their own; and surely to get acquainted with the mind, to regulate, to inform it; to show it its own ignorance and its own nature, does not seem the way to puff it up." Overlooking her own career, More insisted that there was no way that "this sort of reading will convert ladies into authors." If women read "great" male authors, then they will realize that they are incapable of "great" writing. Hack writing of romance novels for and by women would decrease if women were somewhat erudite.[59]

Biographies and histories, More hoped, would demonstrate to young ladies the perimeters of the permissible. The present method of teaching history, however, offered little help. More impugned the mere recitation of dates and names endured by young misses. She believed that instructors should go beyond memorization by rote. At her Park Street School in the 1760s, she had found that careful reading and discussion of documents enabled pupils to trace causes, motives "and accurately to observe the operations of the passions."[60] These exercises led girls to measure themselves against proper ladies and valiant saints celebrated in the chosen accounts, increasing self-knowledge. The most important lesson that More wanted students to grasp was the Evangelical commonplace of innate human corruption. Hence, she barred from syllabi ahistorical Enlightenment portraits of the noble savage, outlawing her own idealizations of African princes in the classroom.[61]

Self-knowledge also meant to More the appreciation of what she and the assigned male authors considered inherent female

---

explicitly blame bad marriages on the study of novels as other Evangelical commentators did. For example, *The Female Aegis* thought that novels "creat[ed] a susceptibility of impression and a premature warmth of young women into a sudden attachment to persons unworthy of their affection, and thus to hurry them into marriages terminating in unhappiness." (p.77)

[59]More, *Strictures, Works*, p.345; Browne, *Feminist Mind*, p.106; Rogers; *Feminism*, p.245.

[60]Ibid., p.346; c.f. Rogers, *Feminism*, p.210.

[61]More, *Strictures, Works*, p.346; for her idealization of Africans, see Hannah More, *The Slave Trade: A Poem, The Works of Hannah More* vol.1 (Philadelphia: Woodward, 1832), pp.27-30.

qualities. It meant understanding of why there was a gender hierarchy, of why women were subservient to men, of why women were women. History was a feminine discipline, More boasted, because humility, especially for women, was the result of historical study. Yet More's recommended exposure to young ladies to worlds beyond the domestic situations of romance carried potential dangers to masculine supremacy. As with teaching the poor to read in her Sunday schools, More forgot that along with the self-knowledge gained from history came critical thinking, a tool to shatter the very sexual archetypes that she so cleverly defended.[62]

Self-knowledge improves self-expression. More parlayed this truism in her *Strictures* to amend fashionable conversation through reform of female education. She complained that superficial reading in boarding schools led to inarticulate aris-tocrats, regardless of sex. The leisured spouted words and coined neologisms without knowing their meaning. Thus More counseled the turning of philology to moral purposes for young rich girls. Clarity of speech calibrated rectitude with no gray areas or subtleties. Definition lay at the root of personal probity. The most moral words to the xenophobic More, of course, were Anglo-Saxon. More wrote that "to this end I know no better method than to accustom young persons very early to a habit of defining common words and things." Feminine famil-iarity with the various definitions of English words in English "would improve the understanding more than barely to know what these words are called in French, Italian, or Latin."[63] Most critically, articulate women, More hoped, would modify the denatured banter of male philosophes. Privileged men needed to recover their frank and serious language. Britain's future

---

[62]More, *Strictures, Works*, pp.346-9; Mary Hays prescribed a very similar list of histories and biographies for young girls. But she wanted them to probe the borders of propriety rather than to accept them. (*Letters and Essays*, pp.97-8).

[63]More, *Strictures, Works*, p.350. The Augustan scholar Elizabeth Elstob made a similar argument about teaching women Anglo-Saxon ninety years before-hand as discussed in Browne, *Feminist Mind*, pp.99-100. The radical philolo-gist Horne Tooke also suggested the benefits of stern Anglo-Saxon words as discussed in Smith, *Politics of Language*, pp.110-153. c.f. the mild endorse-ment of teaching virtue through "the selection of apt moral sentences" in French in *The Female Aegis*, p.20.

depended on it. The doublespeak of posturing tribunes origi-
nated with the fuzziness of feminine vocabularies. The best way
to get male clarity was to reform female conversation and
education.

Joined with More's goal to make male speech less feminine
was her effort to make female patois more masculine. One of
the most nauseating results of a boarding school education, she
observed, was the overuse of interjections, epithets, and hyperbole by supposedly proper ladies. She condemned "the habit of
exaggerating trifles, together with the grand female failing of
excessive mutual flattery, and elaborate general professions of
fondness and attachment." Private letters between women, in
particular, needed to become less effusive; everything was not
so wonderful, *so* interesting, *so* boring etc.[64]

More even linked excessively feminine discourse to overly
intense friendships between two women, blasting schoolgirl
crushes on other girls. More did not shun what Carroll Smith-
Rosenberg has deemed "the female world of love and ritual" in
her own life, maintaining several fast friendships with other
women.[65] She had even lied three years before to preserve her
sister Patty's close emotional relationship with Selina Mills
from the marriage proposal of Zachary Macaulay.[66] Second
thoughts about Patty's crush on Selina and the More sisters'
ultimately unsuccessful attempt to facilitate it at all costs, how-

---

[64]c.f. the wry and similar discussion of female correspondents in Mary Russell
Mitford to Sir William Elford, 28 January 1812, *Letters of Mary Russell Mitford*,
pp.63-8.

[65]Carroll Smith-Rosenberg, "The Female World of Love and Ritual: Relations
between Women in Nineteenth-Century America," *Signs: Journal of Women in
Culture and Society* 1(Autumn, 1975), pp.1-29. For the various kinds of romantic friendships between Western women in the eighteenth and nineteenth
centuries, see also Lillian Faderman, *Surpassing the Love of Men: Romantic
Friendship and Love Between Women from the Renaissance to the Present* (New
York: William Morris & Co., 1989), pp.74-230; Martha Vicinus, *Independent
Women: Work and Community for Single Women 1850-1920* (Chicago: University
of Chicago Press, 1985), pp.157-162, 187-210; Browne, *Feminist Mind*, pp.43-
6; Sylvia Harcstark Myers, *Women, Friendship, and the Life of the Mind in
Eighteenth-Century England* (Oxford: Clarendon Press, 1990), pp.16-20.

[66]For the Mores and the Mills-Macaulay courtship, see Jones, *Hannah More*,
pp.129-32; Hopkins, *Hannah More*, p.13, 119; John Clive, *Macaulay: The Shaping of the Historian* (New York: Alfred A. Knopf, 1973), pp.10-2.

ever, probably led Hannah to judge that "imprudent and violent friendships [between girls were] the most dangerous snares to this simplicity [of language] . . . in those correspondence the young friends often encourages each other in the falsest notions of human life, and the most erroneous views of each other's character . . ." As adults, such girls were likely to lavish promiscuously "vows of everlasting attachment and exclusive fondness" on both male and female friends.[67] In order to stop this verbal pollution, Hannah More urged women to ape masculine simplicity. Ironically, she once again tied the inadequate training of girls to sexual ambiguity, while promoting unladylike force and energy for the conversation of young women.

Borrowing what her contemporaries deemed masculine ways has earned More ill-deserved criticism from at least one male feminist. In his otherwise excellent biography of Hester Thrale Piozzi (a literary acquaintance yet not a friend of Hannah More), William McCarthy congratulates Piozzi for writing like a woman in a man's world, while disparaging More's alleged writing as a man. Hester Piozzi was "intimate, social, and friendly," using hyperbole and apostrophe; Hannah More "shed her sex" by aping male writers.[68] McCarthy even suggests that "in her rhetoric More contrives to identify so entirely with institutional authority—the Parent, the Family, and especially Christianity— that she simply disappears into it, to reemerge as its Voice."[69] McCarthy forgets, however, that More did not echo the conventional father or Anglican most common among the British aristocracy. Unlike More, these men did not want to share "their" tools of self-understanding and were quite content to let ladies babble shallowly and fliply like Hester Piozzi. More subversively rearranged the language of men to help future Mrs. Piozzis clarify their thoughts. It was no coincidence that Mrs. Piozzi, despite her bitterness over More's disapproval of her second

---

[67]More, *Strictures, Works*, p.350; See also p.380.
[68]William McCarthy, *Hester Thrale Piozzi: Portrait of a Literary Woman* (Chapel Hill, N.C.: University of North Carolina Press, 1985), pp.210, 205.
[69]Ibid., p.201. Excerpt reprinted by permission of the University of North Carolina Press. All rights reserved.

husband, labeled More "the cleverest of all us Female wits."[70] And, most strikingly, More did not "shed her sex" in the style of the *Strictures*. This work is rather too conversational, being poorly organized and diffuse.

More chose to save the feminine emotion dispensed in the writing of letters and novels for Evangelical faith, "the most prominent part" of any satisfactory curricula. Indeed, the womanly penchant for sensibility, she claimed, facilitated the teaching of religion to girls. Thus instructors should broach Christian precepts to adolescent females "in a way which shall interest their feelings, by lively images, and by a warm practical application of what they read to their own hearts and circumstances."[71] Lecturing on dry systems was universally boring but was particularly unsuitable to reach the flowery sex. Formality was the recipe by which women saw faith as enslaving instead of liberating. If one taught the Word in a stuffy way to female children, then they came to regard adult independence as the end of their devotions. To More, young ladies "were more capable of being moved with what was simple and touching, and lively, than what was elaborate, abstruse, and unaffecting."[72]

Yet More also wanted to make feminine Christianity muscular. Teachers needed to make girls feel the lonely suffering as well as the ecstatic pleasure which accompanied conversion. Teachers should not sugarcoat Christian isolation for the delicate. In addition, women should not equate faith with feeling only. To More, girls needed what most writers considered "masculine" rationality to balance their natural enthusiasm. They needed to read the sermons of learned divines. They needed to discuss and analyze prayers as an excellent way for self-knowledge, which More defined as self-affirmation of instinctive and distinctive gender roles. In her *Strictures*, More wanted instructors to steer a middle and, in some ways,

---

[70]See the entry of 5 December 1787 in Hester Thrale Piozzi, *Thraliana: The Diary of Mrs. Hester Lynch Thrale (Later Mrs. Piozzi) 1784-1809* vol.2, Katherine C. Balderston, ed., (Oxford: Clarendon Press, 1951), p.699. Mrs. Piozzi also spent considerable time and money in facilitating the translation of More's *Village Politics* into her native Welsh. (*Thraliana* vol.2, p.898)

[71]More, *Strictures, Works*, p.355.

[72]Ibid.; c.f. the similar yet general remarks in *The Female Aegis*, p.17.

androgynous course between what she considered the "masculine" intellectualism of Anglicans and Unitarians and what she characterized as the "feminine" passion of Methodists. This fusion was to mold girls into "excellent women" serving the Lord, not "the indifferent men" proposed by Mary Wollstonecraft.[73]

The *Strictures* sold well, going through five editions and over 19,000 purchased copies.[74] Reviews were mixed. Many missed More's main points (possibly because of the book's diffuse organization.) John Wolcot, the London literary critic with the alias Peter Pindar, mercilessly roasted her verbosity without commenting on her content.[75] Most other pundits nitpicked More's vague doctrinal stands while ignoring her views on female education.[76] Careful readers of More, however, were sympathetic. The perceptive Elizabeth Montagu summarized approvingly More's thesis, predicting that

> If our women lose their domestic virtues, all *the charities* will be dissolved, *for which our country is a name so dear*; the men will become profligate, the public will be betrayed, and whatever has blessed or distinguished the English nation above our neighbors on the Continent will disappear.[77]

The *British Critic*, the organ of the Anglican episcopacy, generally approved of More's recommendations, but predictably insisted "that the female character derives its features and colors from that of the male, rather than the contrary."[78] The

---

[73]More, *Strictures, Works*, pp.355-63, 397-415. c.f. St. Clair, *Godwins and Shelleys*, p.507.

[74]Jones, *Hannah More*, p.119. In Wales Lady Eleanor Butler finished her copy of More's *Strictures* on 20 June 1799 without further comment in her diary as reprinted in Eva Mary Bell, ed., *The Hamwood Papers of the Ladies of Llangollen and Caroline Hamilton* (London: Macmillan, 1930), p.309.

[75]Jones, *Hannah More*, pp.120, 254. John Wolcot had always hated Hannah More largely because she was a female writer.

[76]For instance, see the Reverend Charles Daubeny (a friend of More's), *A Letter to Hannah More on some part of her late publication entitled Strictures on Female Education* (Bath: n.p., 1799).

[77]Elizabeth Montagu to Hannah More, May, 1799, Roberts, *Memoirs* vol.3, p.87; c.f. Barbara Taylor, *Eve and the New Jerusalem: Socialism and Feminism* (New York: Pantheon Books, 1983), p.14.

[78]Review of *Strictures on the Modern System of Female Education, with a View of the Principles and Conduct prevalent among Women of Rank and Fortune. By*

stodgy Dr. Charles Burney, no friend even to the faintest expressions of feminine power, recommended the *Strictures* unreservedly to his famous adult daughter, overlooking its somewhat subversive themes.[79] To her credit, Mary Berry, a friend of the late Horace Walpole, did not overlook these themes and found it "amazing, or rather it is not amazing, but impossible . . . [that Hannah More and Mary Wollstonecraft] agree on all the great points of female education." Berry speculated that "H. More will . . . be very angry when she hears this, though I would lay a wager that she [has] never read . . . [Wollstonecraft.]"[80]

The available evidence does not suggest that More realized how much she agreed with the disgraced Wollstonecraft, and the fragmentary nature of surviving documents makes it impossible to determine the direct influence of the *Strictures*. One can say that it gladdened the Evangelicals. Even Dr. Pretyman, the conventionally Anglican Bishop of Lincoln, was "confident that his sons [would] have better wives" because of the *Strictures*.[81] Furthermore, much to More's delight, the staid royal sisters intended to consult the *Strictures* frequently. Her old friend Mrs. Kennicott reported that the Princess Royal "hoped to make much use of [More's *Strictures*] in the education of her daughters."[82] Other royals did not. The wanton Prince of Wales and his gauche wife Caroline left their infant daughter Charlotte in the care of Lady Elgin, a spineless mediocrity.

Although hardly a knight-errant for learned women, King George III thought that Princess Charlotte, the presumptive heir to the throne, had to have a more extensive education than

Hannah More. Two Volumes. The Third Edition, British Critic 13 (June, 1799), p.644.

[79]Frances Burney to Mrs. Waddington, 20 April 1799 in Joyce Hemlow, ed., *The Journal and Letters of Frances Burney (Madame d'Arblay)* vol.4 (Oxford: Clarendon Press, 1973), p.277. See also Charles Burney to Hannah More, April, 1799, Roberts, *Memoirs* vol.3, pp.69-74.

[80]Mary Berry to an unknown correspondent, 2 April 1799, Lady Theresa Lewis, ed., *Extracts form the Journals and Correspondence of Miss Berry From the Year 1783 to 1852* vol.2 (London: Longmans, Green, and Co., 1865), pp.91-2.

[81]Dr. Pretyman to Hannah More, 5 July 1799, Roberts, *Memoirs* vol.3, p.94

[82]Mrs. Kennicott to Hannah More, 19 April 1799, Roberts, *Memoirs* vol.3, p.84.

most girls. He feuded in true Hanoverian fashion with his son who thought that conventional female education was sufficient for Charlotte. In early 1804, the Prince of Wales gave in to the King's wishes and entrusted Charlotte's instruction to John Fisher, the Bishop of Exeter, who proceeded to teach her Latin, a forbidden subject for ordinary proper ladies.[83]

Several months later, Dr. Robert Gray, prebendary of Durham and an old friend from Bristol, convinced More to write a guidebook to help Fisher to save Charlotte, the heir-presumptive to the throne, from the dangers of conventional female education.[84] In April of 1805 More published her *Hints toward forming the Character of a Young Princess*, developing her themes of the *Strictures*. Intrigued by this opportunity, she not only erected an outline to prepare "a providentially distinguished female" for the most masculine role of leader, but she also tried to clarify her earlier plans for a general improvement in the education of rich young ladies. Once again, however, she wallowed in imprecision and contradiction, trying to push innate sexual differences and androgyny at the same type.

This project presumed a degree of audacity on More's part. A schoolteacher's daughter from Bristol normally did not pontificate on the education of the second in line to the British throne. In the preface, More admitted that it was somewhat brash for any writer to tell the royal family what to do. She was mindful of the "extreme difficulty, as well as the delicacy of [her] present undertaking."[85]

The urgency of this task excused in her mind any unintentional arrogance. To More, the most weighty concern of the Christian West in 1805 was the training of the Princess Charlotte of Wales. It was much more than "a bone of contention" between George III and his son. The future use of the preroga-

---

[83]For the struggles and negotiations over Charlotte's education, see the entries of 17 and 23 December 1804 in Lord Glenbervie's *Diaries* vol.1, pp.411-4; Horace Twiss, *The Public and Private Life of Lord Chancellor Eldon, with Selections from His Correspondence* vol.1 (London: John Murray, 1846), pp.323-30. Lord Chancellor Eldon's biography is a particularly good source here because Eldon served as mediator between George III and his son.
[84]Jones, *Hannah More*, p.186.
[85]Hannah More, *Hints toward forming the Character of a Young Princess*, *The Works of Hannah More* vol.2 (Philadelphia: Woodward, 1832), p.5.

tive of the Crown was at stake.[86] She argued that the expressive freedoms peculiar to Britain countenanced open discussion of this crucial training. She thanked God that she did not have to emulate the Archbishop of Cambray whom French absolutism had driven " to the necessity of couching his instructions under a fictitious narrative, and of sheltering behind the veil of fable, the duties of a just sovereign, and the blessings of a good government."[87]

More also pointed to the lack of conduct books for princesses. She said that she would have never had to write her *Hints* if the royal pupil had been a prince. There were established and creditable courses of study for male royals, but there were none for princesses. Thus she suggested female role models and feminine styles of effective leadership as well as a rigorous curriculum fit for either a prince or a princess.[88]

In several chapters, More outlined her pedagogical program. Only in intensity did this educational curriculum differ from the earlier one that she had suggested for upper and middle class girls. She considered habitual self-denial the most important and tricky end of both royal and regular education. In a sense, this objective was especially urgent for Charlotte, a petulant, tomboyish nine-year-old.[89] In a deeper sense, More echoed in both her *Strictures* and *Hints* the primordial and

---

[86]The phrase "bone of contention" is used by Lord Glenbervie in his *Diaries* vol.1, p.412. Yet an earlier entry shows that Glenbervie shared More's deeper concerns, writing on 17 August 1802; "It is impossible to look at . . . [Charlotte] without thinking a little seriously of the future lot of herself and of the kingdom, which she may have to govern . . . Every look, gesture, word, and act of a child of her high destinies seems to be a fact worth noting and repeating." (*Diaries* vol.1, p.323)

[87]More, *Hints, Works*, p.6.

[88]Ibid. c.f. the radical historian Catherine Macaulay Graham who restricted her hints toward the education of a prince in her *Letters on Education*, pp.223-34. Nevertheless, More's assertion that no conduct books existed for princesses who would govern in the future is not true. For example, see the late medieval Christine de Pizan, *The Book of Three Virtues*, in Katharina M. Wilson, ed., *Medieval Women Writers* (Athens, Ga.: University of Georgia Press, 1984), pp.350-3; Jean Bethke Elshtain, *Woman and War* (New York: Basic Books, 1987), p.125.

[89]For the most recent biography of Princess Charlotte, see Dorothy Margaret Stuart, *Daughter of England: A New Study of Princess Charlotte of Wales and Her Family* (London: Macmillan, 1951.)

global equation of feminine with excesses of either nature or culture. Aristocratic society reflected both extremes of femininity, channeling whims of nature into shopping sprees for culture.[90] Tutors of girls from influential families, whether common or royal, had to insulate their charges from the fashionable with "the soundest, most rational, and . . . most religious education." They had to give their charges an acquired taste for the joys of Christian love and delayed gratification.[91] The inculcation of disciplined virtues, "which every one wishes to see promoted in the lowest ranks of society," were therefore imperative for the most powerful women in the land.[92] It was particularly imperative for future female monarchs to be both tamed and energized because the fates of millions depended on it.

As in her *Strictures*, More emphasized classes aimed at self-understanding rather than at self-indulgence. In doing so, she denigrated courses about Mother Nature and refined culture, the polarities of femininity. More chose passages from Francis Bacon for the princess, but she deemed the mysteries of biology superfluous and even dangerous for a female head of state. A future queen needed to distance herself from the intuition, instinct, and emotion that handicapped lower life forms such as

---

[90]Anthropologists have evidenced the transsocietal, transhistorical phenomenon of male=culture, female=nature. (Sherry B. Ortner, "Is Female to Male as Nature Is to Culture?," in Michael Zimbalist Rosaldo and Louise Lamphere, eds., *Woman, Culture, and Society* (Stanford: Stanford University Press, 1974), pp.67-87; Carolyn Merchant, *The Death of Nature: Women, Ecology, and the Scientific Revolution* (New York: Harper & Row, 1980), pp.xix, 1-41; L. J. Jordanova, "Natural Facts: A Historical Perspective on Science and Sexuality," in Carol P. MacCormick and Marilyn Strathern, eds., *Nature, Culture, and Gender* (Cambridge: Cambridge University Press, 1989), pp.42-69.) Nevertheless, Marilyn Strathern has clarified this phenomenon as males="moderate" mixture of nature and culture, female=excesses of either nature or culture. I find Strathern's revisions most credible. ("No Nature, No Culture: the Hagen Case," in MacCormick and Strathern, *Nature*, pp.176-91, 209-10) For other cogent criticisms off the allegedly universal association of femininity with nature as opposed to exclusively "masculine" culture, see Tomaselli, "Enlightenment Debate on Women," pp.101-24; Jean Bethke Elshtain, "Symmetry and Sophorics: A Critique of Feminist Accounts of Gender Development" in Barry Richards, ed., *Capitalism and Infancy: Essays on Psychoanalysis and Politics* (London:, 1984), pp.55-91.
[91]More, *Hints, Works*, p.7.
[92]Ibid., p.6.

plants, animals, and ordinary women. Natural knowledge would only bring out the wild woman in Charlotte. More wrote that "the royal personage must not be examining plants, when she should be studying laws,"[93] the premier products of masculine reason. The fine arts, a staple in the curricula for rich girls, also wasted valuable time and threatened disaster for a future queen. Studying music and painting, More believed, lessened the dignity of a sovereign whom patriots expected to put forth the aura of masculinity, regardless of the ruler's sex and temperament. Similarly, she ruled out exotic languages and popular novels, standard feminine fare, as distracting and corrupting. She permitted only didactic fiction such as expurgated Shakespeare and periodical essays by Addison and Johnson to seep into her litany of biographies and histories.[94]

The study of political and sacred histories was the fountain of monarchial virtue in More's *Hints*. To More, the past proved human corruption and female inferiority; the public record showed the workings of Providence and the choices of men (for the most part).[95] She emphasized that "history is the glass by which the royal mind should be dressed . . . to apply foregone examples to his own use; adopting what is excellent, shunning what is erroneous and omitting what is irrelevant!"[96] History was peculiarly crucial for a female royal. More judged that interpretation and exposure were the sources of self-improvement, but the sex and habits of a royal female largely excluded her from exposure. A wandering queen would be a national disgrace. A princess had, in a greater degree than her brothers, to depend upon knowledge in vicarious accounts. Although her personal experience had to be limited by her sex, her better-

---

[93]Ibid., p.9; Other commentators worried that botany was a veiled form of sex education, and demanded that it be dropped for encouraging promiscuity. For example, see Polwhele, *Unsex'd Females*, pp.8-9.

[94]c.f. Maurice Quinlan, *Victorian Prelude: A History of English Manners 1700-1830* (New York: Columbia University Press, 1941), p.146.

[95]But More devoted most of her *Hints* to discussing in some details the lives of eminent queens. Advocates of legal equality for women were less contradictory; they found that the lives of eminent women disproved innate female inferiority. For example, see Hays, *Appeal*, pp.34-5.

[96]More, *Hints, Works*, p.16.

ment from perusing primary sources written by men, More claimed, it was substantial.[97]

More's *Hints* has definite biases in the teaching of history. In assigning historians to Charlotte, More preferred Christian advocates over impartial journalists, although allowing bowderlized versions of pagan and skeptical authors. Historians such as Joinville were especially appropriate for impressionable young girls who read uncritically. More did not recommend the reciting of trivial facts and unrelated yarns common to the lesson plans of governesses. To the Evangelical More, Charlotte had not only to be culturally literate, but she also had to be able to trace the human decisions and efforts willed by God.[98]

More thought that Charlotte should have at least a cursory familiarity with antiquity, a masculine pursuit usually denied to young ladies. Given the recent perversion of terms such as liberty, equality, and property, Latin authors could help Charlotte "to be more accurate in her definitions, as well as more critically exact and elegant in the use of her own language."[99] Unlike most royal preceptors, however, More did not glorify classical culture. She highlighted the causes of Greco-Roman decline, noting that poor treatment of women was one of the destructive seeds.[100]

Yet More presented relatively recent English and European history as the centerpiece of her royal syllabi, picking role models for Charlotte to emulate. Quite expectedly, More believed that Charlotte would learn more from the triumphs and tragedies of queens rather than of kings. More, in particular, idolized the submissive Mary II, the wife of William of Orange. She held that Mary's "goodness was the most unostentatious, her gentleness the most unaffected, her piety the most inwoven into her habits,her charity the best principled, and her generosity the most discriminating!"[101] She approved of Mary's adroit handling of sycophants. She implored her audience to compare

---

[97]Ibid. pp.16-7.
[98]Ibid., pp.16, 254-31.
[99]Ibid., p.8.
[100]Ibid., p.22.
[101]Ibid., p.61.

the "forsaken deathbed of Elizabeth" with the family scene around the supine Mary.[102]

But More thought that Charlotte and, to a lesser degree, her other female readers would learn far more from the assertive Elizabeth than from Mary, devoting an entire chapter to the Virgin Queen. She stressed that Elizabeth's native intelligence blossomed through a masculine education. The last Tudor understood Greek authors such as Xenophon and Thucydides without translation, and quoted Scripture on demand.[103] Personal hardships helped, too. The judiciousness that Elizabeth had to exercise at the court of her Catholic half-sister taught her prudence. The ensuing quandaries impelled her to self-control. More attributed Elizabeth's tenacity in the face of papist aggression to that youthful self-discipline. To More, Elizabeth "probably never would have acquired such an ascendancy over the mind of others, had she not early learned so absolute a command over her own."[104] More concluded that "her early years [were] sedulously employed in laying a large stock of materials for governing well" during an "illustrious reign of forty-five years."[105]

Elizabeth usually overcame feminine weaknesses through her masculine upbringing. To More, Elizabeth's emotions were naturally intense due to her sex, and were not always under control. In some instances, More surmised that powerful "feminine" feelings in Elizabeth's psyche canceled out opposite "masculine" passions of equal ferocity. Through the direction of Providence, the queen's eventually dominant "masculine" mood generally favored the commonweal.[106] More also found that Elizabeth's superb and "manly" education attenuated her "feminine" favoritism, her intense passions, her violent attach-

---

[102]Ibid., p.35.
[103]Ibid., p.8; c.f. the disparaging reference to Queen Elizabeth's Latin in Hayes, *Appeal*, p.277.
[104]More, *Hints, Works*, p.33.
[105]Ibid., p.8.
[106]c.f. the similar portrait of Elizabeth in Sir Walter Scott's historical novel *Kenilworth*, W. M. Parker, ed., (London: J. M. Dent, 1969)[orig. pub. 1821], pp.177-95. For a lucid discussion of Scott's Elizabeth, see Baker, *History of English Novel, Volume VI*, pp.185-6, 214.

ments, and even her congenital cheapness.[107] Thanks to her
tutors, she picked effective ministers who respected her as an
intellectual equal. Male parliaments bore Elizabeth's "preemp-
tory" treatment of them because they found the interests of the
country were safe in her hands. More speculated that scholars
would not vaunt the reign of Elizabeth as an ideal use of executive power if ignorance had been coupled with her inherent
feminine liabilities (which More never clearly enumerated). She
admitted that Elizabeth fell short of conventional feminine
propriety. To More, "if we look at the woman, we shall see
much to blame." Yet as an instrument of an omniscient God
implementing the most strenuous undertakings in crises, Elizabeth was magnificent. Her "manliness" saved England from
the Armada.[108]

More wanted the princess to appreciate the tragedy of Elizabeth's last years. Vanity and deceit finally did the queen in;
More attributed Elizabeth's downfall to the victory of the
impetuous woman over the "manly" sovereign in her psyche.
The trenchant mind of Elizabeth did not protect her against
potent onslaughts of flattery. To More, the perils of adulation
escalated "when the female character [was] combined with the
royal." Elizabeth's "masculine spirit" was as susceptible to the
most transparent lines as the most frail of her sex. All her
commendable wariness could not see through male sycophants
who bet on the feminine prevailing over the masculine within
the queen's personality.[109] Here More also told Charlotte to be
on guard against flatterers of her own sex. The domineering
duchesses around Queen Anne influenced public policy unduly
because they knew how to push Her Majesty's sapphic but-

---

[107]Advocates of legal equality for women went beyond marveling at exceptional queens like Elizabeth. They argued that remarkable female sovereigns
with masculine educations proved that any woman with the same education
could "equal men in the sublime science of politicks." For example, see Hays,
Appeal, p.28.

[108]More, *Hints, Works*, p.34. In reference to Elizabeth's alleged hatred of war,
Hester Thrale Piozzi celebrated the "female" preference for peace.
(McCarthy, *Piozzi*, p.221)

[109]More, *Hints, Works*, p.47.

tons.[110] More found that these scoundrels gambled wisely because the woman in both Elizabeth and Anne won.

Indeed, More warned Charlotte not to emulate "feminine" monarchs, whether they be effete kings or impulsive queens. She condemned the bisexual James I for letting his male lovers run the government. In reference to James' public absolutism and his private idiosyncrasies, she suggested that "sovereigns the most arbitrary [unpredictable like Mother Nature] to their subjects, were themselves the tools of favourites."[111] Most purveyors of the divine right of kings did not escape More's censure. She stripped the appellation "the Great" from Louis XIV because of the Sun King's "feminine" love of pomp and luxury.[112]

More wanted Charlotte and her other female readers to learn from the intensely masculine Alfred the Great of Anglo-Saxon England and Peter the Great of Russia. They were truly great because they allegedly practiced the godly virtues. Here More expressed the conventional equation of masculinity with God. In a lop-sided comparison of Alfred the Great and Christina of Sweden, More juxtaposed the ungovernable passions of Christina with the self-discipline of Alfred. Christina lost her riches and throne due to her theatrical recklessness. Alfred gained wealth and power through compliance with the arduous accountability of Christian virtue.[113] Peter also showed unmistakable evidence of greatness in his constant preference of "masculine" practicality and perseverance over "feminine" splendor and popularity. He was not a "tinsel hero."[114] More wanted Charlotte to subdue the woman in her soul through a

---

[110]Ibid., p.48. c.f. the far more sympathetic comments on Anne's favorites by the whig hostess Lady Holland in the entry for 21 June 1798 was her *Journal* vol.1, pp.192-4.

[111]More, *Hints, Works*, p.46.

[112]Ibid, p.76; c.f. the similar attack on Louis XIV's manhood by the Foxite whig James Mackintosh, *Vindicae Gallicae: Defense of the French Revolution* (London: G. G. J. and J. Robinson, 1791)[Woodstock reprint, 1989], pp.19-20. Yet *The Monthly Review*, a whiggish literary magazine, objected to this hatchet job on Louis XIV in its otherwise favorable commentary on More's *Hints, Young Princess, Monthly Review*, 47(June, 1805), pp.181-4).

[113]More, *Hints, Works*, pp.68-9.

[114]Ibid., p.75.

similar exercise of the godly virtues. In maligning femininity, More ironically approached the unisexual feminism that she wrongly accused Wollstonecraft of advocating.

But More qualified her denigration of femininity, making her last chapters go beyond pious "afterthoughts."[115] It is true that More thought men kept a Christian secular morality best, but she also held that men frequently and vainly refused to acknowledge God's suzerainty because of their natural hubris. Women were, More claimed, naturally disposed to surrendering themselves to Christ. Thus, queens made better stewards of the Anglican Church than kings. They picked better bishops than kings; they preserved protestantism at critical junctures. Elizabeth, Mary II, Anne, and Princes Sophia of Hanover were God's instruments, despite their licentious relatives and inferior gender.[116] Here More assured Charlotte that she could be a divine tool, despite her promiscuous parents and innate femininity. An Evangelical preceptor like Hannah More, of course, would help.

The reaction to this often rambling treatise was astonishing even to its author. As with her *Strictures*, most reviewers seemed perplexed by More's jumbled style or her doctrinal positions and were largely silent on her pedagogy.[117] *The London Review*, however, recommended her *Hints* "as a system, or hints for a system, of female education in general."[118] Indeed, the polite rushed to buy More's latest work, making Cadell quickly publish (in two volumes at 12 shillings for the pair) six editions. Once again, King George and Queen Charlotte were pleased and had

---

[115]c.f. Jones, *Hannah More*, p.189.

[116]More, *Hints, Works*, p.105, 110-3.

[117]Review of *Hints towards forming the Character of a Young Princess*, British *Critic*, 26 (September, 1805), pp.249-50; Review of *Hints toward forming the Character of a Young Princess*, Monthly Review, 47(June, 1805), p.187; Review of *Hints towards forming the Character of a Young Princess*, Edinburgh Review, 7(October, 1805), p.92.

[118]Review of *Hints towards forming the Character of a Young Princess*, *The London Review and Literary Journal*, 48(September, 1805), p.205; More did say in passing that her *Hints* were appropriate for a princess, not rich women in general. Nevertheless, she underscored elsewhere that her reading list was within the reach of many intelligent individuals, regardless of royal blood or female sex. c.f. Lerenbaum, "Mistresses of Orthodoxy," p.295.

no qualms about the Bishop of Salisbury reading aloud portions of More's *Hints* to the Princess.

At sixteen, young Charlotte still did not like More's suggestions, saying in her diary that she was "not quite good enough for that yet."[119] Yet by late adolescence her Evangelical upbringing and, then, her marriage to Prince Leopold of Saxe-Coburg tended to dispel her earlier petulance, making her a demure yet intelligent young woman to contemporaries. Significantly, many saw Charlotte as a possible new Elizabeth, after stingy grandparents and incontinent parents.[120] In an address to the Prince Regent on the marriage of Princess Charlotte in 1816, Kent magistrates felt that Charlotte would make an even better queen than Elizabeth, for the simple reason that Charlotte was a married woman.[121] In other words, Charlotte could have become both Mary II and Elizabeth (a synthesis later accomplished by Queen Victoria), probably much to the delight of Hannah More. Yet tragically, Charlotte died in childbirth in November of 1817, predeceasing her grandfather George III by roughly two years.[122]

More had forbidden novel-reading from Charlotte's routine. In both her *Strictures* and *Hints*, she had identified light fiction as a leading cause of pernicious female influence. Despite More's well-received warnings, the number of novels and novelists (mostly women) ballooned at the turn of the century. Frustrated by her lack of success in combatting these hacks, More once again decided to use a rapier of Satan against him (or, more likely, in the case of novelists—her).[123] In the 1780s she had used the usually light form of society verse to evangelize the

---

[119]Princess Charlotte of Wales to Mercer Elphinstone, 16 November 1812, A. Aspinall, ed., *Letters of the Princess Charlotte 1811-1817* (London: Home & Van Thal, 1949), p.28 as quoted in Jones, *Hannah More*, p.190.

[120]For example, see *The Times* (London), 2 May 1816, p.3.

[121]*The Times* (London), 20 June 1816, p.3.

[122]For the causes of Charlotte's death, see Sir Eardley Holland, "The Princess Charlotte of Wales: A Triple Obstetric Tragedy," *Journal of Obstetrics and Gynaecology of the British Empire*, n.d. 58(1951), pp.905-19. For reactions to Charlotte's death, see my *Political and Religious Responses to Royal Ritual: The Funeral of Princess Charlotte in 1817*, Vanderbilt University M.A. thesis, 1988.

[123]A point made by Marlene Alice Hess, *The Didactic Art of Hannah More*, Michigan State University Ph.D. dissertation in English, 1983, pp.140, 142-3.

rich. In the 1790s she had used the usually dirty chapbook to exhort the poor. Hence, only three years after censuring novels in her *Hints*, More published her first and only novel, *Coelebs in Search of a Wife*, in 1808, further exploring her earlier themes about female education and gender bewilderment.

More's *Coelebs* directly rebuked the sexual ambiguity in Madame Germaine de Stael's *Corinne, or Italy*, a novel which had come out the previous year.[124] This admonition had a personal angle.[125] As a budding dramatist in the 1770s, More had conversed frequently (at the Garricks) with Stael's famous parents, Jacques and Suzanne Necker. This couple apotheosized the godly virtues.[126] The fiscal watchdog of the old regime, Jacques Necker was an incorruptible Huguenot banker. An exponent of protestant earnestness among the fashionable, Suzanne Necker performed exemplary philanthropy. They were happily married, following the prim sexual conventions of their class and religion. Suzanne Necker taught her daughter rigorous morals and formidable academic subjects, paralleling the unconventional suggestions of Hannah More. [127] But Germaine de Stael was different than her parents, although equally bright

---

[124]Against her own advice to shun novels, More could not put *Corinne* down. She wrote that "though like Pistol I swallowed and execrated [*Corinne*], yet I went on swallowing." See Hannah More to Sir William Weller Pepys, 1808, Roberts, *Memoirs* vol.3, p.258. More's ambivalence was not unique. Like More, Maria Edgeworth was "dazzled with the genius [of *Corinne*] & provoked by the absurdities." (Quoted in Marilyn Butler, *Maria Edgeworth: A Literary Biography* (Oxford: Clarendon Press, 1972), p.210.)

[125]This dimension has been missed by literary critics. They still echo Alfred Owen Aldridge's dated belief that Hannah More and Madame de Stael lived in mutually exclusive worlds of discourse. For Aldridge's influential comparison, see "Madame de Stael and Hannah More on Society," *Romantic Review*, 38(1947), pp.330-59.

[126]In old age, however, More denigrated the Neckers in a private critique of Stael's biography of her parents. The Revolution had soured her opinion of Jacques and Suzanne Necker. Of the latter, she wrote "with great abilities, I thought her too studiously ingenious to be agreeable, and too recherchee ever to seem easy; in short she seemed to have been formed to be the admiration of Mr. Gibbon [More's least favorite historian]." (Hannah More to Mrs. Huber, 1820, Roberts, *Memoirs* vol.4, pp.142-5.)

[127]For the Neckers, see the concise and revealing portrait in Simon Schama, *Citizens: A Chronicle of the French Revolution* (New York: Alfred Knopf, 1989), pp.88-95.

and serious. She disregarded bourgeois sexual protocol; she was confidently adulterous and extremely outspoken.[128]

Thus it came as no surprise to the disapproving More that expected sex roles and paternal authority make everyone ill and unhappy in Stael's *Corinne*.[129] Oswald, the major male protagonist, is a weak and indecisive narcissist who breaks the heart of Corinne, a strong-willed Sibyl. A precious Romantic anti-hero, Oswald has left cold England to get over this father's death in sunny Italy, meeting fellow expatriate Corinne in Rome. After traipsing up and down the peninsula, they decide (any decision was hard for Oswald) to get married even after both have told each other about the troubles through which protestant virtue has put them. Then, Oswald is called back to England by his regiment. Reacclimated to what his native country considers proper feminine behavior, Oswald reluctantly dumps the rebellious Corinne for the boring Lucile, the half-sister of Corinne. This politic match is largely due to the wishes of his dead father and Corinne's evil stepmother, a caricature of a female mouthpiece for paternal and Evangelical "oppression." Avriel Goldberger has wisely attributed Oswald's indecisiveness to the tension within himself between conformity to and rebellion against expected gender behavior.[130] By marrying Lucile, he finally chooses to play the manly protector of the proper lady over the personally fitting role of second fiddle to an acclaimed writer. At any rate, Oswald's "feminine" vacillations prove too much for Corinne's "masculine" mettle. A secret eyewitness to her betrayal, Corinne slowly dies of "feminine" heartbreak, while Oswald (and the reader) almost drown in his consequent maudlin melancholy.

More inverted Stael's plot, having Evangelical and filial piety solace those characters who do not stray from the straight and

---

[128]For biographies of Stael's colorful life, see J. Christopher Herold, *Mistress to An Age: A Life of Madame de Stael* (New York: Bobbs-Merrill, 1958); Helen B. Postgate, *Madame de Stael* (New York: Twayne, 1968).

[129]For the best translation of this novel, see Madame Anne-Louise Germaine de Stael-Holstein, *Corinne, or Italy*, 1807, Avriel H. Goldberger, trans. & ed. (New Brunswick, N.J.: Rutgers University Press, 1987).

[130]Introduction to Stael, *Corinne*, Goldberger, p.xl.

narrow.[131] In *Coelebs*, Charles, the celibate in the title, resolves to find the perfect wife. As Robin Reed Davis points out, both Charles and Oswald travel soon after the death of their father. Even at the beginning, More underscores the benefits of filial piety. Since Charles had steadfastly nursed his dying father, he basks in the Evangelical faith still emanating from the paternal decline. In contrast, Stael's Oswald mortally wounded his father with selfish indiscretions in revolutionary France. He hates himself for precipitating his father's passing.[132]

Davis also notes that both men feel an excessive need to please their dead fathers through selection of the woman of whom Daddy would approve. Both eventually marry their father's choice, a dutiful daughter of a paternal chum.[133] Davis overlooks the most obvious similarity. Lucile marries Oswald; Lucilla marries Charles.[134]

The paths of Oswald and Charles to marriage, however, are very different. Charles never leaves England, journeying between London and surrounding countryside. Along the way, he rejects various potential mates from the pathologically "feminine" and fragile through would-be men, selecting Lucilla, who agreeably combines the best in feminine and masculine qualities. Charles knows from the start what kind of woman that he and his father would prefer—a lady who is a good cook, a fine mother, an intellectual soulmate, and a spiritual companion.[135]

---

[131]c.f. Baker, *History of English Novel: Volume VI*, p.52, n.1 Katherine Sobba Green argues that More not only inverted Stael's plot, but "the usual courtship schema by featuring a male protagonist 'in search of a wife.'" (*The Courtship Novel 1740-1820: A Feminized Genre* (Lexington, Kentucky: University Press of Kentucky, 1991), p.113)

[132]Robin Reed Davis, *Anglican Evangelicalism and the Feminine Literary Tradition: From Hannah More to Charlotte Bronte*, Duke University Ph.D. in English, 1982, pp.73-4.

[133]Ibid., p.74.

[134]A point made in passing in Kasbekar, *Power Over Themselves*, p.293.

[135]In particular, see Hannah More, *Coelebs in Search of a Wife, The Works of Hannah More* vol.22 (Philadelphia: Woodward, 1832), pp.308-9; c.f. Browne, *Feminist Mind*, pp.70, 110-1; Rogers, *Feminism*, pp.209-10; Elisabeth Jay, *The Religion of the Heart: Angelical Evangelicalism and the Nineteenth-Century Novel* (Oxford: Clarendon Press, 1979), pp.134-5; Anderson and Zinsser, *A History of Their Own*, p.127.

Following paternal guidelines single-mindedly, however, dehumanizes Charles, denying him many natural feelings. As the novel progresses, he becomes an increasingly tedious robot who glacially scorns those women (and men) who do not quite cut it by his father's impossible standards. In response to Charles' haughty condescension, twentieth-century readers have fairly called him "a totally uninteresting prig."[136] Yet literary critics who dismiss *Coelebs* out of hand because of its priggish protagonist forget that stuffy male paragons were not restricted to Evangelical fiction. Samuel Richardson's Sir Charles Grandison was the prototype for the too-good-to-be-true Georgian man of granite. Thomas Holcroft, one of the radical defendants at the state trials of 1794, constructed in his novels and plays many "Jacobins" as prudish and stiff as More's Charles.[137] In addition, most literary critics fail to realize that More purposely overdid Charles' sense of direction to show up the rudderless darlings like Oswald who passed for masculine in the fashionable world. She knew that contemporary female readers would probably prefer the crashing bore of *Coelebs* as a potential husband over Oswald who painstakingly dithers between the disagreeably aggressive Corinne and his "correct" and conventionally demure choice.[138]

---

[136]Jones, *Hannah More*, p.194. See also Betsy Aiken-Sneath, "Hannah More (1745-1833)," *The London Mercury*, October, 1933, p.532; Quinlan, *Victorian Prelude*, p.151-2; A. G. Newell, "Early Evangelical Fiction," *Evangelical Quarterly*, 38(1966), p.10; Davis *Evangelicalism and the Feminine Literary Tradition*, p.75.

[137]See Holcroft, *Anna St. Ives*, pp.48-9, 152-5, 381-2; Kelly, *English Jacobin Novel*, pp.17-8. See also Robert Bage, *Hermsprong: or, Man As He Is Not* vol.3, Stuart Tave, ed., (University Park, Pa.: Pennsylvania State University Press, 1982)[orig. pub. 1796], p.31, 167.

[138]A point raised (more generally) in Christine Krueger, *The Reader's Repentance: Women Preachers, Women Writers, and the Victorian Social Discourse*, Princeton University Ph.D. dissertation in English, 1986, p.125. The indecisiveness of Oswald ironically and unintentionally corresponds to the vacillations of More's first and only *fiancé*, William Turner. Perhaps Charles was overly decisive because of lingering memories of Turner. For More and Turner, see Mary Alden Hopkins, *Hannah More and Her Circle* (New York: Longman, Green & Co., 1947), pp.32-7. In addition, Oswald's "hot-and-cold" hesitations about marriage also resemble Gilbert Imlay's dithering toward Mary Wollstonecraft, a drama familiar to contemporaries because of William

Lucile and Lucilla are as dissimilar as Oswald and Charles. Stael describes Lucile as an ice princess with "the grace of that youthfulness, of that fair skin, that blond hair, that innocent image of the springtime of life."[139] Her almost ethereal beauty immediately fascinates Oswald, who found himself "lost in a dream of the celestial purity of a young girl who, always at her mother's side, knows nothing of life but daughterly affection."[140] But after the wedding Oswald quickly comes to view Lucile "as a coldly beautiful person, fulfilling her duties and loving him to the extent that she was capable of love."[141] In contrast, More presents Lucilla as both physically pretty and mentally acute, a switch from the stock dowdiness of the learned woman. Charles finds that Lucilla's pulchritude flows from her intelligence, which he saw written all over her exquisite face. She also has a warm glow (the only character in *Coelebs* who has a pulse!) about her, expressing her love through the religion of the heart.[142]

Lucile could have been Lucilla if she had had the same education. Unlike Lucilla but like most young ladies, Lucile learns only frivolous diversions and social rules.[143] This conditioning cripples Lucile's personality. She can not convey her true feelings to Oswald because her slim schooling rendered her inarticulate and, hence, outwardly cold. Given that the primary object of conventional female education was to allure men, Oswald ironically finds Lucile less attractive and feminine because of her acquired failure to communicate emotion coherently.[144] On his visits in *Coelebs*, Charles turns down many Luciles, choosing "not to risk [his] happiness with women who could not contribute her full share toward spending a wet winter cheerfully in the country."[145]

Godwin's biography. For Imlay and Wollstonecraft, see Flexner, *Wollstonecraft*, pp.180-218; Tomalin, *Wollstonecraft*, pp.145-50, 167-94.

[139] Stael, *Corinne*, p.341.
[140] Ibid. p.317.
[141] Ibid. p.389.
[142] In particular, see More, *Coelebs*, *Works*, pp.334-5, 341-3.
[143] Stael, *Corinne*, pp.253, 259, 322.
[144] Ibid., pp.384-5, 387.
[145] More, *Coelebs*, *Works*, p.314.

Lucilla, on the other hand, is able to charm a male pedant such as Charles because of her early acquaintance with "great" books written and read almost exclusively by men. More went beyond the usual exploration of inner feelings and repressed thoughts by female novelists and presented a heroine holding her own in intellectual engagement.[146] Lucilla enlivens dry historical and theological debates between the men at Stanley's Grove with erudite precision. In these disputes and discussions, she shares Charles' taste for John Milton and aspires to be Eve in *Paradise Lost*, mesmerizing Charles. Like her creator, how-ever, Lucilla interprets for her own needs the misogynist language of Milton. She sees in Milton's Eve a role model for the use of considerable female power in a man's world. Thus rather than degrading women, Milton in Lucilla's reading actu-ally trumpets the stranglehold that Eve had over Adam. Milton suggests to Lucilla and More than women had the necessary leverage to promote and nurture godly behavior in"their" men through example and conversation. Putting Milton's insights to good use would increase feminine influence, giving rich women "all the dignity of equality" without the superfluous legal guar-antees.[147]

Lucilla's parents gauge her education to avoid the rambunc-tious Charbydis as well as the dainty Scylla. No where is this tinkering more evident than in deciding how far to teach Lucilla classical cultures and languages. To understand the nuances of this decision requires a very brief detour through contemporary responses to female classicists. It is a truism to say that intimacy with Greco-Roman literature and history opened the door to aristocratic cliques of males in the early nineteenth century. Classical studies were meant for gentlemen

---

[146]For the type of novel that women wrote and were expected to write, see Katharine A. Rogers, "Inhibitions on Eighteenth-Century Women Novelists: Elizabeth Inchbald and Charlotte Smith," *Eighteenth Century Studies*, 11(Fall, 1977), pp.63-78.

[147]More, *Coelebs, Works*, p.306-7, 335, 363, 387, 413; c.f. Quinlan, *Victorian Prelude*, pp.150-1; Agress, *Feminine Irony*, p.37; Davis, *Evangelicalism and the Feminine Literary Tradition*, pp.77-9; Hess, *Hannah More*, pp.162-3; Poovey, *The Proper Lady*, p.33; Beth Kowaleski-Wallace, "Milton's Daughters: The Education of Eighteenth-Century Women Writers," *Feminist Studies* 12(1986), pp.288-90.

(and possibly the next queen) only.[148] To the Georgians, women who attempted to ,master this road to status were therefore unladylike. Most scholars, however, overlook how deeply female writers internalized this hatred. Anna Seward maliciously derided Mrs. Piozzi (who, according to her latest biographer, always wrote "like a woman!") for using "strange breakteeth" Latin words that no woman could ever hope to comprehend. Jane Austen even ridiculed More for using the "pretentious" Latin word *Coelebs* in her title.[149] Female classicists usually kept their study secret to avoid controversy. Before her London debut in 1773, More had led the court official Robert Beringer to believe that she as a young schoolmarm knew very little about lyric poems and Horatian epistles.[150] In 1801 Lord Glenbervie was too embarrassed to tell his friend George III how far Lady Glenbervie had progressed in her private study of classical languages.[151] Fifteen years before, More had displayed her knowledge of antiquity overtly and had embarrassed Glenbervie's father-in-law Lord North at Twenty Questions because her knowledge of classical allusions far exceeded that of the former prime minister.[152]

More thus wanted to bring classical study by females out into the open. She suggested in *Coelebs* that it ought to take place under paternal supervision similar to the way that her father had taught her in the 1750s. Like Jacob More, Mr. Stanley, Lucilla's father, "at first . . . [merely] meant to give Lucilla as

---

[148]Smith, *Politics of Language*, pp.6, 13. c.f. the unconventional remarks of Edward Tighe in Caroline Hamilton's journal as reprinted in Bell, *The Hamwood Papers*, p.330.

[149]For Austen, see her letter to her sister Cassandra, 30 January 1809, R. W. Chapman, ed., *Jane Austen's Letters to Her Sister Cassandra and Others* (Oxford: Oxford University Press, 1979), p.259. For Seward, see her letter to Mrs. Knowles, 25 July 1789, A. Constable, ed., *Letters of Anna Seward Written Between The Years 1784 and 1807* vol.2 (Edinburgh: George Ramsay & Co., 1811), p.289.

[150]Hannah More to Richard Beringer, 1 April 1770 or 1771?, Historical Manuscripts Commission, eds., *The Manuscripts of J. B. Fortescue, Esq., Preserved at Dropmore* vol.1 (London: Eyre and Spottiswoode, 1892), p.160.

[151]For Glenbervie, see entries of 29 January 1801 and 1 September 1801 in his *Diaries* vol.1, pp.149, 248.

[152]Hannah More to her sisters, 17 February 1786, Roberts, *Memoirs* vol.2, p.12.

much Latin as would teach her to grammatize her English." Her alacrity for learning Latin compels Stanley, however, to "read over with her the most unexceptionable parts of a few of the best Roman classics."[153] Stanley feels confident that he can guide Lucilla to learn what boys regularly did without her losing "feminine" qualities.

Flabbergasted guests of Stanley still wonder "how Lucilla could be so utterly void of pretension" to overt political and cultural power if she knows the classics designed for men. Sapphic classicists were usually "forward in conversation, deficient in feminine manners, and destitute of domestic talents." The late Elizabeth Carter was the exception that proved the rule.[154]

In response, Stanley notes that women could not show off through speaking a dead language. Men read the classics for inner growth and self-knowledge, not external exhibition. So would intelligent women, a deserving yet underdeveloped elite which Stanley guessed made up one-sixth of the female population in Britain. Playing sonatinas by Muzio Clementi and arranging birds-of-paradise in porcelain vases, on the other hand, were far more likely than reading Virgil to make women hubristic because they could be easily flaunted in mixed company. One of the male guests agrees, further suggesting that teachers of daughters substitute Latin "which abounds with writers of supreme excellence" for the all-too-common study of "the language spoken at Rome in its present degraded state, in which there are comparatively few authors to improve" girls.[155]

The above proposal is one of the many constructions that More employed to dissuade her female readers for pursuit of the "Italian" option of Corinne. Madame de Stael had made the alternative of an independent female life beyond nearly all social and sexual convention very attractive. Although (and

---

[153]More, *Coelebs, Works*, pp.404, 405.
[154]Ibid., pp. 404, 405; Frances Burney in her novel *Camilla* (1796) exposed the cruelties and hostilities that classically educated women encountered. See the discussion of this novel's character Eugenia in Margaret Anne Doody, *Frances Burney: The Life in the Works* (New Brunswick, N.J.: Rutgers University Press, 1988), pp.240-4.
[155]More, *Coelebs, Works*, p.405.

because!) she is a genius and a virago, Corinne has no problem arousing male suitors. Although at the top of her chosen fields, she excels in the "feminine" fine arts. [156] More's main answer to Corinne is Miss Sparkes, a neighbor of the Stanleys who also has "the reputation of being a wit and an Amazon." [157] Unlike Corinne, however, Moss Sparkes repels men. She remains unmarried and unloved at forty-five. Even her name is a pun on this loneliness; to be a Miss Sparkes is to miss the sparks, a contemporary synonym for beaus. The happily single More made it clear, however, that Miss Sparkes is celibate through no choice of her own. No lesbian or nun, Miss Sparkes pines for the company of men, who, in turn, tend to be somewhat amused by her oddness. But these male acquaintances thank the Lord that their wives, daughters, and sisters are not like her. [158] In contrast, More stressed that "the woman who derives her principles from the Bible [like Lucilla] . . . will not pant for beholders." [159] Miss Sparkes is far too competitive for conventional tastes. Unlike the artiste Corinne, she beats men at their most strenuous and public games. With "the cap, the whip, . . . the loud voice, [and] the intrepid look," Miss Sparkes races country gentlemen on horseback, lectures Oxford grads on politics, and works the crowds on the hustings. [160] In response to Stael's equation of female independence with the realization of talent, More linked freedom from gender constraints with the ridiculous and overcompensating "masculinity" of Miss Sparkes.

The right kind of education, More claimed, can prevent future Miss Sparkes. In doing so, a curricula had to "tame" the wild end of femininity, the ungoverned passions of Mother Nature. Stanley "tames" his youngest daughter Phoebe "the

---

[156]Stael, *Corinne*, pp.19-47, 270-1.

[157]More, *Coelebs*, *Works*, p.382.

[158]The introduction of Miss Sparkes in *Coelebs* is a dramatization of a traditional tactic to scare heterosexual women away from expressing or adapting "masculine" qualities. See the less dramatic and very conventional Dr. James Fordyce, *Sermons to Young Women*, 1766 as reprinted in Hill, *Eighteenth-Century Women*, p.23.

[159]Quoted in Seamus Deane, *The French Revolution and Enlightenment in England 1789-1832* (Cambridge, Mass.: Harvard University Press, 1988), p.33.

[160]More, *Coelebs*, *Works*, p.382.

nickname of Artemis, the androgynous Greek goddess of the moon), "who has a superabundance of vivacity," through teaching her arithmetic and "a tincture" of algebra, subjects usually reserved for boys. To Stanley, "nothing puts such a bridle on the fancy as" mathematical proofs. He surmises that if Phoebe had been weaned on the typical snippets of poetry and fiction assigned to young ladies, then she would have become unbridled like Miss Sparkes. Stanley had initially doubted that Phoebe's exposure to long division would keep her impulses under control. He had worried that if Phoebe came across fiction, she would quickly forget the discipline of mathematics. Stanley's metaphor here is revealing. He notes that "as in the case of the cat in the fable, who has metamorphosed into a lady, nature will break out as soon as the scratching of a mouse is heard."[161]

To inoculate Phoebe completely, Stanley substitutes "a few of the best things" in fiction such as *Gulliver's Travels* for further study of algebra. To Stanley's delight, her mathematical training has made her critical of unbelievable flights of fantasy in these works. Stanley's use of mathematics with Phoebe, therefore, "was precisely the same which the ingenious Mr. Cheshire makes of his steel machines for defective shapes, to straighten a crooked tendency or strengthen a weak one." Once the goal of "curing a wrong bias" had been accomplished, both Cheshire and Stanley "discard their apparatus." (Significantly, so did Jacob More fifty-two years before with the twelve-year-old Hannah.) Continued study of mathematics, Stanley (and Jacob More) thought, would defeminize Phoebe (Hannah More), and he "never meant to make a mathematical lad," a scholarly version of Miss Sparkes. In other words, More once again urged a measured amount of "masculine" subjects for women to preempt sexual ambiguity.[162]

Reactions to *Coelebs* were hotly divided. As with her *Strictures* and *Hints*, reviewers weighed More's style rather than her content. Some of the religious periodicals balked at the use of a novel to proselytize; quite a few of the literary magazines

---

[161]Ibid., p.405.
[162]Ibid.

yawned loudly at the lack of incident in *Coelebs'* thin plot.[163] More's friends (with a few painful exceptions) rushed to her defense. With the ensuring brouhaha, sales boomed.[164] Davis notes that "*Coelebs* .. had more editions and earned its author more money than [Sir Walter Scott's blockbuster] *Waverly*."[165]

The most damning review in this web of controversy was written by the Reverend Sydney Smith in the *Edinburgh Review*.[166] In the 1790s Smith had used the tracts of Hannah More at his own Sunday school near Bath.[167] In the next decade, he became a credible mouthpiece for radical whigs and a nemesis of More, although he helped to shape the *Edinburgh Review* as a champion of bourgeois probity.[168] Smith thought More's ideal characters would alienate readers from virtue and exposed the stilted artifice and triteness of Stanley's Grove. He pointed out that More had attacked the phoniness of the fashionable only to supply her own simulated asceticism.[169] One can agree with Smith that Charles is an unbelievably flat charac-

---

[163]For reviews of *Coelebs*, see *British Critic*, 22(1809, pp.481-94; *Christian Observer*, 8(1809), pp.109-21; *Critical Review*, 16(1809), pp.252-64; *European Magazine*, 56(1809), pp.196-201, 283-7, 373-8; *Evangelical Magazine*, 17(1809), p.289; *Gentleman's Magazine*, 79(1809), p.151; *London Review*, 1, (1809), pp.424-44; *Monthly Magazine*, 27(1809), pp.663-7; *Monthly Review*, 58(1809), pp.128-36; *Literary Panorama*, 6(1809), pp.259-67; *Satirist*, (1809), pp.384-90; *Scots Magazine*, 71(1809), pp.435-41, 516-24; *Universal Magazine*, 11(1809), pp.327; 336, 515-24; Hess, *Hannah More*, pp.143-52, 202; Davis, *Evangelicalism and the Feminine Literary Tradition*, pp.83-6.

[164]For the commercial success of *Coelebs*, see Sam Pickering, Jr., "Hannah More's *Coelebs in Search of A Wife* and the Respectability of the Novel in the Nineteenth Century," *Neuphilogische Mitteilungen*, 78(1977), pp.81, 85; Newell, "Evangelical Fiction," pp.6-7.

[165]Davis, *Evangelicalism and the Feminine Literary Tradition*, p.71.

[166]The review articles in the *Edinburgh Review* were unsigned, but a letter indicates that Smith wrote this assessment of *Coelebs*. See the Reverend Sydney Smith to Francis Jeffrey, 7 March 1809, Nowell C. Smith, ed., *The Letters of Sydney Smith* vol.1 (Oxford: Clarendon Press, 1953), p.155.

[167]For example, see the Reverend Sydney Smith to M. H. Beach, 2 April 1795, *Letters of Sydney Smith* vol.1, pp.3-4.

[168]John Clive points out that although the Whiggish *Edinburgh Review* bitterly attacked Evangelicals and Methodists, both the *Review* and its godly victims contributed to making of "the nineteenth-century English middle-class ethic." (*Scotch Reviewers: The Edinburgh Review 1802-1815* (London: Faber and Faber Ltd., 1957), p.150)

[169]Review of *Coelebs in Search of a Wife*, *Edinburgh Review* vol.14, 27(April, 1809), pp.145-51; Jones *Hannah More*, pp.197-8.

ter. Completely asexual, Charles does seem at times to be the sixty-three-year-old Hannah More in the guise of a young man.[170] As for Lucilla, Smith echoed the sentiments of Mary Mitford about ideal feminine characters—"A book laden with an impeccable heroine ought to be covered all over with cork jackets, not to sink ... How do I hate those over-good bookpeople!"[171]

Even the astute Smith overlooked the only important artifice to emerge from More's *Coelebs*—her continued insistence on exclusive gender qualities. The educational programs of her *Strictures, Hints,* and *Coelebs* at key points fused gender identities supposedly different. With Stanley and his daughters, Evangelical civilizing from above took on gender dimensions. Nevertheless, More kept on maintaining artificial distinctions between male and female with a straight face. Here the reaction to *Coelebs* by Madame de Stael is instructive. She loved it.[172] Why? Because Stael had been given the same curricula as Lucilla and, then, went on to have three bastards, to harass the most powerful male autocrat in Europe (Napoleon) publically and personally, and to write critically acclaimed fiction. Germaine de Stael knew that Hannah More's strictures were Trojan horses, even if Miss More did not.

---

[170]Philip Child long ago contended that "the god Eros is not allowed to meddle [at Stanley's Grove because Hannah] had not allowed Eros to meddle in her own life." (Portrait of a Woman of Affairs—Old Style," *University of Toronto Quarterly,* 3(1933), p.94) Recently, however, Christine Krueger has detected faint hints of Eros at Stanley's Grove. (*Reader's Repentance,* pp.125-6)
[171]Mary Russell Mitford to Mrs. Hofland, 18 March 1819, *Letters of Mary Russell Mitford,* p.158.
[172]*The Constitutionnel,* no.18, 18 January 1817 as quoted in Jones, *Hannah More,* p.196.

Chapter VII

The Elder Churchwoman

Hannah More continued writing until her death at eighty-eight, confounding the custom of dormant aged spinsters. Old women in the West were supposed to be extremely passive, serenely happy, and resigned to their fate.[1] Many women regarded this maxim as instructive, but More was not about to retreat into idle repose. To More, Evangelicalism and its reformation of English society remained central throughout her adulthood and frequently required her dynamic action and undivided attention. She soon discovered that her almost insatiable love of socializing, lobbying, and writing endured and, at times, intensified as she entered her seventies. Meeting fifty people one week in the 1820s, More noted that retirement was "a thing that . . . [she] knew only by name."[2] Obviously, the inactivity deemed correct for venerable women did not sit well with More's ongoing desire to write. She relieved this tension between convention and reality by projecting expectations for elderly passivity and resignation upon her audience of poor laborers and ordinary housewives.

Old age bestowed mixed blessings upon More's literary career. It is true that her long experience as a writer helped to solidify her identity as one of the most eminent Evangelical advocates in the 1810s and 1820s. It is also true that her link to the age of Garrick and Johnson left her ideas stranded in the

---

[1]In reference to elderly women in history, this chapter relies heavily upon the seminal insights of Terri L. Premo, *Winter Friends: Women Growing Old in the New Republic, 1785-1835* (Urbana, Ill.: University of Illinois Press, 1990), pp.130-54. Premo limits herself to the young United States, but her discussion of middle-class white protestant women there could apply to those kind of women in Britain just as well.

[2]Quoted in Mary G. Jones, *Hannah More* (Cambridge: Cambridge University Press, 1952), p.226.

last century and, to a large degree, separated her from contemporary political and economic conditions. Hannah More, a perceptive survivor of disorienting revolutions, could not stomach any more drastic personal or national reforms. She recognized anew the importance of stability during the explosion of postwar unrest and reaffirmed the religious and literary precepts of her youth, but the mere repackaging of previous works left her increasingly out of touch with the acceleration of political, social, and literary change after Waterloo. Her reputation as a writer suffered at the hands of the romantic poets, and the recasting of the *Cheap Repository* between 1817-1819 failed miserably from both a stylistic and commercial perspective in comparison with the original tracts of the 1790s.

Inevitable yet unwanted change affected Hannah More's personal as well as literary life. The deaths of all four of her sisters during the 1810s finally caused her to realize fully the fragility and subjection of spinsterhood. Thieving servants even made her leave her home, beloved Barley Wood. More gained comfort and emotional support from her clerical and genteel friends, but the main bedrock in her difficult last years was, of course, her faith in God. She felt that she could help young people to find this faith through popularizing and simplifying Christian doctrine. Handing down this legacy was a conventional desire for any grandmother or maiden aunt, but More here exuded an intensity and energy which, at times, belied her superficial conformity to the mild image of a woman over 65.

Her first book after *Coelebs* promoted habits of retirement and moral purity for the aged that she also hoped would serve as examples to younger Anglicans for many generations. In March of 1811, More addressed *Practical Piety: or the Influence of the Religion of the Heart on the Conduct of the Life* to "herself as a Christian who must die soon, [and] to Christians who must die certainly."[3] In the preface, she justified the repetition of her previous arguments. She first stressed that one has to teach a subject regularly in order to understand it fully and then

---

[3]Hannah More, *Practical Piety: or the Influence of the Religion of the Heart on the Conduct of the Life, The Works of Hannah More* vol.1 (Philadelphia: Woodward, 1832), pp.416-7.

declared that "the world does not require so much to be informed as reminded." More identified herself with the "simple herald" who frequently told the hubristic Philip of Macedon, "REMEMBER THAT THOU ART MORTAL," and whose routine, she contended, was more influential over Philip than the "impassioned orations" of the king's eloquent enemy, Demosthenes. Here Demosthenes represents male commentators who "boldly" campaign against evils in high places yet are ineffective because of their abrasiveness. The "simple herald," through gently harping on the same themes, had at least the king's ear. Accordingly, the "plain and practical" nature of her latest "slight sketch" would reach, not repel, an audience. Hoping for the widest possible readership, More as "simple herald" fit well within the confines of the ideal elderly lady. Dropping the censorious tone of her essays of the 1780s and 1790s, More was ready to take a grandmotherly posture to put forth her Evangelical agenda.[4]

As an old, female repository of truisms against a backdrop of change, More labeled herself a "moderate," whatever that may mean. She portrayed those on her ill-defined extremes in religion and politics as cantankerous, impractical, and ultimately unchristian. Argumentative ideologues (from her experience, almost exclusively male) were concerned with impractical abstractions, a conventionally male preserve, and with uncritical applause from like-minded zealots. In religion, the purveyors of both "uncharitable bigotry" and its allegedly polar opposite, "general benevolence," tried to ambush "those [such as More] who . . . [could not] go all lengths with either." From earlier criticisms of her works, More expected that religious "extremists" such as Unitarians, hyper-Calvinists, or Laudian Anglicans would find her either too close-minded or too willing to compromise. Revealingly, she presented Evangelicalism as a woman between two implicitly male criminals, "one [who] distorts her lovely lineaments into caricature, and throws her graceful figure into gloomy shadow [and] the other . . . [who] daub[s] her over with colours not her own, renders her form

---

[4]Ibid., p.416.

indistinct, and obliterates her features."[5] Unlike the criminals, however, More knew how to dress this "woman" in loose yet recognizable garments "feelingly, if not scientifically" and with "experience, in default of skill."[6]

More also knew from her long history that "a slighter drapery, if it be a new one" might attract far more younger readers to Christianity than "a richer garb to which the eye has been accustomed." In other words, a new book by an old lady might be more accessible to young people than venerable classics written by prominent men. More, then 66, felt especially attuned to the next generation. Even though most of her friends from her youth had died, "fresh links . . . have continued to attach her to society." More found herself "singularly happy in the affectionate regard of a great number of amiable young persons" and thought these personal ties would attract adolescent readers who ordinarily did not buy devotional treatises. In turn, her old age would brighten "if she could hope that any caution here held out, any principles here suggested, any habit here recommended, might be of use to any one of them" long after the time when her pen eventually fell silent.[7]

It would be tedious to recount the verities of *Practical Piety* which More hoped to transmit to her fledglings. She cast typically Evangelical precepts in her "diffuse and heavily antithetical style,"[8] a way of writing no longer in vogue. Most inspired, however, were More's chapters on death. She previously had glossed over final preparation. Now with her own death unavoidably closer than ever before, she focused on hopes and fears about the end of life. Although expressing her own natural concerns as an old woman, she also knew that a discussion of death would interest people of all ages because of high mortality among the young in late Georgian Britain. In order to entice younger readers further, *Practical Piety's* chapters on "happy deaths" prescribe constant vigilance and diligent self-

---

[5]Ibid.; c.f. Robin Reed Davis, *Anglican Evangelicalism and the Feminine Literary Tradition: From Hannah More to Charlotte Bronte*, Duke University Ph.D. in English, 1982, pp.88-9.
[6]More, *Practical Piety, Works*, p.417.
[7]Ibid.
[8]Jones, *Hannah More*, p.199.

examination for the dying who Hannah More broadly defined as the alive. Endorsing ardently protestant ways attractive to the energetic, these chapters scorn customary expectations of non-chalant resignation deemed especially appropriate for elderly women.[9]

Practical Piety sold extremely well with both the old and young. It was More's most commercially successful book; as Mary G. Jones points out, it surpassed even her extremely popular novel *Coelebs* in both editions and the number of copies sold. As More predicted, extremists such as the hyper-Calvinists attacked her on a number of obscure doctrinal points. The ensuing controversy did not hurt sales, however, and did not stop her from publishing a sequel, *Christian Morals*, in December of 1812.[10]

Christian Morals was a kinder, gentler version of More's earlier addresses to aristocrats. Once again, More hoped that the godly reformation of the affluent—those rich enough to buy this volume in sepia cloth—would bring their dependents to Christ. She thought that this reformation had started and felt that the London elite, in particular, was more serious than in the days of bewigged macaronis. She acknowledged this ostensible change by toning down her criticism of the quality Her optimism about fashionable seriousness was somewhat misplaced and, due to frequent illness and country living, was based largely upon second-hand accounts by deferential fans in contrast to her own acute (and detailed) observations of 1788 and 1790. As a result, she overlooked the outlandish levity of Beau Brummells, scions notoriously obsessed with personal appearance and dress. She also ignored or, at times, inadvertently contributed to the banal pettiness of second-generation Evangelicals. Her age here had both dulled and deluded her muse.[11]

---

[9]More, *Practical Piety, Works*, pp.485-501.

[10]Jones, *Hannah More*, p.200. For individual reactions to *Practical Piety*, see the letters from Mr. Stephen to Hannah More, 30 April 1811, from Lord Teignmouth to Hannah More, 28 May 1811, from Lord Barham to Hannah More, 1811, and from Dr. Magee (from Dublin), 7 September 1811, Roberts, *Memoirs* vol.3, pp.336-44, 352-4.

[11]Hannah More, *Christian Morals, The Works of Hannah More* vol.2 (Philadelphia: Woodward, 1832), pp.137-50, 172-83. For the social extravagance of the Regency, see Joanna Richardson, *The Regency* (London: Collins, 1973), pp.33-

However oblivious to the nuances of cultural change, *Christian Morals* is an intriguing if not unique attempt by Hannah More to gain direction along that final path through the valley of the shadow. Given her advancing age, More revealingly devoted several chapters to the use of time and retirement. As hard on herself as others, she worried that her own improper use of time—"worthless employments, frivolous amusements, listless indolence, idle reading, and vain imaginations"—would soon plunge her into the ever burning flames of hell.[12] Such grim apprehension was perhaps more common in the gloomy seventeenth than in the relatively optimistic nineteenth century, although concern with death and the preparation for it was by no means an exclusively puritan characteristic. More, like most Christian commentators, felt it her duty to scare the young into regulating their hours conscientiously. One of the best ways both to spend a typical day and to avoid the everlasting fire, More contended, was "to entertain serious thoughts of death." Dwelling upon one's demise and the consequent divine judgment, however seemingly distant, was the "most likely method for rectifying tempers, for conquering propensities, for establishing principles, for . . . relinquishing enterprises and pursuits" in order to placate a demanding if forgiving God.[13]

Counsel to focus on the afterlife offered the most succor for world-weary retirees, but a morbidly contemplative life for the elderly was not what Hannah More had in mind. More, an old busybody who never retired, publically wrestled with the dangers and advantages of retirement in *Christian Morals*. She observed that although both statesmen and milliners can not wait to escape their irksome occupations, they quickly find out that retirement "has produced no change, except from the idleness of tumult to that of ennui in one sex, and from levity to apathy in the other." For the mature rich, staying at a rural seat was excruciatingly boring (even with the delightful undertakings of agriculture) and, to More, could only be enlivened

---

44, 71-9, 81-98; R.J. White, *Life in Regency England* (London: Batsford, 1963), pp.4-10, 50-1, 74-5, 126-7.
[12]More, *Christian Morals, Works*, p.144.
[13]Ibid., p.146.

through fully accepting the Word. She stressed that practical moral and ethical instruction could never begin too late. Old dogs could indeed teach themselves and others new tricks. She noted the elderly's significant role in anchoring Christ's kingdom here on earth and lauded the increased energy among converted and committed retirees. With ascetic activity, "they will grow not so much to endure retirement as to rejoice in it, not so much to subsist without dissipation as to soar above it."[14]

In *Christian Morals*, Hannah More never climbed as far out on ecclesiastical and speculative limbs as male writers and thus pleased affluent laypeople content with a recapitulation of familiar Evangelical generalities. A few Anglican clergymen scoffed at her all-too-vague references to providential intervention, but most readers of *Christian Morals* did not seem to care. As Mary G. Jones writes, "eleven editions were published and nearly ten thousand copies were sold."[15]

Fed by this series of commercial successes, More's interests suddenly expanded. In January of 1815 she published her first and only attempt at literary biography, *An Essay on the Character and Practical Writings of St. Paul*. "It . . . [was] with no little diffidence that" More presented this work "to the public eye." Indeed, her apprehension in the preface went far beyond the hackneyed expressions of feminine self-depreciation. She was extremely aware that a writer of a Pauline biography needed the broad background in ancient languages, biblical exegesis, and doctrinal subtleties to which she as a woman could "make out no fair title." She admitted that explaining the apostle Paul was a flourishing industry and that the ground she covered was particularly well trodden.[16]

More thought that she could tell a better story because she was a elderly female amateur, however. More was unable to use primary and secondary sources in Greek because of sex and age

---

[14]Ibid., p.169.
[15]Jones, *Hannah More*, p.200. See also Hannah More to an unnamed correspondent, 21 November 1812, The Houghton Library, Harvard University, Autograph File; Mr. Stephen to Hannah More, 1813, Roberts, *Memoirs* vol.3, pp.389-93.
[16]Hannah More, *An Essay on the Character and Practical Writings of St. Paul*, *The Works of Hannah More* vol.2 (Philadelphia: Woodward, 1832), p.216.

and thus could not plumb the innermost sources of Paul's actions. Yet More, "who had no skill to penetrate . . . [Paul's] depths," possessed the skill of compromise learned through years as a woman in male preserves.[17] She thus aspired to synthesize sharply contradictory views of the saint in English through avoiding what she considered the needless controversy of male Christian experts. She also "avoid[ed] whatever might be considered as a ground for the discussion of any point not immediately tending to practical utility." More limited herself to the presentation of "St. Paul's character as a model for . . . general imitation, and his practical writings as a store-house for our general instruction." She wanted to humanize or to popularize Paul for everyday use and did not need "the dignity of the expositor" or "the details of the [academic] biographer." More recognized that the typical reader would find "a devoted Martyr" hard to imitate, but she suggested that the aspects of his life and letters brought out by her treatise might induce others to examine their own behavior.[18]

More's critical biography of Paul tells much more about her than it does about him. She passed over ambivalent and conflicting passages from his epistles concerning women's place in the church and surrounding society, but she did champion the relatively inclusive Christian discourse of the mature Paul over what she considered the male-centered ethos of the Hellenistic Saul of Tarsus. The recent revival of pagan philosophy in revolutionary France, More contended, not only went against the progress of history as symbolized by Saul's conversion, but also restricted the language of moral authority to male elites. Obscure and arid metaphysics excluded "the people," especially women, who required an accessible set of beliefs ministering to common human needs and sufferings. More and Paul were on the side of "the people," even though both directed a significant portion of their efforts toward converting the aristocracy. More's somewhat misleading portrait of the great missionary as simple, straightforward, and eloquent revealed how she saw herself. Paul effectively overwhelmed learned opponents; she

---

[17]Ibid.
[18]Ibid., p.217.

hoped to do the same as an elderly female dilettante. She had no need to underscore those lines in Romans and 1 Corinthians that sanctioned or seemed to sanction womanly preaching. More assumed or tried to assume the role of Paul.[19]

What further attracted More to Paul was his deference to constituted authorities with whom he disagreed. She found that Paul's politics mirrored her own and thus were appropriate as a model for Christians, regardless of sex or age. More noted that she, like Paul, "knew how to unite a respect for the government, with a just abhorrence of the vices of the governor." More stressed that she, like Paul, was not an advocate of passive obedience and, despite common support of the powers that be, "would not connive at any formal power of injustice." Men and women following Paul's example could publically criticize the morals of a ministry, but ought to obey the temporal dictates of any cabinet. He also "well knew . . . [the] wayward motions of the mob" and never manipulated "the multitude, as an engine to lift himself into power or popularity." More particularly liked Paul's aversion to demagoguery; it was the wisdom of God that He could never tempt her to become a demagogue because of her gender.[20]

Yet although both Paul and More refrained (and were formally excluded from) palace as well as popular politics, their preaching was designed to inform and reform the political and social order. Paul "enjoined on the people those industrious habits which are the very soul of order [and] was a most rigorous punisher of idleness, that powerful cherisher of insubordination in the lower orders."[21] More presented Paul and herself as the best friends of order, charging that the very intellectuals who complained about Christianity's weakening of states were

---

[19]Ibid., pp.217-30, 261-70. More had briefly made these arguments about pagan philosophy in her *Remarks on the Speech of M. Dupont* (1793), The Works of Hannah More vol.1 (Philadelphia: Woodward, 1832), p.305. See also the excellent discussion of More's *Remarks* in Christine L. Krueger, *The Reader's Repentance: Women Preachers, Women Writers, and the Victorian Social Discourse*, Princeton University Ph.D. dissertation in English, 1986, pp.109-11.
[20]More, *St. Paul, Works*, p.279.
[21]Ibid.

themselves "the strenuous subverters of order, law, and government."[22]

It would be easy to conclude that More's identification with
Paul and his politics was merely the grandiose and harmless
fantasy of an old woman, but it would be wrong. Influential
readers of this biography took her very seriously.[23] Indeed,
"urgent representations . . . from the highest quarters" in 1817
implored her to reissue and recycle her *Cheap Repository* tracts
from the 1790s.[24] Faced with unprecedented political unrest
and economic distress, the embattled Liverpool ministry turned
to More, then 72, and in mourning over the recent loss of three
of her sisters.

To appreciate the desperation of the ministry and the appreciably different (as compared to the 1790s) content of her tracts
requires a detour through the difficult years after Waterloo.
Peace brought depression on the land and in London. Swings
between boom and bust in both agriculture and manufacturing
occurred most sharply in the 1810s. Encouraged by big profits
and poor weather between 1793 and 1812, farmers had grown
crops on chemically inferior or previously inaccessible land.
They also had tilled more rationally than before because of a
wave of enclosure legislation. Yet given better weather and
lower prices after 1812, capital investment by farmers in the
previous decade, coupled with their cultivation of fens and
mountaintops, spelled trouble for the landed interest. Considerable debts had to be paid in deflationary times, while farming
on marginal soils was no longer remunerative. Excessive quan-
tities of all sorts of produce, or a general glut, were grim reali-
ties in the countryside. Banks became very reluctant to extend
credit and thus further inhibited demand for manufacturing as
well as agricultural goods. Unemployment rapidly increased,
and the unemployed and underemployed, many of them

---

[22]Ibid., p.280.
[23]For example, see Lord Teignmouth to Hannah More, 1815, Roberts,
Memoirs vol.3, pp.448-9.
[24]Hannah More to William Weller Pepys, 24 January 1817, Roberts, *Memoirs*
vol.4, p.11 as quoted in Jones, *Hannah More*, p.201.

returning servicemen, looked for political saviors or scape-goats.[25]

Temporarily high food prices during 1816 and 1817 gave false hope to employers, but this spurt of inflation nearly toppled the Liverpool administration. The summer of 1816 was the exception in the spate of good weather between 1812 and 1822. Seasonably warm temperatures never occurred because emissions of a volcano in the Dutch East Indies enveloped the Northern Hemisphere. As a result, grain harvests failed in 1816 from Galicia and Transylvania in the east to Kentucky and Pennsylvania in the west, from the Papal States in the south to Scandinavia in the north. Wheat yields in England were the worst of the nineteenth century, and the market price of grains doubled.[26]

The ministry justly feared a repetition of Paris, 1789. Once again, "the people" and their self-appointed leaders held an allegedly corrupt and anachronistic political establishment, not the freakish weather, responsible for a scarcity of bread and employment. Most worrisome to the elite was the wave of inexpensive radical propaganda linking their fiscal extravagance to the current economic distress. Most culpable for convincing discontented workers to blame high taxes and government spending for their plight was the journalist William Cobbett, Hannah More's former friend turned bitter enemy. During the grim winter of 1816-17, Cobbett reprinted articles from his *Weekly Political Register* as unstamped twopenny broadsides intended for the widest possible audience. Through bombast and invective easily understood by the semi-literate, Cobbett recommended parliamentary reform as the vehicle to cut taxes, to pay off the deficit, and to put people back to work. This attractive message gave a focused edge to the demonstrations

---

[25]Ian Christie, *Wars and Revolutions: Britain, 1760-1815* (Cambridge, Mass.: Harvard University Press, 1979), pp.158-61; Boyd Hilton, *Corn, Cash, Commerce: The Economic Policies of the Tory Governments, 1815-1830* (Oxford: Oxford University Press, 1977), pp.3-30.

[26]For a modern study of the consequences of this terrible weather for the West's economy, consult John D. Post, "A Study in Meteorological and Trade Cycle History: The Economic Crisis following the Napoleonic Wars," *Journal of Economic History*, 34(1974), pp.315-49.

and riots of the following spring with working-class marchers on London spouting, in the words of Norman Gash, "Cobbettite doctrine in its crudest vernacular form."[27]

The ministry was ill-equipped to counter radical dissent. Aware of popular sentiment, Lord Liverpool had made deep cuts in both domestic and defense spending and had accepted the defeat of the hated property tax in 1816. At least at Westminster, he had gracefully disinfected economy of sedition and had gained the crucial support of swing voters in Parliament such as the Grenvillites and rural whigs. Yet, as J. E. Cookson notes, "hard as the ministers laboured, their work received scant acknowledgement" outside Westminster.[28] Angered by the lack of public gratitude and forbearance, the ministry shepherded (in March, 1817) repressive legislation through Parliament that, among other things, suspended *habeas corpus* for suspected traitors. Lord Liverpool knew, however, that the strength of the British establishment depended upon its relatively libertarian and moral image as compared to the tyrants of the Holy Alliance. "The people" had to accept this image once again, preferably through persuasion.[29] Having no consequential newspaper to defend their probity and legitimacy before the masses, the ministry recalled the commercial success of Hannah More's *Village Politics* and *Cheap Repository* tracts twenty years before. In January of 1817, unnamed senior officials asked for her "powerful assistance in supplying antidotes to the spreading poison" of William Cobbett, ironically the distributor of the *Cheap Repository* in America during the nineties.[30]

More quickly said yes. She shared William Wilberforce's disapproval of agent provocateurs and domestic spies used by the Home Secretary, Lord Sidmouth, and had never really forgiven Sidmouth for his initial opposition to her schools during

---

[27]Norman Gash, *Aristocracy and People: Britain, 1815-1865* (Cambridge, Mass.: Harvard University Press, 1979), p.79. Reprinted by permission of Harvard University Press, Copyright © 1979 by Norman Gash. c.f. E. P. Thompson, *The Making of the English Working Class* (New York: Pantheon Books, 1963), pp.636-46, 668-9.

[28]J. E. Cookson, *Lord Liverpool's Administration: The Crucial Years, 1815-1822* (Hamden, Connecticut: Archon Books, 1975), p.123.

[29]Ibid., p.110.

[30]Jones, *Hannah More*, pp.202-3.

the Blagdon Controversy. Yet she, like Wilberforce, viewed the Liverpool ministry on the whole as "a virtuous government."[31]

The Chancellor of the Exchequer, Nicholas Vansittart, was an Evangelical and a friend, and Lord Liverpool himself "set a quiet example of regular religious observance" of family prayers and Sabbatarian strictures.[32] These Christian soldiers were fighting that coarse drunkard Cobbett and, most gratifying to More, outright blasphemers such as William Hone whose anti-Anglican satires sold over 100,000 copies in 1817. More jumped at the chance to help rebut the radical evildoers, even though, as she self-effacingly reassured astonished male friends, she "did not think to turn ballad-monger in . . . [her] old age."[33]

More certainly controverted the passive, reclusive ideal of a seventy-two-year-old woman. She contributed short pieces to the *Anti-Cobbett or Weekly Patriotic Register*, a ministerial newspaper published at 1 1/2 d. per edition between February and April of 1817. The *Anti-Cobbett* was not commercially successful, and simply declared victory and shut down after Cobbett fled to the United States in April in the wake of the suspension of the Habeus Corpus Act. More popular than the *Anti-Cobbett* was More's recasting of *Village Politics* as *Village Disputants* and composition of several new tracts such as *The Market House Orator*. A central committee of London socialites distributed most of these stories, but More personally handed out pamphlets in her native Somerset.[34]

---

[31]Ibid., p.203; John Pollock, *Wilberforce* (New York: St. Martin's Press, 1977), pp.264-5.

[32]Norman Gash, *Lord Liverpool: The Life and Political Career of Robert Banks Jenkinson, Second Earl of Liverpool, 1770-1828* (Cambridge, Mass.: Harvard University Press, 1984), p.201. Reprinted by permission of Harvard University Press, Copyright © 1984 by Norman Gash.

[33]Hannah More to William Weller Pepys, 24 January 1817, Roberts, *Memoirs* vol.4, p.10; Hannah More to Mr. Harford, 21 April 1817, Roberts, *Memoirs* vol.4, p.18. For Hone's satire, see his tracts reprinted in Edgell Rickword, ed., *Radical Squibs & Loyal Ripostes: Satirical Pamphlets of the Regency Period, 1819-1821 Illustrated by George Cruikshank and others* (New York: Barnes & Noble, 1971), pp.35-58, 83-106, 135-208, 269-310. For the ministry's perception that atheism and anticlericalism underpinned radicals, see Jonathan Clark, *English Society 1688-1832* (Cambridge: Cambridge University Press, 1985), p.384.

[34]Jones, *Hannah More*, p.203.

While More rejected mature resignation through her example, she was less successful (from a literary standpoint) than in the 1790s in urging resignation on the down and out. Her tracts of 1817-19 lack not only the vigor and ingenuity of the *Cheap Repository* but much of its preaching about ascetic paternalism. They simply belabor in cliche and rhyme that dearth and depression stemmed not from bad policy, but from the will of God. The cold and rainy summer of 1816, in particular, was a punishment from the Lord for the treasonous impiety so prevalent among the lower orders in Britain. The disenfranchised ought to yield to His will and ought not to claim an absurdly human omnipotence. More had emphasized selective providential intervention as the cause of the dearth of 1794-5, but a generation later that was all she stressed. These tracts do not scold Regency decadence and have no advice to the affluent about philanthropy. They are so concerned with defending the unreformed Parliament that they have no room for the constructive criticism of the rich so prominent in the *Cheap Repository*. The cleverest female wit of the last century had become an out-of-touch anachronism in the post-war era.[35]

Advocating the political passivity that she herself had eschewed, More paled in comparison with the always colorful Cobbett. She was right to point out that voting rights and budget cuts would not ease economic distress. Indeed, it is a modern truism that the worst move for a policymaker during a depression is to decrease public expenditures. Yet even if Cobbett was dead wrong about fiscal matters, he had the flair and sting that Hannah More used to have. A former admirer and distributor of More, Cobbett had also learned most of her propaganda tricks well. Like More in the 1790s, Cobbett posed as a populistic anti-intellectual who expressed the hopes and concerns of typical John Bulls, characterizing his well-to-do opponents as effete shills for an alien arbitrary government. Like the middle-aged More, he conveyed his concern for the rural poor in part by pointing out how far removed his cosmopolitan opponents were from the corporeal worries of

---

[35]In particular, see Hannah More, *The Loyal Subject's Political Creed*, *Collected Works* vol.10 (London: n.p., 1853), p.277.

the victims of depression and dearth. Cobbett recaptured nationalistic tones and symbols for radical causes and thus, to the elderly More, was the most noxious of the libertarian politicians.[36]

Hannah More, however, did not relinquish easily those powerful patriotic themes that she had been using in her works since her London debut nearly a half-century before. Soon after the demise of the *Anti-Cobbett*, she tried to take back this discourse for Evangelicals with her *Moral Sketches of Prevailing Opinions and Manners, Foreign and Domestic: with Reflections on Prayer*. Suddenly bitter about the course of recent history, More showed that she still had some of her old verve with this relatively pungent essay, published for a middle-class audience in July of 1819. For the first time in years and, as it turned out, for the final time, More honestly wrote as the self-conscious cultural outsider that she had always been. Unlike her recent tracts, her *Sketches* rail against sophisticated aristocrats as well as subversive reporters (such as Cobbett).

Indeed, her *Sketches* are filled with brisk if dated invective against French society and its English admirers. She blamed lingering depression on English consumption of French luxury goods; she attributed chronic unrest to genteel abandonment of the countryside for the sinful pleasures across the Channel. Her hatred of Gallic influence was clear and common, but it was also paradoxically out of phase. Her journalistic outlines of polite society in London are far more descriptive of the alien fashionable world in the 1780s than of the relatively indigenous social splendor of the Regency. Considerably fewer British aristocrats after the Revolution than before looked to Paris for

---

[36]For Cobbett, see George Spater, *William Cobbett: The Poor Man's Friend* vol.2 (Cambridge: Cambridge University Press, 1982), pp.337-50; Raymond Williams, *Cobbett* (Oxford: Oxford University Press, 1983), pp.54-81; Olivia Smith, *The Politics of Language, 1791-1817* (Oxford: Clarendon Press, 1984), pp.227-33; Gertrude Himmelfarb, *The Idea of Poverty: England in the Early Industrial Age* (New York: Vintage Books, 1985), pp.207-29; Ian Dyck, "From 'Rabble' to 'Chopsticks': The Radicalism of William Cobbett," *Albion*, vol.21, 1(Spring, 1989), pp.56-87.

the latest fads in costume and behavior. Hannah More was living in her usable past.[37]

Yet her past provided instruction for her present. In a particularly revealing sketch, More maintained that the elderly French *salonières* of her youth showed how not to be an old lady. More first iterated the conventional wisdom about old age "as a season of repose, reflection, and preparation for death." She, like any ardent protestant, reasoned that God "sent . . . [old age's] infirmities, sufferings, and debility, as gracious intimations of our approaching change." Mocking God's wishes, the courtesans of the Enlightenment tried "to cheat old age of itself—of its present inconveniences, its decays, and its prospective views" by "divert[ing] the stage of infirmity into a scene of superinduced gayety and increased levity." These fun-loving matrons did not act their age and, most egregious to More, wanted to be senior citizens equal before the law. She here advocated conventional passivity for old women such as herself, but in her own political and moral activism she was much more a senior citizen (actually if not legally) than Madame du Deffand had ever hoped to be.[38]

It would be a mistake, however, to assume that More's sex, age, and prominence during the 1810s and 1820s insulated her from high-brow censure and derision. Samuel Taylor Coleridge, the poet and critic, ate dinner at the Mores as an unknown student sometime in the early 1790s. Coleridge was vindictive, returning her courtesy with ridicule of Hannah's intimate manners and simple convictions. More predictable than Coleridge's venom was Lord Byron's satire. Hannah More had dared to read the cynical and bohemian Byron and then conclude that no one ought to read him. Byron had dared to read the prim and proper More and then add "Coelebs' wife in search of lovers" to his *Don Juan*, published in 1818. Yet most damaging

---

[37]Hannah More, *Moral Sketches of Prevailing Opinions and Manners, Foreign and Domestic: Reflections on Prayer, The Works of Hannah More* vol.2 (Philadelphia: Woodward, 1832), pp.434-54; White, *Regency England*, p.8; Gerald Newman, "Anti-French Propaganda and British Liberal Nationalism in the Early Nineteenth Century: Suggestions Toward a General Interpretation," *Victorian Studies*, 18(1975), pp.404, 414-8.

[38]More, *Moral Sketches, Works*, p.445.

to More's reputation as a writer was the opium eater Thomas de Quincey, the rebellious and literary son of one of More's Evangelical friends. In an antagonistic obituary of More published immediately after her death in 1833, de Quincey correctly portrayed her as a crafty and ambitious woman, but he was overly harsh on her writings. He vilified More in the same sardonic and misogynist way that Lytton Strachey would thrash Florence Nightingale eighty years later. He thus relegated More to literary oblivion.[39]

Insulated by her faith from these barbs, however, More and her career suffered most from constant bereavement and domestic fraud in her seventies and eighties. More was able to write books prolifically and to run charities carefully in part because her four sisters (with whom she lived) had handled her household and social chores since the 1760s. This domestic division of labor collapsed with the deaths of Mary in 1813, Elizabeth in 1816, Sally in 1817, and Patty in 1819. More was suddenly forced to run a household by herself at seventy-five and also suddenly had to entertain alone the endless stream of tourists, from American Episcopal bishops through curious Persian noblemen who were interested in seeing her and her home. She had always been busy, but now she was swamped. Retirement proved shocking as well as cluttered to Hannah More. Chronic illness in the early 1820s followed sadness and confined her to upstairs rooms at her cottage, Barley Wood. Her servants took advantage of her bedridden helplessness. In 1788 More had maintained that if the mistress of the house had good morals, the mistress' servants would emulate her good morals. She was wrong. Her own servants spurned her example and had wild parties by night and shopping sprees by day at her expense. The ever loyal Zachary Macaulay rescued her from these parasites and moved More, then 83, in April of 1828 to another one of her cottages where she died five years later. It was thus no coincidence that she did not publish another significant work after *Sketches*, although she put forth a hastily edited collection of some of her previous essays, *The Spirit of Prayer*, in

---

[39]Jones, *Hannah More*, pp.223-4.

1825 and composed a few verses for the anti-slavery movement throughout the twenties and early thirties.[40]

In a sense, Hannah More faced the private frustrations of spinsterhood at full blast only in her extreme old age. This was fortunate not only for More but also for her readers. Her exceptional and, to a certain extent, sheltered life produced an impressive *oeuvre* well into her seventies, one that, among other things, reflected her admirable desires and efforts to avoid being the conventionally complacent, patiently resigned old maid. It would be easy to dismiss More's final works as "pabulum," but it would be imprecise. Her essays, tracts, and biography of the 1810s present familiar moral principles, but by no means are these principles (with the notorious exception of the tracts of 1817-19) meant to be reassuring to the powers that be. Indeed, both her life and her accomplishments as an old woman defied the dicta of the rapidly changing post-war world. More was out of sorts with the temper of the early nineteenth century; her reputation as a mother of the Victorians came much later. Even at 87 she made a political move against the grain, however subtle, by cutting Thomas Macaulay, son of her rescuer Zachary, out of her will because of Tom's fiery speeches in favor of parliamentary reform.[41] She was ultimately bound to and by the political old order, but she was not the typical Mrs. Grundy of her day.

---

[40]Ibid., pp.225-7. For her verses and activities, see also Hannah More, "The Bazaar," July of 1827, Ford Collection, V Autographs Ms. Miscellaneous, The Pierpont Morgan Library, New York; Hannah More to Thomas Cadell, September of 1828, Norcrose Collection, Massachusetts Historical Society, Boston, Massachusetts; Hannah More, "Who are these Heroes?," 1829, The John Rylands University Library of Manchester, English Mss. 341, fo.232; Hannah More, "Comment on the Psalms of David," Beinecke Rare Books and Manuscript Library, Yale University, Osborn Collection, Mss. Vault File, 29 May 1829; Hannah More, "The Negro Boys Petition," 26 July 1830, McIlvaine Collection, V Autographs Ms. Miscellaneous, The Pierpont Morgan Library, New York.
[41]Jones, *Hannah More*, p.221.

Bibliography

Primary Sources

Manuscripts

BEINECKE RARE BOOK AND MANUSCRIPT LIBRARY, YALE UNIVERSITY

Manuscript Vault File, Hannah More, "Comment on the Psalms of David," 29 May 1829.

Osborn Collection, Edmund Burke, "Case of the Suffering Clergy of France, Refugees in the British Dominions," a contemporary reprint from *The Evening Mail*, 19 September 1792, Shelves c.42; Letter from Hannah More to John Eardley-Wilmot, 27 January 1794, Shelves c.42; Letter from Hannah More to an unidentified correspondent, 18 June 1782, Files 85.11.1.

DUKE UNIVERSITY LIBRARY

William Wilberforce Papers, Letters from Hannah More to William Wilberforce, 1789-97.

FOLGER SHAKESPEARE LIBRARY

Art Collection, William Loftis, "Mr. Wroughton as Douglas," c16, no.1.

Garrick Correspondence, Letter from Eva Garrick to Dr. Wright, 11 February 1784, Mss. 486, No.73; Letters from Hannah More to Eva Garrick, 1789-97, Mss.487-8; Letter from Sarah More to Eva Garrick, 12 December 1799, Mss. 488, fo.32; Letter from Mrs. Joel Mendez Pye to David Garrick, 21 November 1774, Mss. W. b. 489, fo.35.

Garrick Papers, David Garrick, Epilogue to *The Inflexible Captive*, Mss.492, fo.28; Fragment of Rough Draft of Prologue to *Percy*, Mss. Y. d. 156, fo.42.

HISTORICAL SOCIETY OF PENNSYLVANIA

Gratz Manuscripts, 2 letters by Hannah More.

HOUGHTON LIBRARY, HARVARD UNIVERSITY

American Manuscripts, Letter from Hannah More to Miss Adams, 15 June 1782, bMS Am. 1631, (298).

Autograph File, Letter from Hannah More to Cadell and Davies, 27 July 1801; Letter from Hannah More to an unidentified correspondent, 21 November 1812.

MASSACHUSETTS HISTORICAL SOCIETY

Norcrose Collection, Letter from Hannah More to Thomas Cadell, September of 1828.

PIERPONT MORGAN LIBRARY

English Manuscripts, Letter from Hannah More to Eva Garrick, 31 January 1803, R-V Autographs Misc., MA 3751.

Ford Collection, Hannah More, "The Bazaar," July of 1827, V Autographs Ms. Miscellaneous.

McIlvaine Collection, Hannah More, "The Negro Boys Petition," 26 July 1830, V Autographs Ms. Miscellaneous.

NEW YORK PUBLIC LIBRARY

Henry W. and Albert A. Berg Collection, Letters from Hester Thrale Piozzi to the Reverend Thomas Sedgwick Whalley, 1800-01.

JOHN RYLANDS UNIVERSITY LIBRARY OF MANCHESTER

English Manuscripts, Hannah More, "Who are these Heroes?," 1829, Ms. 341, fo.232; Letter from Hannah More to Hester Thrale Piozzi, 15 May 1800, Ms. 556, fo.153.

RUSH RHEES LIBRARY, UNIVERSITY OF ROCHESTER

Manuscript Collection 7, Letter from Hannah More to Frances Boscawen, 23 December 1775.

PRIVATE POSSESSION (THE VISCOUNTESS ECCLES)

Hyde Collection, Firestone Library, Princeton University, 4 letters by Hannah More.

Newspapers and Periodicals

Analytical Review, 1(August, 1788).

Anti-Jacobin Review and Magazine, 1798-1803, select reviews.

British Critic, 1793, 1797-9, 1805, 1809.

Christian Observer, 1802-9.

Cobbett's Weekly Political Register, 1802-6.

Critical Review, 16(1809).

Edinburgh Review, 7(October, 1805), 27(April, 1809).

European Magazine, 56(1809).

Evangelical Magazine, 1801-3, 1809.

Gentleman's Magazine, 49(1779), 79(1809).

Literary Magazine, 2(1757).

Literary Panorama, 6(1809).

London Chronicle, 35(5 April 1774), 39(6-8 May 1779).

London Review, 1805, 1809.

Monthly Magazine, 27(1809).

Monthly Review, 1782, 1786, 1801-2, 1805, 1808-9.

Satirist, 1809.

Scots Magazine, 71(1809).

Sporting Magazine, vol.28, no.168 (September, 1806).

St. James Chronicle, September, 1763; August, 1779.

The Times (London), May-June 1816.

Town and Country Magazine, 24(January, 1792).

Universal Magazine, 11(1809).

Contemporary Books, Diaries, and Published Correspondence

Austen, Jane. *Jane Austen's Letters to Her Sister Cassandra and Others*. Edited by R. W. Chapman. Oxford, 1979.

——. *Mansfield Park*. Edited by Tony Tanner. London, 1985.

——. *Pride and Prejudice*. Edited and introduced by Frank W. Bradbrook. London, 1970.

——. *Sense and Sensibility*. Edited by Tony Tanner. Harmondsworth, 1986.

Bage, Robert. *Hermsprong; or, Man As He Is Not* vol.1. Edited by Stuart Tave. University Park, Pa., 1982.

Barbauld, Anna. *The Works of Anna Letitia Barbauld. With a Memoir by Lucy Aikin*. 2 vols. London, 1825.

Bell, Eva Mary, ed. *The Hamwood Papers of the Ladies of Llangollen and Caroline Hamilton*. London, 1930.

Bentham, Jeremy. *The Correspondence of Jeremy Bentham: January 1802 to December, 1808*. vol.7. Edited by J. R. Dinwiddy. Oxford, 1988.

Berry, Mary. *Extracts from the Journals and Correspondence of Miss Berry From the Year 1783 to 1852*. vol.2. Edited by Lady Theresa Lewis. London, 1865.

Bethune, George W., ed. *Pearls from the British Female Poets*. New York, 1876.

Boswell, James. *Boswell's Life of Johnson*. Abridged and edited by Charles Grosvenor Osgood. New York, 1917.

Bowles, John. *Reflections at the Conclusion of the War*. London, 1800.

Brunton, Mary. *Self-Control. A Novel*. 2 vols. New York, 1811. [Garland reprint, 1974].

Burke, Edmund. *Reflections on the Revolution in France*. Edited by Conor Cruise O'Brien. Harmondsworth, 1986.

——. *The Correspondence of Edmund Burke* vol.3. Edited by George H. Guttridge. Chicago, 1961.

Burney, Frances. *Brief Reflections Relative to the Emigrant French Clergy: Earnestly Submitted to the Humane Consideration of the Ladies of Great Britain*, in *Fanny Burney and the Burneys*. Edited by R. Brimley Johnson. New York, 1926.

——. *Camilla; or, A Picture of Youth*. Edited by Edward A. and Lillian D. Bloom. London, 1972.

——. *Cecilia; or, Memoirs of an Heiress*. Edited by Peter Sabor and Margaret Anne Doody. 5 vols. in 1. London, 1988.

——. *Evelina; or, A Young Lady's Entrance into the World*. London, 1958.

——. *The Journal and Letters of Frances Burney (Madame d'Arblay)* vol.4. Oxford, 1973.

Byng, John. *The Torrington Diaries* vol.2. Edited by C. Bruyn Andrews. London, 1935.

Charlotte, Princess of Wales. *Letters of the Princess Charlotte 1811-1817*. Edited by A. Aspinall. London, 1949.

Chatterton, Thomas. "Bristowe Tragedy or the Dethe of Syr Charles Bawdin," 1772, in *Eighteenth-Century Literature*. New York, 1969.

Cobbett, William. *Letters from William Cobbett to Edward Thornton written in the years 1797 to 1800*. Edited by G. D. H. Cole. London, 1937.

Cowper, William. *The Works of William Cowper. His Life, Letters and Poems*. Edited by Reverend T. S. Grimshawe. Boston, 1866.

Crabbe, George. "The Village," in *Eighteenth Century English Literature*. New York, 1969.

Daubeny, Charles. *A Letter to Hannah More on some part of her late publication entitled Strictures on Female Education*. Bath, 1799.

Day, Thomas. *The History of Sandford and Merton: a Work intended for the Use of Children*. New York, 1818.

Defoe, Daniel. *An Essay Upon Projects*. London, 1697.

DeQuincey, Thomas. "Recollections of Hannah More," *The Collected Writings of Thomas DeQuincey* vol.14. Edited by David Masson. London, 1897.

Doddridge, Philip. *A Course of Lectures on the Principal Subjects in Pneumatology, Ethics, and Divinity with Reference to the most considerable Authors on each Subject*. London, 1763.

Dodsley, Robert. *Cleone: A Tragedy*. London, 1792.

Douglas, Sylvester. *The Diaries of Sylvester Douglas (Lord Glenbervie)*. vol.1. Edited by Francis Bickley. London, 1928.

Eden, Frederick Morton. *The State of the Poor*. London, 1966.

Edgeworth, Maria. *Castle Rackrent*. Edited by George Watson. London, 1964.

——. *Popular Tales. New Edition*. Philadelphia, 1867.

——. *The Bracelets, or, Amiability and industry Rewarded*. Philadelphia, 1850.

—— and R. L. Edgeworth. *Essays on Practical Education. A New Edition*. 2 vols. London, 1815.

Ferguson, Moira, ed. *First Feminists: British Women Writers 1578-1799*. Bloomington, Ind., 1985.

Ferrier, Susan. *Marriage. A Novel. Second Edition*. 3 vols. Edinburgh, 1819.

Fielding, Henry. *The History of Tom Jones: A Foundling*. New York, 1967.

Francis, Beata; Francis, Keaty; and Francis, Eliza, eds. *The Francis Letters, by Sir Philip Francis and Other Members of the Family, with a note on the Junius Controversy*, by C. F. Keary. vol.1. London, 1901.

Frere, John Hookham. *The Works of John Hookham Frere*. vol.1. Edited by W. E. and Sir Bartle Frere. London, 1872.

Garrick, David. *Garrick's Own Plays, 1740-1766* vol.1. Edited by Henry William Pedicord and Frederick Louis Bergman. Carbondale, Ill., 1980.

——. *The Letters of David Garrick*. Edited by David M. Little and George M. Kahrl. Cambridge, Mass., 1963.

George, Dorothy, ed. *English Social Life in the Eighteenth Century: Illustrated from Contemporary Sources*. London, 1923.

Gideon's Cake of Barley Meal: A Letter to the Rev. Wm. Romaine on his preaching for the Emigrant Popish Clergy, with Some Strictures on Mrs. Hannah More's Remarks, published for their Benefit. London, 1793.

Gisborne, Thomas. *An Enquiry into the Duties of Men in the Higher and Middle Classes of Society*. vol.1. London, 1793.

Godwin, William. *Caleb Williams*. Edited by David McCracken. London, 1970.

——. *Enquiry Concerning Political Justice*. Oxford, 1971.

Goethe, Johann Wolfgang von. *The Sorrows of Werther*. Translated by Daniel Malthus. Oxford, 1991.

Goldsmith, Oliver. *Collected Works of Oliver Goldsmith*. Edited by William Friedman. Oxford, 1966.

Graham, Catherine Macaulay. *Letters on Education with Observations on Religious and Metaphysical Subjects*. London, 1790. [Garland reprint, 1974.]

Gregory, John. *A Father's Legacy to His Daughters*. London, 1774. [Garland reprint, 1974.]

Hamilton, Elizabeth. *Letters Addressed to the Daughter of Noblemen on the Formation of the Religious and Moral Principle*. vol.1. London, 1806. [Garland reprint, 1974.]

Hays, Mary. *Appeal to the Men of Great Britain in Behalf of Women*. London, 1798. [Garland reprint, 1974.]

——. *Letters and Essays, Moral and Miscellaneous*. London, 1793. [Garland reprint, 1974.]

Hill, Bridget, ed. *Eighteenth-Century Women: An Anthology*. London, 1984.

Historical Manuscripts Commission, eds. *The Manuscripts of J. B. Fortescue, Esq., Preserved at Dropmore* vols.1 & 2. London, 1892.

Holcroft, Thomas. *Anna St. Ives*. Edited by Peter Faulkner. London, 1970.

Holland, Elizabeth Lady. *The Journal of Elizabeth Lady Holland (1791-1811)*. vol.1. Edited by the Earl of Ilchester. London, 1908.

Inchbald, Elizabeth. *A Simple Story*. Edited by J. M. S. Tompkins. London, 1967.

Jenyns, Soame. *Free Inquiry into the Nature and Origin of Evil, The Works of Soame Jenyns, Esq.* vol.3. London, 1790.

———. *A View of Internal Evidence of the Christian Religion, The Works of Soame Jenyns, Esq.* vol.4. London, 1790.

Johnson, R. Brimley, ed. *Bluestocking Letters*. New York, 1926.

Johnson, Samuel. *Lives of the English Poets*. Edited by George Birkbeck Hill. New York, 1967.

———. *The History of Rasselas Prince of Abissinia*. Edited by J. P. Hardy. Oxford, 1988.

———. "The Vanity of Human Wishes," 1749, in *Eighteenth-Century English Literature*. New York, 1969, pp.973-8.

Jones, Vivien, ed. *Women in the Eighteenth Century: Constructions of Femininity*. London, 1990.

Law, William. "A Serious Call to a Devout and Holy Life," *Works of the Reverend William Law* vol.4. London, 1893.

Lennox, Charlotte. *Henrietta*. London, 1758. [Garland reprint, 1974.]

MacDonald, John. *Memoirs of an Eighteenth Century Footman 1745-1779*. Edited by John Beresford. London, 1927.

Mackenzie, Henry. *The Mirror* vol.2, 1779-80, London, 1794.

Mackintosh, James. *Vindiciae Gallicae: Defense of the French Revolution*. London, 1791.

Mahl, Mary R. and Helene Koon, eds. *The Female Spectator: English Women Writers Before 1800.* Bloomington, Ind., 1977.

Mitford, Mary Russell. *The Letters of Mary Russell Mitford.* Edited by R. Brimley Johnson. New York, 1925.

Montagu, Elizabeth. *Mrs. Montagu: "Queen of the Blues." Her Letters and Friendships from 1762 to 1800.* vol.2. Edited by Reginald Blunt. Boston, 1921.

Montagu, Mary Wortley. *Letters from the Levant, during the Embassy to Constantinople 1716-18, with a Preliminary Discourse and Notes Containing a Sketch of her Ladyship's Character, Moral and Literary.* New York, 1971.

——. *The Works of the Right Honourable Lady Mary Montagu, including her Correspondence, Poems, and Essays.* vol.4. London, 1817.

More, Hannah. *Coelebs in Search of a Wife.* New York, 1857.

——. *Letters of Hannah More to Zachary Macaulay,* Esq. Edited by Arthur Roberts. New York, 1860.

——. *Memoirs of the Life and Correspondence of Mrs. Hannah More.* 4 vols. Edited by William Roberts. London, 1835.

——. *The Letters of Hannah More.* Edited by R. Brimley Johnson. New York, 1926.

——. *The Works of Hannah More.* 2 vols. Philadelphia, 1832.

——. *Tragedies.* London, 1818.

More, Martha. *Mendips Annals: or, A Narrative of the Charitable Labours of Hannah and Martha More in Their Neighbourhood. Being the Journal of Martha More. Fourth Edition.* Edited by Arthur Roberts. London, 1861.

Neville, Sylas. *The Diary of Sylas Neville (1767-1788).* Edited by Basil Cozens-Hardy. London, 1950.

Newton, Benjamin. *The Diary of Benjamin Newton, Rector of Wath, 1816-18.* Edited by C. P. Fendall and E. A. Crutchley. Cambridge, 1933.

Opie, Amelia. *Adeline Mowbray; or, The Mother and Daughter*. 3 vols. London, 1805. [Garland reprint, 1974.]

Paine, Thomas. *Rights of Man Parts One and Two*. Edited by Eric Foner. Harmondsworth, 1987.

——. *The Age of Reason: Being an Investigation of True and Fabulous Theology*, in *The Life and Works of Thomas Paine*. vol.8. Edited by William D. Van der Weyde. New Rochelle, N.Y., 1925.

Paley, William. *The Works of William Paley*. Philadelphia, 1831.

Parr, Samuel. *Memoirs of the Life, Writings, and Opinions of the Rev. Samuel Parr, LL.D.* Edited by William Field. London, 1828.

Piozzi, Hester Thrale. *The Piozzi Letters* vol.1. Edited by Edward A. Bloom and Lillian D. Bloom. Newark, 1989.

——. *Thraliana: The Diary of Hester Lynch Thrale (later Mrs. Piozzi) 1784-1809*. vol.2. Edited by Katherine C. Balderston. Oxford, 1951.

Place, Francis. *The Autobiography of Francis Place*. Edited by Mary Thale. Cambridge, 1972.

Polwhele, Richard. *The Unsex'd Females, A Poem*. London, 1798. [Garland reprint, 1974].

Pope, Alexander. *The Dunciad To Dr. Jonathan Swift, Book the First, 1728*, in *The Complete Poetical Works of Alexander Pope, With Life*. New York, 1880, pp.390-401.

Price, Richard. *The Evidence for a Future Period of Improvement in the State of Mankind, With the Means and Duty of Promoting It, Represented in a Discourse, Delivered on Wednesday, 25 April 1787, at the Meeting-House in Old Jewry, London, to the Supporters of a New Academical Institution among Protestant Dissenters*. London, 1787.

Radcliffe, Ann Ward. *The Mysteries of Udolpho*. Edited by R. Austin Freeman. London, 1931.

Radcliffe, Mary Ann. *The Memoirs of Mrs. Mary Ann Radcliffe; Familiar Letters to Her Female Friend.* Edinburgh, 1810. [Garland reprint, 1974].

Reeve, Clara. *Charoba, Queen of Aegypt, reproduced from the Colchester edition of 1785, with a bibliographical note by Esther M. McGill.* 2 vols. New York, 1930.

Ricardo, David. *Letters of David Ricardo to Thomas Robert Malthus 1810-1823.* Edited by James Bonar. Oxford, 1887.

Richardson, Samuel. *Pamela, or Virtue Rewarded: In A Series of Familiar Letters from a Beautiful Young Damsel to her Parents: afterwards in her exalted Condition, between her, and Persons of Figure and Quality, upon the most Important and Entertaining Subjects, in Genteel Life.* Edited by William M. Sale. New York, 1958.

——. *The History of Sir Charles Grandison In a Series of Letters* vol.3. Oxford, 1931.

Rickword, Edgell, ed. *Radical Squibs & Loyal Ripostes: Satirical Pamphlets of the Regency Period, 1819-1821 Illustrated by George Cruikshank and others.* New York, 1971.

Robinson, Henry Crabb. *Diary, Reminiscences, and Correspondence of Henry Crabb Robinson, Barrister-at-Law, F.S.A.* vol.1. Edited by Thomas Sadler. Boston, 1870.

Romilly, Sir Samuel. *Memoirs of the Life of Sir Samuel Romilly, Written by Himself; With a Selection from his Correspondence.* vol.2. London, 1840.

Scott, Sir Walter. *The Antiquary.* Edited by William Parker. London, 1969.

——. *Kenilworth.* Edited by William Parker. London, 1969.

Sevigne, Madame Marie de. *Letters of Mme. de Sevigne to her Daughter and her Friends.* Edited by Richard Aldington. London, 1937.

Seward, Anna. *Letters of Anna Seward Written Between the Years 1784-1807* vols. 1 & 2. Edited by A. Constable. Edinburgh, 1811.

Sheridan, Frances. *The Plays of Frances Sheridan*. Edited by Robert Hogan and Jerry Beasley. Newark, 1984.

Smith, Adam. *An Inquiry into the Nature and Causes of the Wealth of Nations*. Edited by Edwin Cannon. New York, 1937.

Smith, Charlotte Turner. *The Young Philosopher. A Novel*. London, 1798. [Garland reprint, 1974.]

Smith, Sydney. *The Letters of Sydney Smith* vol.1. Edited by Nowell C. Smith. Oxford, 1953.

Smollett, Tobias. *Travels Through France and Italy*, Letter VII, 12 October 1763, in *Eighteenth-Century Literature*. New York, 1969, pp.954-8.

Spencer, Edward. Truths, *Respecting Mrs. Hannah More's Meeting-Houses, and the Conduct of her Followers; Addressed to the Curate of Blagdon*. Bath, 1802.

Stael-Holstein, Madame Anne-Louise Germaine de. *Corinne, or Italy*. Edited and translated by Avriel H. Goldberger. New Brunswick, N.J., 1987.

Tatham, Edward. *Letters to the Right Honourable Edmund Burke on Politics*. Oxford, 1791.

The Female Aegis; or, The Duties of Women from Childhood to Old Age and in Most Situations of Life Exemplified. London, 1798. [Garland reprint, 1974.]

Trimmer, Sarah. *The Oeconomy of Charity*. London, 1787.

Wakefield, Priscilla. *Reflections on the Present Condition of the Female Sex, with Suggestions for its Improvement*. London, 1798. [Garland reprint, 1974.]

Walpole, Horace. *The Castle of Otranto*. Introduced by Sir Walter Scott and Caroline Spurgeon. New York, 1923.

——. *The Letters of Horace Walpole, Fourth Earl of Orford* vols.14 & 15. Edited by Paget Toynbee. Oxford, 1905.

Wilberforce, William. *A Practical View of the Prevailing Religious System of Professed Christians in the Higher and Middle Classes in this Country Contrasted with Real Christianity*. Boston, 1799.

——. *The Correspondence of William Wilberforce*. vol.1. Edited by Robert Isaac and Samuel Wilberforce. London, 1840.

Williams, Helen Maria. *Julia. A Novel*. 2 vols. London, 1790. [Garland reprint, 1974.]

Wilson, Katharina M., ed. *Medieval Women Writers*. Athens, Ga., 1984.

Wollstonecraft, Mary. *Letters Written During a Short Residence in Sweden, Norway, and Denmark*. Edited and introduced by Carol H. Poston. Lincoln, Neb., 1976.

——. *The Works of Mary Wollstonecraft*. vol.1. Edited by Janet Todd and Marilyn Butler. London, 1989.

——. *Vindication of the Rights of Woman*. Edited by Miriam Brody. London, 1988.

Yearsley, Ann. *Poems, On Several Occasions*. London, 1785.

Secondary Sources

Articles & Books

Agress, Lynne. *The Feminine Irony: Women on Women in Early-Nineteenth-Century English Literature*. Cranbury, N.J., 1978.

Aiken-Sneath, Betsy. "Hannah More (1745-1833)," *The London Mercury*, October, 1933, p.532.

Aldridge, A. O. "Madame de Stael and Hannah More on Society." *Romanic Review*, 38(1947), pp.330-39.

Altick, Richard. *The English Common Reader: A Social History of the Mass Reading Public, 1800-1900*. Chicago, 1957.

Anderson, Bonnie S. and Judith P. Zinsser. *A History of Their Own: Women in Europe from Prehistory to the Present*, vol.2. New York, 1989.

Anstey, Roger. *The Atlantic Slave Trade and British Abolition, 1760-1810*. Atlantic Highlands, 1975.

Armstrong, Nancy. "The Rise of the Domestic Woman" in Nancy Armstrong and Leonard Tennenhouse, eds., *The Ideology of Conduct: Essays on Literature and the History of Sexuality*. London and New York, 1987.

Auerbach, Nina. *Communities of Women: An Idea in Fiction*. Cambridge, Mass., 1978.

Baker, Ernest A. *The History of the English Novel, Volume V: The Novels of Sentiment and the Gothic Romance*. New York, 1961.

——. *The History of the English Novel, Volume VI: Edgeworth, Austen, and Scott*. New York, 1961.

Balleine, George R. *A History of the Evangelical Party in the Church of England*. London, 1908.

Bauckham, R. J. "Sabbath and Sunday in the Protestant Tradition," in D. A. Carson, ed., *From Sabbath to Lord's Day*. Grand Rapids, Mich., 1982.

Bebbington, D. W. *Evangelicalism in Modern Britain: A History from the 1730s to the 1980s*. London, 1989.

Beier, A. L. *The Problem of the Poor in Tudor and Early Stuart England*. London, 1983.

Bellenger, Dominic. "The Emigre Clergy and the English Church, 1789-1815," *Journal of Ecclesiastical History*, 34(1983), pp.392-410.

Best, Geoffrey. "Evangelicals and the Victorians," in Anthony Symondson, ed., *The Victorian Crisis of Faith*. London, 1970.

Bindman, David. *The Shadow of the French Revolution: Britain and the French Revolution*. London, 1989.

Birrell, Augustine. *In the Name of the Bodleian and Other Essays*. London, 1906.

Black, F. G. *The Epistolary Novel in the Late Eighteenth Century: A Descriptive and Bibliographical Study*. Eugene, Ore., 1940.

Blaug, Mark. "The Myth of the Old Poor Law and the Making of the New," *Journal of Economic History*, 23(1963), pp.151-84.

Bohstedt, John. *Riots and Community Politics in England and Wales 1790-1810*. Cambridge, Mass., 1983.

Booth, Alan. "Popular Loyalism and Violence in the North-West of England, 1790-1800," *Social History*, 8(October, 1983), pp.295-313.

Bradley, Ian. *The Call To Seriousness*. New York, 1976.

Briggs, Asa. *The Age of Improvement*. London, 1959.

Brown, Ford K. *Fathers of the Victorians: The Age of Wilberforce*. Cambridge, 1961.

Brown, Philip Anthony. *The French Revolution in English History*. New York, 1965.

Browne, Alice. *The Eighteenth-Century Feminist Mind*. Brighton, Sussex, 1987.

Butler, Marilyn. *Jane Austen and the War of Ideas*. Oxford, 1975.

———. *Maria Edgeworth: A Literary Biography*. Oxford, 1972.

———. *Romantics, Rebels, and Reactionaries, English Literature and its Background 1760-1830*. Oxford, 1981.

Canovan, Margaret. "Paternalistic Liberalism: Joseph Priestley on Rank and Inequality," *Enlightenment and Dissent*, 2(1983), pp.23-37.

Cash, Arthur H. *Laurence Sterne: The Later Years*. London, 1986.

Child, Philips. "Portrait of a Woman of Affairs—Old Style." *University of Toronto Quarterly*, 3(1933), pp.87-102.

Christie, Ian. *Wars and Revolutions: Britain, 1760-1815*. Cambridge, Mass., 1979.

———. *Stress and Stability in Late Eighteenth-Century Britain*. Oxford, 1984.

Claeys, Gregory. *Thomas Paine: Social and Political Thought.* Boston, 1989.

Clark, G. Kitson. *The Making of Victorian England.* London, 1962.

Clark, Jonathan. *English Society 1688-1832.* Cambridge, 1985.

Clarke, Martin Lowther. *Paley; Evidences for the Man.* Toronto, 1974.

Clive, John. *Macaulay: The Shaping of the Historian.* New York, 1973.

———. *Scotch Reviewers: The Edinburgh Review 1802-1815.* London, 1957.

Colley, Linda. "The Apotheosis of George III: Loyalty, Royalty, and the British Nation, 1760-1820," *Past and Present,* 102(1984), pp.94-129.

———. "Whose Nation? Class and National Consciousness in Britain, 1750-1830," *Past and Present,* 113(1986), pp.97-117.

Conkin, Paul. *Prophets of Prosperity: America's First Political Economists.* Bloomington, Ind., 1980.

———. *The Southern Agrarians.* Knoxville, Tenn., 1988.

Conn, Walter E., ed. *Conversion: Perspectives on Personal and Social Transformation.* New York, 1978.

Cookson, J. E. *Lord Liverpool's Administration: The Crucial Years, 1815-1822.* Hamden, Conn., 1975.

———. *The Friends of Peace: Anti-War Liberalism in England, 1793-1815.* Cambridge, 1982.

Cott, Nancy. *The Bonds of Womanhood: Woman's Sphere in New England, 1780-1835.* New Haven, 1977.

Courtney, Luther Weeks. *Hannah More's Interest in Education and Government.* Waco, Texas, 1929.

Cox, Stephen. "Sensibility in Argument," in Syndy McMillen Conger, ed., *Sensibility in Transformation: Creative Resistance to Sentiment from the Augustans to the Romantics*. London and Toronto, 1990.

Cunningham, Hugh. "The Language of Patriotism, 1750-1914," *History Workshop*, 12(1981), pp.8-33.

Cunningham, Valentine. *Everywhere Spoken Against: Dissent in the Victorian Novel*. Oxford, 1975.

Davidoff, Leonore and Catherine Hall. *Family Fortunes: Men and Women of the English Middle Class, 1780-1850*. London, 1987.

Davies, Kathleen. "The Sacred Condition of Equality—How Original Were Puritan Doctrines of Marriage ?," *Social History*, 5(1977), pp.563-78.

Davis, David Brion. *The Problem of Slavery in Western Culture*. Ithaca, 1966.

——. *The Problem of Slavery in the Age of Revolution*. Ithaca, 1975.

——. *Slavery and Human Progress*. New York, 1984.

Deane, Seamus. *The French Revolution and Enlightenment in England 1789-1832*. Cambridge, Mass., 1988.

Dickenson, Harry T. "Popular Conservatism and Militant Loyalism 1789-1815" in Harry T. Dickenson, ed., *Britain and the French Revolution*. New York, 1989.

Dobrzycka, Irena. "Hannah More—Forerunner of the English Social Novel." *Kwartalnik Neofilologiczny*, 27(1980), pp.133-41.

Donnelly, F. K. "Levellerism in Eighteenth and Nineteenth-Century Britain," *Albion*, 20(1988), pp.261-70.

Doody, Margaret. *Frances Burney: The Life in the Works*. New Brunswick, N.J., 1988.

Dozier, Robert R. *For King, Constitution, and Country: The English Loyalists and the French Revolution*. Lexington, 1983.

Dunkley, Peter. *The Crisis of the Old Poor Law in England, 1795-1834*. New York, 1982.

Dworkin, Gerald. "Paternalism," in Richard A. Wasserstrom, ed., *Morality and Law*. Belmont, 1971.

Dyck, Ian. "From 'Rabble' to 'Chopsticks': The Radicalism of William Cobbett," *Albion*, 21(Spring, 1989), pp.56-87.

Elshtain, Jean Bethke. *Public Man, Private Woman: Women in Social and Political Thought*. Princeton, 1981.

——. "Symmetry and Sophorics: A Critique of Feminist Accounts of Gender Development," in Barry Richards, ed., *Capitalism and Infancy: Essays on Psychoanalysis and Politics*. London, 1984.

——. *Women and War*. New York, 1987.

Emsley, Clive. "An Aspect of Pitt's 'Terror': Prosecutions for Sedition During the 1790s," *Social History*, 6(May, 1981), pp.155-75.

——. "Repression, 'Terror' and the Rule of Law in England During the Decade of the French Revolution," *English Historical Review*, 100(October, 1985), pp.801-25.

——. "The Impact of the French Revolution on British Politics and Society," in Ceri Crossley and Ian Small, eds., *The French Revolution and British Culture*. Oxford, 1989.

Faderman, Lillian. *Surpassing the Love of Men: Romantic Friendships and Love Between Women from the Renaissance to the Present*. New York, 1981.

Fairchilds, Cissie. *Domestic Enemies: Servants and Their Masters in Old Regime France*. Baltimore, 1984.

Ferguson, Moira. "Resistance and Power in the Life and Writings of Ann Yearsley," *The Eighteenth Century: Theory and Interpretation*, 27(Fall, 1986), pp.247-68.

Flexner, Eleanor. *Mary Wollstonecraft: A Biography*. New York, 1972.

Ford, Franklin L. *Europe 1780-1830*. London and New York, 1989.

Forster, E. M. *Marianne Thornton: A Domestic Biography*. New York, 1956.

Fothergill, Brian. *The Strawberry Hill Set: Horace Walpole and His Circle*. London, 1983.

Fox-Genovese, Elizabeth. "Placing Women's History in History," *New Left Review*, 133(1982), pp.5-29.

Friedman, Barton R. *Fabricating History: English Writers on the French Revolution*. Princeton, 1988.

Gallagher, Catherine. *The Industrial Reformation of English Fiction: Social Discourse and Narrative Form, 1832-1867*. Chicago, 1985.

Gascoigne, John. "Anglican Latitudinarianism and Political Radicalism in the Late Eighteenth Century," *History*, 71(February, 1986), pp.32-6.

Gash, Norman. *Aristocracy and People: Britain, 1815-65*. Cambridge, Mass., 1979.

———. *Lord Liverpool: The Life and Political Career of Robert Banks Jenkinson, Second Earl of Liverpool, 1770-1828*. Cambridge, 1984.

George, M. Dorothy. *London Life in the Eighteenth Century*. New York, 1965.

Gilbert, Sandra and Susan Gubar. *The Madwoman in the Attic: The Woman Writer and the Nineteenth-Century Literary Imagination*. New Haven, 1979.

Gill, Stephen C. "'Adventures on Salisbury Plain' and Wordsworth's Poetry of Protest 1795-97," *Studies in Romanticism*, 11(1972), pp.48-65.

Ginter, Donald E. "The Loyalist Association Movement of 1792-3 and British Public Opinion," *The Historical Journal*, IX, 2(1966), pp.179-90.

Goodwin, Albert. *The Friends of Liberty: The English Democratic Movement in the Age of the French Revolution*. Cambridge, Mass., 1979.

Green, Katherine Sobba. *The Courtship Novel 1740-1820: A Feminized Genre*. Lexington, Ky., 1991.

Hagstrum, Jean. *Sex and Sensibility: Ideal and Erotic Love from Milton to Mozart*. Chicago, 1980.

Halevy, Elie. *A History of the English People in the Nineteenth Century*. 6 vols. London, 1924-47.

——. *The Birth of Methodism*. Translated and edited by Bernard Simmel. Chicago, 1971.

Harland, Marion. *Hannah More*. New York, 1900.

Harmon, Lesley D. *The Modern Stranger: On Language and Membership*. Berlin, 1988.

Harrison, Brian. *Peaceful Kingdom: Stability and Change in Modern Britain*. Oxford, 1982.

Hay, Douglas. "Property, Authority, and the Criminal Law," in the compilation *Albion's Fatal Tree: Crime and Society in Eighteenth-Century England*. New York, 1975.

Hecht, J. Jean. *The Domestic Servant Class in Eighteenth-Century England*. London, 1956.

Hennell, Michael. *John Venn and the Clapham Sect*. London, 1958.

Herold, J. Christopher. *Mistress to an Age: A Life of Madame de Stael*. New York, 1958.

Hill, Bridget. *Women, Work, and Sexual Politics in Eighteenth-Century England*. Oxford, 1989.

Hill, Christopher. *Puritanism and Revolution*. New York, 1964.

Hiltner, Seward. "Toward a Theology of Conversion in Light of Psychology," *Pastoral Psychology*, 17(September, 1966), p.36.

Hilton, Boyd. *The Age of Atonement: The Influence of Evangelicals on Social and Economic Thought, 1795-1865*. Oxford, 1988.

——. *Corn, Cash, Commerce: The Economic Policies of the Tory Governments, 1815-30*. Oxford, 1977.

Himmelfarb, Gertrude. *The Idea of Poverty: England in the Early Industrial Age.* New York, 1984.

Hole, Robert. "British Counter-revolutionary Popular Propaganda in the 1790s," in Colin Jones, ed., *Britain and Revolutionary France: Conflict, Subversion, and Propaganda.* Exeter, 1983.

——. *Pulpits, Politics, & Public Order in England 1760-1832.* Cambridge, 1989.

Holland, Sir Eardley. "The Princess Charlotte of Wales: A Triple Obstetric Tragedy," *Journal of Obstetrics and Gynaecology of the British Empire,* n.s., 58(1951), pp.905-919.

Hooks, Bell. *Feminist Theory: From Margin to Center.* Boston, 1984.

Hopkins, Mary Alden. *Hannah More and Her Circle.* New York, 1947.

Horne, Thomas A. "'The Poor Have a Claim Founded in the Law of Nature': William Paley and the Rights of the Poor," *Journal of the History of Philosophy,* 23(1985), pp.51-70.

Howse, Ernest M. *Saints in Politics.* Toronto, 1952.

Hughes, Everett C. "Social Change and Status Protest: An Essay on the Marginal Man," *Phylon,* 10(1949), pp.58-65.

Hunt, Lynn. *Politics, Cultures, and Class in the French Revolution.* Berkeley, 1984.

Hunt, Margaret. "Literary Success, a Hundred Years Ago." *Living Age,* 2 October 1880, pp.48-53.

Jaeger, Muriel. *Before Victoria.* London, 1956.

James, William. *The Varieties of Religious Experience.* Edited by Joseph Ratner. New Hyde Park, N.Y., 1963.

Jay, Elisabeth. *The Religion of the Heart: Anglican Evangelicalism and the Nineteenth-Century Novel.* Oxford, 1979.

Jones, Mary Gladys. *Hannah More.* Cambridge, 1952.

Jordanova, L. J. "Natural Facts: A Historical Perspective on Science and Sexuality," in Carol P. MacCormick and Marilyn Stathern, eds., *Nature, Culture, and Gender*. Cambridge, 1980.

Katz, David S. *Sabbath and Sectarianism in Seventeenth-Century England*. E. J. Brill, 1988.

Kelly, Gary. *English Fiction of the Romantic Period 1789-1830*. London, 1989.

Ketton-Cremer, R. W. *Horace Walpole: A Biography*. Ithaca, 1966.

Kiernan, V. G. "Evangelicalism and the French Revolution," *Past and Present*, 1(1952), pp.44-56.

Klatch, Rebecca E. *Women of the New Right*. Philadelphia, 1987.

Kleinig, John. *Paternalism*. Totowa, N.J., 1983.

Knight, Helen Cross. *A New Memoir of Hannah More; or, Life in Hall and Cottage*. New York, 1862.

Knox, E. V. "*Percy*: The Tale of a Dramatic Success." *London Mercury*, March, 1926, pp.509-14.

Kowaleski-Wallace, Beth. "Milton's Daughters: The Education of Eighteenth-Century Writers," *Feminist Studies*, 12(1986), pp.275-93.

Kramnick, Isaac. "Religion and Radicalism: English Political Theory in the Age of Revolution," *Political Theory*, 5(1977), pp.511-2.

——. *Republicanism and Bourgeois Radicalism: Political Ideology in Late Eighteenth-Century England and America*. Ithaca and London, 1990.

——. *The Rage of Edmund Burke: Portrait of an Ambivalent Conservative*. New York, 1977.

Landry, Donna. *The Muses of Resistance. Laboring-class Women's Poetry in Britain, 1739-1796*. Cambridge, 1990.

Langford, Paul. *A Polite and Commercial People: England, 1727-1783*. Oxford, 1989.

Laqueur, Thomas Walter. *Religion and Respectability: Sunday Schools and Working Class Culture. 1780-1850.* New Haven, 1976.

Leites, Edmund. "The Duty to Desire: Love, Friendship, and Sexuality in Some Puritan Theories of Marriage," *Journal of Social History,* 15(1982), pp.384-408.

Leranbaum, Miriam. "'Mistresses of Orthodoxy:' Education in the Lives and Writings of Late Eighteenth-Century English Women Writers," *Proceedings of the American Philosophical Society,* 121(August, 1977), p.295.

Lerner, Gerda. *The Majority Finds Its Past.* New York, 1979.

Lipking, Lawrence. *The Ordering of the Arts in Eighteenth-Century England.* Princeton, 1970.

Malcolmson, Robert W. *Popular Recreations in English Society 1700-1850.* Cambridge, 1973.

Mandler, Peter. "The Making of the New Poor Law Redivivus," *Past and Present,* 117(1987), pp.131-57.

Marshall, J. D. *The Old Poor Law 1795-1834.* London, 1968.

Macaulay, Thomas Babington. *Review of Walpole's Letters to Horace Mann, Edinburgh Review,* October of 1833, in *Critical and Miscellaneous Essays.* vol.2. New York, 1863.

MacLeod, Arlene Elowe. *Accommodating Protest: Working Women, the New Veiling, and Change in Cairo.* New York, 1991.

Martin, Bernard. *John Newton: A Biography.* London, 1950.

McGovern, Trevor. "Conservative Ideology in Britain in the 1790s," *History,* 73(1988), pp.238-47.

McKendrick, Neil. "The Commercialization of Fashion," in idem., John Brewer, and J. H. Plumb, eds., *The Birth of a Consumer Society: The Commercialization of Eighteenth-Century England.* Bloomington, Ind., 1982.

McKenzie, Lionel. "The French Revolution and English Parliamentary Reform: James Mackintosh and the Vindicae Gallicae," *Eighteenth-Century Studies,* 15(1980), pp.264-82.

Meacham, Standish. *Henry Thornton of Clapham, 1760-1815.* Cambridge, Mass., 1964.

Meakin, Annette. *Hannah More: A Biographical Study.* London, 1919.

Merchant, Carolyn. *The Death of Nature: Women, Ecology, and the Scientific Revolution.* New York, 1980.

Morris, David. *The Religious Sublime: Christian Poetry and the Critical Tradition in 18th-Century England.* Lexington, 1972.

Mullen, Shirley A. "Women's History and Hannah More," *Fides et Historia,* 19(1987), pp.5-21.

Myers, Mitzi. "Reform or Ruin: A Revolution in Female Manners," in Henry Paine, ed., *Studies in Eighteenth-Century Culture,* vol.11, 1982, pp.199-216.

Myers, Sylvia H. *The Bluestocking Circle: Women, Friendship, and the Life of the Mind in Eighteenth-Century England.* Oxford, 1990.

Newby, Howard. *The Deferential Worker: A Study of Farm Workers in East Anglia.* Madison, 1979.

Newell, A. G. "Early Evangelical Fiction," *Evangelical Quarterly,* 38(1966), pp.3-21.

Newman, Gerald. "Anti-French Propaganda and British Liberal Nationalism in the Early Nineteenth Century: Suggestions Toward a General Interpretation," *Victorian Studies,* 18(1975), pp.385-418.

——. *The Rise of English Nationalism: A Cultural History 1740-1830.* New York, 1987.

Nicoll, Allardyce. *The Garrick Stage: Theatres and Audience in the Eighteenth Century.* Athens, Ga., 1980.

Oates, Wayne E. "Conversion: Sacred and Secular," in *The Psychology of Religion.* Waco, Texas, 1973.

O'Gorman, Frank. *British Conservatism: Conservative Thought From Burke to Thatcher.* New York, 1986.

Ortner, Sherry B. "Is Female to Male as Nature is to Culture?," in Michelle Zimbalist Rosaldo and Louise Lamphere, eds., *Woman, Culture, and Society*. Stanford, 1974.

Parker, Kenneth L. *The English Sabbath: A Study of Doctrine and Discipline from the Reformation to the Civil War*. Cambridge, 1988.

Paulson, Ronald. *Popular and Polite Art in the Age of Hogarth and Fielding*. Notre Dame, 1979.

Pederson, Susan. "Hannah More Meets Simple Simon: Tracts, Chapbooks, and Popular Culture in Late Eighteenth-Century England," *Journal of British Studies*, 25(1986), pp.84-113.

Perkin, Harold. *The Origins of Modern English Society*. Toronto, 1969.

Perry, Elisabeth Israels. *Belle Moskowitz: Feminine Politics and the Exercise of Power in the Age of Alfred E. Smith*. New York, 1987.

Pickering, Samuel. "Hannah More's *Coelebs in Search of a Wife* and the Respectability of the Novel in the Nineteenth Century," *Neuphilologische Mitteilungen*, 78(1977), pp.81, 85.

———. *The Moral Tradition in English Fiction*. Hanover, N.H., 1976.

Pitcher, Edward W. "On the Conventions of Eighteenth-Century British Short Fiction: Part Two: 1760-1785," *Studies in Short Fiction*, 12(1975), pp.327-41.

Pocock, J. G. A. *The Machivellian Moment: Florentine Political Thought and The Atlantic Republican Tradition*. Princeton, 1975.

———. "The Political Economy of Burke's Analysis of the French Revolution," *Historical Journal*, 25(1982), pp.331-49.

———. *Virtue, Commerce, and History: Essays on Political Thought and History, Chiefly in the Eighteenth Century*. Cambridge, 1985.

Pollock, John. *Wilberforce*. New York, 1977.

Poovey, Mary. *The Proper Lady and the Woman Writer: Ideology as Style in the Works of Mary Wollstonecraft, Mary Shelley, and Jane Austen*. Chicago, 1984.

Porter, Roy. *English Society in the Eighteenth Century*. London, 1982.

Post, John D. "A Study in Meterological and Trade Cycle History: The Economic Crisis following the Napoleonic Wars," *Journal of Economic History*, 34(1974), pp.315-49.

Postgate, Helen B. *Madame de Stael*. New York, 1968.

Poynter, J. R. *Society and Pauperism: English Ideas on Poor Relief 1795-1834*. Toronto, 1969.

Premo, Terri L. *Winter Friends: Women Growing Old in the New Republic, 1785-1835*. Urbana, Ill., 1990.

Price, Cecil. *Theatre in the Age of Garrick*. Totowa, N.J., 1973.

Quinlan, Maurice. "Anti-Jacobin Propaganda in England, 1792-94," *Journalism Quarterly*, 16(1943), pp.9-15.

——. *Victorian Prelude: A History of English Manners 1700-1830*. New York, 1941.

Rendell, Jane. *The Origins of Modern Feminism–Women in Britain, France, and the United States, 1780-1860*. New York, 1984.

Richardson, Joanna. *The Regency*. London, 1973.

Roberts, David. *Paternalism in Early Victorian England*. New Brunswick, N.J., 1979.

Rogers, Katharine A. "Inhibitions on Eighteenth-Century Women Novelists: Elizabeth Inchbald and Charlotte Smith," *Eighteenth Century Studies*, 11(Fall, 1977), pp.63-78.

Rogers, Katharine M. *Feminism in Eighteenth-Century England*. Urbana, Ill., 1982.

Rose, R. B. "The Priestley Riots of 1791," *Past and Present*, 18(November, 1960), pp.68-88.

Rosman, Doreen. *Evangelicals and Culture*. London, 1984.

Rubenius, Aina. *The Woman Question in Mrs. Gaskell's Life and Works*. Cambridge, Mass., 1950.

Rule, John. *The Experience of Labour in Eighteenth-Century Industry*. New York, 1981.

Saintsbury, George. *A History of Nineteenth-Century Literature: 1780-1895*. New York, 1896.

Samuel, Raphael. "Introduction: The figures of national myth," in idem., ed., *Patriotism: The Making and Unmaking of British National Identity, vol.3–National Fictions*. London, 1989.

Sangster, Paul. *Pity My Simplicity: The Evangelical Revival and the Religious Education of Children, 1730-1800*. London, 1963.

Schama, Simon. *Citizens: A Chronicle of the French Revolution*. New York, 1989.

Schofield, Thomas Philip. "Conservative Political Thought in Britain in Response to the French Revolution," *Historical Journal*, 29(1986), pp.605-11.

Scott, Joan Wallach. *Gender and the Politics of History*. New York, 1988.

—— and Louise A. Tilly. *Women, Work, and Family*. New York, 1978.

Sekora, John. *Luxury: The Concept in Western Thought, Eden to Smollett*. Baltimore, 1977.

Shellabarger, Samuel. *Lord Chesterfield and His World*. Boston, 1951.

Shklar, Judith N. *Men and Citizens*. Cambridge, 1969.

Sklar, Kathryn Kish. *Catherine Beecher; A Study in American Domesticity*. New Haven, 1973.

Slack, Paul. "Books of Orders: The Making of English Social Policy, 1577-1631," *Transactions of the Royal Historical Society*, 30(1980), pp.1-22.

Smith, Florence M. *Mary Astell*. New York, 1916.

Smith, Olivia. *The Politics of Language 1791-1817*. London, 1984.

Smith, Ruth L. and Deborah M. Valenze. "Mutuality and Marginality: Liberal Moral Theory and Working-Class Women in Nineteenth-Century England," *Signs: Journal of Women in Culture and Society* vol.13, 2(Winter, 1988), pp.277-98.

Smith-Rosenberg, Carroll. "The Female World of Love and Ritual: Relations between Women in Nineteenth-Century America," *Signs: Journal of Women in Culture and Society* vol.1, 1(Autumn, 1975), pp.1-29.

Snell, K. D. M. *Annals of the Laboring Poor: Social Change and Agrarian England 1660-1900*. Cambridge, 1985.

Soloway, R. A. *Prelates and People: Ecclesiastical Social Thought in England 1783-1852*. Toronto, 1969.

———. "Reform or Ruin: English Moral Thought During the First French Republic," *Review of Politics*, 25(January, 1963), pp.114-6, 119-21.

Spater, George. *William Cobbett: The Poor Man's Friend*. vol.2. Cambridge, 1982.

Spencer, Jane. *The Rise of the Women Novelist: From Aphra Behn to Jane Austen*. Oxford, 1986.

Spender, Dale. *Mothers of the Novel: 100 Good Women Writers Before Jane Austen*. London, 1986.

Spinney, G. H. "Cheap Repository Tracts: Hazard and Marshall Edition," *The Library*, 20(1939-40), pp.295-340.

Spitzer, Leo. *Lives in Between: Assimilation and Marginality in Austria, Brazil, and West Africa, 1780-1945*. Cambridge, 1989.

Spring, David. "The Clapham Sect: Some Social and Political Aspects," *Victorian Studies*, (September, 1961), pp.35-48.

Stafford, William. "Religion and the Doctrine of Nationalism in England at the Time of the French Revolution and the

Napoleonic Wars" in Stuart Mews, ed., *Religion and National Identity*. Oxford, 1982.

Strathern, Marilyn. "No Nature, No Culture: the Hagen Case," Carol P. MacCormick and Marilyn Strathern, eds., *Nature, Culture, and Gender*. Cambridge, 1980.

St. Clair, William. *The Godwins and the Shelleys: The Biography of a Family*. New York, 1989.

Stevenson, John. "The Moral Economy of the English Crowd: Myth and Reality," in Anthony Fletcher and John Stevenson, eds., *Order and Disorder in Early Modern England*. London, 1985.

Stone, George Winchester and George M. Kahrl. *David Garrick: A Critical Biography*. Carbondale, Ill., 1979.

Stone, Lawrence and Jeanne C. Fawtier Stone. *An Open Elite? England 1540-1880*. Oxford, 1984.

Stonequist, Everitt. *The Marginal Man: A Study in Personality and Culture Conflict*. New York, 1937.

Straus, Ralph. *Robert Dodsley: Poet, Playwright, and Publisher*. London, 1910.

Stuart, Dorothy Margaret. *Daughter of England: A New Study of Princess Charlotte of Wales and Her Family*. London, 1951.

Sypher, Wylie. *Guinea's Captive Kings: British Anti-Slavery Literature of the Eighteenth Century*. New York, 1969.

Tabor, Margaret E. *Pioneer Women*. London, 1927.

Taylor, Barbara. *Eve and the New Jerusalem: Socialism and Feminism*. New York, 1983.

Thompson, Dorothy. *Queen Victoria: The Woman, the Monarchy, and the People*. New York, 1990.

Thompson, E. P. "Patrician Society, Plebeian Culture," *Journal of Social History*, 7(1974), pp.384-90, 394, 399-400.

———. *The Making of the English Working Class*. New York, 1963.

———. "The Moral Economy of the English Crowd in the Eighteenth Century," *Past and Present*, 50(February, 1971), pp.76-136.

Thompson, Henry. *The Life of Hannah More*. London, 1838.

Thouless, Robert H. *An Introduction to the Psychology of Religion*. New York, 1923.

Tinker, Chauncey Brewster. *The Salon and English Letters: Chapters on the Interrelations of Literature and Society in the Age of Johnson*. New York, 1915.

Todd, Janet. *Sensibility: An Introduction*. London, 1986.

Todd, Margo. *Christian Humanism and the Puritan Social Order*. Cambridge, 1987.

Tomalin, Claire. *The Life and Death of Mary Wollstonecraft*. New York, 1974.

Tomaselli, Sylvana. "The Enlightenment Debate on Women," *History Workshop Journal*, 19(Autumn, 1985), pp.101-24.

Trumbach, Randolph. "London's Sodomites: Homosexual Behavior and Western Culture in the 18th Century," *Journal of Social History* 11(1977), pp.12-3, 17-8, 22-4.

Turberville, A. S. *English Men and Manners in the Eighteenth Century*. New York, 1957.

Twiss, Horace. *The Public and Private Life of Lord Chancellor Eldon, with Selections from His Correspondence*. vol.1. London, 1846.

Valenze, Deborah M. *Prophetic Sons and Daughters: Female Preaching and Popular Religion in Industrial England*. Princeton, 1985.

Vance, Norman. *The Sinews of the Spirit: The Ideal of Christian Manliness in Victorian Literature and Religious Thought*. Cambridge, 1985.

Vicinus, Martha. *Independent Women: Work and Community for Single Women, 1850-1920*. Chicago, 1985.

Waldron, Mary. "Ann Yearsley and the Clifton Records" in Paul Korshin, ed., *The Age of Johnson: A Scholarly Annual* vol.3. New York, 1990.

Ward, William Reginald. *Religion and Society in England, 1790-1850*. London, 1972.

Webb, R. K. *The British Working-Class Reader 1790-1848*. London, 1955.

Weiss, Harry B. "Hannah More's Cheap Repository Tracts in America," *Bulletin of the New York Public Library*, 50(July-August, 1946), pp.539-49, 634-41.

Wells, Roger. *Wretched Faces: Famine in Wartime England, 1793-1801*. London, 1988.

Western, J. R. "The Volunteer Movement as an Anti-Revolutionary Force, 1793-1801," *Historical Journal*, 71(1956), pp.603-11.

White, R. J. *Life in Regency England*. London, 1963.

Whitmore, Clara H. *Woman's Work in English Fiction: From the Restoration to the Mid-Victorian Period*. London, 1910.

Will, George. "Slamming the Doors," *Newsweek*, 117(March, 1991), p.65.

Williams, Raymond. *Cobbett*. Oxford, 1983.

Yonge, Charlotte M. *Hannah More*. Boston, 1888.

Zimmer, Anne Y. *Jonathan Boucher: Loyalist in Exile*. Detroit, 1978.

Unpublished Theses

Barry, Jonathan. "The Cultural Life of Bristol 1640-1775." University of Oxford D.Phil. in history, 1985.

Chambliss, Joanne Schrader. "The French Revolution, Gender, and the British Response: Toward a More Complex Understanding of the Early Origins of Victorian Domesticity." Vanderbilt University M.A. in history, 1989.

Davis, Robin Reed. "Anglican Evangelicalism and the Feminine Literary Tradition: From Hannah More to Charlotte Bronte." Duke University Ph.D. in English, 1982.

Ford, Charles Howard. "Political and Religious Responses to Royal Ritual: The Funeral of Princess Charlotte in 1817." Vanderbilt University M.A. in history, 1988.

Hess, Marlene Alice. "The Didactic Art of Hannah More." Michigan State University Ph.D. in English, 1983.

Kasbekar, Veena P. "Power Over Themselves: The Controversy about Female Education in England 1660-1820." University of Cincinnati Ph.D. in English, 1980.

Krueger, Christine L. "The Reader's Repentance: Women's Preachers, Women Writers, and the Victorian Social Discourse." Princeton University Ph.D. in English, 1986.

Peroutka, Shirley A. "The Cheap Repository Tracts: The Archeology of an Early Mass Media Propaganda Movement." Ohio University Ph.D. in communications, 1989.

Raven, James R. "English Popular Literature and the Image of Business 1760-1790." Cambridge University Ph.D. in English, 1985.

Index

Studies in Nineteenth-Century British Literature

Series Editor:
Regina Hewitt

Books in this series examine the poetry and prose produced by British writers from the time of the French Revolution to the death of Queen Victoria. Historical events—rather than traditional literary categories or dates—define the scope of the series because they better convey a sense of the social consciousness that animates literary undertakings during this age. While the series includes a wide range of approaches to nineteenth-century British works, its special focus is on studies that relate this literature to its cultural context(s). Manuscripts addressing their subjects' social, political, or historical situations, ideals, influences, or receptions are especially welcome; manuscripts analyzing the implications of classifying this literature as "Romantic" or "Victorian" or of separating it into genres are also encouraged. Authors should write in English, though they may appropriately compare British works with those in other languages.

Authors wishing to have works considered for this series should contact:

Regina Hewitt
c/o Heidi Burns
516 North Charles Street
Baltimore, MD 21201